Born in Melbourne and educated in Brisbane, Peter Thompson now lives in London after a successful career as a journalist in the UK. His most recent books are *Pacific Fury*, *The Battle for Singapore* and, with Robert Macklin, *The Big Fella: The Rise and Rise of BHP Billiton*, which won the Blake Dawson Prize for Business Literature in 2010.

ANZAC FURY

THE BLOODY BATTLE
OF CRETE 1941

PETER THOMPSON

WILLIAM HEINEMANN: AUSTRALIA

A William Heinemann book
Published by Random House Australia Pty Ltd
Level 3, 100 Pacific Highway, North Sydney NSW 2060
www.randomhouse.com.au

First published by William Heinemann in 2010
This edition published in 2011

Addresses for companies within the Random House Group can be found at www.randomhouse.com.au/offices.

National Library of Australia
Cataloguing-in-Publication entry

Thompson, Peter Alexander.

Anzac fury

ISBN 978 1 86471 131 8 (pbk)

World War, 1939–1945 – Campaigns – Greece
World War, 1939–1945 – Campaigns – Crete
World War, 1939–1945 – Participation, Australian
World War, 1939–1945 – Participation, New Zealand

940.542195

Cover photographs: Front: Infantry attack in the swirling sands of the Western Desert: Libya, World War II. (National Library of Australia)
Back: German soldiers take aim with their light weapons against the enemy artillery in Crete. (Australian War Memorial Negative Number 106490)

Cover design by Christabella Designs
Maps by James Mills-Hicks
Internal text and picture-section design by Midland Typesetters, Australia
Typeset in Goudy Old Style by Midland Typesetters, Australia
Printed in Australia by Griffin Press, an accredited ISO AS/NZS 14001:2004 Environmental Management System printer

10 9 8 7 6 5 4 3 2 1

Michael Clarke, Anzac hero

Dedicated to Michael Clarke, John Peck and Keith Hooper
– and to the Anzac spirit of sacrifice, mateship, courage
and endurance that sustained them and thousands of their
Australian and New Zealand comrades during the darkest
days of World War II

John Peck, Anzac hero   Keith Hooper, Anzac hero

CONTENTS

ACKNOWLEDGEMENTS

Anzac Fury – a companion volume to *Pacific Fury*, published in 2008 – commemorates the 65th anniversary of the end of World War II in Europe when thousands of Anzac prisoners of war captured in Greece and Crete were released from captivity. It is 70 years since the 2nd AIF arrived in the Middle East to begin their extraordinary adventures in battles against the German and Italian armies in North Africa, mainland Greece and Crete prior to the outbreak of the Pacific War.

The immense contribution made by the New Zealand Division to the new Anzac Corps gives the book an exciting added dimension. Wherever possible, I have combined the personal memories of Anzac combatants with combat action. I have also returned to the original sources of many existing works on the battles of Bardia, Tobruk, Greece and Crete, including the war diaries and histories of units involved in those encounters, the official reports of commanding officers and the memoirs and/or biographies of the main participants.

I am enormously grateful to Louise Morris, Lieutenant Michael Clarke's daughter, for her recollections about her father and for permission to quote from diaries and letters in his extensive archive at her home in Tallarook, Victoria, and from his self-published memoir, *My War*.

I am similarly grateful to Barbara Daniels, daughter of Lieutenant John Peck, an Anzac soldier who joined the Special Operations Executive (SOE) while on the run from the Germans and assisted the escape of hundreds of Allied prisoners of war from Italy. In 1950, John Peck wrote an account of 'the strictly personal experiences of a young man caught up in unusual circumstances of war after being in action as an infantryman in Libya, Greece and the Battle of Crete'. It was, he explained, 'almost a diary which could not be written at the time and reflects the immediacy of the events and impressions without the benefits of hindsight, explanations or literary merit'. It is a fascinating and insightful document and I have quoted extracts from it in this work.

Special thanks go to Dr Sally Vickery of Brisbane for permission to quote from family records concerning her mother, Sister Mabel Johnson, and Mabel's cousin, Sir Charles Spry, Australia's post-war spymaster and keeper of the nation's secrets.

I would like to thank the following people for interviews: Joan Bright Astley, Les Cook, Miriam Dillon, Keith Horton Hooper, Watty McEwan, Anthony Madden, Arthur Midwood, Desmond Morris, Ann Robertson, Bill Rudd, Norman Simper, Harry Spencer and Katrina Swift. The Imperial War Museum Sound Archive, London, provided audio interviews with the following: Admiral Desmond McCarthy (HMS *Ajax*), Leo Brown (HMS *Ajax*), Herbert Rawlings (HMS *Barham*), Albert Pitman (HMS *Barham*), Adrian Holloway (HMAS *Nizam*), Frederick Winterbotham (Ultra), Ken Taylor (HMS *Formidable*), Major-General Michael Forrester (Queen's Royal Regiment), Denis Vellacott (RAF), Lord (John) Harding (General O'Connor's chief of staff), General Sir Richard O'Connor, Richard Green (HMS *Hasty*), Frederick De Fries (HMS *Formidable*) and Peter Wilkinson (SOE).

Anzac Fury also commemorates the outstanding service of Royal Australian Navy ships attached to the Mediterranean Fleet, particularly those involved in the Battles of Cape Spada and Matapan, and to the heroic crews of all ships that took part in the extremely hazardous and sometimes fatal evacuations of the Anzac Corps from mainland Greece and Crete. In all naval matters, I have consulted Lieutenant-Commander Mackenzie Gregory, RAN (retired) and am most grateful for his guidance.

I am also grateful for the assistance of Bill Richards, Australian National Maritime Museum, Sydney; Peter Johnson, Australian Government Department of Defence; the Research Centre of the Australian War Memorial, Canberra; the National Archives, formerly the Public Record Office, Kew; the Reading Room at the Imperial War Museum, London; the British Library, London; the Mitchell Library and State Library of New South Wales, Sydney; the State Library of Victoria, Melbourne; the Oxley Library and State Library of Queensland, Brisbane; and the Library of the Reform Club, London. Robert Macklin, my frequent co-author in Canberra, and Rod O'Loan in Melbourne were incredibly helpful with comments and advice on the work-in-progress.

Nikki Christer, my publisher at Random House Australia, was a tower of strength throughout the publishing process, while Patrick Mangan and Mark Evans are to be congratulated on their excellent editing and production work. Finally, my thanks go to my agent Andrew Lownie for encouraging me to write this book in the first place.

Regarding style, I have taken the liberty of using the present tense – for example, 'he says' or 'she recalls' – when a specific recollection may in fact have taken place years earlier. All interviews are clearly flagged in the References and notes section. The ranks of many service personnel changed during the course of World War II. While I have kept track of some promotions in this work, more usually I refer to the rank at the time of a particular incident. In several instances, I have retained the offensive terms 'Dago', 'Jerries', 'Huns' and 'blacks' in direct quotations taken from memoirs or official histories. I sometimes refer to 'Greece and Crete' as meaning 'mainland or continental Greece and Crete'. Please see Appendix C for the spelling of place names in mainland Greece and Crete used in this book.

Peter Thompson
February 2010

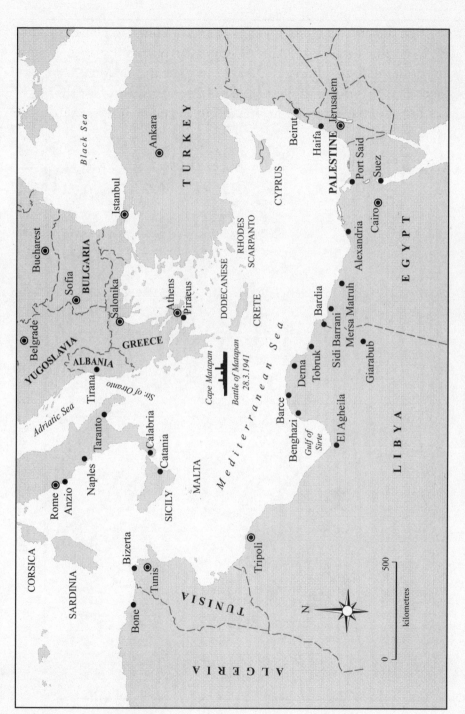

The eastern Mediterranean as it was in 1941, highlighting the battlefields of North Africa and the Battle of Matapan

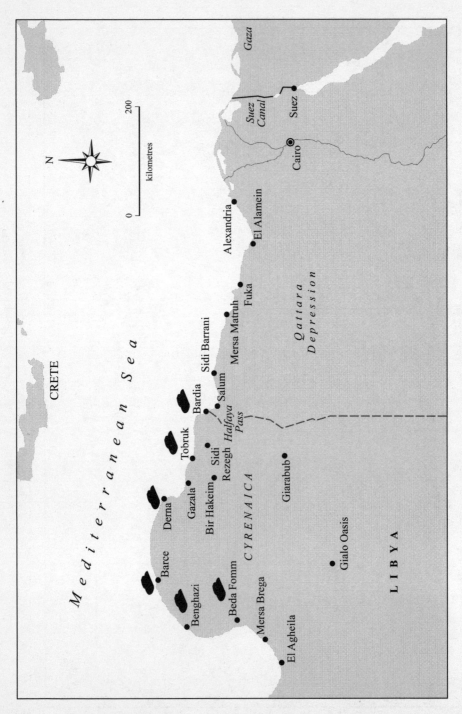

N

CRETE

M e d i t e r r a n e a n   S e a

Barce

Derna

Gazala

Bir Hakeim

Sidi
Rezegh

Tobruk

Bardia

Sidi Barrani

Salum

*Halfaya
Pass*

Benghazi

Beda Fomm

Mersa Brega

El Agheila

C Y R E N A I C A

Giarabub

Gialo Oasis

L I B Y A

Mersa Matruh

Fuka

Alexandria

El Alamein

*Qattara
Depression*

Cairo

Suez

*Suez
Canal*

Gaza

0

200

kilometres

The North African battlefields showing the AIF victories of January/February 1941

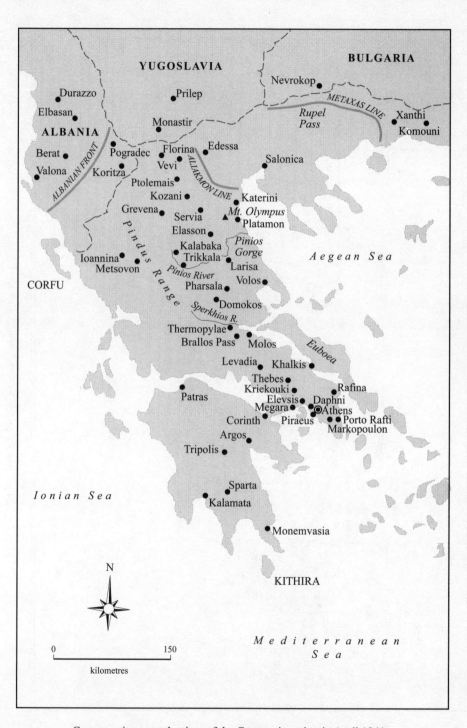

Greece as it was at the time of the German invasion in April 1941

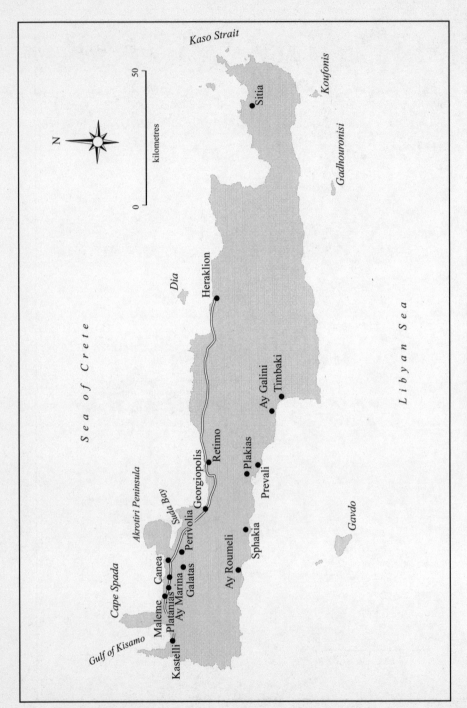

Kaso Strait

Koufonis

Sitia

Gadhouronisi

S e a   o f   C r e t e

Dia

Heraklion

Akrotiri Peninsula

Suda Bay

Georgiopolis

Retimo

Ay Galini

Timbaki

L i b y a n   S e a

Cape Spada

Canea
Maleme
Platanias
Ay Marina
Galatas
Perivolia

Plakias

Prevali

Ay Roumeli

Sphakia

Gavdo

Gulf of Kisamo

Kastelli

N

50

kilometres

0

The island of Crete as it was in May 1941

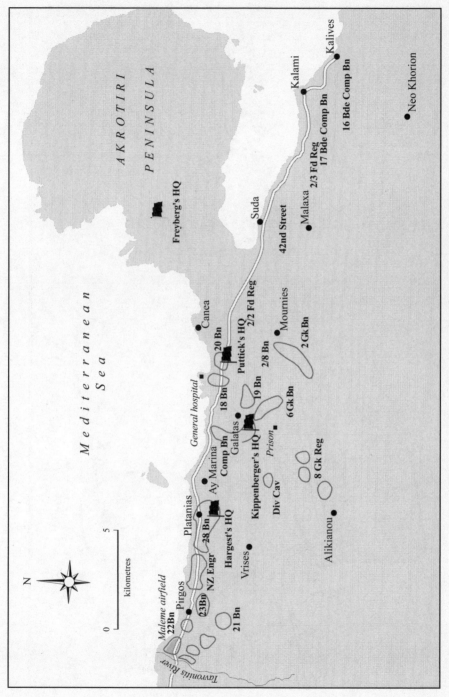

The main positions around Canea and the Akrotiri Peninsula, May 1941

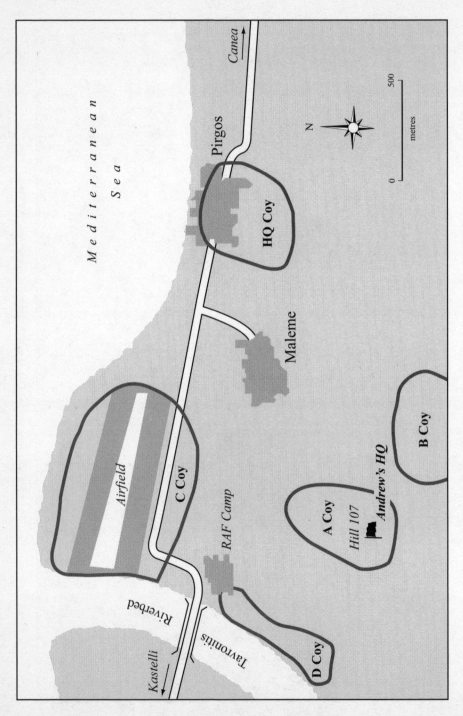

Maleme airfield on 20 May 1941, showing the dispositions of the 22nd New Zealand Battalion

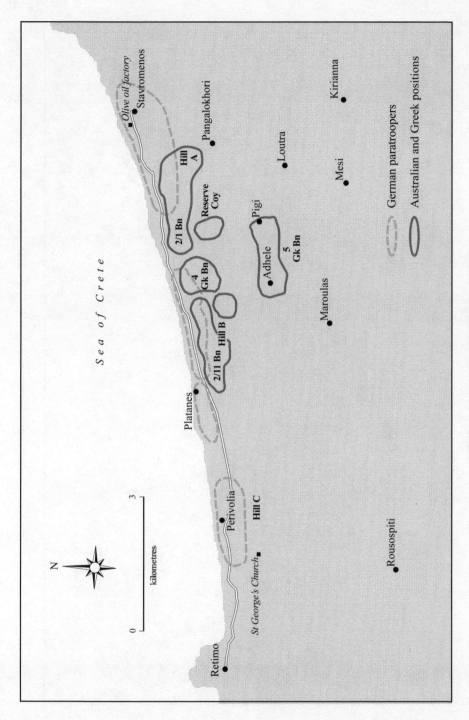

N

Sea of Crete

kilometres
0   3

Retimo

St George's Church ■

Perivolia

Hill C

Platanes

2/11 Bn Hill B

4
Gk Bn

2/1 Bn

Reserve
Coy

Hill
A

Olive oil factory
Stavromenos ■

Pangalokhori ●

Adhele ●
Pigi ●

5
Gk Bn

Maroulas ●

Loutra ●

Kirianna ●

Mesi ●

Rousospiti ●

- - - German paratroopers
—— Australian and Greek positions

Allied positions at Retimo, 20 May 1941

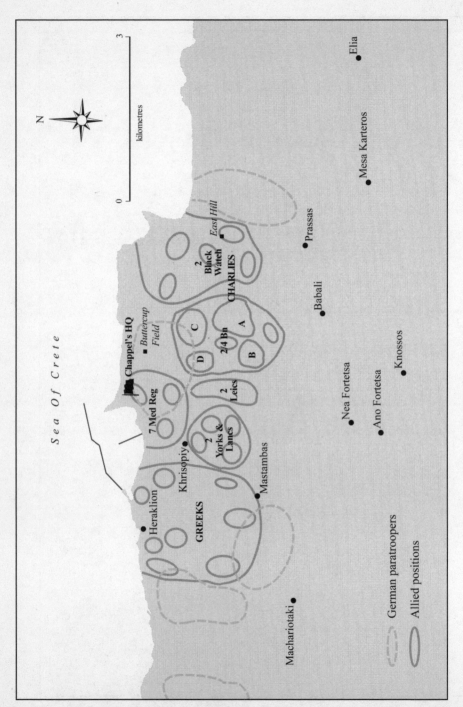

Sea Of Crete

N

0   3
kilometres

Heraklion

Khrisopiy

GREEKS

Mastambas

Chappel's HQ

7 Med Reg

2
Yorks &
Lancs

2
Leics

Buttercup
Field

D

C

2/4 Bn

B

A

2
Black
Watch

East Hill

CHARLIES

Macheriotaki

Nea Fortetsa

Ano Fortetsa

Knossos

Babali

Prassas

Mesa Karteros

Elia

German paratroopers

Allied positions

Positions at Heraklion, 20 May 1941

INTRODUCTION

Anzac Fury

At 8.30 pm on 8 May 1945, Lieutenant Michael Clarke flew out of Germany in a United States Air Force Dakota. The war in Europe was over and he was a free man at last. Michael Clarke had fought at Tobruk and in Greece, where he was wounded. He had commanded one of the last two field guns in the Battle of Crete, holding the Germans at bay while thousands of men were lifted to safety. He had been a prisoner of war for one month short of four years. But the Nazis had failed to break his spirit: he was still a gunner, still an officer in the 2nd AIF, still one of the new Anzacs.

Almost three decades after Churchill had sent the first Anzacs to Gallipoli, Michael Clarke was among 6500 Australian and 7000 New Zealand troops thrown into a desperate battle on the Greek island of Crete against a huge German force of parachute and airborne troops. He had been captured 13 days later with 4794 other Anzacs, the vast majority of whom had been left behind on the beaches during a hurried evacuation. Even today – 65 years after the end of the Second World War – there is a huge question mark over why the troops were on Crete in the first place. And no amount of myth-making can obscure the fact that they were sacrificed for political reasons.

Michael Clarke was held captive in four camps in Germany, where he and his fellow Australian and New Zealand POWs were subjected to what he describes as 'controlled starvation and calculated sadism'. His last camp was Stalag 7A, a notorious prison at Moosburg, Bavaria, where 100,000 prisoners were crammed into shabby, lice-ridden barracks intended for 10,000.

Eight days before Germany's surrender, tanks and infantry from General George S. Patton's conquering United States Third Army stormed the camp, disarmed the guards and liberated the prisoners. Clarke was given an American V-mail letter form to let his family in Melbourne know he was alive. He wrote to his mother, 'Great relief to walk about without a machine gun covering me from a sentry box.' It was an even greater relief to be able to raid the camp kitchens and eat a decent, filling meal.

Yet when the Anzacs who had been prisoners in Europe returned home they said little about their experiences. One POW told this author, 'We heard what a terrible time the prisoners of the Japanese had had in South-east Asia, so we kept quiet.' Thus *Anzac Fury* gives voice to the experiences of men who were sent on Churchill's orders from the victorious battlefields of Libya on a disastrous mission to Greece and Crete. 'We should have chased the Italians out of North Africa and then considered Greece,' says Sergeant Keith Hooper, the son of an Anzac, who was wounded and captured on Crete.

> Greece was a disaster waiting to happen. It was another one of Churchill's great ideas and it didn't work, but as usual Churchill had to have his way. We were up against ten German divisions which had fought in Poland, Holland, Belgium and France – these fellows weren't the Afrika Korps, these were the real bastards. At the head of them was Hitler's favourite

division, the *Leibstandarte* SS Adolf Hitler Division. We never had a chance to settle down as a defending force. We were accused of running away but we didn't run away – we fought them all the way down the Greek archipelago and one of the New Zealanders, Sergeant Jack Hinton, won the Victoria Cross attacking the Germans right at the very end. [1]

Every one of the new Anzacs was conscious of the fact that he was fighting just a couple of hundred kilometres from the shores of Gallipoli. And when the evacuation began – ironically, on Anzac Day 1941 – the men behaved with great dignity. 'Churchill said if the Anzac Corps got into difficulties in Greece, we could be left behind,' Hooper says.

> He was prepared to sacrifice us; as it was, half the 6th Division was lost in Greece and the New Zealanders lost about a quarter of their division. The Germans didn't destroy the Anzacs but they made a hell of a mess of us. Then we had to fight them all over again in Crete when we had lost many of our arms, including all of our artillery. [2]

There has never been a battle like the Battle of Crete and there probably never will be again. It was, according to one of the participants, 'a head-on crash of the world's latest homicide appliances'. [3] To give the battle its rightful place in the context of the Second World War – and to introduce the key figures – *Anzac Fury* begins with the arrival of the new Anzacs in the Middle East in January 1940. The narrative follows their adventures in the Western Desert, when the 6th Australian Division under General Iven Mackay performed brilliantly at Bardia, Tobruk, Derna and Barce in driving the Italian Army out of Cyrenaica.

Dreaming of a united Balkan front against Hitler, Churchill then ordered the commander-in-chief, Middle East, General Sir Archibald Wavell, to undertake an armed intervention in

Greece instead of allowing the Australians to capture Tripoli and drive the Italians out of Libya. 'Churchill had this vision of attacking "the soft underbelly of Europe",' says Les Cook, a member of the 1st Australian Corps Signal Group and a survivor of the Battle of Greece.

> If it hadn't been for his obsession, we would never have gone to Greece, and if we hadn't gone to Greece the Germans probably wouldn't have invaded Greece and Yugoslavia. It's a wonder the Greeks don't hate us. We didn't need to go there to help them; they would have beaten the Italians with one hand tied behind their backs.[4]

In fact, the British Prime Minister lost his enthusiasm for the plan when Turkey and Yugoslavia refused to join his alliance and even the Greek Prime Minister, General Metaxas, turned him down. It was only Anthony Eden, the British Foreign Secretary, allied with General Wavell, who kept the Greek campaign alive.

In the northern spring of 1941, a totally inadequate expeditionary force of 58,000 troops reached Greece from Egypt and Palestine. The vast majority of the fighting units were Australian and New Zealand, yet as at Gallipoli – and despite a complaint by the head of the AIF, General Sir Thomas Blamey – the commanding officer was British: the lumbering General 'Jumbo' Wilson.

The issues raised in *Anzac Fury* are twofold: whether Australia and New Zealand's political and military leaders were deceived into supporting the Greek campaign, and whether the Anzac name was used as a cover to gloss over the incompetence behind its inevitable failure. The very first sentence of the official British history, written by a general, admits, 'The British campaign on the mainland of Greece was from start to finish a withdrawal.'[5] In other words, the men would be fighting against impossible odds, with no chance of winning.

Wavell later confessed that 'the whole expedition was something in the nature of a gamble, [but] the dice were loaded against it from the first'.[6] He makes no mention of the fact that plans for the evacuation of the troops had to be carried out secretly because of his rigid opposition to any such scheme.

The troops were still digging in when the Germans attacked on 6 April 1941. Within a matter of days, the 6th Australian Division and the 2nd New Zealand Division were heavily involved with the enemy on two fronts. On 12 April, General Blamey announced the formation of 1st Anzac Corps at the request of Major-General Bernard Freyberg, the New Zealand commander, and with Wavell's blessing. 'The task ahead, though difficult, is not nearly so desperate as that which our fathers faced in April 26 years ago,' Blamey told the new Anzacs. 'We go to it together with stout hearts and certainty of success.'

The 'certainty of success' was nothing but a forlorn hope. As huge German forces advanced down the archipelago and Greek resistance collapsed, the hopelessly outnumbered Anzacs made a fighting retreat through mountainous terrain while under constant attack from the Luftwaffe. By the end of April, many of the Anzacs had been evacuated to Egypt, but thousands more were among the 30,000 troops who got only as far as Crete, Hitler's so-called 'Isle of Doom'. General Freyberg was ordered by Wavell to take charge of the island's defences, with Brigadier George Vasey commanding the Australian units.

On Anzac Day 1941, Hitler signed Directive No 28 ordering Operation Mercury, the German airborne assault on the island. On 20 May, 9530 parachute and glider troops, supported by 650 bombers, fighters and transport planes, attacked the island's three airfields in one of the most spectacular, hardest-fought and controversial battles of the war. The Battle of Crete was the first airborne invasion in the history of warfare. It was the first time the deciphered German Enigma code played a decisive part in a battle (with disastrous results for the Allies). And it was the first time invading German troops, finally numbering more than 22,000, encountered mass resistance from a civilian population.

The battle remains the only operation in which a major strategic objective was attacked and captured solely by airborne troops. But it cost the Germans more than 4000 deaths – the heaviest enemy losses of the war up to that point – and Hitler never again sanctioned the use of a parachute strike force.

'For a couple of months, we were Anzacs again,' says Les Cook, 'and we were the only Anzacs in the Second World War. I'm proud of that.'[7]

No one was more emblematic of the Anzac tradition than John Peck of the 2/7th Battalion AIF. Captured during the fall of Crete, Peck escaped from the Germans a dozen times. After making his way to neutral Switzerland, he returned to Italy to join an organisation which escorted more than 1500 Allied prisoners of war to safety using the Italian railway system.

And it is through one of the strange twists of history that the story of the new Anzacs actually begins in the unlikely setting of an Italian railway station …

PROLOGUE

Lighting the Fuse

The Battle of Crete was born of one man's vanity. At 11 am on Monday 28 October 1940, Benito Mussolini met his Axis partner-in-crime, Adolf Hitler, on the platform of Santa Maria Novella, the main railway station of Florence. 'Führer,' the Italian dictator beamed, 'we are on the march!'[1]

Intensely envious of Hitler's military successes in Western Europe, Mussolini wanted victories of his own in a 'parallel war' centred on the Balkans and North Africa. Just hours before Hitler's armoured train *Amerika* had pulled into Florence, the Italian Army had stormed across the border of occupied Albania to invade Greece.[2]

Without informing Nazi Germany, Mussolini had started a campaign which would trigger a British pledge to protect Greek independence and lead to the re-forming of the Anzac Corps during the Battle of Greece and its decimation on the bloody battlefields of Crete.

As a brass band struck up the German national anthem and steel-helmeted troops presented arms, Hitler shook Mussolini's outstretched hand and returned his smile.[3] Inwardly, though, he was seething. Mussolini's invasion had derailed his 'peripheral strategy' of maintaining peace at the Balkan end of the Mediterranean to keep vital raw materials – crucially, oil – flowing to the Third Reich from Romania and Yugoslavia.[4]

Mussolini guided his guest into an open-topped limousine which, flanked by motorcycle outriders, set off for the Palazzo Vecchio ('Old Palace'), a onetime Medici fortress that now served as the city hall.

Despite this show of unity, trust was not one of the hallmarks of the Rome–Berlin Axis. Hitler had neglected to share his plans for the attacks on Czechoslovakia, Poland, Norway and France with Italy, believing as he did that 'every second Italian was either a traitor or a spy'.[5] And when the two dictators had met at the Brenner Pass, between Austria and Italy, earlier that month, Hitler had failed to mention that German troops were about to occupy Romania.

Mussolini was infuriated by this latest snub. 'Hitler always faces me with a fait accompli,' he complained to Count Galeazzo Ciano, the Italian Foreign Minister who was also his son-in-law. 'This time I am going to pay him back in his own coin. He will find out from the papers that I have occupied Greece.'[6]

At the eleventh hour, he had sent a letter to Hitler detailing his plans but slyly back-dated it by five days to give the impression it had been delayed in transit.[7] Hitler's train was crossing the German border when he received the news via his mobile telegraph office. 'This is downright madness,' the Führer raged. 'How can he do such a thing?'[8] He was incredulous that any military strategist worthy of the name could be so stupid as to launch a campaign in the rain, slush and snow of a Balkan autumn.[9]

As an omen of things to come, it was raining heavily as Hitler's open-topped limousine passed Florentine buildings draped with red, white and black swastika flags. In leather greatcoat and field marshal's cap, the German conqueror acknowledged the tribute of the Tuscan crowds with his limp-wristed Nazi salute.

During the meeting in the Machiavelli Room at the Palazzo Vecchio, Hitler kept his feelings in check. According to his Luftwaffe adjutant Nicolaus von Below, 'The conversation followed its usual very friendly course and Hitler gave no hint of his annoyance.'[10] Instead, he offered military assistance. German troops, he said, could keep the British out of Greece and safeguard the Romanian oilfields from British bombers. He also offered to send a division of paratroopers to Crete to prevent a build-up of British forces there.[11]

Mussolini, however, was enjoying his moment of glory. Italian forces in North Africa had already crossed the Egyptian border with the intention of driving the British out of Egypt, seizing control of the Suez Canal and gaining access to Britain's oil supplies in Iraq. He wanted to avoid German help in the belief that he, not Hitler, might bring Britain to her knees and thus enable Italy to take her place among the great powers.

Night had fallen by the time Hitler boarded his train for the journey back to Berlin. Mussolini's parting gift was 'The Plague in Florence' by Hitler's favourite Austrian painter Hans Makart.[12]

From that day on, things started to go disastrously wrong between the two Axis powers. The fuse that had been lit in Florence would set the Balkans ablaze, destroying the Italian Empire and bringing down the Duce. It also dislocated Hitler's plans to invade Russia and arguably cost him the war.

PART I

Desert Glory

CHAPTER 1

Sons of Anzac

George Vasey shivered inside his greatcoat as the liner SS *Strathallan* sailed up the muddy waters of the Gulf of Suez on a chill winter's morning. A blood-red sun was rising over the Sinai and the desert glowed pink in the harsh light. Vasey had been here before. As a 20-year-old artillery officer – tall, lean and fresh out of Duntroon, with 'an easy flow of bad language'[1] that would earn him the nickname 'Bloody George' – he had first arrived in Egypt in December 1915, just as the battered Anzac legions who had left the Middle East eight months earlier 'with careless and daredevil self-confidence'[2] were returning from Churchill's failed campaign in the Dardanelles.[3]

For a quarter of a century, he had lived with the memories of those proud Australian and New Zealand troops, many of them bearing the scars of battle and including such heroes as the Victoria Cross winner Albert Jacka, marching into Tel el Kabir,[4] the vast encampment in which Vasey's brigade, the 4th Field Artillery, had been placed after its arrival from Australia.

'The Great Mound' was midway between Cairo and Ishmalia on the Suez Canal.[5] It was here that the Gallipoli heroes were reinforced and then re-grouped into four divisions for the coming battles against the Kaiser's armies in France. In early 1916, Vasey's brigade had sailed from Alexandria to Marseilles with the 2nd Australian Division, heading for the Western Front, where he had taken part in the campaigns in which he would distinguish himself as a soldier – on the Somme, at Passchendaele and the assault on the Hindenburg Line.

It was now January 1940 and once again – largely due to the self-interest of the Versailles peacemakers: 'the Peace to end Peace', in Wavell's apt phrase[6] – the Free World was facing a deadly new peril. And once again, Colonel George Alan Vasey, now a 44-year-old married man with two sons, was in Egypt on his way to fight the Germans. As senior officer of the advance party of the 6th Division, 2nd Australian Imperial Force, he had sailed to Egypt with Brigadier Basil Morris, commander of the Australian Overseas Base, and some 200 Australian and New Zealand personnel to make preparations for the arrival of the Australasian expeditionary forces.

After completing their training and being issued with modern weapons, these sons of Anzac – the 6th Australian Division and the 2nd New Zealand Division (hereafter called the New Zealand Division) – would head for France to join the Anglo–French armies facing the Wehrmacht across the Maginot Line. History, it must have seemed to George Vasey, was repeating itself in the grimmest possible way.

Vasey's advance party had reached Suez on 7 January, three days before the first Australian contingent – the 16th Brigade Group, commanded by Brigadier Arthur 'Tubby' Allen – sailed from Sydney in the liners *Otranto*, *Orcades*, *Orford* and *Strathnaver*. While tugs and steamers sounded their hooters and sirens and ferries blew their cock-a-doodle-dos, Gracie, a cabaret singer from the Palms nightclub, sang 'Now is the Hour' through a megaphone while pitching and tossing in a small boat.

Outside Sydney Heads on 10 January, the four liners joined

six ships carrying the first echelon of the New Zealand Division – the 4th Brigade and associated units. Escorted by the British battleship HMS *Ramillies* and the Australian cruisers HMAS *Canberra* and HMAS *Australia*, the nucleus of the new Anzac Corps then steamed south.

Two days later outside Port Phillip Bay, the *Empress of Japan* took on board 600 Australian divisional and base troops, including Private John Peck, a Victorian of just 17 summers but claiming to be 21 in order to qualify for overseas service. 'I was droving sheep in northern Victoria when war broke out,' he says. 'I was thrilled that I might be able to join the army and have some adventures so I added four years to my age and enlisted in October 1939.'[7]

Farewelling these soldiers in Melbourne, Major-General Thomas Blamey, commander of the 6th Division, exhorted them 'to do all in their power to maintain the good name of Australia abroad and to uphold the glorious tradition of the 1st AIF'.[8]

The troops had no idea where they were going and were taking bets on it. But the Nazis knew somehow. As the convoy cruised west towards Fremantle, the scar-faced traitor Lord Haw-Haw announced on German radio that the new Anzacs 'would have to be good swimmers to get to Egypt'.[9]

On their first day in Egypt, George Vasey and Basil Morris were driven to Cairo by the Australian trade commissioner, Colonel Cyril E. Hughes,[10] to meet General Sir Archibald Wavell, the British commander-in-chief in the Middle East. They met the man who would hold sway over the destiny of Australian and New Zealand troops for the next two years at his headquarters, Grey Pillars, two blocks of flats next to the British Embassy in tree-lined Garden City. The British Ambassador, Sir Miles Lampson, had strolled across the lawn to join them.

Wavell was then in his 57th year. Once sturdy, upright and

'apparently hewn from weathered oak',[11] he was now bow-legged, his face creased and sun-bronzed, his hair a patrician shade of ash-grey, but he still rode most mornings at the Gezira Sporting Club and played a good game of golf. Nor was he averse to flirtatious relationships. Freya Stark, the writer and traveller, fell for 'his genial expression, a look of gaiety and youth'.[12] 'Freya Stark was in love with Wavell,' says Ann Dove, who worked for the Special Operations Executive in Cairo. 'She had an absolute crush on him.'[13]

For a classics scholar who liked to quote poetry, Wavell could be infuriatingly taciturn, so taciturn that the actress Lady Diana Cooper thought him 'very deaf'.[14] Wavell was not deaf but in order to avoid answering awkward questions from people like Lady Diana, he simply pretended he hadn't heard them. 'He was an extraordinary mixture,' says one of his confidantes, Joan Bright Astley (who addressed her letters to him as 'Darling Archie'[15]). 'He had this tremendous facility with his pen, yet out would come this croaky voice [when he spoke]. It was sad because beautiful English just poured from his pen.'[16]

Wavell had been commissioned into the Black Watch three days after his 18th birthday. He had fought for his country in South Africa (against the Boers), France (against the Germans, losing his left eye in the Second Battle of Ypres) and Palestine (against the Turks). He had been in Cairo since the formation of Middle East Command in August 1939. His command covered 3.5 million square kilometres stretching from Egypt, Transjordan, Iraq and Cyprus down to British Somaliland, Aden and Kenya. On paper, he controlled 86,000 troops but apart from the British garrison on the Nile and the 7th Armoured Division (the fabled 'Desert Rats'[17]) in the fortress at Mersa Matruh, most of his forces were scattered the length and breadth of Africa.

Wavell had met many famous Australian soldiers during World War I when he served in Palestine under General Allenby and had written extensively about their role against the Turks. But he was very wary about Australian troops. He had told Lieutenant-General Vernon Sturdee, head of an earlier delegation, that he 'did not want the Australians running riot around Cairo as in World War I'. For that reason, they would be based not in Egypt but in southern Palestine.[18]

Vasey and Morris knew all about the riots that had taken place in 'The Wozzer' – the Haret el Wasser, a street of brothels and drinking dens behind luxurious Shepheard's Hotel in central Cairo – in 1915 when Anzac troops had 'evened the score' by bashing pimps, sly-grog sellers and pickpockets and setting fire to joints such as Tiger Lil's in the red-light district.

As they drove back to the canal, Cyril Hughes told them that the decision to base the Australians in Palestine was in fact political. 'Young King Farouk refused to have us in Egypt, though he has not objected to New Zealanders,' Vasey wrote to his friend Brigadier Sydney Rowell in Melbourne. 'He little knows the error of his choice!'[19]

Farouk was anti-British[20] and despite the protests of Sir Miles Lampson large numbers of Italian spies still roamed around Cairo; some even worked inside the palace as advisers to the King. It didn't help Lampson's case that his much younger second wife, Jacqueline, was half-Italian. Farouk loudly proclaimed, 'I'll get rid of my Italians when he gets rid of his.'[21] The Ambassador and his wife were known in Cairo society as 'Lampson and Delilah'.

The Australian campsites in Palestine were at Gaza, Julis and Qastina on the road to Tel Aviv. The area was rich in history as the scene of the Battle of Beersheba in which Sir Harry Chauvel, commander of the Australian and New Zealand Mounted Division, had unleashed the 4th Australian Light Horse on a magnificent cavalry charge that had overwhelmed the Turkish guns at Beersheba at the foot of the rocky red Judean hills and seized its vital water supply.[22]

Vasey did not like what he saw. The terrain consisted

mainly of open, sandy flats devoid of trees, totally unsuitable for training soldiers who were expecting to fight in the heavily wooded French countryside. On the plus side, the blue waters of the Mediterranean lapped on to sandy shores to the west, while green valleys stretched away to the east. Winter was ending in heavy rains and the hills and fields were covered in a mantle of red and blue wildflowers.[23]

Vasey and his staff took over the Hotel Fast next to the Jaffa Gate in Jerusalem. On Australia Day 1940 the Commonwealth flag was broken out above the hotel and Vasey found himself caught up in the whirl of expatriate social life. 'Everyone has been very kind to us – we've been to a party of one kind or another nearly every night,' he wrote. 'There are lots of Australians here in civil jobs – police and various Government departments. Tonight we are having cocktails ...'[24]

On 12 February, the first Australian–New Zealand convoy of the war reached Suez, where the Secretary for the Dominions, Anthony Eden, was on hand to meet them with Wavell, Ambassador Lampson and General Maitland 'Jumbo' Wilson, commander of British Troops in Egypt (BTE). 'The cheerfulness and outspoken enthusiasm of the men, their splendid physique and the spirit in which they had made this journey, expressed Empire loyalties more eloquently than fine speeches,' Eden noted in his diary.

> I had been to Australia and New Zealand 14 years before, but this meeting took my thoughts back farther, to the month of April 1918, a dark period in the First World War, when we had been in the line alongside the Australians at Villers-Bretonneux, and to September 1916 and the capture of Flers in the Battle of the Somme, when the New Zealanders had been on our left. No tougher fighting neighbours could be dreamed of.[25]

That night, the Australians disembarked at Kantara at the head of the canal and boarded a train for the journey across the Sinai to their camp at Julis, where two British battalions – the 2nd Black Watch and 1st Hampshire Regiment – had pitched tents. Tubby Allen established a divisional headquarters eight kilometres away at Qastina and ordered both camps to be smartened up: paths were gravelled and bordered with white stones and beds of flowers, trees were planted and signs announced places such as 'Wagga', 'Kings Cross' and 'Ingleburn'.[26]

Private John Peck was having the time of his life. The young drover had been posted to Headquarters Australian Overseas Base in Jerusalem and was delivering supplies from the quartermaster's store to the Australian messes. John Desmond Peck, known to his mates as 'Dainty Des' on account of his dapper appearance, had been born at Woollahra on 17 February 1922. His father Harry Peck was a member of the Royal Australian Navy based at Jervis Bay. When he was transferred to Flinders Naval Depot in Victoria, the family moved to a house named 'Bellevue' at Crib Point on Westernport Bay.

Harry and his wife Phyllis had six children but Phyllis died of pneumonia in 1929 when John was seven and his father remarried his wife's divorced sister-in-law Jean. There was friction between John and his stepmother/aunt from the beginning. At just 13, he ran away from home to work on a farm at Craigieburn, north of Melbourne, and a year later went droving sheep in the company of older men. He grew up fast.

'It's pay day today and I'm having a celebration,' he wrote to his father from Jerusalem on 24 April 1940. 'I'm taking out a swell little thing from Gay Paree. She's a blonde with big blue eyes and yours truly has got her by the hind legs. I know you are broadminded and can be sure my morals are still intact.'[27] But his date did not go as planned. 'Got tanked on Victorian beer last night and the French piece wiped me,' he wrote. 'Ended up with a brawl with an Arab taxi driver and Huck [Private Kenneth Huxtable] got two front teeth knocked out. I woke up this morning with blood all over me.'[28]

*

Wavell visited Gaza on 20 February and addressed the 16th Brigade. He left the troops in no doubt about his feelings. 'I need hardly tell you,' he began,

> that I am very glad and proud to have Australian troops under my command. I served out here in the last war, and knew well the Australian Light Horse units, which did such magnificent work in Allenby's campaign, and like everyone else who knew them, had the greatest admiration for their fighting qualities and endurance. They left a very great reputation as soldiers out here, which I am quite sure you will maintain and increase. But they also left in some of the countries of the Middle East a reputation of another kind, for a lack of restraint and discipline, which I am sure you will not wish to maintain but to remove.

Britain's military position in Egypt was absolutely vital and he intended to maintain the best possible relations with the Egyptians. But as a result of certain happenings during the last war, the Egyptians had 'a very lively apprehension' of what Australians might do in Cairo and elsewhere in Egypt. 'I look to you,' Wavell croaked, 'to show them that their notions of Australians as rough, wild, undisciplined people given to strong drink are incorrect.'[29]

Standing on the hallowed ground of the 1st AIF, the troops shuffled uncomfortably. Wavell's comments reflected badly on their fathers and elder brothers – and, indeed, on their officers – who had fought for Britain and her Empire. It was an inauspicious beginning, but the commander-in-chief hadn't finished. 'I should like to try to impress on you what this war means, not only to Great Britain, not only to the British Empire, but to the whole civilised world,' he continued.

> You do not, perhaps, realise as we do, owing to your remoteness from Europe, what we are up against in the Nazi attempt to dominate the world. The issue of this struggle is absolutely

vital to everything that we, and other democracies, hold most important: freedom of speech, freedom of thought, justice, toleration, and a decent standard of life. We are fighting a crusade which is far more important than all the crusades which were led against this country of Palestine nearly a thousand years ago.[30]

The assumption that these citizen soldiers, who had actually volunteered to fight the Nazis, knew little about the perils of Nazism because of their 'remoteness' from Europe caused a certain amount of ill-feeling. Considering the hammering they would take in Greece, Crete, Malaya, Singapore and the Dutch East Indies as a result of Wavell's command decisions, his comments would be recalled with bitterness.

Over in Egypt, Brigadier Edward Puttick, commander of the 4th New Zealand Brigade, was enjoying a warm reception from the Egyptians. Puttick was a World War I veteran who had led a battalion of the New Zealand Rifle Brigade at Passchendaele. His three battalions – the 18th, 19th and 20th plus associated units – now occupied the Maadi camp on the edge of the desert 13 kilometres south of Cairo, with the Pyramids of Giza silhouetted in the distance.

The terrain was no more suitable than Gaza for training troops for combat in Europe but at least it was close to the Egyptian capital. The camp lacked a swimming pool so the 6th Field Company built one. The New Zealand Division's commanding officer, Major-General Bernard 'Tiny' Freyberg, a champion swimmer in his youth, donned his trunks to take the first plunge.[31]

At the opening of the Gallipoli campaign on the night of 25 April 1915, Freyberg had swum ashore to a beach in the Gulf of Xeros and lit oil flares to divert the Turks' attention from the landings being made elsewhere on the peninsula. He was awarded the DSO for that 'gallant and picturesque' exploit and, in 1916, won the Victoria Cross at Beaucourt in France for 'splendid personal gallantry' and 'utter contempt for danger'.

Freyberg had been born at Richmond, Surrey, on 21 March 1889 and had been raised and educated in New Zealand. He started the First World War as a sub-lieutenant in the Hood Battalion of the Royal Naval Division and ended it as an acting major-general of the 29th Division. He had been a great friend of Rupert Brooke and was one of the pall-bearers who had carried the tragic poet up to an olive grove on the island of Skyros and buried him there.

Freyberg was wounded nine times. His friend Winston Churchill once asked him to show him his wounds. 'He stripped himself,' Churchill writes, 'and I counted 27 separate scars and gashes. But of course, as he explained, "You nearly always get two wounds for every bullet or splinter because mostly they have to go out as well as in."' Churchill called him 'the Salamander of the British Empire', the salamander being 'protector' or 'supporter' in heraldic terms.[32]

After the war, Freyberg had remained in England and in 1922 married a wealthy widow, Barbara McLaren. His best man was his friend the *Peter Pan* author J. M. Barrie. In September 1939, he was on the reserve list, but had offered his services to the War Office and had been given command of the Salisbury Plain Area. When the New Zealand Government offered him the New Zealand Division, he flew back to Wellington, stopping en route in Melbourne to confer with his Australian counterpart.

He found that Tom Blamey was in no hurry to leave Australia. Less than a year earlier, the Australian commander had married Olga Farnsworth, an attractive 35-year-old fashion artist, and he was seeking permission for her to accompany him to Palestine.[33]

CHAPTER 2

Best of Enemies

Thomas Albert Blamey was a curious mixture of truculence and affability, a heavy drinker and womaniser who read serious literature, loved animals, collected wild orchids and had a share in a ladies' haberdashery, Le Rêve (The Dream), at the newly opened arcade of the Hotel Australia in Collins Street, Melbourne.

Blamey and Olga lived in a fashionably furnished house in Punt Road, South Yarra. AIF headquarters was just a short walk away through the Botanic Gardens in an Edwardian mansion block at 441 St Kilda Road. His appointment as commander of the 6th Division had caused a certain amount of controversy, even though he had a good record in World War I. On 25 April 1915, he landed at Gallipoli as an intelligence officer on the staff of Major-General William Bridges, commander of the 1st Australian Division, and ended the war as chief of staff to Sir John Monash, commander of the Australian Corps in France. But despite his undoubted brilliance as a staff officer, he had never commanded troops in battle.

Blamey quit the regular army in 1925 after being appointed

chief commissioner of the Victoria Police, an appointment marred by scandal and terminated by disgrace. Knighted in 1935, he continued to command the 3rd (Militia) Division but relinquished that post after being dismissed as police commissioner in 1936 for lying to protect the reputation of one of his senior police officers. When he went on the unattached list the following year, his military career appeared to be over.

Blamey, however, had friends in high places, notably the Prime Minister, Robert Menzies, and two of his ministers, Sir Henry Gullett and Richard Casey. Menzies had been Victoria's attorney-general during Blamey's time as police commissioner and, in common with the ruling Unionist Party in Canberra, had applauded his willingness to use brutal methods to suppress industrial unrest.[1] In 1938, Blamey was appointed chairman of the manpower committee, a task which put him in charge of registering the human resources that Australia would need in the event of war.

At the urging of Defence Secretary Frederick Shedden, the Prime Minister had chosen the controversial right-winger to command the 6th Division in preference to Lieutenant-General John Lavarack, a former chief of the general staff with whom Menzies and Shedden had argued,[2] or Major-General Gordon Bennett, the most senior officer on the active list, with whom the entire staff corps (the permanent officers of the Australian Army) had argued.

Blamey was short, fat and aggressive and, unlike Freyberg who shrank from confrontation, pursued vendettas to the bitter end. Yet according to Sir John Monash there was inside his great cranium 'a mind cultured far above the average, widely informed, alert and prehensile'.[3] His staff work was impeccable, his orders models of lucidity and precision; it was to his country's detriment that his feuds with fellow officers – and the cunning methods he employed to dispose of them – would destroy his popularity and diminish the reputation of his command.

'He had a mind which comprehended the largest military

and politico-military problems with singular clarity,' the official historian Gavin Long writes, 'and by experience and temperament was well-equipped to cope with the special difficulties which face the commander of a national contingent which is part of a coalition army in a foreign theatre of war.'[4]

To protect his position and his powers in that coalition army, Blamey asked for – and received – a charter from the Federal Government which stated that the 2nd AIF must be recognised as an Australian force under its own commander, who had an inalienable right to communicate directly with Canberra. No part of the force could be detached without his consent; however, it was accepted that all troops would be under the operational control of the commander-in-chief of the theatre in which they were serving.[5]

The first recruits enlisted in the 2nd AIF – 'the Thirty-Niners' – were a wide cross-section of men ranging from World War I veterans to the young drover John Peck to Sir Henry Gullett's 25-year-old son. Henry Baynton Somer Gullett, known as 'Jo', was a journalist on the Melbourne *Herald* and a contemporary of the war correspondents Alan Moorehead and John Hetherington. He had been in the cadets at Geelong Grammar School and was a member of the Oxford University Officer Training Squadron for two years while at Oriel College. Determined to carry a rifle and not a typewriter into battle, Gullett saw it as his duty to volunteer for service. His father had been an artillery officer in the 1st AIF and had later served as official AIF war correspondent in Palestine. 'We knew England's position was very serious,' Jo Gullett says, 'and that we should help her as our fathers had done. It was the order of things.'[6]

One of Gullett's friends who shared his patriotic views was Michael Clarke, a 24-year-old barrister who had joined the militia as a gunner after returning to Melbourne from Oxford where he had completed two law degrees with honours.

For months, the two young men discussed the deteriorating situation in Europe. Now that war had been declared, the bureaucratic wheels were moving too slowly for their liking.

'There is still neither news nor indication of any military activity in Australia and it appears that we are going to remain quiescent while the remainder of the empire goes to war,' Michael Clarke complained to his diary on 5 September 1939.

> If the militia is not going to serve overseas, I will do my best to secure a transfer to some more active part of the world. I don't want such a stigma of non-activity during warfare as has clung to Bob Knox and Mr Menzies,[7] and the latter appears once again most unwilling to engage in military activity.[8]

As Australia had been at war for just 48 hours, his impatience might have seemed premature and his reference to Knox and Menzies a bit presumptuous but Michael Clarke was used to mixing in such company: in fact, Sir Robert Knox, a leading businessman, was his uncle and he had met Menzies back in 1936 at a 'Town and Gown' dinner in Oxford. 'We helped him down the stairs at eleven o'clock,' he told his diary later that night.[9]

Michael Alastair Clarke – 'Mick' to his men in the militia, where his privileged background was 'a severe handicap to my military popularity'[10] – had been born on 28 September 1915 at the Clarke family's Sunbury mansion 'Rupertswood', birthplace of the Ashes.[11] He had spent his early years in a large house at 249 Domain Road, South Yarra, with his father, the Honourable Russell Clarke, his mother Frances, known as 'Lute', his brother John, sister Marjorie and four servants, including his personal French nanny, whom he called 'Mam'selle'.

His first school was Melbourne Grammar. Then in 1928 the sandy-haired, blue-eyed boy had been packed off to England – 'exiled for seven and a half years', in his words – to get an English public school education, first at Hawtreys Preparatory School in

Wiltshire and then at Churchill's alma mater, Harrow (where one of his closest friends was John Profumo, the War Minister who would find lasting notoriety through his affair with the prostitute Christine Keeler). He was a good student. In his mid-term report at Harrow in 1932, his housemaster commented, 'Very clever boy. Thinks independently.' His full-term report for that year commented, 'Final place 1. Outstanding.'[12]

At the outbreak of war, Michael was working in chambers as a barrister and serving in the 22nd Militia Field Brigade, commanded by Edmund 'Ned' Herring, a prominent Melbourne King's Counsel. Herring, Blamey and Clarke were all members of the Melbourne Club. Michael Clarke's cousin was the baronet Sir Rupert Clarke, his uncle was Sir Frank Clarke, president of the Victorian Legislative Council, and his father Russell Clarke was vice-chairman of the Moonee Valley Racing Club. In fact, it was at a race meeting at 'the Valley' in July 1935 that he had first met Tom Blamey. Conscious of Clarke's social connections among Victoria's landed gentry, Blamey invited him to his wedding and became his military adviser and sponsor.

Clarke was called up on 25 October 1939 – 'delighted to be on the active list at last'[13] – but then nothing happened until he bumped into Blamey outside his house in South Yarra on 5 November. Inviting him in for a drink, he explained that he was anxious to get an AIF posting as soon as possible. Blamey suggested he 'come along to my HQ in the morning at nine o'clock sharp'.

Reporting to the bare, carpetless building in St Kilda Road, Michael was given the service number VX123 and offered a posting as intelligence officer of the 2/3rd Field Regiment. The 5th Battery was being raised in South Australia and the 6th Battery would come from Western Australia and the Northern Territory. Michael was ordered to take the evening train to Adelaide. That, however, would mean missing the most important date in the racing calendar: the Melbourne Cup, which was being run at Flemington the following day.

'Bloody hell,' Blamey erupted when Clarke explained the problem. 'Do you expect the war to stop for the cup?'

'No, sir,' Clarke replied.

'I expect you also want to take some girl to a bloody dance after the cup?'

'If it is convenient – yes, sir.'

'It is *not* bloody convenient,' Blamey roared. 'You have a damned nerve accepting a plum job one minute and then asking me to cater for your social life the next.'

'Maybe we could forget about the dance, sir.'

'What's your tip for the cup?'

'Rivette, sir.'

'Not a hope. She's already won the Caulfield Cup and no mare has ever won the double.'

Nevertheless, Blamey signed a new travel warrant and Clarke had the satisfaction of watching Rivette win the cup *and* attending the dance. He left Melbourne on 8 November for Woodside camp, South Australia.[14]

Blamey was still in Melbourne in late February 1940 when the War Cabinet formed a second AIF division, the 7th Division, thus creating an Australian corps. He was promoted to commander-in-chief of 1st Australian Corps with the rank of lieutenant-general.

Sydney Rowell and Cyril Clowes, both Duntroon graduates, were named as chief of staff and commander of artillery with the rank of brigadier. Neither man could be described as a Blamey crony, but there were also 'jobs for the boys' in some of his other appointments. As aides de camp, Blamey chose Norman D. Carlyon, the 37-year-old managing director of the Hotel Australia, and John C. Wilmoth, a solicitor whom he had known in the militia. The functions manager of the Hotel Australia was recruited to run his mess, a dry-cleaner to act as batman, a garage owner to drive his car and a jockey to groom his horse. His friend Wally Condor, a former manager at J. C. Williamson Theatres, was given the rank of major and appointed to provide entertainment for the troops.

The possibility of reviving the Anzac tradition arose on 4 March 1940 when Bob Menzies cabled New Zealand's Labour Prime Minister, Michael Savage,[15] to suggest that the New Zealand Division might be incorporated with the 6th and 7th Australian Divisions in a new Australian and New Zealand Army Corps.

Savage, a radical Australian, was an outspoken critic of Britain's Imperial Defence strategy. However, he had been stricken with cancer so his Cabinet asked General Freyberg for his advice. 'New Zealand,' Freyberg replied, 'desires to assist in the manner best conforming to the British war effort and may not wish to be associated automatically with a possible aggressive Australian attitude regarding strategy.' Menzies' initiative also fell on stony ground at the War Office, where the planners foresaw the likelihood of the New Zealand Division being detached from such a corps on the battlefield and placed under British officers.[16]

Tom Blamey's first concerns were not with British or New Zealand generals but with his enemies in the Australian officer corps. Virtually his first action was to veto 'Joe' Lavarack's appointment as commander of the 6th Division, claiming that Lavarack's 'defects of character' – a reference to his quick temper – disqualified him from that post. At one stage of World War I, Lavarack had worked under Blamey, an experience that had created a life-long antipathy between them.[17] When the appointments were announced in April, Blamey had indeed succeeded in preventing Lavarack from getting the 6th Division, but there was nothing he could do to stop him being put in command of the new 7th Division (especially as he was willing to step down one rank to major-general to take the post).

The 6th Division passed to Major-General Iven Mackay,

a no-nonsense Grafton-born schoolmaster who had been an exceptional company commander on Gallipoli – he had led the charge at Lone Pine – and had commanded a battalion and brigade in France. Mackay, now 58 years old, arrived in Palestine on 17 May with the Australian second contingent, including 6th Division headquarters, the 17th Brigade, commanded by Brigadier Stanley Savige, and the Divisional Artillery, commanded by Brigadier Ned Herring.

'The second contingent arrived in awful weather – it was 112 degrees in the shade and there wasn't much shade about,' John Peck wrote to his father on 21 May. 'You want to try carrying full equipment (96 lb) in that heat.'

One of Mackay's staff – GSO-3 (operations) – was Captain Charles Chambers Fowell Spry, the future director of Australia's intelligence service ASIO. At 29, he was a high-flyer who had already experienced overseas service with the Duke of Wellington's Regiment in India, where he had taken part in operations on the North West Frontier.

The 17th's three battalions – the 2/5th, 2/6th and 2/7th – went into camp at Beit Jirja between Julis and Gaza. Beit Jirja, they discovered, meant 'home of George' so the Arabs called them 'Georges'. The 19th Brigade – the 2/4th, 2/8th and 2/11th Battalions – was based at Kilo 89 to await the arrival of their commanding officer, Brigadier Horace 'Red Robbie' Robertson, who was still in transit from Australia.

Both Savige and Herring were close friends of Blamey and all three were militia officers, as was Tubby Allen, commander of the 16th Brigade. Their appointments had been made in accordance with a prime ministerial injunction that, as in the 1st AIF, citizen soldiers should hold the majority of senior commands in the 2nd AIF, a political bias which had generated a great deal of animosity among the staff corps.

The hostility surfaced in early June when George Vasey was joined at Gaza by fellow Duntroon graduates Colonel Frank Berryman, the 6th Division's GSO-1 (senior operations staff officer or chief of staff), and Brigadier Robertson, the only regular army officer to have been given one of the 6th Division's high commands. Robertson, a red-headed Gallipoli veteran, was back on familiar ground, having led the first cavalry charge ever made by Australian troops – at Magdhaba in Sinai in 1916.

The Duntroon men's main target was Stanley Savige, a butcher's son like his friend Blamey, who had risen to the rank of brigadier in the militia while they had marked time as majors in the peacetime army. In fact, Vasey and Berryman had disagreements with all three militia commanders, Allen, Savige and Herring.[18] Loyalties, however, weren't split solely between the militia and the regular army. There was also tension between Vasey and Berryman over the running of headquarters, with the former describing the latter as 'a slave to procedure' and 'selfish as be damned'.[19] This feud had its origins at Duntroon, where Vasey and Berryman had taken a dislike to one another.

Vasey was a heavy drinker, Berryman abstemious, but they both found Tubby Allen 'aggressive and tiresome'[20] and 'hot-tempered and garrulous'[21] in drink. Furthermore, Allen and Savige resented Ned Herring, who was a member of Blamey's Melbourne Club set. All these personality clashes would generate great friction in the AIF and create dangerous situations for the troops when the 6th Division went into battle.

The New Zealand Army had internecine issues of its own, many of them stemming from the infamous 'Colonels' Revolt' of 1938 when four senior Territorial Force officers had taken the unprecedented step of criticising the government's defence policy. The rebels were former brigade commanders who had been reduced to the rank of colonel as part of an austerity drive. Two of them, Neil Macky and Harold Barrowclough, were World War I veterans who worked together as partners in a successful Auckland legal practice. They were also prominent members of society – Macky as commodore of the Royal Yacht Club and Barrowclough as a member of the right-wing National Defence League of New Zealand.

The 'Four Colonels' confronted Frederick Jones, the Minister of Defence in the Labour Government, with demands that he acknowledge the deficiencies of New Zealand's peacetime army. When Jones failed to do so, the colonels published a manifesto attacking the decision to spend defence funds on building up an air force and arguing that the Territorial Force in its present form was incapable of defending New Zealand.

As the army's adjutant and quartermaster-general, it had fallen to Edward Puttick to put down the revolt. At his insistence, the officers were suspended for a breach of King's Regulations and posted to the retired list. 'I am afraid I am too much of a Tory to kow-tow to a bootmaker as a minister of defence,' Macky admitted. This was a reference to Fred Jones' time as a boot clicker – a shoemaker who cuts out the leather for making the uppers. In fact, Jones expanded the Royal New Zealand Navy, created an air force and improved the leadership qualities of the Territorial Army.

Appeals to the governor-general failed to have the men reinstated, but with the advent of war they were quickly forgiven. Macky was given command of the 21st Battalion and Barrowclough was put in charge of the 6th Brigade.[22]

The commander of the 5th Brigade was James Hargest, a 48-year-old farmer-turned-politician. Now red-faced and plump, Jimmy Hargest had ended the First World War as the much-decorated commander of the 2nd Battalion, Otago Regiment. He had a reputation for bravery, tactical flair and organisational ability. Between the wars, he had risen to the rank of brigadier in the Territorial Force and had been elected to parliament as a member of the National Party.

When war broke out, Hargest had sought a senior post in the New Zealand Expeditionary Force, but had failed his medical examination owing to the effects of shell-shock –

post-traumatic stress – suffered in the last war. Using his parliamentary connections, he persuaded Peter Fraser, the acting Prime Minister,[23] to overrule the doctors. It was a decision that the New Zealand Army would come to regret, especially during the dark days ahead on the island of Crete.

The Italian dictator Benito Mussolini dreamed of making Crete an integral part of his new Roman Empire.[24] His socialist father had given him the middle name Amilcare in honour of the Italian anarchist Amilcare Cipriani, who had fought with Garibaldi for Italy's independence from Austria. As a 15-year-old in 1898 during the Greco–Turkish War, Mussolini had yearned to join Cipriani's *Legione Garibaldina* to free Crete from the Turks.[25]

Following the collapse of the Ottoman Empire, Italy had grabbed Libya in North Africa in 1911 but held only the Mediterranean coastline. In 1930, Mussolini ordered Major-General Rodolfo Graziani to crush all resistance to Italian rule. Graziani unleashed his soldiers in orgies of raping, burning and looting and within a year had whipped the western provinces of Tripolitania and Fezzan into line.[26]

Next to suffer were the nomadic Bedouin tribes, members of the Senussi sect, who were holding out in Cyrenaica. Graziani herded the entire population of the Jebel Achdar (literally 'Green Highlands') – the cultivated 'bulge' of the Libyan coastline south of Benghazi – into concentration camps, where many thousands died of starvation, disease and maltreatment.[27] Italian settlers were then handed large plots of fertile land to colonise the province. To the Arabs, Graziani became known as *El Jazar*, 'the Butcher'.

Mussolini then launched an invasion of Ethiopia (Abyssinia) in October 1935 in a campaign that pitted Italian tanks, artillery, bombs and poison gas against the rifles and spears of Emperor Haile Selassie's tribesmen. Italy, he explained, had the same rights as other European powers to 'a small place in the African sun'.[28] As he considered Ethiopia to be nothing more than 'a conglomerate of barbarian tribes', he felt entitled to add its territory to his new Roman Empire.[29] In fact, Ethiopia was a devoutly Christian country which had inflicted a never-to-be-forgotten defeat on the Italian Army in 1896 in the Battle of Adowa.

Nine Italian divisions, commanded by the elderly, white-bearded Fascist icon General Emilio De Bono, drove over the border from Italian-held Eritrea in long convoys of Fiat trucks, while Graziani attacked with another army from Italian Somalia in the south. Haile Selassie protested to the League of Nations. The League considered the matter and did nothing.

De Bono quickly avenged the humiliation of Adowa, but his attack then faltered. Desperate for quick victories, Mussolini replaced him with General Pietro Badoglio, the ambitious, self-promoting chief of the general staff, who dropped around 1000 mustard-gas bombs on Ethiopian villages and sprayed the lethal chemical as vapour from specially equipped aircraft,[30] killing troops and civilians indiscriminately. Mussolini's eldest son, Vittorio, a pilot in *Regia Aeronautica*, the Royal Italian Air Force, described killing Ethiopians as 'entertaining' and likened war to 'a beautiful sport'.[31]

Everything about the Fascists was bombastic and mock-heroic – the Ethiopian campaign was called *La Marcia della Ferrea Volonta* ('the March of the Iron Will'), although personal comfort was never far from the minds of the officers. Hearing that they had no means of chilling their Chianti, an enterprising Libyan businessman bought every liquid-gas-fuelled refrigerator at the Marshall Field emporium in Chicago and had them shipped to the war zone.[32]

By the time Badoglio's army captured the Ethiopian capital, Addis Ababa, on 5 May 1936, Haile Selassie and his court had been spirited away by the British to London. An ecstatic frenzy gripped the Italian nation and a grateful Italian monarch, weeping with joy, assumed his title of Emperor of Ethiopia.

Badoglio's reward from the Duce was reputed to include half of the deposits in the Bank of Ethiopia.[33]

Four years later, in the Old City of Jerusalem, a group of Australian soldiers walked up a flight of steps behind the Church of the Holy Sepulchre during a sightseeing trip. Through a gateway in an ancient stone wall, they found a group of Ethiopians in the courtyard of a small chapel. This was Deir es-Sultan, home of the Ethiopian Orthodox Church in the Holy Land since the time of the Crusades.

The Australians, a lieutenant and four sergeants of the 2nd AIF, engaged the Ethiopians in conversation and learned of their country's plight. It had a profound effect. Back at camp that evening, they wrote their thoughts down in a letter and sent it to GHQ Middle East. The letter said:

> We have all read about the conquest of small countries by big ones, of the brutal aggression of Hitler and Mussolini. But in Jerusalem, from these simple Ethiopians, we learned for the first time from the lips of the victims what conquest can mean, and what liberation can mean too. We began to see that we are in the Middle East for a reason, and that we have a part to play. We hope that the part we play will be concerned with the liberation of Ethiopia. Hence this letter. It is a formal notification that the undersigned are prepared to volunteer for service, in any operation planned for the liberation of Ethiopia. We should be honoured to fight with any army pledged to bring the Emperor and his exiled followers back to the capital.[34]

The letter was filed away in a drawer at GHQ Cairo together with other documents relating to Ethiopia. It would have been forgotten had it not been for Major Orde Wingate, the strange Christian Zionist who had been given the task of returning Haile Selassie to his throne.

Wingate found the Australians' letter while browsing through the files and it set his imagination on fire. He had little regard for his contemporaries in the British Army, whom he regarded as subsidised clerks or sportsmen in part-time work. The Australians had given him the idea of forming a small band of regular soldiers which he would name Gideon Force after the biblical judge who selected 300 men from 32,000 volunteers to save the Chosen People. Gideon Force would infiltrate enemy-held territory in Eritrea and Ethiopia and recruit patriotic tribesmen to drive out the Italians. 'I should like to have these men report to me at once,' Wingate wrote to Wavell. 'They shall be my first volunteers.'

Wavell was unable to oblige – he had other plans for the Australians – and Wingate went on to achieve his objective with a force of 2000 Africans.

Wingate's enthusiasm for Australians was far from universal. The official Australian historian Gavin Long noted 'a tendency on the part of some British officers to seek in the newcomers some proof of their ready-made conviction that colonial officers were uncouth and their troops ill-disciplined'.[35]

One of the men in that category was Brigadier Bruno Brunskill, administrative officer in Palestine and Transjordan. Brunskill was undoubtedly brave – he had won the Military Cross and lost an eye in World War I – but power had gone to his head. His hostility towards the newcomers surfaced when Lieutenant-Colonel Lindsay Male and Major Edward 'Weary' Dunlop of the Australian Army Medical Corps visited British headquarters at the King David Hotel to discuss the establishment of a convalescent depot in Jerusalem to care for sick and wounded Australian troops. Male was short and dapper and although Dunlop was six foot three inches tall, Brunskill was even taller and more powerfully built. A black patch over his missing eye gave him a fierce, piratical mien.

Dunlop recalls that Brunskill kept them standing, treated the request with contempt and then walked out of the room in mid-conversation. The Australians were furious. The convalescent depot was finally set up well away from Jerusalem at Kafr Vitkin on the coast between Haifa and Tel Aviv. From then on, Brunskill seemed to go out of his way to frustrate the efforts of the Australian medicos.[36]

When the 2/1st Australian General Hospital opened for business in a tented settlement on Gaza Ridge on 16 April 1940, supplies were so inadequate that Matron Connie Fall and her 53 nurses and physiotherapists had to spend their own money purchasing basic items such as spoons and tin openers. There was no running water, bacteria proliferated on the dirt floors – 'mildew & spiders & livestock in every nook & cranny'[37] – and sterilisers had to be heated on Primus stoves, creating a serious fire risk.[38]

By the end of May, the canvas wards were packed with 400 patients. Fortunately, nursing reinforcements arrived with the second convoy, including a contingent of nurses from the 2/2nd AGH under Matron Annie Sage who donned their scarlet capes and white uniforms and pitched in to help their colleagues.

There was also a chronic shortage of equipment for the troops, which placed a great strain on the training of the two Australian brigades now in Palestine. Soldiers were so poorly armed in exercises among the hills surrounding Gaza and Beersheba that sticks with red flags were used as Boys anti-tank rifles and sticks with blue flags were Bren-guns.[39] Transport was almost non-existent – one battalion had only two vehicles: a taxi-cab from Jerusalem and a hired truck.[40]

Alan Moorehead, the *Daily Express*'s 29-year-old Melbourne-born war correspondent, found the Australians 'cursing and complaining. They wanted action instead of route marches in the sand.' At 8 pm on 10 June, the troops were finishing dinner when it was announced over the BBC that Italy had declared war on the Allies from midnight that night.[41]

CHAPTER 3

Whacko, Sydney!

Pandemonium. Italy's entry into the war presented the Allied forces in the Middle East with their first chance to get a crack at one of the Axis powers.

No one appreciated that fact more than Andrew Browne Cunningham, the 57-year-old naval commander of the Mediterranean Fleet known throughout the navy as 'ABC'. Naval tradition demanded that he draw the Italian fleet into battle as quickly and decisively as possible. The watering holes on Alexandria's Mohammed Ali Square, the Fleet Club and the brothels along Sister Street emptied as ratings and officers dashed to their ships.

The Italian battlefleet consisted of six battleships, 19 cruisers, some 50 destroyers and at least 115 submarines, mainly concentrated at Cape Taranto and Naples in Italy, with light forces in the Dodecanese Islands off the coast of Turkey and some destroyers and submarines as far south as the Eritrean port of Massawa on the Red Sea.[1]

By 1 am on 11 June 1940, Cunningham's battle squadrons had weighed anchor, cleared the boom and headed for the jet-black sea to seek out and destroy the enemy in the eastern Mediterranean.[2] The two battleships – HMS *Warspite*, which flew the admiral's flag, and HMS *Malaya* – were actually Queen Elizabeth-class superdreadnoughts. Both had taken part in the Battle of Jutland in May 1916. They each had eight 15-inch guns firing shells weighing 1900 pounds and despite their age were capable of a top speed of 25 knots. The fleet also included the veteran aircraft carrier *Eagle*, the five cruisers of the 7th Cruiser Squadron including HMAS *Sydney* (Captain John Collins) and screening destroyers, including three members of the legendary 'Scrap Iron Flotilla', HMAS *Stuart* (Commander Hec Waller), *Vampire* (Lieutenant-Commander John Walsh) and *Voyager* (Lieutenant-Commander James Morrow). This force swept to the west in search of Italian ships around Crete.

At the same time, General Wavell ordered three groups of Rolls-Royce armoured cars of the 11th Hussars, the famous Cherrypickers, to smash through 'the Wire' – the triple line of mines and barbed-wire barriers at the frontier with Libya – and attack Italian outposts and patrols. That first night, the Cherrypickers shot up a convoy of lorries. Two Italian officers and 59 Libyan soldiers were taken prisoner. The officers had no idea that hostilities had broken out and were most indignant about being captured.

RAF Blenheim bombers attacked the docks at the fortified seaport of Tobruk in conjunction with a bombardment by two of Cunningham's cruisers. The old Italian cruiser *San Giorgio*, which was being used as a floating battery, was set on fire.

Much to Cunningham's dismay, the chief of the Italian naval staff, Admiral Arturo Riccardi, had ordered his fleet to stay in port, but the Italians were far from inactive. One of their submarines sank the British cruiser *Calypso* off Crete and their mine-laying submarines created havoc around the approaches to Alexandria harbour. HMAS *Stuart*, *Voyager*, *Vampire*, *Vendetta* and *Waterhen*[3] were constantly at sea on anti-submarine patrol and discovering and marking new minefields.

The obsolete Australian destroyers had been scorned by Goebbels as 'scrap iron' when they arrived in the Mediterranean in December 1939. Their young crews performed so commendably that Cunningham described them as 'the most lively and undefeated fellows I have ever had to do with'.[4]

Hector Macdonald Laws Waller,[5] commander of the 10th Destroyer Flotilla in HMAS *Stuart*,[6] was a rugged, pipe-smoking bear of a man who wore a knitted navy-blue cap on his close-cropped head at sea in preference to a peaked officer's cap. He had been born in Benalla, Victoria, on 4 April 1900, the youngest of eight children. At 14, he had entered the newly founded Royal Australian Naval College, then based at Osborne House, Geelong.[7] 'I cannot recall anyone having a bad word to say about Hec Waller – he was admired throughout the RAN,' says Lieutenant-Commander Mackenzie Gregory, who started at the naval college in 1936 when Waller was commander there. 'I well remember his sense of humour and quiet efficiency.'[8]

Admiral Cunningham thought Waller 'one of the very finest types of Australian naval officer. Full of good cheer, a great sense of humour, undefeated and always burning to get at the enemy, he kept the old ships of the flotilla – *Stuart*, *Vampire*, *Vendetta*, *Voyager*, *Waterhen* – hard at it always.'

Australia's other great captain in the Med was John Augustine Collins, skipper of HMAS *Sydney*, who had joined the 7th Cruiser Squadron on 26 May. Born at Deloraine, Tasmania, on 7 January 1899, Collins was among the first intake of cadets at the naval college in 1913. 'Collins and Waller had been at Osborne House at the same time – Collins was senior by one year – but they would not have been personal friends at that time,' Mac Gregory says. 'They certainly would not have gone ashore together – you kept strictly to your own year and anyone senior to you was treated with great deference.'

Graduating as midshipmen, Collins and Waller both served with the Royal Navy in battleships which had survived the Battle of Jutland – Collins in HMS *Canada* and Waller in HMS

Agincourt – but while Waller had specialised in signals, Collins had chosen gunnery as his field of expertise.

'Collins and Waller were totally different types of naval officer,' Mac Gregory says.

> Waller was a sailor's captain, with a great sense of humour and more self-effacing than Collins, who knew how to both promote and push himself. But Collins was a dedicated and efficient naval officer and I served with him in HMAS *Shropshire* in 1945, when he was a commodore. If I had to choose between them, I would always come down on the side of Hec Waller.[9]

It was John Collins who struck the first decisive blow against the enemy when *Sydney* was sent on patrol off Crete with five British destroyers. Four of the destroyers, *Hyperion*, captained by Commander Hugh Nicolson, with *Ilex*, *Hero* and *Hasty*, were directed to sweep the Aegean north of Crete from east to west in search of Italian submarines. Captain Collins in *Sydney*, in company with the British destroyer *Havock* (Commander R. E. Courage), was given verbal orders by Admiral Cunningham to head further north to support Nicolson's destroyers, but also to 'operate contraband control' – a means of stopping and identifying enemy craft – in the Gulf of Athens.[10]

Sunrise on 19 July brought the promise of a calm and cloudless day in the waters of the Aegean off the coast of Crete. Nicolson's squadron had reached a point six kilometres from Cape Spada at the tip of the thumb-shaped Rodopos Peninsula on the northern side of the island. The crew of *Hyperion* saw the famous White Mountains gradually rise up from the shadows of the sea. At 7.20 am, her lookout sighted two Italian cruisers, *Giovanni delle Bande Nere* and *Bartolomeo Colleoni*, heading north at a distance of 16 kilometres.

Vice-Admiral Ferdinando Casardi in *Bande Nere* was on

his way from Tripoli to the Italian naval base at Leros in the Dodecanese with his sister ship *Colleoni* to attack British merchant shipping. Nicolson increased speed to 30 knots and turned away from the enemy cruisers. Eager hands swung torpedoes seawards and *Hyperion* and *Ilex* opened fire with their 4.7-inch guns. Knowing that his 6-inch guns could easily outrange the destroyers' armaments (but unsure of whether they were screening a larger force), Casardi increased speed and opened fire.

Nicolson stood no chance in a gun duel with the two cruisers so he turned north to lead the enemy in the direction of *Sydney*. Casardi took the bait and a high-speed chase developed off the west coast of Crete. Nicolson flashed a radio signal to Admiral Cunningham in his flagship *Warspite* at Alexandria that he was engaged with two enemy cruisers. *Sydney*, he thought, was much further north in the Gulf of Athens; Collins, however, had instinctively decided to stay close to the British destroyers.[11] As a result, he was just 64 kilometres away when he heard Nicolson's report.

Neither Nicolson nor Cunningham had any idea that *Sydney* was so near and Collins wasn't about to break radio silence to tell them. Ordering *Havock* by Aldis lamp to follow him, the Australian skipper set off on a south-westerly course to intercept the Italian cruisers. 'With some jubilation, we increased to full speed and turned south,' he says.

> The natural impulse was to tell the destroyers and the C-in-C our position, for both would be anxious, thinking us to be hundreds of miles away. However, I felt justified in keeping them in suspense until action was joined. It seemed clear that the moment we touched a transmitting key the enemy would be aware that other forces were in the vicinity and would escape back to the Mediterranean.[12]

With the warships closing on each other at speeds topping

60 knots, Sydney would be within firing range in less than an hour – time enough for the crew to have a quick breakfast: as Collins noted, 'Everyone feels better after breakfast.'[13]

All stations were closed up again at 8.20 am when Sydney's lookouts reported 'volumes of smoke on the southern horizon'. Six minutes later, the two Italian cruisers came into view, with Bande Nere in the lead. Heavily veiled in early-morning mist, Sydney approached unseen. Commander Mike Singer, the gunnery officer, assured Collins that a good range-plot had been generated on the fire-control table. The Australian skipper broke radio silence and reported his position. Then at 8.29 am, Sydney's four gun turrets, two forward and two aft and containing eight twin-mounted 6-inch guns, rotated on target. The muzzles were raised to maximum elevation and the first salvos roared overhead towards Bande Nere at a range of 19,000 yards.

'She came rushing to the southward, on the port beam of the Italian, guns flashing, battle ensigns streaming,' Hyperion's diarist records, 'and such a smother of foam at bow and stern that from the destroyers one seemed almost to hear the high-tensioned scream of the machinery driving her across the water.'[14]

Huge shell splashes on the port side of his ship were the first indication to Admiral Casardi in Bande Nere that he had fallen into a trap. At 8.32 am, he altered course to the south-east and returned fire at Sydney from all turrets, but his gun crews could see only the flash and glare of her salvos while she was still shrouded in mist.

Collins stayed broadside-on to the enemy to keep all of his guns in action. At 8.35 am, Sydney scored her first hit with a shell that passed through Bande Nere's forward funnel and exploded on deck, killing four ratings and wounding four others. Sydney's gunfire was so intense and accurate that Casardi thought the two ships opposing him must both be 8-inch cruisers. After suffering hits and near misses in the first eight minutes, he turned away to the south-west. Both Italian cruisers made smoke and headed for Libya, zig-zagging to avoid shellfire and torpedoes but enabling *Sydney* to close the gap more quickly.[15]

Deep furrows of foam streaming from her bow, she gave chase towards Cape Spada. Her shells rained down on the rear cruiser, *Colleoni*, while the destroyers in line abreast opened up with their 4.7-inch guns.

At 9.24 am, one of *Sydney*'s shells jammed *Colleoni*'s rudder and she was forced to steam in a straight line. A minute later, several shells – both 6-inch and 4.7-inch – exploded on her lightly armoured bridge, causing great loss of life. Simultaneously, one of *Sydney*'s shells penetrated the boiler room, shutting down electrical power throughout the ship. The Italian cruiser came to a halt eight kilometres to the west of Cape Spada. She was on fire and down by the bows.

Mortally wounded, Captain Umberto Novaro ordered his crew to abandon ship. Leaving *Hyperion*, *Ilex* and *Havock* to rescue survivors and sink the wrecked cruiser, Collins chased after *Bande Nere* with *Hero* and *Hasty*. The three destroyers plucked a total of 545 Italians from the sea despite the attempts of the Italian air force – responding to a radio call for help from Casardi – to attack them; indeed, *Havock* was damaged by a near miss which wounded crew and prisoners alike. At 8.59, *Colleoni* was hit by a torpedo from *Hyperion* and sank with the loss of 121 lives.[16]

Meanwhile, Casardi had circled back to see whether he could help his sister ship. This gave *Sydney*'s gunners another crack at him and a 6-inch shell crashed into his quarterdeck. Casardi turned south-west again and Collins gave chase. *Sydney*'s guns had fired 956 shells and her muzzles were burned black. At 10.37 pm, Cunningham, who had gone to sea in *Warspite* in case the action precipitated a major naval battle, ordered Collins back to port. By this time, *Bande Nere* was out of sight and Collins, low on ammunition and 'with great reluctance', gave up the chase.

At 11 o'clock the following morning, *Sydney* reached Alexandria. As she headed for her berth at the far end of the harbour, the Mediterranean Fleet erupted in a rousing 15-minute ovation.[17] 'We hoisted the Australian Jack as we passed through the boom and steamed down the line of battleships and cruisers,' chief engineer Syd Dalton says. 'All ships cleared lower deck and gave us three cheers as we proceeded and anyone would have imagined that we had won the war.'[18]

The Australian destroyers, each flying seven Australian flags from their masts, formed a guard of honour, with Hec Waller in *Stuart* making the signal 'Whacko, *Sydney*!' It was, said the official Australian historian, 'a great Australian day in Alexandria'.[19] The only damage to *Sydney* was a shellhole in her forward funnel; the only casualty a rating who had been slightly wounded by flying splinters.

Four days later, Captain Novaro of the *Colleoni* died of his wounds in an Alexandrian hospital. He was buried with full military honours, with Captain Collins as one of the coffin bearers. Novaro was awarded the *Medaglia d'Oro al Valor Militare*, Italy's equivalent of the Victoria Cross. Admiral Cunningham asked Collins, who was knighted by King George VI for bravery, how he had managed to get into action so quickly. The Australian flashed one of his toothy grins.

'Providence guided me, sir,' he replied.

'Well,' said Cunningham with a knowing smile, 'in future you can continue to take your orders from Providence.'[20]

The collapse of the French Army, the evacuation of the British Expeditionary Force at Dunkirk and Italy's entry into the war had completely redrawn the war map. On 20 June, when General Blamey stepped ashore with the advanced headquarters of the Australian Corps from a Qantas flying boat at Lake Tiberias, the Mediterranean and Middle East had become independent theatres of war.

Blamey was dressed as though for a day at the races in checked suit and grey felt hat – the flight had passed through several neutral countries, so Blamey and his officers had posed as businessmen. Blamey was no stranger to Egypt. He had been serving at the War Office in London in 1914 and had sailed with Harry Chauvel to join the 1st Australian Division in Egypt as general staff officer, grade 3 (GSO-3 operations). As a lieutenant-colonel, he had returned there from Gallipoli in July 1915 to help form the 2nd Division.

Blamey's command of the 2nd AIF in Palestine started with a warning. 'I've got a trunkful of bowler hats,' he told his officers, 'and any of you who lets me down will find himself back in Australia wearing one.'[21] The first recipient was Major Wally Condor, the entertainments officer, who hired a bunch of second-rate Tel Aviv dancers to put on a girlie show for the troops. The performance was of such low quality that it was booed off stage and there was a near-riot. Blamey sent Condor back to Australia and ordered the Palestine Symphony Orchestra to be brought in from Jerusalem to entertain the troops.[22]

From the beginning, there was friction between Blamey and the press, notably the ABC war correspondent Chester Wilmot and John Hetherington of the Melbourne *Herald*, who knew too much about his time as police commissioner of Victoria. He had been in the job less than two months when on 21 October 1925 the licensing squad raided a Fitzroy brothel run by vaudeville actress Mabel Tracey. In one of the rooms, they found a man who identified himself as a policeman. 'That's all right, boys,' he said. 'I'm a plain-clothes constable. Here is my badge.'[23] He produced police badge 80, the badge that had been issued to the commissioner.[24]

Blamey claimed he had given his key ring, with his badge attached, to a friend who wanted a late-night drink. The friend was supposed to remove a bottle from Blamey's locker at the Naval and Military Club, but instead had visited Madam

Tracey's bordello. Blamey refused to divulge his friend's name and then changed his story, claiming that the badge had actually been stolen from him and then mysteriously returned, even though a senior police officer had seen it on his desk in the intervening period. As a result of the 'badge 80' episode, Blamey became known to his troops as 'the old brothel-basher'.

Chester Wilmot had no doubts that Blamey's time as police commissioner had turned many Victorian recruits against him. 'Knowing that Blamey had the reputation of being a crook, they did not serve happily under him.'[25]

Shortly after his arrival in Palestine, Blamey flew to Cairo and checked into Shepheard's Hotel. He called on General Wavell, who lamented the fact that while he had seven divisional headquarters, he did not have one complete division in Egypt or Palestine – a fact he mentioned because he was already casting avaricious eyes on the 6th Division.[26] He told Blamey he wanted to assign one of his infantry brigades and one cavalry regiment to the Western Desert, where they would serve under British officers. Blamey objected. He referred Wavell to the charter under which no part of his force could be detached without his consent. The matter was dropped – for the time being.[27]

Returning to Gaza, Blamey commandeered the 6th Division's headquarters for himself and established his mess sergeant in an ornate Arab villa. He also acquired a new member of staff when Base HQ discovered John Peck's true age and wanted to send him back to Australia. 'I applied to the commander-in-chief and begged to be allowed to stay in Palestine,' Peck says. 'He said I could work for him in Gaza until I was old enough to join the infantry.' Blamey took a shine to the young man and made him his barman. Contrary to popular belief, Peck says that Blamey 'didn't drink very much – a lot of his staff officers did but he didn't'; indeed, he suffered from gout and was trying to cut down.[28]

In his first order-of-the-day, Blamey urged his troops, 'Keep fit; work hard; play hard. Don't worry about the pinpricks. Be a good comrade and pal to your mates, and when the time comes the Germans will know, "Australia will be there."' Blamey was one of the first casualties of the campaign – confined to bed with a severe attack of gout.

'To someone like me, he was very good,' John Peck says. 'He had a reputation later in the war of being very ruthless towards some of his commanders but to me he was okay – understanding and just.'

In July, Wavell proposed forming a composite '6th Australasian Division' consisting of the 16th Australian and 4th New Zealand Brigades, on the grounds that these were the only formations advanced enough in their training to be able to fight. Blamey and Freyberg rejected the idea, Freyberg writing to Wavell:

> I do not wish to disclose to the New Zealand Government the proposals as outlined by you to break up the New Zealand Forces, as they would make a most unfavourable impression in New Zealand official circles with repercussions you have probably not foreseen. The answer to any such proposal would, I am sure, be an uncompromising refusal.[29]

Meanwhile, the 6th Division had been released from its Palestinian exile. The 16th Brigade was undergoing final training at Helwan camp, 25 kilometres south of Cairo, and many of the men had got their first taste of the Egyptian capital. They found that the class system was still firmly in place. Nothing epitomised this more than an Old Etonians' dinner at which Jumbo Wilson, Arthur Smith – Wavell's one-legged chief of staff at GHQ – and Sir Miles Lampson ragged one another, handed out tickets – impositions – and sang the Eton Boating Song.

Among those most anxious to maintain the peacetime status quo were 'the Gabardine Swine' – hundreds of officers who held staff jobs at Grey Pillars and two other military establishments: the Citadel of Mohammed Ali on the hill above Cairo's Old City Walls and the Kasr el Nil barracks on the Nile. Wavell's headquarters had mushroomed from a staff of half a dozen officers in 1939 to more than 1000, prompting one naval officer to comment that Cunningham's team in Alexandria was 'microscopic compared to the serried ranks of brigadiers in Cairo'.[30]

The Gabardine Swine (named after the material in their formal service dress) took a mandatory five-hour siesta during the hot part of the afternoon, drank whisky in the Long Bar at Shepheard's and attended race meetings or watched the cricket at the Gezira Sporting Club, where one of the batsmen might be Flight Lieutenant (later Squadron Leader) Wally Hammond, the England captain.[31]

Lieutenant Michael Forrester of the Queen's Royal Regiment was astonished at the indolence when he was posted to Grey Pillars as a 23-year-old intelligence officer in 1940. 'Life assumed a very comfortable routine indeed,' he says. 'GHQ hours were from eight in the morning until 12 or half past, then one broke for lunch and there was nothing more in the afternoon until an evening session. It was a nice routine totally removed from war and reality.'[32]

None of this might have mattered had the ennui at GHQ not become a matter of life or death to the fighting troops. Incredibly, Wavell, preoccupied with trying to plug the gaps in his fighting forces, seemed oblivious to one of the main factors contributing to his failure as a commander.

Part of the problem was that none of the senior commanders complained loudly enough or often enough about GHQ's incompetence. Freyberg was too correct to buck the system and Blamey revelled in the decadence of Cairo whenever he visited the capital on AIF business. His generous expenses allowance enabled him to stay at Shepheard's which, in common with the Continental, the Turf and Gezira clubs – and many restaurants and nightclubs – was out of bounds to ordinary soldiers. Instead of the exotica of Madam Badia's '*club nocturno*' or the Roof Garden of the Continental, they were directed to Tiger Lil's in the Wozzer or to the Wagh el Birket – 'the Birker' – scene of a number of medically controlled regimental brothels.

In Jerusalem, Blamey joined Lieutenant-General Philip Neame, VC, commanding officer of British Troops in Palestine, at the King David Hotel, where the cuisine was excellent and the drink flowed. After dinner, Blamey made what his ADC Norman Carlyon describes as 'personal excursions in search of pleasure'. Despite his recent marriage, he was still an incorrigible old roué. His first biographer John Hetherington wrote that his advancing years 'had not reduced either his taste for amorous adventures or his capacity to enjoy them, and in Palestine as well as later in the war he had short-lived intimacies with accommodating women'.[33]

According to Carlyon, 'Blamey was attracted by young and pretty women. When opportunity arose, he had no inhibitions, enjoyed himself to the full – and then moved on.'[34]

Things were about to change dramatically, however. For at a time of extreme danger for Britain and her Empire, when the Battle of Britain was still raging and the Atlantic convoys faced annihilation from German U-boat packs, Churchill demanded action in the only theatre where British land forces could attack the Axis – the Middle East. And while the Gabardine Swine drank whisky at the Long Bar, Blamey's men would be performing great feats of arms.

CHAPTER 4

Spaghetti Western

By the northern autumn of 1940, Mussolini had an army of a quarter of a million men in the Horn of Africa, while in Libya he had deployed a further 215,000 troops in 14 divisions under Marshal Rodolfo Graziani with the intention of driving the British out of Egypt and seizing the Suez Canal.[1] By adding Egypt and the Sudan to his imperial jigsaw, he would be able to link Libya with Italy's East African colonies.

From his Tripoli headquarters, Graziani warned Mussolini and *Comando Supremo*, the Italian high command in Rome, that his army was far from battle-worthy, but his objections were brushed aside. Trusting in the mythical powers of 'Fascist dynamism', the Duce gave the order '*Avanti!*' and on 13 September 1940 the 10th Italian Army in Cyrenaica crossed the border into Egypt. Foreign Minister Count Ciano noted, 'Never has a military operation been undertaken so much against the will of the commanders.'[2]

The 10th Army was commanded by the crafty General Francesco Berti, who wisely remained behind at his headquarters in Tobruk, while Lieutenant-General Annibale Bergonzoli –

known as 'Barba Elettrica' to Italians on account of his blue beard,[3] and 'Electric Whiskers' to Allied troops – took charge of the Italian forces in the field. Spearheaded by a phalanx of motorcyclists and with 200 light and medium tanks guarding the flanks, six Italian divisions, including two of Mussolini's hated Blackshirt divisions from the military arm of the Fascist Party and two divisions of conscripted Libyan troops, advanced en masse along the coast road behind a rolling barrage of shellfire.

Bergonzoli used his artillery boldly in front of the leading infantry against the small force opposing him: the 3rd Battalion of the Coldstream Guards, one battery of the 3rd Royal Horse Artillery and one section of the 7th Medium Regiment, Royal Artillery.[4] Major-General Pietro Maletti's mobile group was supposed to perform an outflanking movement to the south but lost its way to the start-line and had to join the main attacking force.[5]

General Bergonzoli had been unable to find motor transport for more than one full division so the attack plodded along at the pace of the slowest foot soldier. The Italian columns entered the bottleneck at Halfaya Pass – 'Hellfire Pass' – at the northern end of the escarpment leading down to Salum, just over the Libyan border in Egypt. As the first motorised infantry groups slowly descended the unmade road in 10-ton Lancia lorries, British gunners, guided by the flash of sunlight on their windscreens, opened up with 25-pounders and scored many hits. 'The withdrawal of our small force was effected with admirable skill,' Wavell says, 'and there is no doubt whatever that very serious losses were inflicted on the enemy. Our own losses were under 50 men and a small number of vehicles.'[6]

At a speed of less than 20 kilometres a day, the vast caravanserai, tinkling with cooking pots and other impedimenta and with the soldiers' dark green uniforms turned field grey by dust, took three days to pass through Salum and reach the watering hole of Buq Buq. By the fourth day, with temperatures reaching 50 degrees Celsius, the Italians entered the tiny coastal settlement of Sidi Barrani, just 95 kilometres from its start-line. *Comando Supremo* issued a communiqué to an expectant nation claiming a great victory and stating that 'all is quiet and the trams are again running in the town of Sidi Barrani'. There were no trams in Sidi Barrani – indeed, there was no town, just a mosque, police station, a few mud huts and a landing strip – but that didn't stop Italian troops performing the *passo romano*, the Italian version of the goose-step, in front of the bemused inhabitants.

According to Ciano, Mussolini was 'radiant with joy'.[7] He hailed the operation as 'an indisputably brilliant tactical success' and was eager for Graziani to continue to his next objective. This was the heavily defended port and railhead of Mersa Matruh – the little seaside resort where Antony had wooed Cleopatra by the azure waters of the Mediterranean. Nothing, however, could induce Graziani to go any further. He believed British propaganda that Wavell had a huge army at his disposal and, fearing a counter-attack, ordered an arc of fortifications to be built from Sidi Barrani to a depth of 80 kilometres along the rock-strewn desert of the escarpment.[8]

Judging by the extent of the building works, it appeared that the Italians were preparing for a long stay. Well-furnished mess tents and huge green-lined hospital marquees were erected. Spacious sleeping quarters were dug into the rocky surface and surrounded by stone breastworks called sangars. Minefields were laid on all approaches to each camp except the western approaches – to allow access to lorries bringing supplies, including fresh fruit and vegetables from Italian farms in the Jebel Achdar.

For the officers, no expense was spared to make their sojourn in the desert more agreeable: at breakfast, they ate melon and freshly baked bread and drank percolated coffee, while their sleeping quarters were equipped with fresh linen, reading lamps and even book rests. In anticipation of victory, every officer had brought his dress uniform adorned with a sash and an array of medals. The British forces opposing them, dressed in rags after weeks in the desert and existing on a diet of bully beef and hard tack, could only dream of such *dolce vita*.

Mussolini declared himself 'very happy that Italy could score in Egypt a success which affords her the glory she has sought in vain for three centuries'.[9] He assured Hitler during their meeting at the Brenner Pass that the attack on Mersa Matruh would begin on 15 October at the very latest; *Regia Aeronautica* would then move forward and bomb Alexandria to drive the British fleet out of its Egyptian base. Hitler offered to provide specialist forces for the assault on Mersa Matruh but Mussolini coolly replied that he would need no help. However, he reserved the right to request German tanks and dive-bombers for the third phase of his campaign – the conquest of Alexandria.[10]

Wavell ordered the 16th Australian Brigade, which had been training at Helwan for just two weeks, to move up to the Western Desert, while the Victorians of the 17th Brigade moved from Palestine to take their place. Tubby Allen's men took up position at Amiriya, an area of undulating sand covered with scrub on the edge of the Nile Delta and the last line of defence in front of Alexandria.

Further west, the 18th and 19th Battalions of the 4th New Zealand Brigade were transported by the 4th Reserve Mechanical Transport (RMT) Company to join the Western Desert Force at Garawla, a rock-strewn wasteland near Mersa Matruh. From their base at nearby Smugglers' Cove, the RMT drivers, commanded by 45-year-old Major G. H. Whyte, then travelled deep into the desert to plant huge reserves of petrol, ammunition and food at secret field supply depots to be used in future operations.[11]

Tuesday 15 October came and went and there was no sign of an Italian advance. 'We hoped very much that they would go on to Mersa Matruh because we had a plan to annihilate them,' says Lieutenant-General Richard O'Connor, the Governor of

Jerusalem who had been appointed commander of Western Desert Force. The plan was to encourage the Italians to advance as far as Mersa Matruh and then launch the 7th Armoured Division on to their flank from its position south of the fortress. 'But unfortunately they stayed 70 miles short of Mersa Matruh. As they wouldn't come forward to us, I felt we must do something about them and I wrote to Wavell that we should take some sort of action against them.'[12]

At his headquarters, Wavell had pinned a map of the Italian positions on the wall facing his desk and studied it every day through his one good eye. He noted that the forts were not mutually self-supporting and were separated by wide distances – as much as 25 kilometres between the defences at Rabia and Nibeiwa, a gap which invited a counter-offensive.[13] While the Italians controlled the territory within the compass of their camps, the British forces, including the new Long Range Desert Group, roamed free and virtually unchallenged over most of the desert. As there were no Italian patrols to worry about, it would be a relatively simple matter to raid the Italian forts.

'Oddly enough,' O'Connor says, 'Wavell had written a letter to General Wilson saying the same thing, with a copy to me: he had an idea for a five-day raid against the Italians in their present positions.'[14]

Meanwhile, Graziani had been summoned to Rome, where Mussolini ordered him to capture Mersa Matruh without further delay. Again, Graziani prevaricated. He was in the process of building a sealed road, the Via della Vittoria ('Victory Road'), from Sidi Barrani to link up with the Via Balbia, a 2000-kilometre macadam highway built by the former Libyan Governor, the Italian flying ace Italo Balbo,[15] to link Tunis with Tripoli, Benghazi, Tobruk and Bardia. Like a true son of Caesar, Graziani was also constructing an aqueduct to provide water for his troops.

*

This was the situation in the last week of October when Mussolini's attention switched to the Italian invasion of Greece, an attack that had been even more vehemently opposed by his commanders. Mussolini had undertaken the Greek campaign without consulting the Fascist Grand Council and against the advice of Marshal Badoglio.[16] The Italian chiefs of staff had reached the conclusion that the Italian Army would simply be too weak to overcome Greek resistance. And despite Badoglio's advice, Mussolini had failed to occupy Crete, a strategic blunder that would have profound consequences for the Axis Powers and shape the destiny of the Anglo–Anzac forces in the Middle East.

Mussolini shared the guilt with Count Ciano, whose advocacy of the Greek invasion had been so strident that the conflict was called 'Ciano's war'. The decision had been taken after General Sebastiano Visconti Prasca, the commander-in-chief in Albania, assured Mussolini that the plan of campaign was 'as perfect as is humanly possible': he would cross the Pindus Mountains, overrun the provinces of Epirus and Macedonia in ten to 15 days and force the Greek Army to surrender.[17] Mussolini questioned him about the capabilities of Greek troops. Visconti Prasca raised a tinted eyebrow and declared, 'They are not a people who like fighting.'[18]

In a torrential downpour, an Italian force of 70,000 men advanced into Greece along three lines of attack. The main thrust headed from the Albanian town of Koritza along the road to Florina with the ultimate objective of seizing the great port of Salonica. The troops had little winter clothing, few maps, no engineering units and no unified system of command, while thousands of Albanian conscripts promptly defected to the other side. Visconti Prasca's forces were soon tied up in mountainous terrain in which heavy rain had washed away many of the roads, leaving tanks and troop-carrying vehicles wallowing in seas of mud.

The weather was so bad that Italian planes could not take

off to support his forward units and the navy's presence was virtually nonexistent, but in the first three days the invaders encountered little opposition. The Greeks had sensibly kept their forces clear of the border area to prevent charges of provocation. General Alexander Papagos, the hawk-nosed, 57-year-old Athenian who had been appointed commander-in-chief, bided his time while reinforcements were mobilised and rushed to the front as quickly as the Greek Army's antiquated transport system made possible.

Honouring Chamberlain's pledge of 1939 to guarantee Greece's independence, Churchill offered military help to the Greek Prime Minister, General Iaonnis 'Little John' Metaxas. The dictator's *'Ochi!'* – 'No!' – to the Italian ultimatum on the night of the invasion 'was music to Churchill's ears', says Michael Forrester.

> It encouraged him to think that here at last he had the foundations of a Balkan front which had been near to his heart ever since the war started. He was justified to think that whatever we could do for Greece would encourage other Balkan countries to come in on the right side. So the question at the time was how to keep the Greeks going and how best we could support them.[19]

Churchill was also conscious of the fact that the American minister in Greece for the previous eight years had been Lincoln 'Link' MacVeagh, one of President Franklin D. Roosevelt's oldest friends from Groton and Harvard, and one of his staunchest political allies. If MacVeagh reported favourably on Britain's efforts to aid Greece, it would strengthen Roosevelt's hand against the isolationist bloc in Congress.

The wily Metaxas knew that Churchill was plotting to extend the Greco–Italian war into a second front against Germany and he wanted nothing to do with it. He stalled Britain's first overtures but permitted Churchill to send Major-

General Michael Gambier-Parry to Athens with a small British military mission to liaise with the Greek high command. Gambier-Parry was greeted cordially and offered rooms in the Grande Bretagne Hotel on Constitution Square.

Noted for its excellent cuisine and panoramic views of the Acropolis, the hotel had been commandeered as Greek general headquarters, partly because its massive cellars could be used as air-raid shelters. The British general got to work with Colonel Jasper Blunt, the military attaché at the British Legation, on the best ways to help the Greek war effort. Charles Mott-Radclyffe, a former diplomat who had joined the military mission as GSO-3, recalls, 'We were a very happy party under the jovial leadership of General Gambier-Parry whose manner and approach were exactly what the Greeks expected of a British general.'[20]

Gambier-Parry paid tribute to the military 'genius' of General Metaxas for the Greek Army's 'exceedingly clever' dispositions and added that it was impossible to overemphasise the importance of the Greek Army's success in the field since 'it is the first and only success of the Allied armies on land'.[21]

It was ironic that the British were collaborating with Metaxas, a dictator who ran a police state more in tune with the Third Reich than Britain's parliamentary democracy. Indeed, he was a graduate of the German Military College and had ruthlessly suppressed his Venizelist and communist rivals since coming to power on 4 August 1936 at the invitation of Greece's head of state, King George II, to foil a communist-inspired coup.

Metaxas was in the terminal stages of throat cancer and although desperate to save his country before he died, his main fear was that the presence of British fighting units would provoke a German attack. The German minister in Athens, however, assured him that Germany would not consider the presence of British aircraft in Greece as a *casus belli*, provided they were forbidden to use airfields in northern Greece to bomb the Romanian oilfields.[22] Metaxas therefore invited Churchill to send RAF squadrons to support his troops in the field and, at the same time, asked whether the British would take responsibility for the defence of Crete.

Churchill seized the unexpected Greek offer with both hands. 'One salient strategic fact leaped out upon us – CRETE!' he writes. 'The Italians must not have it. We must get it first – and at once.'[23] He ordered British troops to occupy the island immediately and for the long, deep anchorage of Suda Bay to be turned into 'a second Scapa' for Admiral Cunningham's Mediterranean Fleet. While a joint services mission flew to Crete to consult the Greek authorities, Cunningham gathered his naval forces together. The cruisers *Sydney* and *Orion*, on patrol in the Aegean, were recalled to Alexandria. The patrol had taken them as far as the Dardanelles and *Sydney*'s company had gazed in respectful silence at the rugged cliffs of Gallipoli.[24]

Just 24 hours later the first Crete convoy, escorted by the scrap-ironers *Vampire*, *Voyager* and *Waterhen*, sailed from the Egyptian port for Suda Bay. Hoping the Italian navy would come out to attack the convoy, Cunningham took the fleet to sea and roamed around the west coast of Crete. Although the British ships were sighted by Italian aircraft, the Italian navy remained resolutely in port.[25]

On 1 November, the first British troops – the 2nd Battalion of the York and Lancaster Regiment – landed on Crete, followed a few days later by the 2nd Battalion of Wavell's old regiment, the Black Watch. Anti-aircraft guns, supplies and equipment were off-loaded and a refuelling base set up at Suda Bay. Just as Hitler had feared, Crete had become a stepping stone for British forces en route to the Balkans.

On the night of 11/12 November, Cunningham took the fight to the Italians when 21 antiquated Swordfish bombers of the Fleet Air Arm, taking off from Britain's newest aircraft carrier HMS *Illustrious*, attacked the port of Taranto on the heel – the Achilles heel – of southern Italy and torpedoed three battleships and two cruisers. 'A black day ... I thought I would find the Duce downhearted,' Count Ciano writes. 'Instead, he took the blow quite well and does not, at the moment, seem to have fully realised its gravity.'[26]

In fact, the crippling of half the Italian battlefleet restored the balance of power in the Mediterranean just as it was swinging Italy's way. Wildly popular among the Greeks, the action forced *Supermarina* – the high command of the Italian navy – to move its fleet from Taranto to Naples and Brindisi. Three days later, as the worst winter in living memory took hold in the mountains, the ebullient Greek Army launched a counter-offensive along the whole Albanian front.

The first British force to Greece arrived the following day when five British warships berthed at Piraeus and disembarked 4000 RAF and army base personnel. 'British troops are all over town,' Link MacVeagh noted, 'and I must say it's nice to see them.' The troops were sentries, anti-aircraft gunners and ground staff whose job was to look after the five British fighter and bomber squadrons – later raised to eight – that would be operating in support of the Greek Army under the command of Air Commodore John D'Albiac from Eleusis and Menidi airfields near Athens.[27]

The British chiefs of staff then made a serious tactical error. The King had warmed to Gambier-Parry, who had moved mountains to assist his armed forces with planes, guns, ammunition and equipment. There was widespread dismay when, without warning, he was posted to Crete as commander-in-chief of British forces there. His replacement, Major-General Thomas Heywood, a former military attaché in Paris, was an entirely different type: an empire-builder with hard, narrowed eyes who glared at subordinates through a monocle.

Heywood already had 'form'. His glowing reports to the War Office about the competence of the French Army had raised false hopes about its chances against the Wehrmacht in 1940. He arrived in Athens with enough staff to occupy an entire floor of the Grande Bretagne Hotel. Refusing to speak to Jasper Blunt, who knew more about the Greek Army than any other British officer, he installed Colonel Stanley Casson, reader in classical archaeology at New College, Oxford, as head of Intelligence. Casson quickly proved himself a master in the art of 'saying nothing in a rigmarole of earnest nonsense', while his talented young staff indulged in the pointless exercise of marking positions on a huge map of Albania with coloured pins and wool.[28]

Heywood's staff expanded to some 70 officers, the vast majority of whom had little work to do. 'Far too many of us were kicking our heels,' says Charles Mott-Radclyffe, 'while others tripped over our toes.'[29] While the staff doodled, chatted and smoked the hours away, harassed Greek officers in the same building laboured non-stop to provide supplies and reinforcements to the Greek Army in the mountains of Albania. Oblivious to his Ally's sensitivities, Heywood authorised the opening of a huge cocktail bar for his staff on the ground floor of the hotel in full view of the hard-working Greeks. 'The bar was chock-a-bloc before lunch and dinner daily,' says Lieutenant-Colonel Miles Reid, whose reconnaissance unit was attached to the mission. 'It should never for one moment have been tolerated – the British Club was a few minutes away across the road.'[30]

According to Reid, Heywood 'allowed the mission to flounder on with no guidance or control until circumstances disrupted it without it ever having justified its existence or having atoned for its shortcomings'.[31] Heywood's response to the pressures of command 'was to make himself more and more inaccessible until even his own ADC failed to have any idea of his movements'.[32]

It seems inconceivable that General Wavell, who made several visits to Athens during this period, could have been unaware that Heywood's mission was not only undermining British prestige in Greece but also represented an affront to Greek *amour propre*. But if he noticed, he did nothing about it.

Meanwhile, the Greek Army had pushed most of the Italians back over the Albanian border. 'Visibly depressed' by his ally's poor showing,[33] Hitler expressed his displeasure in a letter to Mussolini on 20 November. 'I wanted, above all, to ask you to postpone the operation until a more favourable season, in any case until after the presidential election in America,' he wrote.

> In any event I wanted to ask you not to undertake this action without previously carrying out a blitzkrieg operation on Crete. For this purpose I intended to make practical suggestions regarding the employment of a parachute and of an airborne division.[34]

In his reply, Mussolini apologised to Hitler for these 'misunderstandings'. He had sacked the man responsible for the Greek debacle, General Visconti Prasca, and replaced him with General Ubaldo Soddu, an intriguer known to his colleagues as 'the sly murderer'. The switch did not bode well for Italy's chances: short, fat and bespectacled, Soddu was a music lover who spent his evenings composing film scores.[35] The Duce's embarrassment was plain to see and marked a seismic shift in his relationship with Hitler over whom he had previously enjoyed a certain sway as the longer-serving dictator. From now on, the Führer was in charge.

Anthony Eden, now War Minister in Churchill's government, visited Wavell in Cairo to see whether he could squeeze more Greek aid from Wavell's limited resources. This was the last thing Wavell wanted. He had remained silent about his plans for a counter-offensive against Graziani's forces in Egypt due to what he described as Churchill's desire 'to have at least one finger in any military pie'. He wanted to avoid arousing premature hopes of success and he didn't want Churchill telling him what to do – 'absolute secrecy was the only hope of keeping my intentions from the Italians, who had so many tentacles in Cairo'. Risking interference from No. 10 and a possible security leak, he was now forced to let Eden into the secret to prevent a further drain on his assets.[36]

Churchill had been badgering Wavell for months to use his troops against the Italians.[37] The Australians and New Zealanders, he pointed out, had been training for almost a year and it had been hugely expensive to bring them to Egypt. Was this valuable military asset to be wasted?

Mussolini's relationship with his commanders was abysmal but there were times when Churchill would have run him a close second. 'Wavell has 400,000 men,' he raged on one occasion, ignoring the fact that the vast majority were unarmed base troops. 'If they lose Egypt, blood will flow. I will have firing parties to shoot the generals.'[38] Balfour thought in 1914 that Churchill wanted to rival Napoleon rather than Nelson; in World War II, he seemed to want to rival *both* of them. And there was nobody to stop him.

As Bob Menzies later discovered, the British War Cabinet was full of 'dumb men most of whom disagree with Winston but none of whom dare to say so'; the chiefs of staff 'are without exception Yes-men': the first sea lord, Sir Dudley Pound, was 'too old and past his job' (in fact he was suffering from an undiagnosed brain tumour which would kill him in October 1943), the chief of air staff, 'Peter' Portal, was 'being killed on his feet by the late-night meetings convened by Churchill', and the chief of the general staff, Sir John Dill, was incapable of standing up to the Prime Minister.[39]

Churchill had met Wavell for the first time in August 1940 when he attended a meeting of the War Cabinet in London. The Prime Minister had expected a virtuoso performance from his commander-in-chief on ways of defeating the Italians, but Wavell had clammed up and simply refused to discuss strategy in front of politicians. Churchill, who considered himself a master strategist, made no secret of his disappointment. He had been vocal about Wavell's shortcomings ever since. Wavell, he told Anthony Eden, lacked 'that sense of mental rigour and resolve to overcome obstacles which is indispensable to successful war'.[40] He would make 'a good chairman of a Tory association'.[41]

Churchill's attitude changed miraculously when he was informed by Eden that Wavell was going on the offensive. He 'purred like six cats'[42] and speculated on the 'centre of gravity in [the] Middle East shifting suddenly from Egypt to the Balkans, and from Cairo to Constantinople'.[43] His mood changed again when Wavell refused to divulge the launch date of his offensive and cabled that he felt 'undue hopes [were] being placed on this operation which was designed as raid only'. Churchill was furious. He told Sir John Dill, chief of the imperial general staff, 'If, with the situation as it is, General Wavell is only playing small, and is not hurling on his whole available force with furious energy, he will have failed to rise to the height of circumstances.'[44]

On 4 December, Wavell discussed the final plans for his counter-attack with Admiral Cunningham, the RAF chief Air Marshal Sir Arthur Longmore, General O'Connor and O'Connor's immediate superior, General Wilson. Under Operation Compass, as the offensive was to be called, Dick O'Connor's Western Desert Force – 30,000 men and tanks of the British 7th Armoured Division (the Desert Rats) and the 4th Indian Division (the Red Eagles) and including some additional British regiments – would attack the Italians in their redoubts around Sidi Barrani. Reconnaissance had revealed that the gap between Rabia and Nibeiwa would enable British tanks, infantry and artillery to approach the Nibeiwa camp from the relatively undefended western side, where there was no minefield, no anti-tank ditch and little artillery. While other British forces approached along the coast to threaten Maktila, the easternmost Italian camp, the main force, commanded by Major-General Noel Beresford-Peirse of the 4th Indian Division, would swing north from Nibeiwa and attack Tummar West, Point 90, Tummar East and the other camps inside the defensive circle.

Wavell thought the operation – invoking the same lethal mix of fast-moving armour supported by infantry as the German blitzkrieg in France – would be 'a short and swift one lasting four or five days at most and taking every advantage of the element of surprise'.[45] He told Cunningham, however, that he was 'determined to go all out if the Italians showed signs of making off'.[46]

So Churchill would get his wish of a British fightback in the only theatre of war where his troops could strike at the enemy. Wavell provided the opportunity, but it was Dick O'Connor, the slightly built, quietly spoken, Irish-born commander, who would have to make it happen. 'Jumbo Wilson was a really cosy, chatty man and probably got [O'Connor] to unbutton, which did him good,' says O'Connor's aide de camp, Earl Haig, son of the First World War general. 'But I know he was no help to him when it came to moments of serious decision.'[47]

On Saturday 7 December 1940, Wavell took his wife Eugenie, known as Queenie, and his three daughters to a race meeting at Gezira, the little European enclave on an island in the Nile. While press photographers and Italian spies followed them around the paddock,[48] Longmore's fighters and bombers, including Australian Gladiators from the 3rd Squadron RAAF, attacked Italian airfields in Libya and destroyed many aircraft on the ground. That evening, Wavell was driven in his big black Packard to the Turf Club, where he dined with 15 officers, including Generals Blamey and Freyberg. He appeared unconcerned, almost carefree, and gave no sign that a major offensive was under way.

During 8 December, RAF fighters kept Italian spotter planes at bay while O'Connor's troops crept unseen in heavily camouflaged trucks across 80 kilometres of desert to their assembly areas 24 kilometres south-east of the Rabia–Nibeiwa Gap. The Kiwi drivers of the 4th RMT Company had been entrusted with the job of carrying the three battalions of the 5th Indian Brigade – the 1st Royal Fusiliers, 4/6th Rajputana

Rifles and the 3/1st Punjab Regiment – in their three-ton Bedfords, 'so one knew that they would be sure to arrive at their destination'.[49]

The narrow coastal strip around Sidi Barrani was ideal for bombardment from the sea. By 11 o'clock that night, three ships were in position: the gunboats *Aphis* and *Ladybird* with 6-inch guns and HMS *Terror*, a monitor armed with two 15-inch guns and eight 4-inch guns. Named after the USS *Monitor*, the monitor was a flat-bottomed seagoing barge equipped with battleship-sized guns and intended for bombardment of the enemy coast. As the targets were illuminated by parachute flares dropped by the Fleet Air Arm, they were blasted for 90 minutes, with *Terror* and *Aphis* hitting strongpoints and motor transport in Maktila and *Ladybird* concentrating on enemy positions at Sidi Barrani.

Thirty kilometres to the south, RAF aircraft circled over Nibeiwa to drown the approach of the 7th Royal Tank Regiment's 48 Matilda heavy tanks (officially known as Infantry or 'I' tanks) that would spearhead Operation Compass under the command of Lieutenant-Colonel Roy Jerram. The night was bitterly cold and a freezing wind stirred up a thick duststorm or *khamsin*.[50] In the moonlight, the 11th Indian Brigade was driven through the Rabia–Nibeiwa Gap to their final rendezvous point ten kilometres south-west of Nibeiwa.[51]

At 5 am on 9 December, the 4th/7th Rajput Regiment roused the Italians from their slumber with a diversionary attack on the eastern side of the camp. The shooting lasted for only a few minutes. Such disturbances had been a regular occurrence to familiarise the Italians with them and when the danger seemed to have passed, as it always had done, the camp lapsed into silence. As daylight broke, the Italians stirred again and began preparing breakfast: bread was being baked and coffee beans ground. Breakfast was always served at 7.30 am sharp,[52] but at 7.15 am all 72 artillery pieces of the 4th Indian Division suddenly opened fire on Nibeiwa with high-explosive shells.

Twenty-three Italian light and medium tanks which had been placed outside the perimeter wall as an advanced guard were neutralised while still warming up. As the 25-ton Matilda tanks burst through the wire at the north-west entrance with battle pennants flying and Besa machine guns blazing, the 2nd Queen's Own Cameron Highlanders and 1st/6th Rajputana Rifles poured out of their trucks and followed the tanks in.

The Italian gunners swiftly brought their artillery to bear against the Matildas, but their shells bounced off the heavily armoured turrets and hulls. In despair, the gunners abandoned their guns and made gallant attempts to halt the tanks with grenades, also to no avail. A pyjama-clad General Maletti, the camp's commander, burst from his quarters armed with a machine gun and was killed by fire from one of the Matildas.[53]

By 10.40 am, Nibeiwa was in British hands and half a dozen other fortified camps were under attack. The Kiwi drivers drove headlong through the swirling sandstorm to deliver the Fusiliers and Punjabis to Tummar West, pulling up within 100 metres of the perimeter walls and, although under fire, accompanied the troops into action – the first Anzac soldiers to come to grips with the enemy.

At the same time, the Rajputana Rifles heading for Tummar East ran into a counter-attack by Italian infantry and tanks. Taking the initiative, Sergeant I. R. H. Thomson, a 28-year-old Kiwi driver, led a section of Rajputs in capturing a machine-gun post and holding out until Punjabi reinforcements arrived to deal with the enemy.[54] The following morning Tummar East fell, followed by Sidi Barrani. Italian forces could be seen retreating westward along the coast road with light tanks and armoured cars in pursuit. A young British officer of the 7th Armoured Division flashed a signal to his headquarters, 'Have arrived at the second B in Buq Buq.'[55] As the Italians climbed towards Halfaya Pass, *Terror* and the gunboats were waiting off Salum and saturated the road, now graded and surfaced by Libyan workers, with shellfire.[56]

At sunset on 11 December, Italian troops could be seen throwing away their weapons, while others were on the beach waving their shirts in surrender.[57] O'Connor's three-day 'raid' had bagged 38,000 Italian prisoners (including five generals), 73 tanks, 237 guns and 1000 vehicles and driven the Italians out of Egypt. Churchill cabled Wavell, 'I send you my heartfelt congratulations on your splendid victory, which fulfils our highest hopes.' He urged the commander to pursue the Italians to exact 'the greatest forfeit' from them and added, 'Nothing would shake Mussolini more than a disaster in Libya itself.'

In his office at Palazzo Venezia, the Duce complained about the cowardice of his commanders. 'Five generals are prisoners and one is dead,' he told Ciano. 'This is the percentage of Italians who have military characteristics and those who have none.'[58]

'It looks as though the Italians have cracked good and proper,' Sir Miles Lampson wrote in his diary. 'Serve the brutes damn well right too.'[59] In Berlin, Josef Goebbels was in a rage. 'The Italians have brought the entire military prestige of the Axis crashing down in ruins,' he stormed.[60] It was Britain's first victory of the war, the first beacon of hope in a sea of darkness.

Things were just as bad for the Italian forces in Greece despite the formation of a new-look *Comando Supremo* in Rome to tackle the military crisis. The Italian central divisions had been cut off in Epirus and the other two prongs had to be withdrawn to Albania, with heavy losses. To no avail, Mussolini accepted Badoglio's resignation as chief of the general staff and on 6 December appointed Badoglio's arch-rival, 60-year-old Count Ugo Cavallero, to the post. Badoglio retired to his country estate to shoot pheasant but he would return later in the war to exact an exquisite revenge on the Duce.[61]

By Christmas, the Italians had been driven back into Albania and the Greeks were pressing towards Valona, the principal

Italian supply port. If General Papagos could seize Valona, he could supply his own troops by sea and deliver a knockout blow to the Italians. Conditions at the front were grimmer than ever: Italian soldiers received a supply of new boots but found they were all left-footed, while many Greeks had no boots at all.

Charles Mott-Radclyffe's abiding recollection of a tour of the Albanian front 'was of a cold so intense that it numbed all senses, and of unbounded admiration for the Greek troops, many of whom came from the plains and had little or no experience of mountain warfare'.[62]

On New Year's Eve, General Cavallero sacked General Soddu and assumed the post of Italian commander in Albania himself. Fortune now favoured the Italians: the Greek offensive ran into a blizzard and ground to a standstill; Valona remained tantalisingly out of reach. Half a million Italian troops had been thrown into the battle, 13,744 of whom were killed, 50,000 wounded, 12,000 hospitalised with frostbite and a further 52,000 invalided out of the service with various other ailments.[63] Mussolini's dreams of an Italian *imperium* had crashed in flames. Explaining to Marshal De Bono why he had undertaken the Greek campaign, he said, 'The Army had need of *glory*.'[64]

Mussolini had become the bane of Hitler's life. Piqued by successive Italian defeats, the Führer was forced to revise his entire south-east strategy. At the Reich Chancellery, he issued Directive No. 20 for Operation Marita, under which German forces would invade Greece in the spring of 1941 and drive the British out of the Balkans. They would also seize Crete to secure the Wehrmacht's southern flank for the forthcoming campaign against Soviet Russia.

Hitler had decided in July 1940 – despite the signing of the Nazi–Soviet Non-Aggression Pact a year earlier – to attack his Russian ally (and secret military collaborator) once he had dealt with Britain. 'If we start in May 1941, we would have five months to finish the job,' he told his generals at a meeting in the Berghof, his lair in the Bavarian Alps.[65]

Field Marshal Erich von Manstein, who had led the German invasion of Western Europe, thought the Führer was 'already drunk with a belief in his own infallibility'. The Blitz on British cities raged between September 1940 and May 1941, with appalling loss of life. On 29 December 1940, the City of London witnessed the greatest conflagration since the Great Fire in 1666. The Luftwaffe, however, had failed to win the Battle of Britain, leading to the cancellation of Operation Sea Lion, the invasion of the British Isles across the English Channel. Churchill then treated Hitler's spurious 'appeal to reason' for Britain to reach a negotiated settlement with Germany with icy indifference. 'If Hitler really believed he had won the war after the defeat of France and that it was now merely a matter of bringing this home to Britain, he could not have been more wrong,' von Manstein writes.[66]

Hitler had hoped for British support in crushing Russia but the German leader now changed tack and urged Stalin to send the Red Army southward to invade British India, a move that might have signalled the disintegration of the British Empire – in quick succession, Britain could have lost Egypt and the Suez Canal to the Italians, India to the Russians and Singapore to the Japanese.

During talks in Berlin on 12 and 13 November, Russia's Foreign Minister Molotov turned his nose up at the mention of India. Stalin's territorial ambitions, he said, extended through the Dardanelles into the Balkans – the very thing that Hitler wanted to avoid.[67] As Russia had occupied the Baltic republics and the north-east section of Romania, Hitler now feared that Stalin would seize the Romanian oilfields on which his war machine depended.[68] On 18 December, ignoring the lessons of history, he issued Directive No. 21 for Operation Barbarossa, 'to overthrow Soviet Russia in a rapid campaign', beginning as soon as possible after 15 May 1941 and lasting no more than six months.[69]

That month, December 1940, saw the appointment of

Anthony Eden as Britain's Foreign Secretary for the second time. He had resigned as Foreign Secretary in Chamberlain's government in 1938 over the manner – though not the policy – of appeasing Hitler and Mussolini. From the very first day, he embarked on a two-month odyssey to save Greece from the Nazis, a mission that would have profound consequences for Australian and New Zealand troops in Egypt and Palestine. But for the time being, many Australian fighting units would be fully occupied in North Africa. They had wanted 'action instead of route marches in the sand' and now they were going to get it in a battle that would herald the beginning of five years of combat.

Meanwhile, John Peck's dream of joining a fighting unit had come true. 'I badgered Blamey so much that towards the end of 1940 he kicked me out into the infantry and I joined the 2/7th Battalion,' he says. 'The training was excruciating because for the past 12 months I'd had a very soft life. Marching across the desert with a full pack for 18 hours really tore me to bits.'[70]

CHAPTER 5

Baptism at Bardia

General Wavell dropped his bombshell on 11 December 1940. He informed Dick O'Connor that he was sending the 4th Indian Division, the heroes of Sidi Barrani, to spearhead his invasion of Italian-occupied East Africa and replacing them with Iven Mackay's 6th Australian Division. The switch stopped O'Connor's advance in its tracks. The Australians were untrained in desert warfare and had only just been armed with modern artillery pieces. 'It came as a complete and very unpleasant surprise,' says O'Connor, who knew he had the enemy on the back foot and wanted to keep up the pressure.

> General Wavell told me afterwards, 'I purposely didn't tell you because I thought it might affect your operations.' But really, of course, it put paid to the question of immediate exploitation.[1]

O'Connor was forced to postpone further attacks on Italian forces in Cyrenaica until the New Year, when Italian commanders would have had time to rectify the failings revealed at Sidi Barrani.

Things were going to be difficult for Australian troops in their first battle against an Axis power, but Iven Mackay was confident that they would give a good account of themselves. His entourage took off for the desert in two vehicles: a Ford Mercury with the general's personal lavatory – 'Iven's thunderbox' – strapped to the roof and a station wagon that would serve as his 'battle buggy' when he visited the battlefields.[2] 'The Australians were a very fine lot of troops – very, very fine,' says Lord Harding, formerly O'Connor's chief of staff, Brigadier John Harding. 'They were brilliant fighters and very well led by General Mackay, but they were short of artillery, particularly medium artillery.'[3]

At 1st Corps Headquarters in Gaza, General Blamey eagerly awaited the arrival of his wife Olga. He had used his influence with Robert Menzies and Percy Spender, the Army Minister, to have her passport endorsed for travel to Egypt and Palestine. On 12 December, the War Cabinet – putting aside more urgent matters – had finally granted her a visa to join her husband in the Middle East.[4] While Iven Mackay set up his headquarters in the vast cavern of one of the desert's underground water cisterns at Capuzzo, Blamey threw a 'fabulous Christmas party' in his mess at Gaza.[5] To Mackay, he sent a message asking to be kept informed of the battle.

The 2nd AIF's baptism of fire would take place at Bardia (pronounced 'bar-dear') an insignificant speck on the map consisting of a couple of dozen white-walled stone buildings clustered around a small harbour, with a few more dwellings on the surrounding cliff-tops. General Bergonzoli had been placed in charge of the Bardia garrison after Mussolini had insisted – and Graziani had agreed – that the British must be made to fight for every metre of Libyan territory.

'I have given you a difficult task,' Mussolini told Bergonzoli over the crackling airwaves from Rome, 'but one suited to your courage and your experience as an old and intrepid soldier – the task of defending the fortress of Bardia to the last. I am certain that *Barba Elettrica* and his brave soldiers will stand at whatever cost faithful to the last.'

Bergonzoli replied, 'I am aware of the honour and I have today repeated to my troops your message – simple and unequivocal. In Bardia we are and here we stay.'[6] Bergonzoli, however, was confident that he wouldn't be required to make the ultimate sacrifice of his own life. With more than 45,000 troops, 290 artillery pieces and 127 tanks at his disposal – twice as many men, three times as many guns and twice as many tanks as British Intelligence had estimated – he believed he could withstand whatever force the enemy might throw at him. He assured Mussolini that Bardia was 'impregnable'.

The defences were indeed formidable, more so than at Nibeiwa or Sidi Barrani. A network of fortifications had been built along a 25-kilometre semi-circle ringing Bardia from coast to coast and encompassing long sections of the Via Balbia.[7] The first line of defence consisted of dense barbed-wire barriers and minefields fronted by an anti-tank ditch four metres wide by one-and-a-half metres deep. These defences protected a series of concrete-lined trenches armed with one or two 47-mm guns and from two to four machine guns. The trenches were connected to deep underground shelters which were practically bomb-proof. Three hundred metres behind the forward line was a second line of defence posts consisting of concrete and steel-shuttered pillboxes protected by six well-dispersed minefields.[8] Iven Mackay described the defences at Bardia as 'a miniature Hindenburg Line'.[9] There were 83 posts in all and he could see from maps captured at Sidi Barrani that they were numbered consecutively from south to north, odd numbers for the outer posts and even numbers for the inner. Aerial photographs also showed that many of Bergonzoli's artillery pieces and much of his infantry had been deployed on a switchline, a secondary line of five additional strongpoints running from east to west and defending the southern side of the perimeter.[10]

'What we had to tackle at Bardia and Tobruk was entirely different [from Sidi Barrani],' General O'Connor says. 'They were strong fortresses with wire and a very large anti-tank ditch surrounding them. There was no way of getting the tanks in except to bridge the ditch.' He placed light and medium tanks of the 7th Armoured Division astride the Via Balbia between Bardia and Tobruk, effectively ending any hope Bergonzoli might have had of reinforcements reaching him from that direction.

Nevertheless, Bardia was well placed to fight a siege. It had a good water supply from artesian wells – 200 tons a day were pumped and distributed in pipes to points within the perimeter – and was amply stocked with ammunition and stores. On the other hand, General O'Connor faced a logistical nightmare. Supplies of all kinds, including every drop of petrol and water, had to be transported 320 kilometres by road across the desert or by sea from Mersa Matruh to Salum for distribution by the intrepid Kiwi truckers to a new ring of field supply depots on the dusty, high Libyan plateau. It was George Vasey's responsibility, as quartermaster, to see that the depots were well stocked and that sufficient ammunition was brought forward to the gun-pits.

On 19 December, the first Australian troops reached the Bardia perimeter and went into the line on the south-western side of the Italian perimeter. The Australians were aggressive and in high spirits, despite the freezing winds and ever-present dust. The great fighting tradition of their fathers in World War I had been drummed into them during training and they were bursting to get at the enemy. They would be the first Australian troops to go into action since October 1918.

The biggest problem was that as a fighting force they were totally untried. Mackay's first divisional exercise had taken place as recently as November when the 16th and 17th Brigades had been given the task of attacking the 19th Brigade. His troops were still raw and lacked essential equipment, particularly transport.[11] They arrived at the front with slogans such as 'Look out, Musso, here we come' chalked on the sides of their lorries.[12] Every vehicle was decorated with the 6th Division's symbol: a kangaroo leaping over a boomerang.

For seven nights from 21 December, General Mackay –
known to his staff as 'Mr Chips' on account of his time as
headmaster of Cranbrook School – sent patrols along the
western side of the enemy's line to measure the anti-tank ditch
and the depth of the wire entanglements, and to establish
whether the posts were occupied by Italian or Libyan soldiers.[13]

On Christmas Eve, General O'Connor held a meeting with
Mackay at which the Australian commander was ordered to find
a way of getting Colonel Jerram's Matilda tanks inside the Bardia
perimeter for an assault on the fortress and the town. O'Connor
suggested that the Australians should attack on a narrow
front, although the detailed planning was left up to Mackay,
who handed the task to his most skilled tactician, Colonel
Frank Berryman.[14] Berryman's plan of attack was explained
to commanders at a conference on 28 December. For some
inexplicable reason, Brigadier Savige was not invited to attend
that meeting and although he attended two later conferences
his 'exclusion' from the first one seems to have affected his
judgment, with tragic consequences for his troops.[15]

Bergonzoli probably expected the blow to fall on one of
the entry points of the Tobruk–Bardia or Fort Capuzzo–Bardia
sections of the Via Balbia, which formed a V-shaped wedge as
they ran into the town. Instead, Berryman conceived a set-piece
operation containing an element of surprise, very much like the
ones employed by the Australians in France during 1916–18
which had given them mastery of no-man's-land over the
Germans.[16] The main assault would be made by Tubby Allen's
three battalions where the Italians least expected it: outside the
Australian front between posts 45 and 47.[17]

The point of attack was midway between the two sections
of highway on the western side of the perimeter and it had
the advantage of giving access to a slight incline which would
enable the lumbering Matilda tanks to make a downhill run at
the enemy once inside the perimeter. Reconnaissance had also
discovered that this was the boundary line between two of the

Italian divisions, so some confusion could be expected in their ranks.

During Phase I of the attack, the 2/7th Battalion of Stan Savige's 17th Brigade would act as divisional reserve, while the 2/6th Battalion mounted a diversionary attack on the southern side of the perimeter.[18] In Phase II, Savige's 2/5th and 2/7th Battalions would pass through the breach and roll up the Italian defences in a south-easterly direction, while the 2/6th continued to divert the enemy's attention. The plan pitched 6000 Australian troops into battle against an Italian force of 45,000, giving the enemy a seemingly unbeatable advantage of more than seven to one.

There was no sign of General Blamey in the Western Desert but he sent an observer from 1st Corps to keep him informed. After Christmas, Wavell visited O'Connor and Mackay and accepted the plan of attack. He also agreed that Brigadier Robertson's 19th Brigade should be brought up from the Nile Delta to act as divisional reserve. In response to a plea from Mackay, the drivers of the 4th New Zealand Brigade Group transported the 19th's three battalions over a distance of 560 kilometres from Burg el Arab, west of Alexandria, to the outskirts of Bardia in just 48 hours. Mackay thanked General Freyberg for a 'wonderful piece of work'.[19] The Kiwis' only regret was that they wouldn't be involved in the fighting.

On New Year's Day, Western Desert Force ceased to exist and the Allied forces in Cyrenaica were renamed XIII Corps. The attack on Bardia was due to start the following day but it was postponed for 24 hours after George Vasey pleaded for more time to get additional supplies of ammunition forward to the guns of the 2/1st and 2/2nd Field Regiments.

At the same time, the Italian high command was in disarray. General Berti had gone on sick leave and General Italo Garibaldi, commander of the 5th Army in Tripolitania, had been acting as commander of the 10th Army. Then on 23 December Berti had been permanently replaced by Graziani's chief of staff,

General Giuseppe Tellera, so the 10th Army had had three commanders in as many weeks.[20]

On the eve of battle, Iven Mackay received a letter from his old commander, 75-year-old Field Marshal Lord Birdwood of Anzac – the general who had named the Gallipoli landing place Anzac Cove – wishing him a happy New Year. 'May 1941 bring with it such a smashing blow from our AIF to the Italians that they may just drop clean out!' he wrote. 'What I wouldn't give to be with you for it – just *all* that I have, but alas! Though still active as ever, I fear that *anno domini* rules me out.'[21]

All through the glacial night of 2/3 January 1941, Tubby Allen's men moved to their designated areas west of the Italian perimeter. 'Everyone is happy, expectant, eager. Old-timers say the spirit is the same as in the last war,' Roland Hoffman, the 16th Brigade's diarist, noted. 'Each truckload was singing as we drove to the assembly point in the moonlight.'

The favourite song among the men was 'South of the Border', with altered lyrics:

> *South of Macleay Street,*
> *Near Rushcutters Bay,*
> *I met a chrome* and took her home the other day.*
> *She knew I was stony and I couldn't pay*
> *For I'm only a soldier on five bob a day.*[22]

Reporters were later told the men had sung 'The Wizard of Oz'. *The Age* reported that they also gave voice to the old Anzac favourite, 'Roll out the Barrel'. All ranks had been issued with a tot of rum for a little succour against the cold. Then, through the gloom, the Australians saw the 20 surviving Matilda tanks lined up 'like a fleet of battle-cruisers' on the skyline. A great Australian cheer was carried forward

---

* abbreviation for 'chromo', Australian slang for prostitute

on the wind, but the tanks' four-man crews heard nothing except the roar of their diesel engines: they had removed the mufflers to bluff the Italians into believing they faced a huge armoured column.

Lieutenant-Colonel Kenneth Eather, commander of the 2/1st Battalion (the City of Sydney Regiment), was one of the toughest men ever to don a pair of army boots. At 5.30 am, he led the infantry attack on the enemy frontline behind a ferocious artillery barrage, while the 7th Armoured Division laid down harassing fire from the western side of the perimeter. The Australian companies surged forward from the start-line into the teeth of a sandstorm that flayed them with sheets of icy grit.

As well as his woollen uniform, each man wore a sleeveless leather jerkin and a greatcoat with the skirts buttoned back to give freedom of movement; he had a steel helmet on his head, a gasmask strapped to his chest and a haversack on his back; he carried 150 rounds of ammunition, one or two grenades and three days' rations of tinned beef and biscuits. With a Lee-Enfield rifle and bayonet slung over his shoulder and the dead weight of his 50-pound pack dragging him down, he half-ran, half-stumbled across the stony ground to his first objective – the barbed-wire fences beyond the tank trap. Somewhere on each man's back was a patch of white cloth to enable the following troops to recognise him as one of their own – a precaution first adopted by Australian troops at Lone Pine in August 1915.[23]

The assault troops were accompanied by six parties of 'gingerbeers', the engineers of the 2/1st Field Company, who blasted holes in the wire entanglements using Bangalore torpedoes (long metal tubes packed with explosives). In less than an hour, 100 mines were cleared away and, despite heavy Italian fire, the sheer sides of the anti-tank ditch had been broken down with picks and shovels to make six crossing points for the Matilda tanks.

By 6.35 am, the 2/2nd Battalion (Lieutenant-Colonel

Frederick Chilton) and 2/3rd Battalion (Lieutenant-Colonel Vivian England) were streaming through the breach, with the armoured monsters trundling downhill at 20 kilometres an hour and hammering Italian posts with machine-gun fire and two-pound shells. Within minutes, several posts had fallen and hundreds of Italians had surrendered.

'When we got near the first line of wire and saw the holes cut by the engineers, there was much confusion,' says Corporal Henry Rawson of the 2/3rd Battalion. 'Italian prisoners were trying to get through to our lines and our men had to go through to attack. I have never seen such fear marked on the faces of those prisoners.'[24]

Once inside the perimeter, the Australian battalions fanned out in a great arc from the bridgehead, with the 2/1st heading north towards the Tobruk–Bardia road, the 2/3rd going straight ahead to take the town and the 2/2nd pressing south towards the Fort Capuzzo–Bardia road. All along this arc, Australian platoons engaged the numbered posts, destroying them one by one with bayonets and grenades. Greatcoats swirling behind them and with bulky packs on their back, the attackers appeared to the defenders as grotesque, superhuman figures. The fact that they advanced through a hail of machine-gun fire led the Italians to believe that their shiny leather jerkins must be bulletproof.

Plunging through clouds of dust and smoke, Bren-gunners fired from the hip and shouted war cries, while the tanks, creaking and grinding over the stony terrain, crushed the enemy's protective sangars. In many places, Italian soldiers kept their nerve and fought bravely, exploding the myth that they had no stomach for battle, but they were overwhelmed by the speed and ferocity of the attack. One Italian prisoner, an infantryman who spoke English, later told the *Age* correspondent, 'We were surprised to find the Australians such big men.'[25]

As at Nibeiwa, the Italian artillerymen offered the bravest resistance but once again their shells bounced off the Matildas' thick armour-plating. Even so, some of the tanks were damaged by artillery firing over open sights at point-blank range and hitting their tracks or jamming their turret rings. Gun-pits had to be overrun and the artillerymen bayoneted to death before their guns fell silent. While the Matildas were being refuelled and re-armed to support the attack by Savige's 17th Brigade, Admiral Cunningham laid down a 45-minute bombardment of Bardia with the 15-inch (381-mm) guns of the battleships HMS *Warspite*, *Valiant* and *Barham*. The RAF's sorties against Italian airfields were so effective that Italian aircraft failed to put in an appearance despite a desperate radio plea from Bergonzoli's headquarters to *Regia Aeronautica*, 'All of our aircraft in Libya, come to our assistance.'[26]

At 6th Division headquarters, General Mackay had been receiving progress reports since 7 am but he had gone forward in a light tank at 11 am to see the battle for himself; ignoring Italian shelling, he watched the fighting for two hours. It was during this period that things started to go awry for Brigadier Savige.

There was a distance of four kilometres between his 5th and 6th Battalions and his remaining battalion, the 2/7th – which now included Blamey's erstwhile barman John Peck as a rifleman in C Company – had been split in half to create a brigade reserve. Communications were therefore extremely difficult for Savige and to complicate matters only four of Roy Jerram's Matildas were available to support his Phase II attack following their early-morning exertions.[27]

Then, at 10.30 am, the 2/5th Battalion's headquarters was hit by Italian artillery fire and its commander, Major Hugh Wrigley, seriously wounded. Savige had switched Wrigley – 'a severe man and a soldier through and through'[28] – from the 2/6th Battalion just 12 days earlier to replace Lieutenant-Colonel Tom Cook, who, at 48, was considered too old to lead troops in battle. Now commanded by Major George Sell, one of its company commanders, the 2/5th entered the bridgehead with half of the

2/7th Battalion (Lieutenant-Colonel Theo Walker) and swung south towards the switchline, while the 2/6th (Lieutenant-Colonel Arthur Godfrey) continued its diversionary assault on the southern boundary.[29]

The 2/5th and 2/7th Battalions immediately found themselves in the centre of 'a hive of hostility' in which the Italian 62nd and 63rd Divisions fought tenaciously, pouring fire into the Australian ranks at close range.[30] The main body had been halted with heavy losses, although one small group was able to fight its way down the left-hand flank into the main artillery area of the fortress, while on the right Captain David Green's B Company of the 2/7th knocked out post after post as it advanced south towards the switchline.

At Post 22, Captain Green was taking the surrender of the garrison when an Italian 'popped up from a pit with a rifle and shot him through the chest. The Italian then dropped the rifle, raised his hands and climbed out with a smile on his face.' He was thrown back into the pit by an angry Australian Bren-gunner who emptied his magazine into him. Several Australian soldiers then demanded that Lieutenant Charles McFarlane, who was now the only officer surviving in B Company, should permit them to bayonet the other prisoners. McFarlane refused to give the order and the Italian prisoners remained unharmed.[31]

On the southern side of the switchline, Colonel Godfrey had been chafing at the bit to get at the Italians. With Savige's blessing, he had promoted his diversionary attack into a full-scale frontal assault in violation of Berryman's plan. 'We shall give the enemy such a thrashing,' Godfrey told his company commanders, 'that they will never willingly stand up to an assault by Australian infantry again.'[32]

As an auctioneer in the woolbroking business, Godfrey was used to shouting the odds but he would have been advised to remain silent at Bardia. His artillery support consisted of a single battery of World War I artillery pieces (Colonel Bill Cremor's 2/2nd Field Regiment's 18-pounders and 4.5 howitzers), he had no tanks and, despite numerous night patrols, he had no idea of the enemy's true strength. In fact, his troops faced Post 11, the most heavily fortified and best-manned strongpoint at Bardia, containing 400 well-armed Italians and commanded by a resolute and experienced infantry officer.

This force was deployed in stone sangars and a trench covered with thick wooden planks in front of a concrete and steel-shuttered pillbox on the inside bank of Wadi Muatered, the deep, curving gully – a 'virtual canyon', according to Savige's biographer – which ran right across the battalion's front. Ignoring all of these factors, Godfrey proposed to take Post 11 with just two of D Company's platoons numbering 43 men, with the third platoon in reserve.

D Company's commander, Captain Max Little – 'tall, well-built, with a crisp, military cast of features, a clipped moustache, and a voice to go with them'[33] – passed on Godfrey's orders to his platoon leaders, Lieutenant Jack Bowen, Sergeant Romney Cole and Sergeant Jo Gullett. 'D Company will attack and capture Post 11,' Little said. 'I will see you then in Post 11 tomorrow morning, or I shall not see you at all.'[34]

As soon as darkness fell, Bowen (16th Platoon) and Gullett (17th Platoon) led the attacking platoons through the barbed-wire apron and crossed the wadi, while Romney's 18th Platoon waited in reserve. The Italians held their fire until the Australians had clambered up the precipitous north bank and were charging across level ground towards the encircling outer trenches. Then they opened up with machine guns, rifles and grenades, knocking down almost every one of the attackers. Gullett and a handful of survivors regained their feet, lifted the overhead planks and dived into the trenches where all but four were killed in fierce hand-to-hand fighting with the enemy.

'I don't know why we did it,' says Sergeant Keith Hooper, a former machine-gunner who was in charge of dismounted members of the carrier platoon in the absence of their full quota of vehicles.

> Arthur Godfrey got this damn silly idea in his mind – or Stan Savige did – of raiding the trenches as they used to do in World War I. The Italians were good fighters when they were well led and we had 12 fellows killed that day. We lost more men than any other battalion.[35]

At this point, the 2/6th's war diary records, 'Captain Little reports personally to CO. Ordered to endeavour to hold position gained and use mortar.' By now, 64 of Colonel Godfrey's men were listed as killed, missing or wounded. His battalion was left clinging precariously to the banks of the wadi. One of the dead was Jack Bowen, a large, serious Victorian country boy whose father had been killed in World War I.

Jo Gullett had been shot three times but had been dragged out of the trenches by one of his men and had staggered to safety with three other survivors.[36] Max Little had also been wounded – hit by shrapnel from a mortar shell after entering an adjoining wadi to see what was happening. He lost one of his feet and had a serious chest wound, but survived.

Godfrey's attack had been a rank failure. To make matters worse, Stan Savige had no way of contacting his scattered battalions, a fact that became known at divisional headquarters when he requested air reconnaissance to locate his men. At the end of the first day's fighting, Berryman concluded that although the Australians held two-thirds of the Bardia perimeter and had penetrated more than a kilometre inside it,[37] Savige had lost control of the battle in his area.[38]

On the morning of 4 January, Brigadier Allen's men began to encircle Bardia town itself. The 2/3rd Battalion advanced through a deep wadi, taking thousands of prisoners on the way, and then climbed into upper Bardia on the cliff-tops. In the afternoon, the 2/2nd Battalion, approaching from the south, captured a fort on the opposite headland and entered the lower town.[39] By the end of the second day, the fortress had been cut in half.

The 17th Brigade, however, had been unable to make much progress towards its objectives and at midday Savige had been ordered to halt. General O'Connor had asked Mackay to keep the 19th Brigade fresh for the assault on Tobruk, which would take place as soon as Bardia had fallen, but at Frank Berryman's urging Mackay now asked O'Connor for the use of Robertson's infantry to reinforce the final attack on the southern sectors of the perimeter.

Robertson was instructed to prepare his troops for an attack the following morning when the 2/11th Battalion (the City of Perth Regiment commanded by Lieutenant-Colonel Tom Louch) would pass through the 17th Brigade and clear the southern defences with the support of artillery and the six remaining Matildas. The 2/8th Battalion (Lieutenant-Colonel John Mitchell) would guard the flank and the 2/4th Battalion (Lieutenant-Colonel Ivan Dougherty) would remain in reserve.[40] The new plan effectively marginalised Brigadier Savige but that had not stopped the 2/7th Battalion from fighting on. C Company, commanded by Lieutenant Bev McGeogh, was ordered to attack Post 12. 'While some distance from the post,' the 2/7th's war diary records, 'a loud whistle blew and MG, mortar and shellfire fell on the company from the front and left flank.'

'C Company had one of the narrowest squeaks of the lot,' John Peck later wrote to his father.

> We were sent out at 1.00 hours to take a machine-gun nest which had held up the others all day. Me, Stan and Johnno were sent out to cut the wire entanglements in front of the post and then lead the advance of the rest of the company.

You should have seen us three wirecutters, each with a rifle and bayonet slung across our back, me with a Colt .44 in one hand and the wirecutters in the other. Getting back to the company, we prepared to assault this post but we found we were surrounded by machine guns. They spotted us and opened fire. Down we went like clockwork. In the next broadside, Stan and I were together and he copped it. I was lucky as hell not to get hit but he got a bullet in the thigh and one ploughed a furrow along the side of his head and clipped a bit off his ear. Another half-inch and his brains would have been blown out.

C Company failed to take the post 'but this was no discredit,' Peck continues, 'as the next day mortars and artillery couldn't do it and finally 30-ton tanks were sent in to clean them up.'

On the morning of 5 January, the 16th Brigade advanced north and occupied the remaining Italian posts around the town. It had shown great dash in battle and had advanced so fast that the Italians had not had time to blow up the water supply system.[41]

In the southern sector, Captain Ralph Honner's C Company led the 2/11th Battalion into battle at 9.15 am. Accompanied by the Matildas, the men were quickly under fire. Some of them went to ground only to receive a tongue-lashing from Honner (pronounced 'honour') who had taught them that fast, orderly movement was the best way to minimise casualties under fire.[42]

The 2/11th captured Post 8 and then headed for the troublesome Post 11 half a kilometre further south. At 11.30 am the Australians were nonplussed when the Italian commander of Post 11 defiantly ran up the Italian flag, even though the rest of the fortress had capitulated.[43] But it was a last desperate gesture. Post 11 was trapped between Robertson's tanks, artillery and infantry in one direction and Godfrey's 2/6th Battalion in the other. Wounded himself, the Italian commander decided that surrender was preferable to annihilation. At midday, he hauled down the Italian tricolour and replaced it with a white flag. The Australians were amazed when a huge force of 350 soldiers, including 24 officers, streamed out of the post. Godfrey went forward and shook his adversary's hand.[44]

It was discovered that Post 11 contained an astonishing array of weapons: two field guns, two 3-inch mortars, six anti-tank guns, 12 medium and 27 light machine guns, and 325 rifles.[45] The overwhelming superiority of men and arms in Post 11 made Stan Savige's 'diversionary attack' by fewer than 50 Australians armed with nothing but rifles and grenades look like a suicide mission. Yet on Savige's recommendation, Godfrey was awarded the Distinguished Service Order 'for leadership in the battle of Bardia'.

By 1.30 pm, more than 15,000 Italians had been taken prisoner in this sector for the loss of just three wounded men. The tally of prisoners included four divisional commanders, but there was no sign of General Bergonzoli. Electric Whiskers had deserted his post on the third day, when he and a small group of officers slipped through the Australian lines during heavy fighting. Walking by day and hiding in caves by night, it took them five days to cover the 112 kilometres to Tobruk.[46]

By then, 45,000 Italians had been herded into prisoner-of-war cages at Salum, awaiting transport to Mersa Matruh and Alexandria.[47] Australian losses in the Battle of Bardia amounted to 456 men (130 killed and 326 wounded). 'The plan worked out almost without a hitch,' Wavell's biographer John Connell wrote admiringly. 'It was the Australians' blooding in World War II. From the outset they fought with the utmost dash and self-confidence.'[48]

Stan Savige's performance in command of the 17th Brigade soured the taste of victory at 6th Division headquarters. George Vasey commented that while Tubby Allen and his 16th Brigade had done excellently, 'Not so Stan and his [brigade]. Had Iven any real go Stan would get a bowler hat.'[49]

Describing the battle as 'one of the greatest feats in Australian military history', Chester Wilmot reported to Australia from the ABC's mobile unit with the AIF, 'The Italians had an overwhelming advantage in position, numbers and firepower and our troops had to attack elaborately prepared and strongly fortified positions. Bardia's capture was a triumph of brilliant tactics, courage, speed and the co-ordination of all forces.'[50]

In his account of the Battle of Bardia, Dick O'Connor wrote, 'I was much struck by the excellence of the Staff of the 6th Australian Division and by the determination of its commander, Major-General Mackay. Throughout he showed himself to be the right man in the right place, and his Division thoroughly deserved its success.'[51]

Alan Moorehead's *Daily Express* hailed 'Iven the Terrible' and described the Australians as the 'cream of the Empire troops and the finest and toughest fighting men in the world'. The words that meant most to the men were in the London *Daily Telegraph*: 'The Australians' dash was worthy of the old Anzacs. There is no higher praise.'[52]

'I still can't believe how I got out of it with a whole skin,' Private Peck wrote to his parents.

> We had a good feed today on captured Dago officers' tucker. Wait till I tell you the real news: little me captured an Italian general and his batman. Not bad, eh? He was apparently missed in the general advance and I got him at 4 o'clock in the morning in a dugout. I'll send the souvenirs home as soon as I get back to civilisation.

Later in life, Peck reflected on the effect the Battle of Bardia had had on him: 'After your first action, you get a feeling almost of invincibility – all the shot and shell that was fired at you and missed gave you the impression that you weren't going to be hit. It was always going to be the next bloke.'[53]

CHAPTER 6

Tobruk

While nothing could displace Bardia in the Australian pantheon as the site of the 2nd AIF's first battle of World War II, the 6th Division's next port of call, Tobruk, would become infinitely more famous. Stained with the blood and sweat of thousands of Australian fighting men, it was the one place that Rommel, despite all of his *sturm, schwung, wucht* (attack, impetus, weight), couldn't conquer in his astoundingly successful campaigns of 1941 – the uncrackable nut that denied him victory in Egypt.

Three days after the fall of Bardia two brigades of the 6th Division were bivouacked outside the eastern half of the Tobruk perimeter, a feat which could only have been achieved because the Kiwi truck drivers made the 224-kilometre round trip from Bardia to Tobruk time and again with practically no sleep until the job was finished, drawing the heartfelt gratitude of Dick O'Connor and the Australians.

Even before Bardia had fallen, O'Connor had sent units of the 7th Armoured Division ahead to cut off the roads leading west and south-west from the town. On 13 January, Iven Mackay revealed his plan for the assault on the fortress to his senior officers. Unlike Bardia, Frank Berryman had placed the break-in point in the Australian sector and, to further mislead the enemy, had chosen a point where the Italian artillery was very strong.[1] Once again, Berryman envisaged a two-phase attack under which Allen's 16th Brigade would breach the defences, while Robertson's 19th Brigade exploited the opening and penetrated the inner defences of the port.[2]

General Blamey hadn't visited Bardia and, with Lady Blamey due to arrive by Qantas flying boat on 18 January, he had no intention of going anywhere near Tobruk. However, his military protégé Michael Clarke, now a 25-year-old lieutenant in the 2/3rd Field Regiment, had arrived in Egypt and was heading for the front. Clarke had last seen Blamey at a cocktail party at the Melbourne home of General Sir Harry Chauvel shortly before the young gunner sailed for the Middle East in the *Queen Mary* in May 1940. Fearful of Italian submarines in the Red Sea and an invasion across the Channel, Churchill had diverted the convoy – which included the 18th Australian Brigade under Leslie Morshead and the 6th New Zealand Brigade under Harold Barrowclough – to Britain. The troops had landed at Gourock in the Firth of Clyde on 17 June, the day of the French surrender. The 2/3rd Field Regiment went into camp at Tidworth in Wiltshire, not far from Clarke's old school, Hawtreys. Now commanded by Colonel Horace Strutt, the regiment was going into action as part of XIII Corps in the Battle of Tobruk.[3]

The gunners' first meeting with General Mackay took place on 13 January 1941 at their camp at Ikingi Maryut, near Alexandria. Mackay was a stickler for neatness: a button carelessly sewn on could mean that a man might forget his rations; a spot of rust on a water bottle could spread and prove fatal in the desert.[4]

That day, the regiment had gone into the desert for an overnight exercise but had been caught in a severe *khamsin* and had arrived back in camp covered in sand. 'The General was exceedingly rude to us, condemning us for our filthy appearance,' Michael Clarke says. 'He insulted everyone he met and we were damned relieved when he took himself off to his comfortable billet.' After that experience, the gunners referred to Mackay as 'the bloody headmaster'.[5]

On 16 January, the three troops of the 5th Battery headed west from their camp towards the Libyan desert in a little convoy of quads (armoured Morris trucks towing their 25-pounder field guns), one-ton Fords containing ammunition and supplies, Bren carriers and the Humber staff car of the battery commander, Major Dick Bale – all vehicles painted slate, white and grey to blend in with the terrain. Driving through another violent *khamsin* that stung their faces and reduced visibility to a few metres, they passed through Mersa Matruh, saw the bombed-out remains of Sidi Barrani and the burned-out, bullet-riddled hulks of dozens of derelict tanks and lorries before crawling into Salum on the third day.

On Sunday 19 January, B Troop, commanded by Captain Gordon Laybourne Smith (known to his men as Willie Smith) swung left off the Via Balbia and headed cross-country towards the El Adem road, which ran due south from Tobruk to an abandoned airfield. The desert was sandy, hard and stony, with patches of spindly camel-bush and, scattered here and there, the whitened bones of dead animals. Having travelled the shorter distance from Bardia, the other gunners were already in position, so Clarke's troop quickly unlimbered its four guns.[6]

Tobruk was the Italian Army's main defensive position in Cyrenaica, with 27,000 troops, 220 guns and 65 tanks guarding the fortress and town inside a 48-kilometre semi-circular perimeter. General Tellera, the 10th Army's new commander, and General Bergonzoli had flown from Tobruk to Benghazi, leaving 72-year-old General Enrico Pitassi Mannella to command the garrison against the 'Australian barbarians'.

Tobruk had 128 fortified posts protected by a booby-trapped anti-tank ditch, double-layer minefields and a double apron of barbed wire. The posts were spaced around the perimeter in two lines, the second line covering gaps in the first. The town of Tobruk – a cluster of modern, white-walled residences, town hall, three hotels, shops, post office and restaurants – was occupied by Italian colonisers who had largely displaced the Arab population. It was built on a headland that formed the northern arm of Tobruk's well-appointed harbour. As this was some 15 kilometres inside the perimeter, Pitassi Mannella was confident that his artillery could break up any enemy attack before it became dangerous.

In his final briefing to his brigadiers, Mackay told them, 'It is about time we openly professed the reasons why we are fighting this war.' He wanted the men to go into action 'angry and virile and hating', and using grenades and Bren-guns against the Italians 'until they pray for mercy and are in a proper mood to surrender'.[7]

By the early morning of 21 January, Australian patrols had measured the anti-tank ditch, probed for mines, disarmed booby-traps and placed landmarks to guide the infantry up to the wire. The forward troops, who had been living in shallow trenches, protected from bombs and shellfire but plagued by fleas, lice, dust and desert sores, moved to the start-line under fire from Italian 6-inch guns.[8] There was a brief pause while Australian 4.5-inch howitzers, which had been sited well forward of the main gun-line, opened up with a counter-battery bombardment that silenced the Italian guns in a matter of minutes.

At 5.40 am, 88 British and Australian field guns roared into life and the attack on Tobruk opened between Posts 55 and 57 just east of the El Adem road. The barrage lasted 15 minutes, the range creeping forward every minute. 'We concentrated grimly on this range timetable because we knew that our infantry would be following close behind our shells,' Michael Clarke says.[9]

By daybreak, the engineers had broken through the wire and the leading battalion – Colonel England's 2/3rd – was attacking the first line of posts on a front of 500 metres. After their experiences at Bardia, the men had discarded their greatcoats and gasmasks and carried only their weapons, ammunition and rations. They had retained their leather jerkins for warmth, but wore them inside out to prevent them shining in the moonlight.[10]

The first five posts were quickly destroyed, giving a clear run to the 2/1st and 2/2nd Battalions and 12 Matilda tanks, all that remained battle-worthy from the original force of 48. On the eastern side of the perimeter, the 2/5th Battalion of the 17th Brigade, supported by one battery of the Royal Horse Artillery, launched a diversionary attack under strict instructions to avoid the fate that had befallen the 2/6th at Bardia.

The Australian gunners now concentrated on hitting enemy gun-pits in a rapid-fire program that lasted more than two hours. Despite the pre-dawn cold, many of the men were stripped to the waist as they fed the guns with ammunition. The gun barrels were cooled with water but the issue of one gallon per gun wasn't nearly enough for the purpose, so the men used the contents of their water bottles and went thirsty. They were still firing at 7 am when first light broke over the battlefield.[11]

It was Mackay's intention to 'bite deeply into the defences and get the enemy artillery early'. To that end, the 2/1st Battalion crossed the Tobruk–Bardia section of the Via Balbia in the east and opened additional breaches in the perimeter to let in the 2/2nd Battalion, which charged noisily towards the guns. They were followed by the 2/6th and 2/7th Battalions of the 17th Brigade, whose job was to eliminate all opposition in the eastern sector.[12]

'The Italian artillery was brilliant,' says Sergeant Keith Hooper, who now commanded one of his battalion's Bren carriers.

I was heavily shelled going through the wire in my carrier, then along the right-hand side of the defences. I got down into one of the posts and I was fiddling about with an anti-aircraft gun and the next thing I knew shells were crashing around inside this confined concrete shelter. I was completely deaf for the rest of the day.[13]

At 7.55 am, the 19th Brigade headed north behind a creeping barrage, with two companies of the 1st Battalion, Royal Northumberland Fusiliers (a machine-gun battalion) and two troops of the Divisional Cavalry in Bren carriers protecting their left flank. Brigadier Robertson had given Ivan Dougherty the task of capturing the headquarters of the Tobruk garrison, sited among a cluster of buildings that formed the so-called Fort Solaro on the western side of Tobruk airfield.

The rear-most Italian guns still posed a threat to Dougherty's battalion so the 5th Battery was ordered to move inside the wire to silence them. Michael Clarke deployed B Troop in a gap between two points that were on the receiving end of Italian fire. The men set up their 25-pounders beside the quads in rough country with low sandhills in front and, in company with other gun troops, blasted the enemy gun-pits. After an hour, the Italian guns fell silent.

Meanwhile, the Victorians in the 2/8th Battalion on the left flank of the 19th Brigade had encountered heavy fire from posts round the junction of the Bardia and El Adem roads. The battalion swung west and from 11 am until dusk fought its way along the escarpment. One company lost all but one of its officers and sergeants and nearly half its men to fire from machine-gun posts, artillery and tanks dug into the ground.[14]

Dougherty had taken his battalion to the west and, meeting less hostile opposition, crossed the airfield and overran the Italian headquarters near Fort Solaro. The garrison's commander, General Pitassi Mannella, was found in a bomb-proof cave cut into the escarpment. He was marched in front of Brigadier Robertson, who demanded that he order his troops to surrender to avoid further bloodshed. The old Italian refused to do so, saying the Italians had been ordered to fight to the death.[15]

By nightfall on the 21st, the eastern half of the fortress had been pacified. B Troop was looking forward to an evening meal when it received orders to advance a further six kilometres towards the town. Clarke led the way on his motorbike but in the dark got lost in the huge dust-cloud that now covered the battlefield. When he turned round to check that B Troop was following, only two guns and two ammunition trucks were behind him. Lieutenant Peter Cudmore and the other two guns had vanished.

'I hadn't a clue where we were, except that we were stranded in the middle of an apparently deserted battlefield,' he says. Clarke spent the night in one of the ammunition trucks. He awoke at 4.30 am on 22 January. It was so cold the water had frozen in his flask. The men got out of their vehicles and did physical exercises to warm up.

At first light, Clarke sighted a large vehicle parked 500 metres away and rode over on his motorbike to seek directions. The canvas flap was up and the tailboard down and standing up in the back of the truck in his shirtsleeves was the victorious Red Robbie Robertson. He was shaving, but he turned and recognised Clarke – he had known his uncle, Major-General Sir Granville Ryrie, in World War I.

'Good morning, Michael,' Robertson said. 'A bit fresh, isn't it? Would those be your guns parked over in that minefield?'[16]

While Clarke took in that alarming piece of news, Robertson finished shaving and jumped down on to the ground.

'We are a bit lost, sir,' Clarke admitted. 'What do you suggest that I do next?'

'First say your prayers,' he replied. 'Then go back and tell them to reverse out of it. Then ride over to those vehicles parked over there on the right. They happen to be Artillery HQ and if they are not lost themselves they might be able to give you some directions. By the way, you blokes did some bloody good shooting.'

Clarke's men extricated themselves from the minefield without mishap. At Artillery HQ, a staff captain gave him a cup

of tea laced with rum and showed him B Troop's new position
on a map. By 7 am, all of the 25-pounders of the 5th Battery
were ready to fire on the town but at 11 am a British officer in
a carrier trundled back from the front with the news that the
garrison had capitulated.[17]

Indeed, all resistance had collapsed. Brigadier Robertson
entered Plaza Benito Mussolini with the divisional cavalry to
find thousands of Italian depot troops and naval men, including
an admiral, lining up to surrender. 'The Mayor of Tobruk, with
drooping feather in his Tyrolean hat, was trying his best to be
taken into custody but no one was interested,' says Lieutenant-
Colonel Leslie Le Souef, commander of the 2/7th Australian
Field Ambulance (and Michael Clarke's cousin). Le Souef
remembers Robertson holding a victory lunch with Italian
wines in the large, unfinished Admiralty Building. The final
tally in the Battle of Tobruk in just a day and a half was 25,000
prisoners and 208 field and medium guns. Australian casualties
were 49 dead and 306 wounded.[18]

In the afternoon, the 5th Battery's officers and gun sergeants
were driven around the battlefield to see the results of their
shooting. The official AIF photographer, Captain Frank Hurley,
photographed a group of begrimed West Australians of the
2/11th Battalion inspecting an Italian anti-aircraft gun-pit
which had taken a direct hit that had wiped out the gun crew –
small men in dark green uniforms who had fought bravely and
who looked in death like broken puppets.

In Rome, Ciano confronted his father-in-law with some
unpleasant truths about his crumbling Libyan defences. 'At Sidi
Barrani, they spoke of surprise,' he said.

> Then you counted upon Bardia, where Bergonzoli was, the
> heroic Bergonzoli. Bardia yielded after two hours. Then you
> placed your hopes in Tobruk because Pitassi Mannella, the king
> of artillerymen, was there. Tobruk has also been easily wrested
> from us. Now you speak with great faith of the escarpment

of Derna. I beg to differ with your dangerous illusions. The trouble is grave, mysterious and deep.[19]

After four days of non-stop action, B Troop stripped off their filthy uniforms and plunged into the cool waters of the bay, then camped in the shade of an anti-tank ditch and finally scrounged a decent meal: tinned meat and vegetables, plum pudding, condensed milk and freshly brewed coffee. 'The Italians certainly hadn't been starving,' Michael Clarke says. 'Every one of their dugouts was stocked with food. We were now living like kings.'[20]

While operations against Tobruk were still in their early stages, Churchill had made his next move towards achieving a united Balkan front. On 8 January 1941, despite the doubts of the chiefs of staff, he decided 'by hook or by crook to send Greece the fullest support in our power'.[21] Wavell was ordered by the British War Cabinet to visit Athens and offer the Greeks armoured troops, artillery and anti-aircraft guns to assist their forces in the defence of Salonica and Macedonia.

Dressed in mufti and accompanied by his aide de camp, Captain Peter Coats, and Air Vice-Marshal Arthur Longmore, General Wavell met King George II of the Hellenes, General Metaxas and General Papagos at two conferences at the Greek Ministry for Foreign Affairs on 14 and 15 January. Metaxas informed the visitors that he believed Yugoslavia and Turkey would remain neutral in the event of war with Germany.[22] He added that unless the British could send nine fully equipped divisions with corresponding air support,[23] the presence of British soldiers on Greek soil would simply provoke German aggression without being strong enough to check it.[24]

Britain was able to spare nothing like those numbers – the best Wavell could manage was two or three divisions and a small number of additional aircraft, although only two regiments of gunners and an armoured unit of 60–65 tanks could be dispatched immediately. These forces were declined. 'Had this offer been accepted, it is improbable that it would have been possible to continue the operations in Cyrenaica beyond Tobruk,' Wavell says.[25]

By Friday 17 January, Wavell was back in Cairo, where he took his wife to a ball. 'This nonchalant and amazing soldier is a rather small man with a lined, dry, humorous looking face,' noted Weary Dunlop, who met him in the cloakroom searching for his cap and coat in the absence of Peter Coats. 'The left eye is closed forever (by the absence of an eyeball I should think) and then the keen flash of the other is arresting.'[26]

The success of the attack on Tobruk had stirred Churchill into forgetting his dislike of Wavell. On 23 January, he cabled him:

> I again send you my most heartfelt congratulations on the third of the brilliant victories which have, in little more than six weeks, transformed the situation in the Middle East, and have sensibly affected the movement of the whole war.
>
> The daring and scope of the original conception, the perfection of staff work and execution have raised the reputation of the British and Australian Army and its leadership, and will long be regarded as models of military art.[27]

Meanwhile, Dick O'Connor's XIII Corps had turned the Italian retreat into a rout, with the 6th Division chasing the enemy back to Derna and then Barce on the Via Balbia towards Benghazi, their last major base in Cyrenaica. O'Connor kept them at it. As Frank Berryman said to his chief of staff John Harding, 'Do you know what we call your general? The "Little White-haired Terrier" – because he never lets go.'[28] But events in the eastern Mediterranean were spiralling out of control and not even 'Terrier' O'Connor would be able to hold on to the Australians.

PART II

Greek Gamble

CHAPTER 7

Wily Wavell

At this crucial time, with Australian troops on the brink of a magnificent victory in Cyrenaica, General Blamey took a short holiday with his wife. The Blameys inspected houseboats on the River Nile in which to open a branch of the Australian Soldiers Club. All was in readiness on 2 February when Australia's Prime Minister, Robert Menzies, arrived in Palestine by Qantas flying boat on his way to London to consult with Churchill and the British War Cabinet.

While Syd Rowell moved 1 Australian Corps headquarters from Gaza to Ikingi Maryut prior to taking command of the Allied forces in Cyrenaica, Blamey travelled to Lake Tiberias to meet his political patron. Menzies was pleased to find him 'in good shape'. Blamey had celebrated his 57th birthday on 24 January. He had been following a regime of physiotherapy and exercise, including horse-riding, ever since the chief medical officer, Major-General S. R. 'Ginger' Burston, threatened to send him back to Australia for being unfit.[1]

There was drink in abundance on 5 February when the Blameys hosted a cocktail party for Menzies in the AIF houseboat on the Nile. One of the guests, Air Marshal Sir Arthur Tedder, described the function as a 'devastating party' and noted, 'I don't know how the ship kept afloat.'[2] He described Blamey as 'a tubby little man with a snub nose and expensive complexion, high blood pressure and a scrubby little white moustache. He has a certain amount of commonsense and 20 years ago may have been fairly useful, but –!'[3]

Another guest was the American-born Conservative member of parliament Henry 'Chips' Channon, who had been at Oxford with King George of Greece and the Yugoslav regent, Prince Paul. He had visited Athens and Belgrade in the hope of persuading his royal friends to join Churchill's Balkan front, but had little to show for his efforts. He had just returned from a trip to Palestine and Jordan with his lover, Wavell's aide-de-camp Peter Coats. Later on the evening of the 5th, Channon attended a dinner party for Menzies at the British Embassy and paid tribute to his 'rapier-like intelligence'.[4]

Meanwhile, Hitler had written angrily to Mussolini criticising his handling of the North African campaign. He had already ordered the German 5th Light Division to Libya; now he offered to send an entire panzer division – the 15th Armoured Division, commanded by the former chief of his military bodyguard, General Erwin Rommel. There was one condition: that the Italians did not retreat as far as Tripoli, which the German high command considered indefensible.

Two days later on 7 February Rommel's task became immeasurably more difficult when Benghazi fell to the Australians. To prevent the Italians from escaping into Tripolitania, O'Connor sent units of the 7th Armoured Division racing across the base of the Jebel Achdar to cut the road at Beda Fomm on the Gulf of Sirte. After failing to break through the armoured cordon, the Italians capitulated. O'Connor's triumphal radio message to Wavell announcing the surrender of the 10th Army reflected his commander-in-chief's love of hunting: 'Fox killed in the open.'

Ten Italian divisions had been destroyed with the loss of 130,000 prisoners, 500 tanks and 800 guns. British and Commonwealth forces had lost around 2000 men killed or wounded. The prisoners included General Tellera, who was found mortally wounded inside an Italian tank, and the elusive General Bergonzoli, who had surrendered to the Rifle Brigade.

Alan Moorehead, who was accompanying the 6th Division in the field, found Bergonzoli sitting in the back seat of a car with a rug wrapped around him. He was ill. 'Poor little Bergonzoli,' Moorehead wrote.

> I had expected a blustering, piratical sort of general. But here he was, a soft-spoken little man with a pinched swarthy face that had aged unbelievably since his great days in Spain. His famous *barba elettrica* was a neat, bristly beard parted in the centre. He wore a plain, undecorated green uniform. Among the fascist generals, he was certainly the bravest of the lot.[5]

Meanwhile, Lady Blamey's privileged treatment had caused a public outcry in Australia and the War Cabinet was agitating for her to return home. Blamey, however, had persuaded Colonel Harold Cohen, the Red Cross commissioner with the AIF in the Middle East, to appoint her as a hospital visitor. Dressed in an official Red Cross uniform, she was doing good work among the sick and wounded.

Olga Blamey wasn't the only wife causing problems. She met one of the other troublesome women when she attended a lunch in Menzies' honour at the British Embassy. Ignoring regulations that barred civilian wives from joining their husbands at the front, Hermione, Countess of Ranfurly, had followed her husband, a staff officer in the Sherwood Rangers, to Egypt and had resisted all attempts to send her home. The vivacious, dark-haired 26-year-old had met Menzies in Australia while serving as personal assistant to Lord Wakehurst, Governor of New

South Wales. 'You should not be here at all,' Wavell's chief of staff, Major-General Smith, barked at her. 'You have given us a great deal of trouble.' Hermione wrote in her diary:

> I was very embarrassed. Bob Menzies sat next to me at lunch and we talked of old times in Australia. He told me Billy Hughes is going strong in Canberra and switches off his hearing aid whenever something is said he doesn't agree with. Bob wants to talk to his troops so I suggested that, while he's in Cairo, he pay a visit to the 'Dug-Out' nightclub where most Australian ranks gather at nights when on leave in Cairo. We fixed to do this tomorrow evening.[6]

That night, Menzies dined with Blamey, Wavell, Longmore and Lampson, among others, at the Turf Club. Menzies attempted to discuss Australia's military role with Wavell. 'He simply did not talk at all,' Menzies noted.

> He appeared to be blind in one eye, and this meant that when I sat next to him at table he would swivel his head right round, 90 degrees, fix me with the good eye, and say either 'I see', or 'Maybe', or 'Um', or nothing.[7]

In the morning, Menzies left Cairo for Cyrenaica. He had to forgo his visit to the Dug-Out, a belly-dancing joint at the rear of the Metropolitan Hotel. He caught up with 'Hermy', as he called Lady Ranfurly, when he returned to Cairo and they dined at the rather more respectable Mohammed Ali Club. Despite her irregular status, Hermione worked as confidential secretary to the head of Special Operations Executive in Cairo. She read secret telegrams to and from Churchill and probably knew more about what was going on than any civilian in the region.[8]

On 8 February, Menzies accompanied Blamey on his first visit to Libya. At Tobruk, the Prime Minister chatted to various AIF groups, 'friendly boys wise now in terrible things'.[9] The British had occupied Agheila, a rose-red fort 240 kilometres south-west of Benghazi and close to the border between Cyrenaica and Tripolitania. The road to Tripoli was wide open, with only four demoralised and depleted Italian divisions standing in O'Connor's path. The big question was whether XIII Corps could maintain its lines of communication so deep in enemy territory. General O'Connor was confident he could take Sirte and then advance as far as Tripoli by 20 February. But at that moment the question became academic: the little general received an order from GHQ Middle East to stop his advance.[10]

To plead O'Connor's case, Brigadier Eric 'Chink' Dorman-Smith left O'Connor's headquarters in the Hotel d'Italia at Benghazi and drove through the night to Cairo. At 10 am on 12 February, he walked into Wavell's map room at Grey Pillars and was dismayed to discover that all of the desert maps had been replaced by maps of Greece. 'You see, Eric,' Wavell said, 'I'm starting my spring campaign.'[11]

'I don't think that it entered [Wavell's] head at that moment to go on to Tripoli – he was completely involved in the Greek campaign,' O'Connor says. 'I'm sure we would have got there. I blame myself now that I didn't go on straight away with the Australian brigade I'd used in the Battle of Beda Fomm [the 19th Brigade]. I blame myself very much for not doing it.'[12]

The pendulum had suddenly swung east again with the death of General Metaxas on 29 January following a throat operation – poisoned, German radio alleged, by Peter Coats at a dinner at the Grande Bretagne Hotel during his visit with General Wavell. The new Prime Minister, Alexander Koryzis, governor of the Bank of Greece, was the King's nominee. He had been chosen largely because he favoured accepting a British expeditionary force. Koryzis was a handsome, upstanding, patriotic man but lacked his predecessor's well-honed cunning and dominating personality.

'Immediately after the fall of Benghazi on 7 February,' Wavell wrote in his dispatch,

I received a telegram from the chiefs of staff setting out a new policy for the forces in the Middle East. The new Greek Government had sent a request on 8 February for information as to what help we could afford them in the event of a German attack. The War Cabinet accordingly directed that no operations were to be undertaken beyond the frontier of Cyrenaica, which should be held with the minimum possible force necessary to secure the flank of our Egyptian base, and that it was essential to be able to send the largest possible army and air forces from the Middle East to assist the Greeks against a German attack through Bulgaria.[13]

Churchill's chances of extending the Greco–Italian war into the whole of the Balkan region depended on whether he could persuade Yugoslavia and Turkey to support the Greeks against invasion through Bulgaria and Yugoslavia, even though Major-General Sir John Kennedy, director of military operations, warned him that 'we must not throw away our power of offensive action [in the Middle East] by adopting an unsound strategy in Greece'.[14]

The royal houses of Europe were scattered through the Balkans like plums in a pudding. Ancient rivalries, mixed bloodlines, territorial disputes and personality clashes ran deep. In Yugoslavia, Prince Paul, who was married to Princess Olga of Greece, was under pressure from Hitler to join the Tripartite Pact – the anti-communist alliance signed by Germany, Japan and Italy in Berlin on 27 September 1940 – against the wishes of Olga's cousin, the Greek King. Romania had already signed the pact after George's former brother-in-law, the dissipated King Carol II, had been forced to abdicate in September 1940. In Bulgaria, King Boris III had refused to join Italy's invasion of Greece and was now haggling with the Nazis to retain some vestiges of independence. Turkey, doubting Britain's ability to defeat a resurgent Germany, remained on the sidelines.

Back in Cairo on 10 February, Menzies visited Grey Pillars in another attempt to gain information from Wavell about the future deployment of Australia's three divisions in the Middle East. Echoing Churchill's view, Wavell said it was 'probably not worthwhile' taking Tripoli – a strange statement considering that seizure of Tripoli would have driven the Italians out of North Africa and prevented the Germans from coming in.[15] Wavell did not reveal, as he should have done, that he intended to include Australian formations in his proposed Greek task force.

Churchill now made a decision that would lead to two immediate military disasters – in Greece and Crete – and prolong the war in North Africa by two years.[16] '[Y]our major effort must now be to aid Greece and/or Turkey,' he cabled Wavell on 12 February – the day Rommel arrived at Castel Benito airfield in Tripoli and began planning Operation Sunflower, his counter-attack against British forces in Cyrenaica. 'This rules out any serious effort against Tripoli.'[17]

Wavell was in a class of his own in what Joan Bright Astley described as 'this tremendous facility with his pen'. Carefully tailoring the facts to suit a script in favour of Greece, he replied to Churchill that same day. 'We have naturally been considering problem of assistance to Greece and Turkey for some time.'

> My [telegram] of 11 February to chief of the imperial general staff [Sir John Dill] gave estimate of available resources but [I] hope [I] may be able to improve on this especially if Australian Government will give me certain latitude as regards use of their troops. I have already spoken to Menzies about this and he was very ready to agree to what I suggest. I will approach him again before he leaves.[18]

Menzies hadn't agreed to anything in relation to Greece – it was Wavell who was taking 'certain latitude' with the truth.

His subtle massaging of the facts would return to tarnish his reputation.

Meanwhile, the Australian Prime Minister had returned to Libya. At Barce in the Jebel Achdar, he was introduced to General Sir Maitland Wilson, recently knighted for his role in the Libyan operations.[19] During a drive around the town in his grey Lincoln Zephyr sedan, Wilson had seen two Australians singing 'Waltzing Matilda' around a purloined piano.[20] The impromptu concert was one of several incidents of 'irregular conduct' involving Australian troops which had offended his sense of order.

On meeting Menzies, he complained, 'The Australian soldiers have been troublesome.'

'Yes,' Menzies replied, 'I understand the Italian soldiers have found them very troublesome.'

'It's not that,' Wilson said. 'They're not disciplined, you know.'

No one had ever accused the AIF of being a bunch of angels and it is undeniable there were examples of 'souveniring' enemy possessions and drinking enemy wine after the battles at Bardia and Tobruk. But Menzies wasn't having it. 'These men,' he replied coolly, 'haven't spent their lives marching around parade grounds. They come from all walks of life and they've come over here to do a job and get it over with.'[21]

That night, Menzies wrote, 'Only one of the whole bunch who intelligently understands is O'Connor. Wilson seems tall, fat and cunning.'[22]

Menzies had no sooner arrived back in Cairo than he received an invitation to meet Wavell again. This meeting took place on Thursday 13 February – Menzies' last day in Egypt during which he lunched with President Roosevelt's special envoy to the Balkans, Colonel William 'Wild Bill' Donovan, dashed to Helwan to visit Australian troops in a New Zealand hospital and gave an interview to war correspondents. His meeting with Wavell was sandwiched between a reception at the Turf Club, where he made a speech, and a farewell dinner at the British Embassy. Afterwards, he wrote in his diary, 'Back at 8 pm to an interview with Wavell, who is clearly contemplating the possibility of a Salonica expedition.'[23]

And that was all – just a line scribbled last thing at night after a hectic day. Menzies left for London the following morning without discussing this new 'possibility' with Blamey, who was still at 1st Corps headquarters in Libya. Considering the vague manner in which Wavell had mentioned Salonica, the Australian Prime Minister could be forgiven for having failed to recognise its significance.

Archie Wavell now moved fast. Blamey had scarcely had time to do more than visit the battlefield forward of Benghazi when, on 16 February, a dispatch rider arrived at his headquarters at El Abiar, near Barce, with a message from Wavell ordering him to return to Cairo. The following day, he flew to Heliopolis, where he was informed by his liaison officer at GHQ, Lieutenant-Colonel Ronald Irving, that an expeditionary force was being sent to Greece.[24]

On 18 February, Wavell revealed that the expedition, codenamed 'Lustre Force', would consist of 1st Australian Corps headquarters, the 6th and 7th Australian Divisions, the New Zealand Division, the 1st British Armoured Brigade and a brigade of Polish soldiers.[25] 'I informed him that in my view the matter would require to be referred to Australia,' Blamey later claimed, 'and he stated that he had discussed the possibility of such an operation with the Prime Minister of Australia.'[26] 'Discussing a possibility' was a far cry from securing Menzies' agreement to uproot the exhausted 6th Division from Cyrenaica and cut short the 7th Division's training program in order to send both divisions to Greece to fight against a German army which had been revitalised and re-equipped since its last battle in June 1940.

Nevertheless, orders were issued for the 6th Division and associated units to return to Egypt. The 2/3rd Field Regiment had fought as far as Sirte, 500 kilometres west of Benghazi, when it received an order to turn around. After travelling east all night, it bivouacked at Barce and spent the day clearing sand from its 25-pounders. 'It was a filthy job and the men got covered in grease,' Michael Clarke says. In mid-afternoon, General Mackay appeared at short notice to inspect the guns. Lieutenant Cudmore ordered Sergeant Wally Haines of A Gun to form his crew into a guard of honour. The general was distinctly unimpressed.

'You have the nerve to call this an honour guard?' he raged. 'I never set eyes on such a filthy collection of no-hopers in my life! No hats, no jackets, covered in what looks like grease.'

Turning to Wally Haines, he added: 'If you are the sergeant in charge, you should be bloody well ashamed of yourself.'

Wally Haines looked Mackay up and down. The sleeves of a flannel singlet protruded a few centimetres beneath the general's short-sleeved shirt and the legs of his underpants could be seen beneath his shorts.

'If those are the only comments you can make, sir,' Haines replied, 'you can stick them up your arse.'

Mackay barked at Cudmore, 'Have that man court-martialled for insolence and being disgracefully dressed on parade. See that he is demoted from sergeant to gunner.'

Mackay then stormed off. All the way back to Ikingi Maryut, Cudmore mulled over the general's orders and then filed the matter away in what he called his 'too-hard basket'.[27] Wally Haines kept his stripes.

General Freyberg received the news that his division was joining Lustre Force with characteristic stoicism. 'I never expected to be asked my opinion by the commander-in-chief,' he says. 'He was far from co-operative; he had the secrecy mania.'[28] Wavell had told him on 17 February that the New Zealand Government had agreed to the expedition, yet there is no evidence that the New Zealand Prime Minister, Peter Fraser, had even been consulted.[29] Wavell had successfully forestalled any objections from Blamey and Freyberg by informing them that his plan had their governments' approval.

Wavell's expectations of the Greek expedition were unrealistic and the underhand methods he used to achieve his ends reflect badly on him as both strategist and commander. In his defence, it is pointed out that he was fighting or planning half a dozen campaigns at once – in Cyrenaica, East Africa, the Dodecanese, Greece, Iraq and later Crete and Syria – with extremely limited resources. The fact remains that in bending to the will of politicians he miscalculated the risks to his troops in Greece and the price to be paid in Libya.

No one would pay a higher price than General Morshead and the young men of the 9th Division. Morshead had gone forward as an observer at the Battle of Tobruk and had familiarised himself with the battlefield, an act for which he – and the rest of the Allied world – would soon be eternally grateful.[30]

Leslie Morshead, said Charles Bean, the official AIF historian in World War I, was a man 'in whom the traditions of the British Army had been bottled from his childhood like lightly-corked champagne'. He was born on 18 September 1889 at Ballarat. After training as a teacher, he had taught at The Armidale School, New South Wales, and then Melbourne Grammar School, where he commanded the cadet corps. In September 1914, Lieutenant Morshead was posted to the 2nd Battalion AIF and served as a captain at the Gallipoli landings on 25 April 1915 and as a major at Lone Pine in August. Promoted to lieutenant-colonel, Morshead had returned to Australia to raise the 33rd Battalion in April 1916 and, after training in England, had taken it to France in November of that year. His men could well have been among those who had given Anthony Eden's King's Royal Rifle Corps such memorable support at Villers-Bretonneux in April 1918.

At Julis camp in Palestine, Morshead got down to work with

his senior staff officer, Colonel Charles 'Gaffer' Lloyd, to knock his division into shape. His brigadiers, John Murray (20th Brigade), Arthur Godfrey (24th Brigade) and Ray Tovell (26th Brigade), reported that the men were relatively untrained and short of transport, guns and ammunition. Moreover, the 24th Brigade had only two of its three battalions, the 2/25th having been left behind in Australia to garrison Darwin.

Nevertheless, the 9th Division was subjected to exhausting route marches, tactical exercises, bayonet practice and aggressive night patrolling, while the quartermaster obtained whatever supplies he could get from official sources and scrounged the rest. Knowing the value of endurance, one of Morshead's suggestions was that junior officers 'go without sleep and water for a couple of days' to condition themselves to the rigours of desert warfare.[31]

Morshead's insistence on discipline and hard work brought him the nickname 'Ming the Merciless' (after a character in the popular Flash Gordon comic strip), but he also made sure that his men had time for sport and relaxation. He himself liked nothing better than dancing. As he was only five feet seven inches tall, he chose Sister Mabel Adelaide Johnson, a diminutive (just over five feet tall), 35-year-old captain in the Australian Army Nursing Service, as his dancing partner whenever there was a dance at the officers' mess. 'Morshead wouldn't have anybody else,' she told her daughter, Dr Sally Vickery. 'He'd send a staff car to the hospital to pick me up and Matron had to take me off duty.'

Mabel, a beautiful, intelligent woman with olive skin and bright green eyes, was treating the wounded from Bardia and Tobruk with the 2/6th AGH medical team under Matron Joan Abbott. Mabel also spent some of her off-duty hours with her cousin, Captain Charles Spry, who was on General Mackay's staff. Spry might have been known to his comrades as 'Silent Charles' but to Mabel he was 'Charlie'. He had been born at Mabel's home, 'Yeronglea', in the Brisbane suburb of Yeronga on 26 June 1910, was raised on his father Augustus Spry's bee-keeping farm in north Brisbane and educated at Brisbane Grammar School. He served in the school's cadet corps, entered the Royal Military College, Duntroon in 1928 and graduated at the end of 1931. In his final year, he was judged as 'slow to grasp essentials, a fair horseman, boxes well, a good cricket and tennis player'.[32]

'I saw Charles Spry in Cairo and he took me to dinner and was very good to me,' Mabel wrote to her parents at Yeronga in an undated letter. 'He is a fine fellow and could not have been nicer to me.'

From early March, Operation Lustre took precedence over all other activities. Within a matter of days, Captain Spry and Sister Johnson would be serving in Greece, while General Morshead would move his three brigades, only one of which had anything like its full complement of weapons, to Cyrenaica to join the weak force guarding the vital desert flank. Churchill had traded a secure position in North Africa for an extremely tenuous foothold in Europe, a decision that would have dire consequences for all of the Anzac forces in the Middle East.

CHAPTER 8

Eden's Odyssey

The driving force behind the misbegotten Greek enterprise was Foreign Secretary Anthony Eden, whose homburg hat, double-breasted Savile Row suit and Old Etonian tie became the symbols of Britain's desperate shuttle diplomacy. Eden arrived in Cairo with Sir John Dill just before midnight on 19 February 1941 to make recommendations about the Balkans and Middle East to the British War Cabinet.

'Do not consider yourself obligated to a Greek enterprise if in your hearts you feel it will only be another Norwegian fiasco,' Churchill cabled the British envoys, referring to his ill-prepared raid at Narvik. 'If no good plan can be made please say no. But of course you know how valuable success would be.'[1]

Churchill, however, had given Eden plenipotentiary powers 'in all matters diplomatic and military'[2] and the decision to send an expeditionary force to Greece was actually made at a conference between Eden, Dill, Wavell, Longmore and Cunningham on 20 February without consulting either Blamey or Freyberg, whose forces would provide the vast majority of the fighting troops.[3] Despite many uncertainties and in the absence of any firm evidence, Eden informed Churchill, 'There is a fair chance that we can hold a line in Greece.'

On 22 February, Wavell set off for Athens with Eden and Dill but on the way landed at the El Adem airfield at Tobruk to see Jumbo Wilson, who had been summoned from his new headquarters near Benghazi. Wilson was told he would be in command of Lustre Force if the Greek expedition went ahead. When Wilson pointed out that he had just been appointed Governor of Cyrenaica, Wavell assured him that he was 'by far and away the best choice for this very important job'.[4]

Wilson's place in Britain's military hierarchy was a mystery. He later aspired to the title of Field Marshal Lord Wilson of Libya for reasons which, as Wavell's biographer Ronald Lewin says, 'are difficult to identify and have never been explained'.[5]

After serving in staff posts on the Somme and at Passchendaele, Wilson had been appointed GSO-1 of the New Zealand Division in the First World War. General Freyberg, who had known him since 1919, regarded as 'an amiable yes-man'.[6] His elevation might have had something to do with the fact that he had been one of Wavell's brigade commanders in the 2nd British Division at Aldershot in 1936–37, had succeeded him as commander of the 2nd Division and, in Cairo, shared his house overlooking the Gezira Club with the Wavells.[7]

At ten o'clock that evening in an ornate conference room at the Tatoi Palace outside Athens, the British delegation met with King George, Prime Minister Koryzis and General Papagos. The King and the Prime Minister were prepared to accept a British Expeditionary Force but Papagos remained sceptical so Eden launched into a sales pitch 'with all the enthusiasm at his command'.[8] Sitting at the far end of the conference table, Major Francis 'Freddie' de Guingand listened with mounting concern as the British minister announced that Lustre Force would consist of 100,000 men, 240 field guns, 202 anti-tank guns, 32 medium guns, 192 anti-aircraft guns and 142 tanks.

As a member of the joint planning staff at GHQ Cairo, de

Guingand had prepared the figures for Lustre Force and had seen them dramatically altered on the flight to Athens by one of Eden's aides who thought they should be 'swelled' – inflated – to seem more impressive. 'I felt that this was hardly a fair do,' de Guingand says, 'and bordering upon dishonesty.'[9] Indeed, Eden was foisting British aid on the Greeks not so much to honour Chamberlain's pledge of Greek independence but to entice Yugoslavia and Turkey into joining Churchill's united front against Germany.

Eden then invited Wavell to give his expert opinion. Slowly, the commander-in-chief rose to his feet and began to speak in a low, subdued voice. De Guingand 'almost prayed' that he would inject a note of hard-edged military realism into the situation. The young officer knew that Wavell's intelligence chief Brigadier John Shearer had written a paper highlighting the enormous dangers involved in the Greek campaign.[10] Moreover, the joint planning staff had advised strongly against it. Wavell, however, ignored all advice that contradicted Eden's political wishes.[11]

It was his considered view, he said, that the assistance being offered had every chance of enabling the Allies to prevent a German advance into Greece. De Guingand felt 'a hot wave of anger' surge over him. 'I failed to understand,' he says, 'how it was possible for an experienced officer to say the things he did say.'[12]

The offer of armed assistance wasn't due to go before the British War Cabinet until 24 February but the Greeks accepted it in the early hours of the 23rd. After the meeting had broken up, Freddie de Guingand watched as Eden 'preened himself before the chimney-piece on how well he had swayed the meeting'.[13] Everything about the deal he had cut with the Greeks was precipitate, incomplete and deceitful. The man who had welcomed Australian and New Zealand troops to the Middle East a year earlier was about to throw them into an unwinnable battle against the most formidable fighting force in the world. De Guingand placed the blame for the impending catastrophe squarely on Wavell's shoulders, 'because he failed to stand up to political pressure when he should have done'.[14]

Wavell knew that despite the gloss Churchill had put on Dunkirk, it had been a disaster for the British Army; that thousands of troops and all of the expeditionary force's transport, supplies and mobile workshops had been left behind in France. In Greece, the risk of defeat to a revitalised German Army was unacceptably high, while the chances of a successful evacuation over much longer distances across the Aegean without adequate air cover were appreciably lower.

Menzies, who was staying with Churchill at Chequers on the eve of his first visit to the War Cabinet, was staggered when the British leader suddenly raised the Greek issue with him late that night. 'Momentous discussion later with PM about defence of Greece, largely with Australian & New Zealand troops,' Menzies wrote in his diary. 'This kind of decision, which may mean thousands of lives, is not easy. Why does a peaceable man become a Prime Minister?'[15]

Menzies' comments show that until this point he was unaware of the existence of any plan to send an expeditionary force to Greece, or that Australian and New Zealand troops would form the majority of the force. It is also clear that he was appalled at the prospect of losing 'thousands of lives'. He went into the 5 pm Cabinet meeting in Downing Street the following day 'with some misgivings'. No previous Australian prime minister had ever been so closely involved in decisions affecting military operations.[16] Menzies acquitted himself well. Without him, the matter would have been nodded through in a matter of minutes; as things were, the discussion lasted only three-quarters of an hour and most of that time was spent on questions raised by the Australian visitor.

Churchill opened the meeting with the statement that, on the evidence before him, he was in favour of Operation Lustre going to the rescue of Greece.[17] 'If any of you have misgivings,' he added, 'you should express them now.'[18] Menzies was the first to speak. 'I was the only one to put questions,' he wrote in his diary that night, 'and feel like a new boy who, in the first week of school, commits the solecism of speaking to the captain of the School.'[19]

Menzies insisted that the Australian Cabinet would have to agree to the AIF's deployment in the Greek operation. In his best parliamentary manner, he sought reassurance on two points: 'How long, for instance, would it take to put our troops into Greece in order to take up defensive positions? Could our shipping maintain the strain of the operation?' He was also 'a little uneasy' over the equipment of the 7th Division, which was still completing its training at Helwan. In General Dill's absence, the vice-chief of the imperial general staff, Lieutenant-General Sir Robert Haining, told Menzies that he 'could rest assured that no Australian force would be put into the line without the full establishment of the necessary weapons', a pledge that he singularly failed to honour.[20]

Wavell's view was that German formations assembling in Tripoli would not be ready to attack Libya until May, but Menzies told the meeting that he 'had just come from the Western Desert and that the opinion there was not so sanguine about the dangers of a German counter-stroke, and [he] felt – correctly – that the danger was underestimated'.

Menzies then asked what would happen if the Greek expedition failed: would the price of failure be confined to the loss of equipment? Churchill replied that 'we ought to be able to evacuate safely all but the wounded'. Menzies continued that 'the justification for the enterprise rested upon the prospect of our being able to put up a good fight. If the enterprise was only a forlorn hope, it had better not be undertaken.' Could he tell his colleagues in Canberra that 'the venture had a substantial chance of success?'

To Menzies, success meant stopping the German invasion of Greece, whereas to Churchill (and Eden) it had quite a different meaning: the Greek intervention would be judged a success if it persuaded Yugoslavia and/or Turkey to take up arms against Germany. It must have seemed ironic to Menzies that Churchill had sent the first Anzacs to the Dardanelles to knock the Turks out of World War I and was now sending their sons to the Balkans to bring them in.

'In the last resort,' snapped Churchill, who knew from Ultra decrypts – a top-secret source denied to Menzies – that a vast German army capable of sweeping aside all Anglo–Greek opposition had assembled in Romania, 'this is a question which the Australian Cabinet must assess for themselves on Mr Menzies' advice. In my opinion, the enterprise is a risk which we must undertake.'[21]

And that was it. The War Cabinet authorised Churchill to notify Eden that, subject to agreement from Canberra and Wellington, military aid would be sent to Greece.[22] Sir Alexander Cadogan, head of the Foreign Office, who was present at the Cabinet meeting, wrote in his diary that night that the expedition '*must* in the end be a failure. However, perhaps [it was] better to have failed in a decent project than never to have tried at all. [Anthony Eden] has rather jumped us into this.'[23] As events would show, it was Eden's will that carried the day when serious doubts arose about Operation Lustre; otherwise, the expedition would have been cancelled and the whole history of World War II in the Mediterranean rewritten.

Menzies cabled the acting Prime Minister, Arthur Fadden, that the British War Cabinet was unanimously in favour of the Greek expedition, even though it would be risky and might end in evacuation; in that event, Churchill considered 'the loss would be primarily one of material and that the bulk of the men could be got back to Egypt'.[24] Menzies recommended that despite his own anxieties Australia should agree to Operation Lustre – to do otherwise would have laid Australia open to charges of sabotaging Britain's efforts to help a valiant little ally.[25] So the Australian Government reluctantly concurred, as did New Zealand's, with the proviso that the New Zealand Division should be fully equipped and accompanied into battle by an armoured brigade.[26]

Churchill pronounced himself 'deeply moved' by the decisions of the two governments. 'They have responded magnificently to what was perhaps the most severe proposal ever put before the Dominion Governments,' he added. To Eden, he cabled, 'Full steam ahead.'[27]

The Foreign Secretary and Sir John Dill (known to Churchill as 'Dilly-Dally') then flew to Ankara to prod the Turks into action. The President, Mustafa Ismet Inonu, and Prime Minister, Dr Refik Saydam, regretted that their country could do nothing without military aid from Britain. Dill then told them something they already knew: that all available British aid had already been committed to Greece.[28]

Sir John Kennedy at the War Office noted dryly that 'it had now become obvious that Eden's attempt to establish a Balkan front had been a fiasco'. Turkish obstinacy provoked Churchill into raising the prospect of a possible escape route from Britain's commitment to Greece. He reminded Eden that he was empowered 'to liberate Greeks from any bargains and at the same time liberate ourselves'.[29]

Quite apart from Turkey's reluctance and the hesitancy of Prince Paul of Yugoslavia – 'Prince Palsy' to Churchill – the Greeks had refused to allow the RAF to bomb the Romanian oilfields from Greek airfields and insisted that no British fighting units should arrive in Greece until the German Army had crossed the Danube into Bulgaria. 'This,' Papagos writes, 'disposes of the German assertion that they were forced to attack us only in order to expel the British from Greece, for they knew that, if they had not marched into Bulgaria, no British troops would have landed in Greece.'[30]

Meanwhile, Australian air-crews were already fighting in the skies over Greece. On 28 February, Flight-Lieutenant Richard 'Ape' Cullen, of Newcastle, NSW, flying a newly acquired

Hurricane of 80 Squadron, took part in the RAF's most successful action of the Greco–Italian campaign when 27 Italian planes were shot down over Albania. 'Displaying remarkable skill, Flight-Lieutenant Cullen shot down five of the enemy's aircraft,' his commanding officer wrote in the citation for the award of a DFC. 'He has now destroyed 11 enemy aircraft and has consistently shown great resource and courage.'[31]

The invasion of Greece became a certainty on 1 March when Bulgaria signed the Tripartite Pact, thus giving free passage to German troops on their way to the Greek border. Operation Lustre ran into further difficulties the following day when Eden and Dill returned to Athens to discover that General Papagos had failed to honour a secret agreement with Dill to withdraw four Greek divisions from the Metaxas Line on the Bulgarian frontier. This line protected Greek citizens in eastern Macedonia and Thrace, and safeguarded Salonica, the only port through which the Yugoslav Army and the Greek Army in Albania could be supplied.

The British had envisioned the four Greek divisions joining Lustre Force on the shorter, more defensible Aliakmon Line that followed the edge of the western Macedonian tableland from the mouth of the Aliakmon River up through Veria and Edessa to the Yugoslav border.[32] The left flank of this line would be protected by the Yugoslav Army if Prince Paul could be persuaded to join the Allied cause. However, all efforts to secure such an agreement had failed. Prince Paul had despised Eden since their Oxford days and refused to meet him. Before moving his troops, Papagos needed to know whether any agreement had been reached. Despite repeated inquiries to General Heywood, he had heard nothing.

Heywood had failed to appreciate the importance of Papagos' inquiries and had consequently neglected to tell Wavell that the Greek commander urgently needed a reply. To complete the muddle, Eden hadn't realised that there would be no chance of a deal with the Yugoslavs if Papagos abandoned Salonica. As it was now too late to move the Greek troops before the German attack, they would have to stay where they were.[33]

With its left flank now anchored in thin air, the dangers to Lustre Force were manifest: if German forces could take the town of Monastir on the Yugoslav border, they could swing south to Florina and Kozani, thus penetrating the rear of the Aliakmon Line.[34] Eden summoned General Wavell to Athens, where he went into a huddle with Dill, Papagos and King George at the British Legation in an atmosphere that Eden later described as 'the haggling of an oriental bazaar'.[35]

Situated in Loukianou Street, the legation was a stately pink-and-white villa that had once belonged to Eleftherios Venizelos, the great Greek statesman who had banished King George's pro-German father, King Constantine, during the First World War. In the Ambassador's study, Eden briefed Link MacVeagh on Turkey's decision to remain neutral. He then astonished MacVeagh with the observation that 'even if Germany succeeds in overrunning Greece, I don't see how this will help her. By that time, we shall have cleaned up in the Middle East and be sitting pretty in Africa.'[36]

The mix-up over the original Anglo–Greek agreement and the failure to reach agreement with Yugoslavia and Turkey presented Churchill and the War Cabinet with sound reasons to drop Operation Lustre. This was the first that anyone in London had heard of the agreement between Dill and Papagos about withdrawing Greek troops from the Bulgarian border, and the fact that it was starting to unravel raised fresh doubts about the whole plan. Indeed, Churchill repeated his suggestion that Eden could 'liberate' the Greeks from any undertaking if he chose to do so. Eden pressed on regardless and a compromise deal was hammered out between Wavell, Dill and Papagos a few minutes before midnight on 4 March. Squinting through his monocle, General Heywood read the entire document in French before it was signed by Dill and Papagos.

The new agreement stipulated that the Greek Army would

leave three divisions to defend the Metaxas Line. British forces
would be dispatched to Greece as rapidly as shipping permitted
and would be joined by three other Greek divisions, plus
seven assorted battalions, on the Vermion–Aliakmon–Olympus
position 'on which it is intended that the Greco–British forces
should give battle'.[37] Instead of the 35 battalions first promised,
the Greeks would now provide, at most, 23 battalions, the vast
majority of whom had never fought a battle and were armed, at
best, with captured Italian weapons.[38]

'This was a very unsatisfactory arrangement in comparison
with the original proposal,' Wavell says in his dispatch on
the Greek campaign, 'but it was found impossible to persuade
the Greeks to move back the troops in Macedonia, and the
alternative of refusing to send aid to the Greeks altogether
seemed politically impossible.'[39]

On 5 March, an advanced party of 1st Australian Corps,
led by Lieutenant-Colonel Henry Wells, as well as units of the
6th Australian Division, the New Zealand Division and part
of the 1st Armoured Brigade, embarked in the cruisers HMS
Gloucester, York and *Bonaventure* for the trip to Greece.[40]

Despite the new agreement, there was still time to call
the whole thing off. The case against Operation Lustre grew
stronger that day with the admission in a cable from Eden
and Dill to Churchill that 'our forces, including Dominion
contingents, will be engaged in an operation more hazardous
than it seemed a week ago'.[41] Eden also suggested that Papagos
might be persuaded to co-operate more fully by the award of
'a high decoration' from Britain. Emerging from his siesta that
afternoon, Churchill was shown Eden's telegram and dismissed
the idea with a disgusted gesture. 'Too cheap,' he said.[42]

In his reply to Eden, Churchill accepted that the situation
'had changed for the worse'. 'We must be careful not to urge
Greece against her better judgment into a hopeless resistance
alone when we have only handfuls of troops which can reach
scene in time,' he said. As Australian and New Zealand troops

were involved, their governments' agreement might be doubtful in view of the changing circumstances. To Eden's chagrin, he added that the loss of Greece and the Balkans 'would not be a major catastrophe, provided Turkey remains honest neutral'.[43]

The Foreign Secretary, who thought he had pulled off a major diplomatic coup, bridled at the suggestion that Lustre might now be scrapped. 'I need not emphasise to you the effect of our now withdrawing from the agreement actually signed between chief of the imperial general staff and Greek commander-in-chief,' he told Churchill. 'This seems to me quite unthinkable.' Ignoring the fact that the new agreement was still unauthorised, Eden repeated the words of the British minister to Greece, Sir Michael Palairet, 'We shall be pilloried by the Greeks and the world in general as going back on our word.'[44]

Menzies, however, was prepared to call Eden's bluff. Protesting that the whole affair was being mishandled, he asked for the Greek plan to be re-examined. 'Why the devil should Eden purport to commit us on facts which he must know are most disturbing and which have an Empire significance?' he asked his diary on the night of 5 March.[45]

At the War Cabinet meeting the following day, Menzies protested that the Australian Government had reluctantly accepted the plan for a Greek expedition in the first place but now the situation had worsened. Eden's disclosure of a military agreement between Dill and Papagos was frankly embarrassing and there would be a great deal of resentment if Australia and New Zealand, who would provide three-fifths of Lustre Force, were told they were committed to an agreement which had been signed in Athens without effective consultation with the Dominions.[46]

Churchill immediately cabled Wavell:

We must be able to tell the Australian and New Zealand Governments faithfully that this hazard is undertaken, not because of any commitment entered into by a British Cabinet minister in Athens and signed by the chief of the imperial general staff, but because Dill, Wavell and other commanders-in-chief are convinced that there is a reasonable fighting chance. So far, few facts or reasons have been supplied which could be represented as justifying the operation on any grounds but noblesse oblige. A precise military appreciation is indispensable.[47]

No such appreciation in which the military prospects were clearly distinguished from political considerations was ever provided and for that Sir John Kennedy blamed Wavell. 'Greece, in my opinion, can hardly be regarded otherwise than as an error of military judgment,' he writes. 'It was the first of the series of major mistakes that finally led to Wavell's removal from his command.'[48]

General Sir Alan Brooke, the future chief of the imperial general staff, thought Greece 'a definite strategic blunder'. He says, 'Our hands were more than full at that time in the Middle East, and Greece could only result in the most dangerous dispersal of force.'[49]

The clouds of unreality over Athens thickened with the arrival of Jumbo Wilson. Germany had retained diplomatic relations with Greece throughout the war with Italy and to avoid provoking the Germans Wilson was required to dress in mufti and use the pseudonym 'Mr Watt'. His son Patrick, who was accompanying him as security officer, was 'Mr Watson'.[50] Wilson checked into the British Legation and although he was able to converse with members of the British mission inside the legation's thick bronze doors, he was banned from visiting mission headquarters at the Grande Bretagne Hotel on Constitution Square.

On 6 March, General Papagos visited Wilson to brief him about the three Greek divisions which would join Lustre Force on the Aliakmon Line. Until Wilson's troops reached their positions, the 19th (Motorised) Division – in reality, 2000 mechanics quite untrained in warfare – would hold a front 10,000 metres wide on the coastal plain in front of the Katerini Pass; the 12th Division would be in the Veria Pass and the 20th Division in the Edessa Pass. As British forces came into the line, the 12th and 20th divisions would move to the left to occupy the Vermion Range north of Veria, including the wide Edessa Pass. At Katerini, the New Zealand Division, with the 19th Greek Division on its right, would hold the coastal sector, while the 6th Australian Division would guard the Veria Pass.[51]

These dispositions entailed a great deal of staff work for Wilson but, absurd as it may seem, the Greek restrictions also prevented him from entering his own headquarters when it opened at the Acropole Palace Hotel in Patission Street on 7 March. 'I was not allowed to join them,' he relates, 'as the Greeks insisted on my remaining incognito.'[52]

German spies roamed freely around Athens. The German military attaché, who spoke excellent English and dressed like an Englishman, loitered around the Acropole Hotel noting the comings and goings. The German minister to Greece, Prince Victor zu Erbach-Schönburg, was often seen ambling past with a couple of dachshunds at his heels. 'Guile was one of his greatest characteristics,' says Michael Forrester, who had joined the British mission. 'He was at great pains to convince the Greeks that Germany had no designs on Greece.'[53]

It was possible for the Prince to report directly to Berlin by telephone from his gated mansion in suburban Psychico, but these calls could be monitored, so messages were transmitted by radio from the German commercial office in the basement of a block of flats. British Intelligence wrecked the transmitter by introducing an extra high voltage into the building's normal power supply. There were protests from other occupants, including Link MacVeagh – the American Chancery was in the same building – and a dentist who was drilling a patient's tooth at the time of the surge. The fate of the patient is not recorded.[54]

The enemy was well entrenched in Athenian society, partly through the prestigious German School of Athens, founded in 1896 by Wilhelm Doerpfeld, the archaeologist who had excavated the Acropolis. One of the pupils was Miriam Preston, who had been born to a British couple, Victoria and Overton Preston, in Tasmania in 1922. After the marriage had broken down, Victoria left Hobart and returned to Greece where she had been raised. 'This was in 1931,' Miriam says.

> There was no English school in Athens, so I was sent to the German School. I was about to sit for my Arbitur examinations when war broke out. The British Council coached me and I passed my London matriculation. I spoke English, Greek and German and I got a job with MI6 in a section of the British Legation. One of my jobs was to piece together papers which had been torn up and put in the waste bins of the German Legation.[55]

General Heywood liaised with the Greek high command through the King's cousin, Prince Peter of Greece. Anxious to maintain good relations with the royal family, Heywood's reports to GHQ Cairo gave a misleadingly optimistic appreciation of Greece's fighting capabilities. The more realistic views of Jasper Blunt were filed separately to London and never saw the light of day. 'Jasper Blunt's knowledge and experience weren't utilised quite as they might have been,' Michael Forrester says. '[He] knew more about the Greek Army than anyone in the mission, yet he was sidelined – not deliberately but simply because of the sheer size of the intelligence section.'[56] By now, Stanley Casson's intelligence officers included David Hunt, Monty Woodhouse and Patrick Leigh Fermor – three men who, along with Michael Forrester, would become legendary figures during the Battle for Crete and the island's subsequent occupation.

*

Having witnessed the slaughter at Gallipoli and on the Western Front, Blamey was reluctant to commit Australian fighting troops to the tender mercies of a British commander. He was also concerned about his own position in the military hierarchy. As Australians formed the largest single group of Lustre Force, he protested to Wavell about Wilson's appointment and claimed he should have been considered for the post.[57] Wavell replied that the Australian contingent of 42,000 was only one-third of the total strength of 126,000, but he agreed to inform the British Government that Blamey had raised the issue.

On 26 February, Blamey complained bitterly to Menzies, who raised the matter with the British War Cabinet – only to be told that Wilson's appointment had been made because British troops formed a majority of the force. This was not so – the Australian and New Zealand contingents in the Order of Battle were actual, whereas many of the British units were mere projections and some did not even exist.

That night, Blamey's thoughts were far from Greece. Australia's official war correspondent Kenneth Slessor wrote in his diary:

> In the Dug-Out Cabaret, to my surprise [I] recognised Blamey jazzing fatuously with a blowsy Egyptian girl … This seemed to me to be unwise behaviour for any commander-in-chief who wishes to keep his officers' respect.[58]

On 7 March, Eden cabled Churchill, 'We are all convinced not only that there is a reasonable fighting chance, but that we have here an opportunity, if fortune favours, of perhaps seriously upsetting the German plans.'[59]

This might just have been possible if the RAF and the Greek Air Force could have been given large numbers of new American aircraft under the Lend-Lease scheme but all attempts to purchase 30 fast pursuit fighters had run foul of US neutrality laws. Link MacVeagh admitted in his diary, 'Greece's failure to obtain any planes whatever from the United States of America after three months of effort has been heartbreaking.'[60] Greek hopes rose when Colonel Donovan, Roosevelt's burly, blue-eyed emissary, informed the Greek high command during a visit to Athens that their order might be filled as early as April, a promise that never materialised.[61]

Eden consulted Donovan on his return to Cairo and was galvanised by his descriptions of Greek steadfastness – a steadfastness that was based principally on Donovan's spurious promise of the aforesaid fighter planes. South Africa's Prime Minister, General Jan Smuts, also weighed in with his strenuous support for the Greek venture. After receiving Eden's cable, Churchill swung into the pro-Greek lobby again and exhorted his colleagues in the War Cabinet 'to go forward, making the necessary communications to the Dominions whose forces were to take part in the campaign'.

The wool was then pulled firmly over Bob Menzies' eyes when he was shown a message from Dill which claimed that Wavell had explained the situation to Blamey and Freyberg, who had both 'expressed their willingness to undertake operations under new conditions'.[62] So Menzies in London was assured that Blamey agreed to the operation, while Blamey in Cairo had been told that Menzies concurred. Endorsing Churchill's view that the expedition should proceed, the War Cabinet asked Menzies once again to secure his government's approval.

Blamey denied that his views had been sought. 'On 6 March I was again called in and saw the chief of the imperial general staff (General Sir John Dill) with the commander-in-chief,' he wrote to Army Minister Percy Spender.

> I was informed that following on a visit of the commander-in-chief to Greece there was some doubt as to the plans developing. Although both on this and on the previous visits my views were not asked for and I felt I was receiving instructions, I made enquiries as to what other formations would be available

and when. I was informed that one further armoured division might be looked for at an unknown date, and that beyond that there were no plans for further reinforcing formations owing to the fact that shipping could not be made available.[63]

Blamey was now desperately concerned about the chances of the Greek expedition. The Australian commander had rented a flat on Gezira Island for his excursions to Cairo and it was there he confided to Norman Carlyon that Operation Lustre was doomed to fail because it would be impossible to land these forces in Greece before the Germans attacked. Carlyon urged Blamey to alert the Australian Government.[64]

On 8 March – too late to prevent the first units of Lustre Force from going ashore in Greece – Blamey cabled Percy Spender in Canberra, asking for permission to put his views on the Greek expedition to the War Cabinet. Permission was granted and, in a cable drafted by Sydney Rowell, Blamey stated that neither the 7th Australian Division nor the New Zealand Division had completed their training, whereas the Germans could throw as many divisions into battle as the Greek roads could carry.

The argument in favour of reinforcing Greece was the fear of adverse opinion in Turkey, Yugoslavia and Greece for failing to do so. The argument against was the effect that defeat and evacuation would have on opinion in the same countries, as well as Japan. Blamey considered the operation was 'extremely hazardous in view of the disparity between opposing forces in numbers and training'.[65]

Unaware of Blamey's objections, Menzies cabled Fadden to say that Eden, Dill and Wavell now thought the expedition had a good prospect of success and that Wavell had given assurances that troops could be withdrawn from Cyrenaica without endangering the position on the Benghazi front.[66] He added that 'the overwhelming importance to our position in relation to the world at large and particularly America of not abandoning the Greeks, who have of all our allies fought most gallantly, should be the decisive consideration'.[67]

In retrospect, it is regrettable that Blamey had waited so long before making his very valid points. Lustre Force would not be strong enough to stop the Germans in Greece and its very existence would seriously deplete the forces in Libya.

After spending a year in Egypt and Palestine, the Australian and New Zealand troops arriving in Greece enjoyed the change of scenery. As they moved north in bright spring sunshine, villagers cheered them, threw flowers and called, 'Zeeto ee Australia' (Long live Australia). The fields were green with leaf and blossom and the days were warm and sunny, although snow was still falling in the mountains and the nights were cold. After months in the baking wastes of Libya, the intrepid New Zealand drivers of the 4th RMT Company thought to themselves, 'This could be home.'[68]

'We set up two big supply dumps, one at Athens racecourse and the other at Larisa 150 miles away,' says Anthony Madden, one of the drivers. 'From Larisa, we took munitions and food supplies and made small caches for the troops as far north as the Albanian border – in fact, we might even have gone across it at times.' [69] Sometimes they parked their trucks – Chevrolet three-tonners with a two-speed Eton axle provided by the Americans under Lend-Lease – at wayside inns and sampled the local wine. It was a refreshing change from the desert.

Back in Cairo on 12 March, Kenneth Slessor was once again in the Dug-Out where he 'found to my surprise [the] rather undignified spectacle of Blamey in civilian clothes, jazzing with Lady B and some other women'.[70] The vexed subject of Lady Blamey's presence in Egypt remained unresolved. Blamey informed the Australian War Cabinet that his wife had taken legal advice 'to maintain her rights as a free subject' and that he had proposed 'to withdraw entirely from the matter until legal position determined'.[71] He had no intention of losing Olga, who was doing good work as a Red Cross hospital visitor, as well as ministering to his needs and acting as his hostess. 'If the Government wants my wife back,' he muttered to his staff, 'they'll have to send another expeditionary force to get her.'[72]

Norman Carlyon described his actions regarding his wife as 'indefensibly selfish',[73] while George Vasey wrote, 'What a fool the little man has been over her.'[74] The Blameys were finally separated on 18 March when Blamey sailed for Greece with Sydney Rowell and his personal entourage in the cruiser HMS *Gloucester*. Wavell had wanted the fresh 7th Division to be the first Australian formation into Greece but Blamey was adamant that the 6th Division – exhausted after its desert campaign – should precede it, thus denying Joe Lavarack his moment of glory.

Gloucester docked at Piraeus at four o'clock the following afternoon and Blamey was soon ensconced in his quarters in the Grande Bretagne Hotel. In his first few days in Athens, he visited Henry Wells at the Australian Corps headquarters in the Acropole Hotel and attended planning conferences with General Wilson at the British Legation. At the palace, General Papagos presented him to King George II. 'The King struck me as an easy and friendly man, eager and quick to respond and remarkably youthful in his manner,' Blamey told Kenneth Slessor, who had arrived in Athens to report his first campaign. 'He said how delighted he was to have the Australians in his country, since he had always admired them and had followed their deeds closely.'[75]

From the air, Greece was a country of treeless, ice-capped mountain ranges, with thin brown lines tracing the paths dropping down their sheer sides to huge green hills and high valleys studded with occasional hamlets, while sinuous, coffee-coloured rivers rolled down to ever lower levels of rock and pasture stretching as far as the eye could see. The terrain presented acute difficulties to attacker and defender alike.

On 22 March, Blamey and Rowell drove north through Thermopylae and across the Plain of Thessaly to Larisa, 240 kilometres north of Athens, and thence to General Freyberg's headquarters at the railhead of Katerini on the Gulf of Salonica. Larisa had been hit by an earthquake just 19 days earlier and 80 per cent of its buildings were in ruins. The roads through the mountains were narrow and slippery, with hairpin bends winding down to misty valleys. By the roadside, gangs of women and children repaired potholes with rudimentary implements.[76] The Australian commanders knew that the campaign would come down to a struggle for control of the mountain passes and the few good roads that threaded through them. They considered the Aliakmon Line a position of 'great natural strength' which could only be penetrated from the east through three defiles – the Katerini, Veria and Edessa Passes – each of which led to an open plain where supplies could be stored and reinforcements marshalled for counter-attacks.[77]

Blamey and Rowell were surprised to find the Kiwi troops digging themselves in on a front 25 kilometres wide outside the Katerini Pass. The division's trucks were much in evidence, transporting hundreds of tons of rations, ammunition, barbed wire, explosives and petrol from the dump at Larisa to depots on the vast plain in front of, not behind, the passes. Tiny Freyberg was beset with problems. Wavell's headquarters in Cairo had planned the logistics of the New Zealand Division's move to Greece and his divisional headquarters, which should have been in one of the early convoys, had still not arrived. Then to compound his problems Jumbo Wilson had placed the New Zealanders well forward of the Katerini Pass in line with the dispositions of the 19th Greek Division in that area.

Freyberg told Blamey and Rowell that he wanted to keep a

mobile force in the forward area, hold the mouth of the pass with one brigade and place the rest of his force in reserve on the plain at the rear of Mount Olympus.[78] It was the first time that all of the New Zealand units had been assembled together in one place but, as Freyberg observed, this was 'not a training exercise or a battle rehearsal, but a bitter battle'.[79]

Returning to Athens on 24 March, Blamey complained to Wilson about the New Zealand positions and the British general agreed to make the change but then failed to issue such an order on the grounds that it might upset General Papagos. Freyberg's chief of staff, Colonel Keith Stewart, was appalled at the inefficiency of Wilson's headquarters, which he described as 'a washout'.[80]

Wilson had been cleared to receive Ultra decrypts (a privilege that neither Blamey nor Freyberg enjoyed), which revealed that the Wehrmacht would be able to concentrate 11 to 13 divisions against the four Greek divisions on the Metaxas Line. Once they had broken through, six or seven divisions would then be thrown against the Anglo–Greek forces on the Aliakmon Line.[81] Ultra also disclosed that the Germans would enjoy air superiority of ten to one, with a force of 800 aircraft to the RAF's 80.

Having seen the Aliakmon Line for himself, Blamey didn't need Ultra to tell him that his troops would be fighting a lost cause. Taking Norman Carlyon with him, he quietly left Athens in his Rover sedan and ordered his driver to take the coast road to Corinth and thence into the Peloponnese, where he inspected several beaches which Carlyon was told to mark on a road map. Even before a shot had been fired, Blamey was planning an escape route for his troops.

On 25 March, the stalemate over Yugoslavia ended dramatically when its representatives signed the Tripartite Pact in Vienna. Massive anti-Nazi demonstrations broke out in Belgrade and two days later a group of pro-British generals ousted Prince Paul in a bloodless coup d'etat and installed Prince Peter, the pro-British 17-year-old heir to the throne, as

King. Churchill was overjoyed. In a cable to Arthur Fadden in Canberra, he entertained the rosy vision of an anti-Axis front manned by 70 Greek, Turkish, Yugoslav and British divisions, even though the Turks were still refusing to fight and it would take at least a month to mobilise the Yugoslav Army.[82]

The Belgrade coup induced a fit of convulsive anger in Hitler. He ordered that Yugoslavia should be attacked 'with unmerciful harshness', the country broken up and the pieces given to Hungary, Romania and Italy.[83] 'The beginning of the "Barbarossa" operation will have to be postponed up to four weeks,' he raged. Field Marshal Wilhelm Keitel, chief of the German high command, later wrote, 'The decision to attack Yugoslavia meant completely upsetting all military movements and arrangements made up to that time.'[84]

Meanwhile, Rommel's preparations for Operation Sunflower in Libya were proceeding apace. Since early January, strong German air forces, notably Junkers Ju-87B Stuka dive-bombers and Messerschmitt ME-109s of X Air Corps, had been moved from Norway to airfields in southern Italy and Sicily. X Air Corps was an independent force that specialised in operations against shipping. It strengthened Axis communications between southern Italy and North Africa, enabling a rapid build-up of Italian and German forces in Tripoli.[85]

Instead of dealing with the new menace, Admiral Cunningham was struggling to deliver the full complement of British and Commonwealth troops to Greece. On 27 March, one brigade of the 6th Division, the entire 7th Division, two artillery regiments and the Polish Brigade were still in Egypt. On that day Cunningham learned from Ultra decrypts that the Italian navy, with Luftwaffe air cover, was planning to attack the next Lustre convoy on passage from Alexandria to Piraeus. A four-engined Sunderland flying boat of 230 Squadron RAF, piloted by 26-year-old Flying Officer R. S. Bohm of Rockhampton, Queensland, was sent out to confirm the Ultra intelligence.

Cunningham decided to give the Italian commander-in-chief afloat, Admiral Angelo Iachino, an unpleasant surprise. He cleared the battlefield of merchant ships and their escorts, recalling one convoy to Alexandria and ordering another to stay at Piraeus. RAF headquarters in Greece was alerted to provide reconnaissance and bomber aircraft, while the Fleet Air Arm stood by with torpedo aircraft and fighters at the newly constructed Maleme (pronounced 'mal-ee-me') airfield on the north coast of Crete.[86]

It was the chance the old seadog had been hoping and praying for. And it hadn't come a moment too soon.

CHAPTER 9

Wild Waller

During his trip to Egypt in February 1941, Robert Menzies had been taken to see the legendary scrap-ironers *Stuart* and *Voyager*, and the cruiser HMAS *Perth* which had replaced *Sydney* in Admiral Cunningham's Mediterranean Fleet.[1] As they approached *Stuart*, Cunningham told the Prime Minister, 'And now you are going to meet one of the greatest captains who ever sailed the seas – his name is Waller.'[2]

Captain Hec Waller, commanding the 10th Destroyer Flotilla, had won the DSO and had also earned himself a colourful nickname, 'Hardover Hec', on account of his orders to the coxswain during bomb attacks: 'Hard-a-starboard' or 'Hard-a-port'. Waller had made his mark with Cunningham (an old destroyer man himself) through his bombardment of enemy positions in Cyrenaica, his iron nerve in clearing minefields (sometimes shooting mines with armour-piercing bullets from a rifle)[3] and especially his aggressive pursuit of enemy submarines. Hearing a large number of depth-charge explosions close at hand, Cunningham once remarked to his staff on the bridge of *Warspite*, 'Ahh, I see Waller has rejoined the fleet.'[4]

During World War I, *Stuart* and *Warspite* had gone hunting together in the Mediterranean and later, during the Greco–Turkish and Russian revolutionary wars, the destroyer 'had nosed in and out of Black Sea ports like a terrier in a rabbit warren'.[5] Now, with her big White Ensign flapping from the foremast and the Australian flag at the opposite yardarm, Waller took his destroyers into battle against the Italian fleet 'like so many well-drilled soldiers'.[6]

At 9 pm on 26 March, Admiral Iachino set sail from Naples in his new, 30-knot, 35,000-ton battleship *Vittorio Veneto*, armed with nine 15-inch guns and a secondary armament of a dozen 6-inch guns. Heading south towards Crete, he was joined by six 8-inch gun heavy cruisers, *Trieste*, *Trento*, *Bolzano*, *Zara*, *Fiume* and *Pola* and two 6-inch gun light cruisers *Abruzzi* and *Garibaldi*, plus a screening force of 13 destroyers armed with 4.7-inch guns.

It was a formidable killing machine, but Iachino faced serious problems. Vice-Admiral Eberhard Weichold, the chief German naval liaison officer in Rome, had told him that the Luftwaffe had disabled two battleships at Alexandria – HMS *Warspite* and *Barham* – but both were in fact in good fighting order. Furthermore, the armoured aircraft carrier HMS *Formidable* had just joined Cunningham's fleet to replace the bomb-damaged HMS *Illustrious*, whereas Iachino had no carriers at all (Mussolini having declared that Italy herself would act as one big aircraft carrier for the Mediterranean). And unlike his Italian adversary, Cunningham had the use of radar which would enable him to locate enemy ships even in the dark.

At 12.25 pm on 27 March, Flying Officer Bohm's Sunderland sighted three enemy cruisers – *Trieste*, *Trento* and *Bolzano*, commanded by Vice-Admiral Luigi Sansonetti – 130 kilometres east of Sicily on a course that would take them south of Crete the following morning. Sansonetti reported to Iachino that his cruisers had been spotted but when the Sunderland's radio message was intercepted by cryptographers in *Vittorio Veneto*,

Iachino realised that mist had concealed the battleship and her escorts from the Sunderland's vision.

Unaware that *Vittorio Veneto* was at sea, Cunningham ordered Rear-Admiral Henry Pridham-Wippell – who was awaiting orders in the Aegean with his 7th Cruiser Squadron, including HMAS *Perth* – to take up a position just south of Gavdo Island, a rocky outcrop 30 kilometres south of Crete, at 6.30 am on the 28th. He would join him there with the battle fleet later that day and with a bit of luck catch the Italian cruisers between the two forces.

Cunningham then went ashore with his golf clubs and an overnight bag as though planning to play a round of golf and then spend the night with his wife. One of Rome's most conscientious spies in Alexandria was the Japanese Consul, a keen golfer who was known on account of his squat, pear-shaped build as 'the Blunt End of the Axis'.

For his benefit, Cunningham strolled around the course, but in the evening he slipped back on board *Warspite* and at 7 pm the Mediterranean Fleet cleared the boom and put to sea. The deception worked. The Japanese Consul confirmed reconnaissance reports that the fleet was spending the night in port.

Accompanying *Warspite* were the battleships *Valiant* and *Barham* in their black, white and grey camouflage colours and the carrier *Formidable*, whose crew 'felt like the new batsman walking to the wicket'.[7] The capital ships were escorted by nine destroyers: *Jervis, Janus, Nubian* and *Mohawk* of the 14th Flotilla, under Captain Philip Mack in *Jervis*; and *Stuart, Greyhound, Griffin, Hotspur* and *Havock*, under Captain Waller in *Stuart*.

At 8 am on the morning of the 28th, Pridham-Wippell, known on the quarterdeck as 'Pig and Whistle', located the leading Italian cruisers *Trieste, Trento* and *Bolzano* south of Gavdo Island. Admiral Sansonetti opened fire with his 8-inch guns and Pridham-Wippell turned away and headed south-east to draw the Italians towards Cunningham's battleships.

At 8.55 am, the Italians ceased fire and altered course to the north-west. Puzzled, Pridham-Wippell swung round and began to follow. *Perth*'s lookout, Able Seaman Walter Parry, suddenly spotted Iachino's battleship *Vittorio Veneto* 20 kilometres ahead. Pridham-Wippell realised that *he* had fallen into a trap when the opening salvo of Iachino's 15-inch guns straddled his flagship *Orion*. With enemy cruisers on his starboard quarter and *Vittorio Veneto* to port, he signalled his squadron to make smoke, turn about and 'proceed at your utmost speed'.[8]

Hearing that his cruisers were in trouble, Cunningham ordered Rear-Admiral Denis Boyd, flag-officer in *Formidable*, to attack the enemy ships with aerial torpedoes. At 11.27 am, six obsolescent Albacore torpedo bombers of 826 Squadron found the Italian fleet. All of their torpedoes ran wide, but they broke up Iachino's attack. The presence of the Albacores told Iachino that a British carrier was nearby and, lacking air cover himself, he turned his battle fleet to the north-west and headed for home.

It was not until 3.30 that afternoon that a spotter plane from *Formidable* found the Italian flagship once more: screened by four destroyers, she was now 100 kilometres north-west of *Warspite*. To slow her down, Admiral Boyd ordered another torpedo strike. Skimming along at sea level in his Albacore, Lieutenant-Commander John Dalyell-Stead dropped his torpedo on the battleship's port quarter at a range of 750 metres. As he struggled to gain height, bullets from her machine guns and multiple pom-poms ripped apart the frail fabric of his aircraft. The old biplane struggled valiantly to right itself and then dived straight into the sea, killing Dalyell-Stead and his two-man crew.

At that instant, his torpedo exploded four metres below the battleship's waterline, severing the port outer shaft. The propeller sheared off, thousands of tons of water rushed in and she stopped.[9] On hearing the news, Cunningham signalled Admiral Boyd, 'Well done. Give her another nudge at dusk.'

Vittorio Veneto was soon making 12 knots, rising to 15 and then 19, far short of her top speed of 32 knots but fast enough to stay ahead of Cunningham's big ships. The Italian fleet would have escaped virtually unscathed if it hadn't been for Lieutenant-Commander Ben Bolt, a veteran observer who was catapulted off *Warspite*'s deck in a Swordfish floatplane at 5.45 pm with orders to stay in touch with the enemy fleet. At 6.55, he reported, 'Enemy are concentrating. Total enemy force sighted up to time indicated consists of 1 battleship 6 cruisers 11 destroyers.'

Vittorio Veneto was on a north-westerly course with two destroyers ahead and two astern; on each side of this centre column were three heavy cruisers and, outside them, columns of three or four destroyers.[10] Sansonetti's cruisers *Trento*, *Trieste* and *Bolzano* were in the inner port column, Vice-Admiral Carlo Cattaneo's cruisers *Zara*, *Pola* and *Fiume* in the inner starboard column.

Sunset that evening was at 6.40 pm. Admiral Boyd dispatched six Albacores of 826 Squadron and two Swordfish of 829 Squadron for one final attack under the cover of darkness. Cunningham had decided to engage the Italians in a night action and it was imperative to slow the Italian fleet down.[11]

The very last Swordfish to attack was piloted by Sub-Lieutenant Grainger Williams. He guided his unwieldy biplane through streams of tracer and, at 7.46 pm, his torpedo hit the cruiser *Pola* amidships on the starboard side, flooding three compartments and the forward engine-room boilers. Her electrical system was knocked out and she stopped. *Pola*'s skipper, Captain Mantio de Pisa, radioed Iachino asking for protection and to be taken in tow. Iachino signalled Admiral Cattaneo in *Zara* to turn about and go to *Pola*'s assistance with *Fiume* and his destroyer escort. All three cruisers were of the *Zara* class – 182.8 metres long, 11,700 tons, with crews of 830 men apiece and heavily armed.[12]

The sea was calm, the night clear but moonless. To get an all-round view, Cunningham and his staff moved from the admiral's bridge to join *Warspite*'s skipper, Captain Douglas Fisher, and his own officers on the cramped compass platform. All of the ships were closed up for action and in the gun turrets the excitement of a night action was palpable.

Hec Waller was dressed in duffel-coat, navy polo-necked sweater, grey slacks tucked into sheepskin-lined boots and knitted cap. On *Stuart*'s open bridge, he could hear the eight-man crews of the destroyer's A and B guns below the bridge talking to one another and singing softly. During the destroyer's recent refit in Malta, many members of the original crew had been assigned to other ships and 60 new hands had come on board. The gunners included ordinary seamen who had arrived from Australia only five weeks earlier. Five of B gun's crew had joined *Stuart*, their first ship, in Alexandria as recently as 24 March.[13]

At 10.23 pm, north-west of Crete and south of Cape Matapan in southern Greece, *Stuart*'s chief signals yeoman Posy Watkins spotted an enemy ship on the destroyer's starboard bow. Waller raised the night alarm.

The Italian ships had no idea they were close to the British battle fleet. Half of their crews were absent from their battle stations in readiness to assist *Pola*, while *Fiume*'s crew was actually laying out the towing cables. *Pola*'s lookouts saw the dark shapes of the British ships sliding silently past and Captain de Pisa, believing them to be Italian, fired a red signal rocket to show his position.[14]

Using short-range radio, Cunningham turned his big ships into single line ahead, handling them as though they were destroyers. In *Warspite*'s director tower, the trainer slowly turned the hand-wheel to swing A, B and X turrets on to the moving silhouettes ahead.[15] Then a voice from the director tower calmly announced, 'Director layer sees the target.' The distance was just 3000 metres, point-blank range.

As *Warspite*'s electric firing-gongs sounded, the destroyer *Greyhound* switched on her searchlight and caught the silvery-blue shape of an enemy cruiser in its beam. 'Then came the great orange flash and the violent shudder as the six big guns bearing were fired simultaneously,' Cunningham says.

> Our searchlights shone out with the first salvo and provided full illumination for what was a ghastly sight. Full in the beam I saw our six great projectiles flying through the air. Five out of the six hit a few feet below the level of the cruiser's upper deck and burst with splashes of brilliant flame. The Italians were quite unprepared. Their guns were trained fore and aft. They were helplessly shattered before they could put up any resistance.[16]

The first cruiser to be hit was *Fiume*. Her after turret was blown clean over the side and in its place a pillar of vivid scarlet flame soared skywards. Listing heavily, the cruiser drove out of the line.

'Good!' Cunningham shouted to *Warspite*'s gunnery officer. 'Give the next bugger some of the same!' *Warspite*'s 6-inch guns then fired star shells and in their white glare *Warspite*, *Valiant* and *Barham* all opened up with their big guns on Admiral Cattaneo's flagship *Zara*. *Barham*'s first 15-inch salvo struck the cruiser just below the bridge, while another 19 hits were observed on her superstructure. Admiral Cattaneo and his staff were all killed.[17]

At 10.30 pm, the battleships checked fire. The action had lasted less than five minutes. Fearing a torpedo attack by the Italian destroyers, Cunningham turned his ships 90 degrees to starboard then re-formed them in line ahead on a northerly course. *Stuart* and *Havock* were released to sink the damaged cruisers *Fiume* and *Zara*, while *Greyhound* and *Griffin* set off to chase the enemy destroyers to the westward.

Hec Waller located *Fiume* at 10.59 pm, stopped and ablaze. *Stuart*'s gunners opened fire on the cruiser with their 4.7-inch guns. Three minutes later, Waller shifted fire to a destroyer which suddenly loomed out of the darkness. He had just returned to *Fiume* when he saw a second cruiser slowly circling the burning ship. This was *Zara*, apparently trying to protect her sister-ship.[18]

At 11 pm, Waller ordered his torpedo officer to fire *Stuart*'s full complement of eight torpedoes at the two cruisers and reported a 'dim explosion' which he believed was a torpedo hit on *Zara*. After attacking *Fiume* once again with his guns, he took off after *Zara* in a southerly direction. She hadn't gone far. Waller found the cruiser stopped and listing heavily. He opened fire and heard a loud explosion, which ignited a large fire on her upper decks.

At that moment, another enemy ship appeared at high speed on *Stuart*'s port bow, forcing Waller to change course to avoid a collision. He hit the intruder, most probably the destroyer *Carducci*, with three salvos as she sped past. It was now 11.08 and *Stuart*'s lookouts sighted *Zara* for the second time; her engines were still functioning and she had moved some distance to the south-west.

Waller was heading in that direction to finish her off when he encountered yet another destroyer listing and burning. This was the flotilla leader *Alfieri*, which had been crippled in those first few moments by *Barham*'s huge shells. *Alfieri*'s machine-gunners kept up a steady stream of fire at *Stuart* but at 11.15 pm she capsized and sank.

On board *Fiume*, a fire was still burning fiercely from the site of her after turret. She was listing heavily so her skipper, Captain Giorgio, gave the order to abandon ship. The crew just had time to lower liferafts and jump overboard when, at 11.15 pm, she went down stern first.[19]

At 11.18 pm, Cunningham signalled the fleet, 'All forces not engaged in sinking the enemy retire north-east.' Waller had lost touch with the rest of his destroyer division and started to withdraw as ordered. But the action wasn't over. At 11.45 pm, *Havock* illuminated the area with star shells and the crew were astonished to see yet another warship – a very large one – lying stopped in front of her. This was the cruiser *Pola*, still flying her ensign; she had no power or lights and her guns were pointing uselessly fore and aft.

The cruiser seemed so huge compared with the little destroyer that *Havock*'s captain, Commander Watkins, mistook her for *Vittorio Veneto* and signalled the fleet that he was about to engage the battleship. This came as a surprise to Philip Mack in *Jervis*, who thought he was pursuing *Vittorio Veneto* to the north-west; he abandoned the chase and turned back. Pridham-Wippell had already turned his cruisers around after receiving Cunningham's signal, so *Vittorio Veneto* was now free to proceed home.

It was past midnight on 29 March when *Jervis* arrived back at the scene of the battle. The first ship sighted by Mack was not *Pola* but the stricken *Zara*, which had flames leaping from her upper decks and was spewing oil into the sea. As he sailed past, fires glowed red and orange across the swell and Mack unleashed four torpedoes, two of which hit the target. *Zara* blew up and sank.[20]

Mack ordered *Greyhound* and *Griffin* to pick up survivors, while he inspected the damage to *Pola*. She was low in the water but still on an even keel. Drawing alongside, he found her company in a state of chaos: men roamed her decks, some drunk after breaking open the ship's wine store, some naked after jumping into the freezing waters only to climb back on board because of the extreme cold. Mack rescued Captain de Pisa and 249 officers and crew, and at 4.10 am *Jervis* sank *Pola* with her remaining torpedoes.

At seven o'clock in the morning, Cunningham sailed back to the battlefield. He found hundreds of oil-covered seamen wallowing among wreckage and floating corpses. 'We took some of them on board and gave them our spare clothes,' says Richard Green of HMS *Hasty*. 'Then we gave them some macaroni to eat but they didn't like it at all.'[21]

The destroyers rescued 900 survivors and the figure would

have been higher except for the belated arrival of German dive-bombers which attacked the British ships, forcing Cunningham to cut short his rescue operations. Withdrawing to the east, he signalled the survivors' position to *Supermarina*. The hospital ship *Gradisca* was dispatched to the scene and arrived in time to save another 160 lives.

The Mediterranean Fleet reached Alexandria intact on the afternoon of 30 March. In the Battle of Matapan, the Italians had lost three 8-inch gun cruisers, *Zara*, *Pola* and *Fiume*, the destroyers *Alfieri* and *Carducci* and 2400 officers and men. The British had lost five aircraft (four of them ditching in the sea or crash-landing) and the lives of one air-crew. After Matapan the Italian fleet, 'paralysed by shock',[22] never put to sea again.

Hec Waller received a bar to his DSO. He took *Stuart* back to the Aegean to resume work with the Lustre convoys. 'If we wish to skite,' one of his crew writes, 'we say, "I was with Hec Waller in the Med."'[23]

CHAPTER 10

Fire and Ice

Just ten days after the last shots in the Battle of Matapan had echoed across the Mediterranean, Australian and New Zealand troops were fighting for their lives in the frozen hills of Macedonia. For Churchill and Menzies in London, the spotlight swung from the Western Desert to the eastern Mediterranean, from fire to ice, and everywhere the picture was bleak.

On 31 March, Rommel launched Operation Sunflower at least a month earlier than Wavell had thought possible. Wavell's estimate had been based on Ultra decrypts of Hitler's orders to Tripoli that Rommel should conduct a defensive action in Tripolitania, an order that 'the Desert Fox' had singularly failed to obey.[1]

Stripped of tanks and artillery, Western Desert Force retreated across the Jebel Achdar faster than the German armour could advance in a race dubbed 'the Benghazi Handicap'. Within a matter of days, General Morshead's Australians and a few British units at Tobruk would be the only thing standing between Rommel and the great prize of Egypt.

Surprisingly, there was no co-ordination between Rommel's

operations in the Western Desert and Hitler's plans in the
Balkans, where the Germans had now massed two armies
for the conquest of Greece and Yugoslavia. The 12th Army,
commanded by Field Marshal Wilhelm List and consisting of
13 divisions, would attack Greece and southern Yugoslavia
across the Bulgarian border, while the 2nd Army's 15 divisions,
commanded by Field Marshal Maximilian Von Weichs, would
invade central and northern Yugoslavia from Austria.

The German armies dwarfed Lustre Force. On 3 April,
the headquarters of the 19th Brigade, its 2/4th and 2/8th
Battalions, two artillery regiments – the 2/2nd and 2/3rd – and
Matron Joan Abbott and 49 nurses and five physiotherapists
of the 2/6th AGH landed at Piraeus. The new arrivals brought
Jumbo Wilson's command to 58,000, just under half Lustre
Force's promised quota.

The 19th Brigade was now commanded by George Vasey,
who had been promoted to brigadier after Horace Robertson
had gone into hospital for an operation on his leg. The ebullient
Vasey, who had seen the 19th in action at Tobruk and Derna,
relished the prospect of leading them into battle. As his troops
disembarked, German agents roamed the dockside, noting troop
numbers and colour patches. The leaping kangaroo symbol on
all vehicles identified the troops as members of the 6th Division,
while 'white over green' placed them in the 2/4th Battalion and
'white over red' in the 2/8th.

On 5 April, Jumbo Wilson's Anglo–Greek army was
designated 'W Force'. He would have two headquarters, one in
Athens and a forward HQ at Elasson, south of Mount Olympus.
On the same day, General Blamey reached his corps HQ at
Gerania at the foot of Olympus to take command of Australian
and New Zealand forces. The village consisted of a cluster of
hovels so Syd Rowell had set up tents in a nearby wood. Blamey,
however, decided he needed a roof over his head and moved
into a small farmhouse. To reach his sleeping quarters, he had to
cross a muddy paddock and walk through a chicken coop and a

pigsty. His bedroom had creaking timbers and broken windows and reeked of barnyard smells.[2]

For the first time since World War I, Anzac troops would be fighting side by side. Blamey issued a special order-of-the-day recalling that it was 26 years since the Anzacs had landed at Gallipoli. 'We have now landed again in these regions,' he said, 'to fight alongside the Greek Army to overthrow once more a German effort to enslave the world.'

The convergence of time and place stirred memories in General Freyberg, who wrote to his Prime Minister, Peter Fraser, 'We are now linked with the 6th Australian Division; thus the Anzac Corps is again in being.' Privately, Freyberg had no doubts that the outcome in Greece would be identical to that at Gallipoli. He wrote in his diary, 'The situation is a grave one; we shall be fighting against heavy odds in a plan that has been ill-conceived and one that violates every principle of military strategy.'[3]

At 5.30 am on 6 April (a Sunday, the same day as Hitler's other invasions), the German minister presented a note informing the Hellenic Government that Germany had been at war with Greece since midnight. At the same time, the XVIII Mountain Corps under Lieutenant-General Franz Boehme, consisting of the 2nd Panzer Division, the 5th and 6th Mountain Divisions, the 72nd Infantry Division and the 125th Infantry Regiment, attacked the Greek forts on the Metaxas Line with the full force of the blitzkrieg.

In southern Yugoslavia, General Georg Stumme's 40th (Motorised) Corps – the 9th Panzer Division, the 73rd Infantry Division and the black-uniformed *Leibstandarte* SS Adolf Hitler Division[4] – charged across the Bulgarian border, while the Luftwaffe launched a three-day blitz of Belgrade, codenamed Operation Punishment, which reduced the capital to rubble and slaughtered as many as 17,000 of its citizens.

W Force was far from prepared to meet the German challenge. The 16th Brigade was digging in at Veria, the 19th Brigade was in transit to the Kozani sector and the 17th Brigade was still in Alexandria; there was no armoured support for the troops and only one regiment of medium artillery had taken its place in the line.[5] In the south, the Allied cause was about to be dealt a blow from which it never recovered.

On the evening of 6 April, Brigadier Bruno Brunskill, Jumbo Wilson's senior administrative officer, learned from an RAF member of the Ultra liaison unit over dinner at the Grande Bretagne Hotel that the Luftwaffe planned to bomb the Piraeus dockside that night. 'He suggested that we watch it together from the roof of the hotel,' Brunskill writes, '[and] added that there was plenty of time for us to finish our dinner.'[6]

It seemed strange that a senior British officer could regard bombing as something to be watched like a spectator sport, but then Brunskill was a strange man. His father had died before his first birthday and his mother had struggled to put him through Sandhurst. He had spent the early years of his professional career in the Indian Army, where he had enjoyed polo, pig-sticking and 'shooting black and red bear in the Himalayas'. The most important female in his life was Susie, his wire-haired terrier, whom he had brought to Greece to keep him company.

While Brunskill was eating his pudding, no one warned the naval officer in charge of the docks about the impending air raid for the simple reason that no such officer had ever been appointed.[7] When the air-raid sirens sounded at 8.35 pm, small craft were darting among the black hulls of ships in bright moonlight, returning libertymen from leave, delivering stores, or ferrying cargo to shore.

Captain Herbert Giles and most of his crew had remained on board the freighter Clan Fraser while she unloaded 350 tons of TNT explosive into two barges. At 10 pm, the ship was hit by three bombs and caught fire. Commander John Buckler of the Royal Naval Reserve and the crew of the little tugboat Stag made valiant efforts to tow the barges, packed with explosives, away from the side of the blazing vessel.[8] They had made little progress when, at 2 am on 7 April, *Clan Fraser* blew up.

White-hot remnants of her deck and superstructure flew into the air like shrapnel and started fires all around the docks. At the Grande Bretagne Hotel, 10 kilometres away, Brigadier Brunskill had retired for the night after watching the air raid. The blast blew him out of bed. Quickly dressing, he ordered his car and was driven down to the port. There were no organised fire-fighting units in action but he found a group of New Zealand engineers, who had dashed to the scene from their nearby hotel.[9]

At 2.45 am, a second ammunition ship, the *Goalpara*, exploded at No. 3 berth, destroying the Sea Transport office and killing several soldiers who were working with the salvage parties. Fifteen minutes later, a third ammunition ship, *City of Roubaix*, blew up, scattering blazing debris on to the transport *Clan Cumming*. Brunskill commandeered two rowing boats and ferried the New Zealand sappers over to the blazing ship, where they doused the flames with buckets of water.[10]

The blasts had sunk seven merchant ships, 60 lighters and 25 caiques, killed Commander Buckler and his tug crew, knocked Captain Giles unconscious on his bridge and killed or maimed his crew, wrecked quays, offices and shops, and put the telephone system out of action. The Nazis could not have hoped for a greater stroke of luck. The port had to be closed completely for two days, delaying the disembarkation of troops and supplies.[11]

At the King George Hotel on Constitution Square that night, John Buckler's wife kept a lonely vigil for her husband. He had retired from his post as sea transport officer but had gone down to Piraeus to see if he could help. Weary Dunlop heard 'the poor woman next door, walking up and down, up and down, wondering what had happened to her husband'.[12]

*

At the same time, General Blamey received the devastating news that Wavell was retaining Lavarack's 7th Division and the Polish Brigade in Egypt to reinforce Tobruk against the Afrika Korps. 'I must admit,' Wavell cabled Churchill, 'to having taken considerable risk in Cyrenaica after capture of Benghazi in order to provide maximum support for Greece.'[13] It was the worst of all possible worlds: at a stroke, W Force – Britain's 'maximum support' for Greece – had been cut in half. Once again, Blamey had not been consulted about a crucial decision involving the AIF and he was rightly furious.

In eastern Macedonia, the Wehrmacht's heavy armour, supported by Stuka dive-bombers and Messerschmitt 109s, methodically dismantled the Metaxas Line. The Greeks fought courageously, with no chance of imposing more than a few days' delay on the enemy. The collapse of the partly mobilised, poorly armed Yugoslav Army then allowed the 2nd Panzer Division to thrust south along the Axios River valley towards Salonica, the only port through which the Greek armies in Macedonia and Albania could be supplied.

In southern Yugoslavia, Field Marshal List ordered Stumme's 40th Corps to swing south through the Monastir Gap into the Florina Valley and attack the Anglo–Greek defenders on their poorly protected left flank at the barrack town of Kozani, where roads radiated eastwards to Veria and Salonica. To sharpen the spearhead, the 5th Panzer Division was detached from General Ewald von Kleist's 1st Panzer Group and given to Stumme so his forces now consisted of two armoured divisions and two infantry divisions.[14]

Given the paucity of numbers and the lack of preparation, the Aliakmon Line could never have detained the German Army for more than a few days. 'The impossibility of preventing any serious attack from breaking through was obvious,' Blamey wrote at the time.[15] Even the tanks of Brigadier 'Rollie' Charrington's 1st Armoured Brigade at Edessa and Amindaion near the Yugoslav border weren't much use: many were practically worn out after their exertions in the desert and badly needed overhauling.[16]

At Katerini, Blamey pulled the Kiwis back to a more defensible position at the mouth of the pass but by then they had used most of their engineering supplies, barbed wire and anti-tank mines in fortifying the original, now-redundant line.

There were also serious concerns about the fitness of the 12th and 20th Greek Divisions who, as agreed with Papagos, were holding the high ground north and west of Salonica. The Greeks were poorly armed, badly trained and had virtually no motorised transport, relying instead on donkeys, mules and ox-wagons that moved more slowly than a walking man.

Tubby Allen's 16th Brigade was positioned high up in the Veria Pass and so scattered that it took three hours to climb from one end of the 2/2nd Battalion's line to another. Ammunition and stores had to be manhandled across the high peaks which even sure-footed Greek donkeys could not traverse. Mountain streams were frozen, so snow was melted to provide water.[17]

On the evening of 8 April, the 19th Brigade was concentrated around Kozani when Brigadier Vasey was informed that the enemy was heading straight for him through the Monastir Gap. Jumbo Wilson had learned about the German threat from Ultra decrypts and ordered Iven Mackay to form a defensive line on the vital flank near the Macedonian village of Vevi, south-east of Florina, to 'stop a blitzkrieg down the Florina Valley'.

Watching the Florina Valley from Amindaion was a mixed Allied force under Brigadier E. A. Lee consisting of the 3rd Royal Tank Regiment, the 27th New Zealand Machine-gun Battalion (less two companies) and part of the 64th Medium Regiment of the Royal Artillery. Two battalions of Vasey's 19th Brigade, with the addition of the 1/Rangers Battalion as its third battalion, the 2/3rd Australian Field Regiment and the 2/1st Australian Anti-Tank Regiment (less one battery), would go into the line at Vevi, where they would be joined by Brigadier Lee's force. The 4th Hussars (the light tank regiment of the 1st Armoured Brigade) would form a screen at Edessa to protect the 12th and 20th Greek Divisions.

Mackay Force was an ill-balanced assortment of arms amounting to little more than a brigade group with the support of artillery and tanks (six of which broke their tracks before they had fired a shot).[18] Nevertheless, it was ordered to hold the enemy at Vevi until the night of 12/13 April to enable the 12th and 20th Greek Divisions to withdraw through the Edessa Pass and cross the Florina Valley to stabilise the situation in western Macedonia. The 16th Brigade and the New Zealand Division would then pull back from the mountain passes to a new defensive line running from east to west along the Aliakmon River just north of Mount Olympus.

On 9 April, however, the Eastern Macedonian Army surrendered unconditionally and Salonica, trailing plumes of black smoke from its blazing oil installations, fell to General Boehme's XVIII Corps. Boehme then sent his mountain troops racing west to attack Australian and New Zealand troops in the passes.

That same day, forward patrols of the SS Adolf Hitler Division entered the Monastir Gap. The *Leibstandarte*, or 'bodyguard', who wore Hitler's name and insignia on their sleeves, was at brigade strength and had been reinforced with an assault-gun detachment and additional anti-aircraft and artillery weapons.[19]

Commanded by Hitler's favourite bodyguard, the short, squat, cold-blooded assassin Josef 'Sepp' Dietrich, this SS unit had committed one of the worst atrocities in the Battle of France. On 28 May 1940, the *Leibstandarte* herded the 2nd Battalion Royal Warwickshire Regiment into a barn at Wormhoudt. Grenades were thrown into the building and then the wounded were led out five at a time and machine-gunned. All told, about 80 British soldiers were massacred.[20]

*

By nightfall on 9 April, three rifle companies of Colonel Ivan Dougherty's 2/4th Battalion were dug in on a five-kilometre front centred on snow-swept Hill 1001 just south of Vevi (pronounced 'vee-vee') near the Yugoslav border. Dougherty was minus one company which had been left behind to guard Jumbo Wilson's advanced headquarters near Elasson.[21]

The 2/4th had arrived at five o'clock that morning with the Rangers Battalion, an inexperienced Territorial outfit raised in the London area which had been trained to fight with tanks and armoured cars. 'We are high up on the pass, and it is bitterly cold and raining,' Private Dick Parry of the 2/4th wrote in his diary.

> March four miles and dig in. Then march about five miles and dig in. Then march about five miles and dig in ... We try to sleep, but rain turns into sleet and ice. Our blankets and clothes are wet through. Hard luck: we move again and dig in for the third time in one night.[22]

The main road from Monastir and Florina ran past Vevi's hilltop huddle of white-walled, red-tiled houses. One fork led through fields green with young crops and flecked with poppies to Edessa and Salonica in the east; the other south through harsh, stony countryside to the Klidi Pass and on to Kozani.

The pass varied in width from 100 to 500 metres. Mackay placed the Rangers on either side of the Kozani road to the right of the 2/4th's positions. Two of the Rangers' companies were at the top of a slope north-east of Vevi village and one in the foothills north-west of the road.[23] The 2/1st Australian Field Company had blown up this road and planted an anti-tank minefield along the front. The New Zealand machine-gunners would support the Rangers and the 2/8th Battalion when it had taken up its positions around Hill 997. The two-pounders of the 1st Australian Anti-Tank Regiment were on the forward slopes, with good observation of the road from Vevi.

Brigadier Ned Herring set up Mackay Force's three regiments of field and medium artillery – the 2/3rd Field Regiment, the 2nd Royal Horse Artillery and the 64th Medium Regiment – mainly in the hills to the south of Vevi, although some of the 2/3rd's guns were sited at a position eight kilometres to the north.

'The 5th Battery moved up, leaving the village of Vevi on our right, and we advanced north-westward through the hamlet of Itea,' Michael Clarke recalls.

> Ahead of us lay the border hills. The railway and the road to the pass were on our left. We followed a track through the fields to some low ground just short of the frontier hills. It was a fine morning and we were an ideal target from the air. The gun positions had already been selected, and we set feverishly to work to dig in.[24]

Within two hours, the battery had unlimbered its guns, erected camouflage nets, unloaded ammunition and dispersed its vehicles to the rear. Signal wire was run up from the guns to three observation posts (OPs). By mid-afternoon, Captain Willie Smith, commanding B Troop, was registering fire on the roads and tracks to his front. It was a fine day, but for men who had been in Egypt just a week earlier, it was unpleasantly cold that night when snow showers swept in on a freezing wind.[25]

There were no tanks to protect any of Mackay Force's forward positions. As soon as the Germans had advanced across the Macedonian Plain, the 1st Armoured Brigade had retired along stony paths and greasy roads packed with Greek soldiers and refugees through the Edessa and Veria Passes towards Kozani.[26] General Papagos suggested that Charrington should move north to engage the enemy around Monastir and 'hinder his advance as much as possible'. Jumbo Wilson, however, knew that the engines and tracks of many of his tanks were almost worn out and held them back as a reserve force.[27] He placed one squadron of the 3rd Royal Tank Regiment and one squadron of the 4th Hussars with the Northumberland Hussars (also known as the 102nd Anti-Tank Regiment) on the Sotir ridge nine kilometres from the front to cover the exit of the Vevi–Klidi Pass.[28]

George Vasey's headquarters were in camouflaged trucks near the village of Xinon Neron, six kilometres south of his men, in the only stand of trees that provided cover anywhere near the front. Iven Mackay was even further south on the Kozani road in the town of Perdika, where he was joined by two troops of the New Zealand Divisional Cavalry in Bren carriers and Rollie Charrington's headquarters.

In the absence of ciphers, messages were passed over the field telephone system in what were called 'oblique conversations'. Charles Mott-Radclyffe had been attached to Miles Reid's reconnaissance unit at Kozani as liaison officer between British, Australian and New Zealand units. One message from Mackay's headquarters asked him to 'stop those funny-hat whiz-bang wheels going to Kozani'. An obliging Australian officer interpreted the message for him as: 'Stop the New Zealanders from withdrawing a 25-pounder battery to Kozani'.[29]

Meanwhile, scouts of the SS Adolf Hitler Division had been astonished to find the Monastir Gap undefended. By 8.30 pm on the 9th, a motorcycle company with Spandau machine guns mounted on sidecars had crossed the border and was pressing forward into the uplands of the Florina Valley.

Dawn on 10 April was cold and wet, with heavy mist shrouding the hills and valleys. First contact with the enemy was made early that morning when a motorised Allied patrol including three Marmon Herrington armoured cars commanded by Lieutenant Darcy Cole of the New Zealand Divisional Cavalry headed up the road towards Monastir. 'We were escorting British engineers to blow bridges just across the Yugoslav border,' says Trooper Harry Spencer, a member of C Squadron who was in one of the cars.

The engineers were demolishing a stone bridge when the German Army turned up. One of our boys, Corporal 'Lofty' King, was up front when Germans on motorbikes and sidecars came down this narrow, winding road. They were leading a column of trucks and armoured cars and they didn't expect to find us in Yugoslavia. Lofty opened fire with his Bren-gun.[30]

The German column jerked to a halt and SS troops jumped out of the trucks and replied with mortars and machine guns, forcing the Kiwis to abandon the bridge. The patrol leader, Captain P. G. Page of the 4th Hussars, ordered the engineers to return to Vevi. 'We got them out of the way,' Harry Spencer says, 'and then decided to burn down a couple of wooden bridges near the border. We set them on fire all right but then found we were cut off by another lot of Germans.'

This group had moved east along the road from Florina and were guarding the next bridge. Once again Lofty King opened fire with his Bren-gun, forcing the Germans to retire and giving the armoured cars an opportunity to dash over the bridge. King was awarded the Military Medal.[31]

At 11 am that morning, the same German force was spotted on the Itia–Vevi road approaching Mackay Force.[32] The trucks halted at a spot within 2000 metres of the Vevi Line, where they disgorged dozens of SS troops. From 1 pm onwards, British and Australian field guns fired at long range on the German vehicles. One shell from the very first salvo fired by the 64th Medium Regiment scored a bullseye. 'Out first ball,' Iven Mackay commented.[33] The 5th Battery did even better, hitting five vehicles before the Germans could pull back. The battery's war diary reads, 'The contact with German Forces on 10–12 April resulted in this regiment being the first Australian artillery unit to engage German forces in this war.'[34]

From their OPs, infantry and artillery observers watched British bombers and Hurricane fighters harassing the long, slow column of German tanks, trucks and artillery pieces as they crept across the Florina Valley to take cover behind the low Lofoi ridge.[35]

When news of the German advance reached Athens, Link MacVeagh noted in his diary, 'I hazard the prediction that the British will lose Greece (and all those fine Australians and New Zealanders). Man to man the Australian or New Zealander is a better soldier than the German, but they are so few. The hordes of the mechanised barbarians are too numerous for the few free peoples brave enough to fight for their freedom.'[36]

All this time, Colonel Mitchell's 2/8th Battalion had been struggling to take up its position around Hill 997, the vital high ground to the right of the Rangers in the valley below. The men had been shuttled north in cramped railway wagons and had spent the night of 9 April in the snow. Having marched 18 kilometres during daylight hours on the 10th, the battalion faced a steep climb to reach their position before nightfall. They had just crawled into shallow trenches scraped in the rocky terrain when German patrols began moving stealthily among the widely spaced platoons, grabbing unsuspecting troops and spiriting them away for interrogation. Five Australians, some New Zealand machine-gunners and six Rangers were taken prisoner.

Just after midnight on 11 April – Good Friday in the Western calendar – Michael Clarke followed the signal wire through blinding snow to his regiment's forward observation post above the Rangers' trenches. When the snow abated, he directed the fire of all three troops of 5th Battery on to enemy vehicles which could be dimly seen on the road south from Vevi. At the same time, the first mobile German guns had caught up with the forward SS units and had opened fire, causing casualties among the Australian anti-tank gunners on the forward slopes. Clarke expected to hear return fire from the Rangers but there was none. He phoned Willie Smith 'to voice my strong suspicions that there were no bloody infantry in front of me, unless they were holding fire until they could see the whites of the enemy's eyes'. In fact, the company of Rangers beneath his OP had been pulled out of the line at 3 am.[37]

At daybreak, snow was still falling on the high ground and after a miserable night without hot food or blankets the men of the 2/8th were cold, wet and hungry, but they extended their line to fill the gap left by the Rangers and waited for the German attack. George Vasey's three battalions – the 2/4th, the 1/Rangers and the 2/8th – were now spread across a 16-kilometre front that dominated the heights and overlooked the pass between Vevi and Klidi on the main road to Kozani, with the 21st Greek Regiment on the extreme left of the line and the Dodecanese Regiment on the extreme right.

During the morning, two battalions of the SS Adolf Hitler Division advanced along the main road towards the 2/8th Battalion but were stopped by artillery fire when they were 750 metres from the forward posts. At 4.50 pm, B Company of the 2/4th Battalion on the left of the Rangers' position was attacked in strength by five companies of German troops who had crept forward under cover of a snowstorm. They were driven off by small-arms fire and dashed towards the railway line, where they sought shelter behind a coal dump, providing a good target for the 2nd Royal Horse Artillery, who 'blew the tripe' out of them. The barrage provoked a fresh infantry attack on the 2/4th which was also repulsed by heavy fire.[38]

'You may be tired,' George Vasey told his troops in an order-of-the-day relayed through his officers. 'You may be uncomfortable. But you are doing a job important to the rest of our forces. Therefore you will continue to do that job unless otherwise ordered.'[39]

At 6.30 pm that day, 11 April, General Blamey was summoned to a meeting at Jumbo Wilson's northern headquarters at Elasson. Wavell had flown in. The three commanders dined together, then discussed the campaign for a further three and a half hours. It was decided to unite the Australian and New Zealand divisions in a new Anzac Corps, with Blamey in command.[40]

The cable from Canberra to the New Zealand Government announcing the change of name from 1st Australian Corps to 1st Anzac Corps stated that it had been made 'at the request of the New Zealand Division and with Blamey's full agreement'.[41] Understandably, Freyberg did not want his men to serve in an Australian corps. While relations between Freyberg and Blamey were cordial, the New Zealand general was determined to maintain his division's independence.

Early on the morning of 12 April – Easter Saturday – Blamey informed his commanders in a written order:

> As from 1800 hrs 12 Apr I Aust Corps will be designated ANZAC CORPS. In making this announcement the GOC ANZAC CORPS desires to say that the reunion of the Australian and New Zealand Divisions gives all ranks the greatest uplift. The task ahead though difficult is not nearly so desperate as that which our fathers faced in April 26 years ago. We go to it together with stout hearts and certainty of success.[42]

Handing Blamey's message to Captain R. Morrison of the 25th New Zealand Battalion for dispatch to General Freyberg's headquarters, Syd Rowell said, 'I'll let you know what's in it. It will save you opening it on the way home!' He read out the message and Blamey chipped in, 'There you are, sonny, you have only got to live till 6 o'clock tonight to be a bloody Anzac.'[43]

CHAPTER 11

Anzacs Again

That Easter Saturday, it seemed as though all of Greece was on the move. Remote mountain paths that had rarely seen motor vehicles echoed to the scream of petrol-driven engines powering six-wheeled German armoured cars, gun tractors and troop-carriers. Squadrons of tanks shook village churches as old as antiquity in which women in black sought solace in their Orthodox faith. Greek forces moving across the Florina Valley to new positions in the western passes mingled with thousands of refugees fleeing south from the Nazis.

Brigadier Stan Savige's 17th Brigade and the 2/11th Battalion, the missing battalion of George Vasey's brigade, disembarked at Piraeus that afternoon. The dockside stank of gunpowder and oil from the *Clan Fraser* disaster. Within hours, the troops had boarded trucks and railway carriages and were heading north to Lamia and thence to Larisa to block the enemy's approach from the west via the road from Kalabaka. The 2/6th Battalion was now commanded by Lieutenant-Colonel Hugh Wrigley, who had recovered from his wounds at Bardia. 'The Greek Army had been pretty well thrashed, so it was two Anzac divisions versus ten German divisions,' says Keith Hooper. 'I had a lot of sympathy for the Greeks. You'd see them going up to the line with no weapons and often no shoes.'[1]

From General Wilson's advanced headquarters at Elasson, Kenneth Slessor drove north to see the Vevi front for himself. 'Up to the line go camouflaged trucks with loads of ammunition, petrol, food and supplies in a heartening and ceaseless stream,' he wrote in a dispatch to Australian newspapers.

> Down from the line come Greek soldiers caked in mud, hobbling with utter weariness. In between come the refugees. They are the saddest sight of all. Some trudge on foot, others are on gaunt farm horses or walk beside tiny mules tottering under their loads. Each has all that he can call home rolled up in a blanket.[2]

Slessor was forbidden to report that men were falling out of the Vevi Line suffering from frostbite, exhaustion and altitude sickness.

The campaign had reached its most crucial phase. General Papagos informed the staff at Jumbo Wilson's rear headquarters in Athens that he would withdraw his III Corps in Albania to reinforce the Allied left flank at Vevi, provided the 1st Armoured Brigade moved into the Florina area to protect its withdrawal. Wilson's staff, who 'seemed to spend most of their time in the British Club or taking afternoon tea', was out of touch with the fighting but they gave that assurance without consulting their commander.[3]

By now, General Boehme's troops had reached the Vermion–Olympus Line from the east and heavy fighting had broken out around the Edessa, Veria and Servia Passes. Wilson issued an order at 3.45 am on 12 April that all formations under his command – including his tanks – should move to new positions 'as soon as possible'. This decision caused grave offence to the Greek commander, who felt that Wilson had abandoned his forces.

Starting at 8.30 am on the 12th, German infantry launched a ferocious, three-pronged attack on the Vevi Line, striking at the Dodecanese Regiment, attacking the Rangers astride the road and assaulting Vasey's headquarters with mortars. 'Jerry was all around us on three sides,' Lieutenant Cecil Chrystal of the 2/4th writes, 'and the fighting was pretty solid. I moved to the rear of our position before lunch and tried to get some trucks out but had to leave them. I saw a lot of other chaps from other units withdrawing so went back to company headquarters as fast as I could …'[4]

German patrols had concluded that the weakest point on the Vevi front was the junction between the Rangers and the 2/8th Battalion, so the heaviest assault fell on this section. The most forward Australian platoon was overrun with the loss of all but six men. The Germans were driven off by enfilading fire from posts on the left and right but at 11 am the Rangers, believing the position had been lost, withdrew three kilometres down the Kozani road, much to the chagrin of the Australians, who had simply moved 100 metres up the slopes of Hill 997.

From the heights, Colonel Mitchell's men fired down on German infantry advancing behind tanks and, later that afternoon, staged a well-organised counter-attack that regained some of the lost ground. The enemy, however, continued to press forward and it was only the fire of the Royal Horse Artillery, the two remaining Australian anti-tank guns and the Vickers machine guns of a New Zealand platoon that held up the German advance.[5]

'They attacked under cover of a snowstorm which raged for nearly two days,' Chester Wilmot reported to Australia in his ABC dispatch. 'Our troops felt the cold particularly badly – many of them had never seen snow before and they'd certainly never had to spend days and nights in a snowstorm without any chance of getting warm.'[6]

*

General Wavell had been quick to applaud the advent of the Anzac Corps, noting that 'the revival of this historic title Anzac was welcomed with pride by all in the corps'. Such hopes were completely lost on the infantrymen of Tubby Allen's 16th Brigade, who were unaware that the Anzac Corps had been re-created. All through the night of 12/13 April, they slogged over mountain paths from Veria to the Aliakmon River and then up to the village of Velvendos on the right flank of the main Servia Pass defences, a distance of 50 kilometres.

Blamey had ordered that the 2/1st, 2/2nd and 2/3rd Battalions withdraw entirely on foot over the mountains rather than make the trip in a matter of hours in road transport. He feared that German tanks might break through Vasey's forces in the upper Aliakmon valley and crash into the retreating columns. It was a decision that inflicted great hardship on the men and cost the brigade much of its heavy equipment. The German attack hadn't even started when Blamey issued his order and the men would have been able to reach safety in their trucks long before there was any threat.

As things were, each man was weighed down with 100 rounds of ammunition, five days' rations, his greatcoat, blanket, groundsheet and haversack. Much of the route was ankle-deep in slush which turned to ice. And then it snowed, obliterating the track. On the steep, slippery slopes, men stumbled with fatigue. If a man fell down, his mates pulled him back to his feet, redistributed his load and helped him along.[7]

Colonel Fred Chilton of the 2/2nd Battalion walked every step of the way with his men, describing it as 'a frightful march full of frightful memories for us all'.[8] Roy Waters, leading a skinny little donkey loaded with equipment, had filled his water bottle with brandy. 'My old donkey had a ton of guts,' he says, 'and with the aid of my biscuits and kind words stood up well.'[9]

As 6 pm approached on the Vevi Line, there were many of George Vasey's men who would not see the appointed Anzac hour. The 2/4th and 2/8th Battalions had been instructed to make for their trucks at the rear of their positions at 8 pm, while the Rangers acted as rearguard at the head of the Klidi Pass. The Rangers would then fall back through the 1st Armoured Brigade a few kilometres south at Sotir.[10]

Vasey had been fairly happy with the way things were going and had assured Iven Mackay that his men were holding their own. When he was informed that the Rangers had already pulled out, he refused to believe it. In fact, the British battalion was well on its way to Sotir after suffering heavy losses in the earlier fighting.

By 4.30 pm, German tanks accompanied by 500 infantry were inflicting serious punishment on the forward posts of the 2/8th Battalion. The Germans severed the telephone wire running through the Rangers' position to brigade headquarters, cutting Colonel Mitchell's contact with Vasey. With the Klidi Pass no longer available as a line of retreat, his men had no choice but to fall back over the crest of Hill 997 and head down to the floor of the valley.

Vasey suddenly realised that his men were in mortal danger. It must have shaken him, but he remained characteristically cool. At 5 pm, he telephoned the 2/4th's headquarters with a message for Ivan Dougherty. 'Tell him the roof is leaking,' he said in the 'oblique conversation' code. 'He had better come over so we can cook up a plot.' Dougherty knew this meant he should extricate his men from their positions as quickly as possible and move towards brigade HQ. As it was no longer safe for the trucks to come forward, the men would have to make a cross-country hike of 20 kilometres and meet them at the crossroads south of Sotir near the village of Rodona.[11]

General Mackay ordered Colonel Horace Strutt of the 2/3rd Field Regiment to form a rearguard with his 5th and 6th Batteries covering the exit of the Klidi Pass. Strutt ordered all gun troops: 'Prepare all-round defence areas. Have machine guns ready at hand. Enemy troops may break through under cover. We are to stay here and fight them off.'

'I reported to the colonel at regimental headquarters down in a creek bed and was told that the British troops in the centre had packed up and left our flanks in the air,' Captain Smith says. 'The whole force was falling back to a line at Servia. I was to go forward to the mouth of the pass and shoot the battery until our infantry were clear.'[12]

Camouflage nets were pulled back, dial sights exchanged for open-sight telescopes and the guns were moved forward. At a range of a few hundred metres, the 6th Battery fired on the first panzers to appear through the pass. As daylight faded, the quads began to arrive and the guns ceased firing one troop at a time, with 5th Battery dropping further back to cover the 6th while its gunners dragged their guns out of the thick mud. Messerschmitt 109s flew up and down the road firing incendiary bullets which destroyed two of the gunners' trucks.

For the next two hours, 5th Battery fired over open sights as German foot soldiers advanced on their right flank, shooting at them with Schmeisser submachine guns.[13] 'It was not the easiest withdrawal,' the regimental historian writes. 'The snow had left the ground slushy and the guns had to be manhandled down from their hilltop positions.'

The main body of the 2/8th Battalion had fanned out and was making its way overland to the Rodona crossroads. The men were ordered to ditch any weapons or equipment that might slow them down. Having walked huge distances to reach the front only 48 hours earlier, they plodded wearily into the freezing night over steep hills and slippery ridges.

At 8.30 pm on Hill 1001, German infantry climbed the forward slopes as the last sections of the 2/4th pulled out of their positions under heavy enemy artillery fire. The 1st Armoured Brigade had come under Iven Mackay's command that afternoon and he could have moved the tanks forward from Amindaion to Vevi to cover the withdrawal but he was informed that the tanks had run into enemy panzers on their way from Amindaion to Sotir and would be lucky to get out themselves.

Heavy fighting was heard in the hills as the 19th Brigade's trucks, plus half a dozen Kiwi three-tonners, moved towards the rendezvous point. 'Down from the hills straggled small parties of weary Australians,' the official historian of the 4th RMT Company writes, 'some without rifles and one or two even without boots, and one by one the vehicles filled and smartly moved off.'[14] Just 250 men of the 2/8th Battalion, 200 of whom were no longer bearing arms, reached Rodona. Seventy members of one of the 2/4th's three companies were captured after exchanging fire with a German patrol and then losing their way in the dark and walking into enemy lines.[15]

Iven Mackay watched the troops stream into Rodona. It was obvious to him that the Rangers Battalion was 'in a state of fright' and would be incapable of supporting Charrington's rearguard if he got through. While the 2/8th Battalion was driven south to Servia, Mackay ordered the 2/4th to join the Rangers in the rearguard. 'There was not a murmur from any of the men of my tired battalion,' Ivan Dougherty says. 'They went into it with resolution and determination ... I felt proud of my battalion.'[16]

The 2/4th were driven a couple of kilometres to Sotir, where they manned the right-hand side of a ridge stretching across a narrow neck of land surrounded by marshes. Dougherty was ordered to hold this position until 9 am on 13 April. Just before dawn that day, he and Vasey crept forward to observe the enemy in their weapons pits 1000 metres ahead of the battalion's advanced units. Vasey was wearing a white raincoat and at first light the Germans spotted him and opened fire with machine guns. The two commanders crawled back on their hands and knees, while the Australians provided covering fire. Unbeknown to them, 100 Allied prisoners of war were corralled in no-man's-land between the two forces and some 30 of them were killed or wounded in the firefight.

*

At sunrise on 13 April, the rearguard of Tubby Allen's 16th Brigade reached the heights overlooking the muddy waters of the Aliakmon River. Down below, the brigade's three battalions – fingers, feet and socks frozen and covered in layers of snow[17] – were being ferried across the fast-flowing river in an antiquated punt.

Once ashore, they were astonished to find Father Paddy Youll, a Catholic priest, and Padre Harold Hosier of the Salvation Army manning a tea point after carrying their gear up the mountainside on the back of a donkey. The men were also offered reviving tots of Johnnie Walker Black Label whisky and packets of Sao biscuits.[18] A four-hour climb then took them to the village of Velvendos, where they bivouacked for the night; in the morning, they made a further climb up to their battle positions.[19]

By now, Rollie Charrington's tanks had reached Sotir and as the Germans were dug in and showing no signs of attacking, George Vasey authorised Ivan Dougherty to start withdrawing his men at 7.30 am. 'We feel pretty shaky at the idea of having to run about 300 yards up the slope,' Dick Parry says.

> The first man in our platoon to poke his head up gets a bullet through it and drops back dead. Not so good. One after another the boys jump up and start to run, while the volume of fire increases. I watch one of our section halfway back. As he runs the earth spurts up all around him: he runs through the lot and disappears over the rise, safe for the moment.[20]

At 8.55 am, the last of the battalion's trucks was heading towards Kozani and the bridge over the Aliakmon River. While the tanks of the 33rd Panzer Regiment pursued the remnants of Mackay Force, the SS Adolf Hitler Division were ordered to give up the chase and wheel west to cut off the Greek forces withdrawing from Albania. That afternoon, as the panzers rumbled into Ptolemais, a town halfway between Vevi and

Kozani, they came under heavy artillery and anti-tank fire from the Allied rearguard.

The cruiser tanks of the Royal Tank Regiment and the light tanks of the 4th Hussars attacked the German armour and destroyed four panzers but suffered even heavier losses themselves. Nevertheless, the action had delayed the enemy advance. Rollie Charrington detached his bloodied and battered brigade and made for Mount Olympus. He had lost so many tanks – mostly to mechanical breakdown rather than enemy action – that it was now a brigade in name only.[21]

On the Olympus Line, the 4th and 5th New Zealand Brigades guarded the passes and the 16th Brigade held the snow-swept heights above Servia. The Australians were so far from the front that the only people they were likely to encounter were Greek shepherds. The 19th Brigade, however, was cut off in rough country on the western side of the Aliakmon River and would be the first to make contact with the enemy. As its numbers had been severely reduced, Blamey reinforced it with the 26th New Zealand Battalion.[22]

The New Zealanders were noticeably muted in their enthusiasm for the revival of the Anzac Corps. General Freyberg cabled Blamey, 'All ranks NZ Div welcome reunion of Australian and New Zealand Divisions with greatest satisfaction. Will you please send this message to our comrades [in the] 6th Division.' But according to Colonel Stewart, the new Anzac Corps 'could never be more than a name when all the personnel on the headquarters were Australian'.[23] It was a fair point. There was a strong suspicion that the Anzac name was being used as a cover to gloss over the political and military incompetence that had placed the fighting troops of both nations in an impossible position.

At 3.30 pm on 13 April, advance enemy elements could be seen approaching the Aliakmon River but before they could reach the three steel-trussed spans of the bridge Australian engineers detonated their charges and dropped two of the spans into the river.[24] On the eastern side of the river, the 2/3rd Field Regiment unlimbered its guns in the hills behind the 20th New Zealand Battalion, commanded by Lieutenant-Colonel Howard Kippenberger. No sooner had the guns been laid out and camouflaged than the Luftwaffe appeared overhead. Although the planes failed to spot the 25-pounders, New Zealand troops digging in on the steep slopes above Servia were given their first taste of strafing and sustained several casualties.

During the night of 14/15 April, German and Austrian infantry crossed the river in portable boats and headed towards two anti-tank ditches which had been dug in the road to Elasson and Larisa.[25] The German commanders had been led to believe that the passes were only lightly defended, even though the two towns were vital points on W Force's withdrawal route. In fact, three companies of the 19th NZ Battalion were stationed on a narrow, precipitous ridge at the mouth of the Servia Pass, supported by the 31st New Zealand Anti-Tank Battery and a platoon of Australian machine-gunners.

Just before dawn on the 15th, sentries in the Wellington Company's 7th and 8th Platoons heard footsteps approaching their position. In response to a challenge, there were cries of 'Greko! Greko!' Private Jack Barley left his trench and walked down the road to the first tank ditch. He could vaguely discern a party of soldiers, led by a man in Greek uniform, negotiating the first tank obstacle. Throughout the day, Greek soldiers had passed through the New Zealand lines and it was pointless questioning them, even through a Greek-speaking interpreter, because they mostly came from the eastern provinces and spoke only Turkish. Barclay signalled the party to proceed and returned to his position.[26]

Some 50 soldiers crossed the first tank trap and headed towards the second. As soon as they reached the cover of a cutting between the two obstacles, they opened fire on the forward New Zealand posts. At the same time, the Wellington Company's 9th Platoon fired on the intruders from its position above the road. The Hawke's Bay Company and two of the Australian Vickers machine guns joined in, trapping the enemy troops in the cutting.

Meanwhile, the number of enemy troops in the first tank ditch had swollen to 250 and these troops provided covering fire to their comrades until a red Very light from 8th Platoon signalled the Bren-gunner in No. 7 Section to open fire on the ditch. There were cries of 'Kamerad!' and white handkerchiefs were waved in surrender.

By eight o'clock in the morning, the surviving enemy troops were sheltering behind bushes on the hillsides or fleeing back towards the Aliakmon River.[27] Total enemy losses were estimated at 400, compared with two Kiwis killed and six injured.[28] A body in Greek uniform was found among the enemy dead; it is probable that the Germans had placed a prisoner of war at the head of their column to deceive the Kiwis.[29]

Elsewhere along the New Zealand line, the 28th New Zealand Battalion and other units of the 4th and 5th Brigades clashed with the enemy. 'Our infantry are magnificent and held their line against overwhelming attacks,' Captain Willie Smith writes.

> The Maori Battalion [the 28th] showed the Germans some bayonet tricks that they will remember for ever. The buggers did not stay for a second helping. We did some very pretty shooting and B Troop alone stopped an attack on the left flank, catching the poor bloody Huns crossing the icy-cold river, and absolutely wiping out the whole show.[30]

Meanwhile, General Freyberg had made an 800-kilometre round trip by car to visit all of his detachments. He arrived at Anzac Corps headquarters at Elasson to discover that the situation had changed dramatically. The Germans had broken through the Greek forces on the left flank and Savige Force – the 2/5th, 2/6th, 2/7th and 2/11th Battalions – was occupying a line in the

Kalabaka area to cover Larisa against an attack from the west. Blamey told Freyberg that Anzac Corps was being pulled back 160 kilometres on the orders of Jumbo Wilson. The new line would be across the narrow neck of land at Thermopylae.[31] 'I call on every Anzac to grit his teeth,' Blamey ordered his men, 'and be worthy of his father.'[32]

CHAPTER 12

Thermopylae

The Thermopylae line stretched from the Aegean to the Gulf of Corinth – a distance of 48 kilometres – and covered the Thermopylae, Brallos and Delphi Passes. When General Papagos met General Wilson at Elasson on 16 April, he raised no objection to the British withdrawal; in fact, the Greek commander-in-chief suggested it would be better if Lustre Force left Greece altogether.

At the same time, General Wavell, Admiral Cunningham and Air Chief Marshal Longmore concluded at a meeting on board *Warspite* that evacuating the force from Greece was the only sane option to prevent wholesale slaughter. On 17 April, Churchill agreed to Operation Demon, as the evacuation was designated, provided the Greek Government gave its consent.[1]

Thus the withdrawal to Thermopylae (literally the 'Hot Gates') became the first step in the evacuation of Lustre Force from Greece. As the whole force had to pass through the dangerous bottleneck of Larisa, it would be accomplished only with great difficulty.[2] And as Wavell had refused to permit his planning staff at Grey Pillars to draw up an evacuation plan lest its very existence erode troop morale, Demon would inevitably have to be cobbled together at the last minute. Weeks earlier – even before the first troops had reached Greece – Freddie de Guingand had anticipated the need for an exit strategy and was actually working on an evacuation plan. 'The commander-in-chief is very annoyed about it,' Arthur Smith, Wavell's chief of staff, told him, 'and I'm afraid you will have to stop.'[3]

Meanwhile, the 19th Brigade, which would hold the vital Brallos Pass during the early stages of the evacuation, crossed the Aliakmon River over a hastily constructed footbridge, which meant abandoning its anti-tank guns and much of its equipment. Colonel Kippenberger received no notification that the Australians and the 26th New Zealand Battalion had withdrawn, leaving the left flank of his 20th New Zealand Battalion completely exposed.[4]

Tubby Allen was attempting to extricate his three battalions from the precipitous mountains east of Servia when he was confronted with a new danger. Against all expectations, the main threat to W Force emerged not from the Germans on the left but from those on the right-hand flank. Colonel 'Polly' Macky of the 21st New Zealand Battalion, which had been holding the coastal village of Platamon, reported to Sydney Rowell at Anzac Corps HQ that he was under heavy attack on the seaward side of the Vale of Tempe, the great volcanic gash that forms the gorge of the Pinios River on its way to the Aegean. Unless this German advance could be stopped, the enemy would cross the Plain of Thessaly and seize the road junction at Larisa, cutting the Allied forces in half.

Tensions had been simmering between Rowell and Blamey throughout the campaign and this sudden crisis brought them to the boil. Rowell had always been critical of Blamey's drinking and womanising but he now decided that Blamey 'was quite incompetent as a field commander in modern war'.[5] The flashpoint was reached when Rowell suggested that Brigadier Cyril Clowes, Anzac Corps' imperturbable artillery commander, should be attached to the 21st Battalion to liaise with Colonel Macky over what action needed to be taken to halt the Germans. As Blamey considered Clowes – a Queenslander like Joe Lavarack – a contender for his own position, he was reluctant to give him an important operational role. When Rowell insisted, Blamey 'agreed with very ill grace' and Clowes set off at 1 am on the 16th.[6]

When he reached Macky at the eastern end of the gorge ten hours later, German tanks and motorcycle troops were moving along the railway line towards the Pinios River. Clowes learned from Macky that one of his companies and part of another were missing, while the rest of his men were dispersed under mulberry and poplar trees or entrenched in patches of wheat covering the area.[7]

Clowes instructed the New Zealand commander that it was 'essential to deny the gorge to the enemy till 19 April, even if it meant extinction'. He promised that support would arrive within 24 hours.[8] He then explained the situation to Rowell, who immediately ordered Colonel Fred Chilton to divert his 2/2nd Battalion to the western end of the gorge near the village of Tempe. Blamey was unhappy about Rowell's decision – he thought a few New Zealand Bren-carriers would suffice as reinforcements – and another argument ensued. Finally, Blamey seemed to appreciate the danger of the situation and ordered the 2/2nd and 2/3rd Australian Battalions, the 4th New Zealand Field Regiment (less one battery), a troop of New Zealand anti-tank gunners and 11 New Zealand Bren-carriers into the gorge. He placed these forces under the command of Tubby Allen.

Blamey then left Elasson and drove to his new Anzac Corps headquarters at Soumpassi, where he was completely out of touch with the fighting in the Pinios Gorge and also with the troops retreating from the north. When Rowell suggested that either he or Blamey should go back to help Iven Mackay and Bernard Freyberg, Blamey 'said he couldn't go himself and wouldn't let me go'. Rowell raised the matter twice more and, according to Charles Spry who witnessed the exchange, Blamey finally snapped, 'Well, go your bloody self.'[9]

Rowell drove back along the congested roads and saw both commanders, who were keeping the convoys moving. Mackay rode up and down the long column on the back of a motorbike, urging the drivers to keep going despite the dive-bombing and strafing of German Stukas and Messerschmitts. The Stukas were notoriously inaccurate and at one point Mackay deliberately sat out in the open during an air raid to show there was little danger. At night, his Ford Mercury drove with its lights on to encourage the truck drivers to do the same. Well aware that the enemy had not perfected taking off and landing at night, he reprimanded any soldier who screamed that German pilots would see them.[10]

General Freyberg was also in the thick of it, casually ignoring an enemy aircraft as it tried to machine-gun him, while his large, barrel-chested figure was later seen calmly sorting out a traffic jam.[11]

When Rowell got back to Soumpassi, he discovered that Blamey had decamped yet again – for Levadia on the road to Thebes, some 50 kilometres south of the Thermopylae Line. Rowell later wrote that he was 'of the opinion that the Corps General failed in his first task, *viz.*, the exercise of command'. General Wilson, who was loath to criticise Blamey, nevertheless observed that Rowell was 'a brilliant officer who carried Blamey'.[12]

Meanwhile, all arrangements for the evacuation had been left to the Grey Funnel Line, as the Royal Navy was affectionately known. Admiral Cunningham appointed Rear-Admiral 'Tom' Baillie-Grohman, former captain of HMS *Ramillies*, to organise the naval side of Operation Demon in Greece, while Vice-Admiral Pridham-Wippell would be in charge of operations afloat. An inter-service triumvirate consisting of Group Captain Claude Pelly of the RAF, Commander Alec Fearn of the Royal

Navy and Major Douglas Packard, a Royal Artillery officer, would be responsible for getting fighting units, base troops, RAF personnel, and Palestinian and Cypriot labourers to the evacuation points. Based at the Acropole Hotel in Athens, Pelly thought his comrades 'excellent stout-hearted chaps'. He had been at Dunkirk and Fearn had organised the pullout from Narvik in Norway, 'so between us we knew quite a bit about evacuation'.

In response to a plea for guidance from Air Marshal Longmore, Churchill issued a directive to his Middle East commanders on 18 April which would seriously jeopardise Operation Demon's chances of success. 'You must divide [your efforts] between protecting evacuation and sustaining battle in Libya,' he wrote.

> *But if these clash, which may be avoidable, emphasis must be given to victory in Libya.* Crete will at first only be a receptacle of whatever can get there from Greece. Its fuller defence must be organised later. *Victory in Libya counts first, evacuation of troops from Greece second.*[13]

This directive led to allegations that Churchill was prepared to abandon Anzac Corps in Greece. Bob Menzies pleaded in the War Cabinet for more air cover for the troops but Churchill insisted that Libya must have first claim on Longmore's overstretched resources.[14] The most immediate effect of Churchill's directive was to place a heavy burden on Rear-Admiral G.H. Creswell, who was responsible for marshalling the Greece-bound convoys in the harbour at Alexandria. Creswell had been told that 'no preparatory action for Demon was to be undertaken unless demanded by GHQ Middle East', so he could only 'earmark' merchant ships for Greece and not hold them in readiness, in case they were needed for Libya.[15]

Eventually, the Royal Navy and Merchant Marine scrambled together an evacuation force. It comprised eight cruisers;

24 destroyers and escort vessels; three huge landing ships, infantry (LSIs) – *Glenearn*, *Glengyle* and *Glenroy*; the assault ship *Ulster Prince*; 14 troopships; five flat-bottomed landing craft, tanks (LCTs capable of holding 900 men); and numerous smaller landing craft.[16] In Greece, beachmasters were placed in control at each of the eight evacuation points which stretched from Rafina, Port Rafti and Megara in the Athens area to Mylio, Nauplion, Tolos Bay, Monemvasia and Kalamata in the Peloponnese.

Meanwhile, W Force's sappers were demolishing the very roads, bridges and railway lines on which Greece's largely rural economy depended, contributing towards the widespread famine which would grip the nation within a matter of weeks. 'The astounding thing about it is that the Greeks helped us throughout,' Group Captain Pelly comments. 'Both in Athens and outside, they were friendly and co-operative. It was pathetic but, at the same time, a magnificent attitude. They certainly have played their part in this war, with honour.'[17]

As an airman, Pelly knew that fighter cover was the key to minimising losses during an evacuation but he noted with alarm that British aircraft had almost disappeared from the skies. 'As the Army retired,' he writes, 'we lost aerodromes and the Huns got their vast numbers of aircraft nearer and nearer. They gradually made our aerodromes untenable and our tiny fighter force was soon reduced to nothing.'[18]

Allied air cover was seriously damaged on 15 April when the Luftwaffe destroyed 30 British fighters and bombers on the ground at Larisa airfield and then a few days later Air Commodore D'Albiac's force virtually ceased to exist when a sustained attack was launched on airfields in the Athens area. 'Out in the open,' one eye-witness recalls of an air raid on Menidi airstrip, 'a bunch of eight Aussie soldiers having a late breakfast alternated between taking mouthfuls of tinned sausage and rifle-potting the passing aircraft.'[19]

An even graver crisis faced W Force when the vast Greek

forces in the north-west, starved of supplies since the fall of Salonica and with no means of getting further aid, collapsed. On 17 April, General Wilson met with King George and his advisers at his Athens palace to discuss the crisis. He found a mood of despair: the country was bleeding to death and fatalism had become endemic. Later that day, the Greek Prime Minister Alexander Koryzis told the King he felt he had failed in the task entrusted to him. Overnight, he went into his study, put a revolver to his greying temple and shot himself.

At 7.30 am on 18 April, the Anzac force in the Vale of Tempe encountered German tanks advancing over the slopes of Mount Olympus and along the single-track railway line on the northern side of the gorge. German infantry waded across the Pinios River. Though raked with machine-gun fire, many succeeded in clambering on to the southern bank. The battle raged all day and towards dusk the German commanders sent in a large force of tanks, supported by air cover, which drove the Anzacs out of the gorge and into the hills.

At nightfall on the 18th, German tanks crossed the river and were pressing against Tubby Allen's rearguard. The commander of the leading German tank made the mistake of standing up in his turret to see where he was going. Colonel Jimmy Lamb, commanding the 2/3rd Battalion, shouted to his men, 'Make every shot tell, men; these tanks can't fight us in the dark.'[20] The tank leader was riddled with bullets. All of the panzers then wheeled and stopped and began firing indiscriminately into the dark.

The 2/3rd Australian Field Regiment had withdrawn from the Servia Pass with the 4th New Zealand Brigade and had set up its guns in the hills near Elasson to cover the withdrawal of the 6th Brigade. Early on the morning of the 18th, tanks and mobile guns of the 2nd and 9th Panzer Divisions were spotted at extreme range emerging from Mount Olympus. B Troop fired super-charged shells at maximum range to break up the formation as it tried to force its way through the 6th Brigade.

'This was our big day,' Willie Smith writes. 'I don't think that we were expected to get out. We ourselves almost gave up hope when we saw the massed tanks.'[21] All guns fired continuously, pausing briefly when the Stukas and 109s arrived in batches of up to 60 at a time to bomb and strafe their positions.

'At mid-afternoon, the New Zealanders started to come back in open order over an old Roman arched bridge, so casually they might have been out for a Sunday exercise,' Michael Clarke says. 'We concentrated our fire on the tanks to give the retreating infantry as much cover as possible.'

At 9 pm, both batteries received orders to pull out. As the guns on B Troop's right started to move, German tanks could be seen gathering for another attack. 'For two hours we stuck to it and hammered them until the attack faded away and darkness fell,' Willie Smith writes. 'On the day, I gave orders myself for 1500 shells to be fired. We pulled out after dark and the whole covering force got safely away.' The regiment had fired 6000 rounds, a record for a day's shooting. The gunfire had blackened the barrels of the guns and some of the crews were haemorrhaging from burst eardrums.[22]

The south-bound troop convoys snaked through the mountain passes at night hoping to reach cover by dawn. 'By now, it was impossible to do anything by daylight,' Claude Pelly says. 'The Hun was everywhere and we were unable to put up any opposition. He did as he liked and roads, troops, ships were bombed and gunned all day long.'[23] Some of the drivers heard rumours that Germans in Greek uniforms were joining the convoys in captured Allied trucks; once in the line, they were leading other vehicles into an ambush. As a result, the passenger windscreen of each big Chevrolet was knocked out and a Bren-gunner posted up front with his mount resting on the bonnet and orders to open fire on any suspicious vehicle. 'It was just a rumour,' Signalman Les Cook says, 'but it was typical of the paranoia at that time.'

Cook had been a member of the 19th Brigade's liaison party

attached to the 12th Greek Division on the Yugoslav border. 'I stayed with them till halfway down Greece just past Larisa and then the whole thing broke up and everybody went their own way,' he says.

Savige Force had been guarding W Force's left-flank line from just west of Kalabaka to Larisa when, on the 18th, all units were ordered to pull out. The 2/11th marched through Kalabaka and boarded trucks for the journey south, crossing the Pinios River in a punt and rejoining the 19th Brigade on the Thermopylae Line. Colonel Louch had been hospitalised with a damaged shoulder and Major Ray Sandover took over as battalion commander, with Captain Ralph Honner as second-in-command.

The train carrying the 2/6th and 2/7th Battalions hadn't gone much further south than Larisa when it was attacked by enemy aircraft and brought to a halt. Keith Hooper says, 'We lost our train driver – he pissed off – but fortunately we had a fellow [Corporal Douglas Taylor of the 2/7th Battalion] who'd driven trains before and he took over and brought us down to Lamia, where I picked up my Bren-carrier.'[24]

By dawn on 19 April, all of the Anzacs were south of Larisa and the following day they were in position on the Thermopylae Line, with the New Zealand Division on the coastal plain and Mackay's 6th Division on the left of the line in the Brallos Pass and in the surrounding mountains.

In 480 BC, Leonidas and 300 hand-picked Spartans had made their last stand in the narrowest part of the mountains but over the centuries the silting of the Sperkhios River had widened the pass and it was no longer a secure position. Regardless, Brigadier Vasey told his men, 'Here you bloody well are and here you bloody well stay!'[25]

Heading for the road-and-rail bridge over the Corinth Canal, Les Cook's party hitched a lift in a truck loaded with 25-pounder ammunition. The driver went to sleep at the wheel and drove into a ditch. The men were looking for another lift when they were strafed by a Messerschmitt 109. Cook had armed himself with a Boys anti-tank rifle and his mates had .303 rifles but they were useless against the German fighter. 'It was the first time we'd seen a 20-mm canon firing through the propeller blades, whereas conventional fighters had eight guns, four in each wing,' he says.

> We took shelter in a cemetery at the side of the road. It was a strange place: each body was buried above ground level in a stone coffin. Once the strafing ended, we got up and were heading back towards the road when we heard a muffled voice. We couldn't see anything and were a bit shaken, so we kept going. Then somebody said, 'There's got to be somebody there. Let's go back and have a look.'
>
> So we went back and one of the blokes noticed that the slab on top of one of the graves was slightly skewed. We pushed it aside and there was an English bloke inside the grave. He couldn't talk for a while – he was a bit distressed – but he was a truck driver and when the cannon shells started to explode around him he'd pushed the slab aside, got into the grave and lowered the slab on top of himself so he was quite safe but because the grave was so shallow he couldn't get the leverage to lift the lid off again. He was trapped in there with the bones and would have stayed there if we hadn't found him.[26]

General Wavell arrived in Athens on 19 April to discuss Operation Demon with General Wilson and King George. The King was defiant but his ministers were in various degrees of nervous prostration.[27] General Papagos despaired over the fact that the Greek Army had been isolated in Epirus and couldn't hold out much longer. The Greek commander repeated his suggestion that W Force should leave Greece to save the country from devastation. Wavell replied that the Thermopylae Line would hold so long as the Greek Army continued to protect the left flank. In view of Wavell's optimism, the King agreed to defer a decision on evacuation.

Tired, depressed and suffering from giddy spells,[28] Wavell drove north to meet Blamey at Anzac Corps headquarters at Levadia, near Thebes. At 2 am on 20 April, heavy rain thundered down as they studied the map on which Blamey had marked suitable evacuation beaches.[29] According to Wavell, he also quizzed Blamey on whether he had been happy with Jumbo Wilson's command of the campaign and had received an affirmative answer.

All hope of holding the Germans at Thermopylae vanished soon after Wavell arrived back in Athens later that day when General Georgios Tsolacoglou, the self-appointed commander of the Greek Army of Epirus, contacted Sepp Dietrich of the SS Adolf Hitler Division and announced his willingness to surrender his entire army. He wanted to capitulate to the mighty Wehrmacht rather than the despised Italians. The surrender was unauthorised and General Papagos was furious (as was Mussolini, who wanted to take the surrender in front of Italian movie cameras).[30] Nevertheless, Wavell informed King George that W Force would now have to be evacuated as soon as possible.[31] Link MacVeagh wrote, 'There will be a grand rumpus now in Parliament and what will Australia and New Zealand say?'[32]

During a meeting in Athens, Wavell told Freddie de Guingand, 'It looks as if we shall have to consider evacuation. You now have my authority to discuss this matter with Brigadier Brunskill and of course General Wilson if you see him but with no one else.'[33]

Meanwhile, Bob Menzies had called Sir John Dill to Australia House to discuss the vexed question of Australia's place in the Anglo–Anzac high command structure. Menzies was furious about Wavell's appointment of a British officer, Major-General Sir Noel Beresford-Peirse, as commander of Western Desert Force. The Prime Minister had a 'long and frank talk with Dill' in which he maintained that Blamey should have been given the command 'instead of some unknown major-general with a hyphen in his name'.[34]

Beresford-Peirse, a decorated World War I veteran, could hardly be described as unknown. Following his exploits at Sidi Barrani in December 1940, he had been knighted for leading the 4th Indian Division in the 53-day Battle of Keren, one of the greatest Allied infantry victories of the Second World War.[35]

After listening to Menzies' complaints, Dill cabled Wavell about 'the possibilities of strong and dangerous political reaction in Australia'. 'Menzies foresees,' he wrote, 'that the cry in Australia will be that not for the first time Australian troops have been sacrificed by incompetent imperial generals.'[36] Having just spoken to Blamey in Greece, Wavell replied that the Australian commander was 'emphatic' that the crisis in Greece owed everything to the collapse of the Yugoslav and Greek armies and that General Wilson and his staff could have done no more. He continued:

> He said he hoped no political trouble would be made of what had occurred. He was quite calm and accepted the situation coolly. Blamey has shown himself a fine fighting commander in these operations and fitted for high command. Suggest now for your consideration that he be appointed deputy commander-in-chief, Middle East, as soon as he can be spared from Greece.[37]

Blamey's appointment as Wavell's deputy, which owed everything to Menzies' political agitation rather than his fine fighting qualities, was duly listed in the *London Gazette*.

On 21 April, as the embattled Anzacs held the Germans on the Thermopylae Line, Sister Mabel Johnson was with the 2/6th AGH medical team under Matron Abbott treating the wounded in a British hospital among the scented pines at Kifisia on the outskirts of Athens when the order came through that Australian and New Zealand nurses were to be evacuated from Greece. Mabel writes:

> We were given two hours to pack and get out. We carried our own luggage down the drive from the lovely home we were living in and sat ready at the gate. Our truck arrived and we set off for the port. The people cheered us all the way but we felt like curs running away from our jobs. Then the air raid siren sounded.

The hospital ship *Aba* had berthed among the wreckage at Piraeus and some of the nurses of 2/6th AGH started to scramble aboard.

> When we reached the port we could see German planes dive-bombing the shipping. One truckload of sisters had been taken on the ship but the remaining two had missed the boat. So back we drove to the hills.

Matron Abbott and 24 nurses sailed off in the hospital ship, but Mabel and the other nurses had to return to Kifisia. 'We lived in an empty house,' she says, 'sleeping on the marble floor and working in the English hospital, where all the wounded had been brought.'

Meanwhile, another group of Australian nurses under Matron Katie Best had been looking after AIF wounded in the 2/5th AGH, which had been set up in tents at Ekali, a few kilometres from Kifisia. The commanding officer of the 2/5th AGH, Colonel W. E. Kay, was determined to remain with his patients. On 21 April, he asked Matron Best to choose 44 nurses and physiotherapists for evacuation, while 40 would remain at the hospital. Matron told the nurses to write their names on a slip of paper with the word 'stay' or 'go'. 'I gathered the slips to catalogue them,' she says, 'but not one sister wrote "go" on her paper.' She then had the grim task of choosing the 39 nurses who would remain with her in Greece.[38]

That day, the Wehrmacht had two armoured and two mountain divisions moving slowly along the bomb-damaged road from Larisa to Lamia. Keith Hooper and his two-man crew reclaimed their carrier and set off in the direction of Thermopylae. 'We were bombed and machine-gunned and I jumped out and hid behind some rocks,' he says.

> When I went back, the carrier was riddled with so many bullet holes it looked like a colander. The 2/11th Battalion was falling back to the Brallos Pass and I hopped on the side of one of their trucks. A bomber came along and everybody jumped off and it blew the truck to pieces. I continued across country and waded across a creek and continued on to Brallos, where I was 'captured' by the 2/5th Battalion. I had walked into their lines and discovered that the 2/6th was on the other side of the road. I've never been so happy in my life.[39]

The first columns of motorised German infantry reached Lamia and hurried across the plain to a bridge over the Sperkhios River to gain access to the pass. They were repelled by accurate shooting by two 25-pounders of the 2/2nd Field Regiment, which had been pushed to the brink of a narrow ledge on the escarpment overlooking the bridge. Early in the morning of 22 April, German guns engaged the Australians in an artillery duel. At 1 pm, one of the Australian 25-pounders was knocked out.

Lieutenant John Anderson then saw that German infantry had reached the foot of the escarpment and were attempting to scale it. Just as the Persians had discovered a secret track to outflank Leonidas, the enemy had found another route up to the pass. Anderson and his men lifted the tail of their remaining gun and aimed the barrel at the Germans. They fired another 50 rounds before the gun suffered a direct hit, forcing the Australians to withdraw with the loss of six killed and three seriously wounded.

The regiment's historian writes: 'For these dead gunners there could well be repeated and paraphrased, the message of Leonidas, "Go stranger, tell at Melbourne that we who lie here died content."'[40]

PART III

Vertical Warfare

CHAPTER 13

Retreat to Crete

On the evening of 21 April, Jumbo Wilson and Admiral Baillie-Grohman met General Blamey at Anzac Corps HQ at Levadia. With the Germans pressing forward on both flanks, it was decided that W Force would be evacuated at the earliest possible date, most probably starting on the night of 24/25 April. A curtain was to be drawn on the Greek campaign and the stage set for the Battle of Crete.

On the morning of 22 April, Blamey called a conference with General Mackay, his senior staff officers and Colonel Wells, the liaison officer who was to take the evacuation orders to General Freyberg.[1] According to Sydney Rowell, Blamey 'was physically and mentally broken. He was almost in tears and gave Mackay, who was always a model of calm, such garbled orders that I was forced tactfully to intervene and get him straight. After it was all over, I took Mackay, Sutherland and Prior [Mackay's senior staff officers] out on to the side of the hill and we went through the whole thing again in proper sequence.'[2]

Back in Athens, there was feverish activity among the diplomatic corps as German panzers moved inexorably closer to the capital and German fighters roamed the sky looking for targets. Bags were packed and confidential papers and codebooks incinerated. The Yugoslav and Turkish envoys were most anxious to leave Greece before the Germans arrived in Athens, while thousands of refugees from the Nazis, including many Sephardic Jews from Salonica, tried to find transport to other countries.

On 23 April, King George, his brother Crown Prince Paul, his new Prime Minister, Emmanuel Tsouderos – like the unfortunate Koryzis, a governor of the Bank of Greece – and the British minister, Sir Michael Palairet, flew out of Scaramanga flying boat base near Athens for Crete. There, they joined the King's family and his English mistress Joyce Britten-Jones at the Villa Ariadne, former home of the British archaeologist Sir Arthur Evans at Knossos.

The King, who had been divorced from his Queen Consort, Elisabeth of Romania, since 1935, had met the alluring Mrs Britten-Jones during a state visit to India, where her husband, a captain in the Black Watch, was aide-de-camp to the Viceroy. Too fond of liquor, he had lost his wife to the charming monarch.[3]

Link MacVeagh packed two suitcases 'for departure at a moment's notice' but had received no orders to leave so was asked to look after the British Legation and pay any of the military mission's outstanding bills.[4] General Heywood had left Athens without settling the accounts and, indeed, without carrying out an order from GHQ Cairo to destroy 1500 tons of British aviation fuel at Drapetzona, near Athens, a misdemeanour for which he was later severely criticised.[5]

At 10 pm on 23 April, Blamey was summoned to Jumbo Wilson's headquarters at the Acropole Hotel. Arriving at midnight, he learned that Wavell had ordered him to leave Greece with six members of his staff. Iven Mackay and Bernard Freyberg were also ordered to abandon their commands and return to Egypt as soon as possible.

Wavell was anxious to avoid the risk of his senior commanders in Greece falling into German hands after Generals O'Connor, Neame and Gambier-Parry had all been captured by Rommel within the space of 48 hours while fleeing from the Germans in Libya. General Wilson's staff would now supervise the evacuation, a task it was demonstrably ill-equipped to perform.[6]

Returning to Anzac Corps HQ, Blamey told Rowell that he had been recalled to Egypt 'to prepare a plan for the defence of the Western Desert'. Rowell was sceptical. 'I don't believe you,' he said bluntly. Blamey insisted that it was true. Rowell felt strongly that Corps HQ should stay behind to ensure that Australian and New Zealand troops were successfully evacuated. Indeed, Blamey would have been justified in appealing to Wavell to allow him to stay with his men but he had had a bellyful of Greece and raised only a token objection; he also had no intention of allowing Sydney Rowell to show him up by staying behind with the troops.

'I don't propose to go,' Rowell said.

'I order you to go,' Blamey replied.[7]

Blamey then instructed Norman Carlyon to take down the names of the six officers who were to accompany him, starting with Sydney Rowell. Colonel Henry Wells, Colonel Lloyd Elliott and Major Eric Woodward – three officers who would form the nucleus of the supposed new Western Desert headquarters – were next on the list; then Blamey told Carlyon to add his own name.

When it came to the sixth and final place, Carlyon suggested Brigadier Bill Bridgeford, Blamey's senior administrative officer. 'No,' Blamey said, 'Bridgeford will stay here and take over from Rowell.' Other candidates were suggested and rejected for one reason or another until Blamey's purpose was finally revealed. 'Well,' he said at last, 'we might as well take young Tom.'[8] 'Young Tom' was his 28-year-old son, Major Thomas Blamey, who had been seconded from his artillery unit to serve as a liaison officer at Anzac Corps headquarters.[9]

When Blamey read out the list to his staff, Bill Bridgeford whispered loudly, 'He *would* take his bloody son.' Blamey's moustache twitched but he said nothing. 'Blamey was in a horrid mood, scared out of his bloody life,' Rowell says. 'He arrived in his car draped with suitcases.'[10] Bridgeford later claimed that Blamey had 'acted like a coward. While the battle for Greece was on, he stayed at his headquarters and lived sumptuously on champagne' – an exaggeration, but one that captured the spirit of Blamey's command, if not the substance.[11]

'We heard he'd flown his son out of Greece with him and that was not considered the thing to do,' Les Cook says. 'It was only a rumour at the time but it was the start of his fall from grace. Blamey was an excellent staff officer but his problem was that he didn't understand his own troops.'[12]

Tiny Freyberg doggedly refused to leave Greece. He cabled Wilson's headquarters in Athens that he was in the middle of a battle at the Thermopylae Pass. 'I was being attacked by tanks, fighting a battle on a two-brigade front, and asked who was to command the New Zealand troops if I left,' he says. 'I was given the answer of "Movement Control" [a euphemism for Force headquarters]. I naturally went on with the battle.' Freyberg's 18-year-old son Paul Freyberg was a private in the 23rd New Zealand Battalion, yet it never occurred to him to ask for preferential treatment for him during the evacuation. Incredibly, Freyberg later faced a British military court of inquiry to answer charges that he had stayed with his rearguard instead of organising the beach defences in the south. He was exonerated.[13]

As Blamey flew out of Scaramanga for Alexandria at 5 am on 24 April, the Germans renewed their attack on the Thermopylae Line. On the coast road, the New Zealanders knocked out a dozen panzers which tried to break through, while George Vasey's 19th Brigade beat off a detachment of mountain troops in the Brallos Pass. During the afternoon, both brigades started to break contact with the enemy and head south towards their evacuation points.[14]

Churchill wrote to Roosevelt, 'The Anzacs have been fighting all day in the Pass of Thermopylae. But, Mr President, you will long have foreseen the conclusion of these particular Greek affairs. I wish we could have done more.'[15] Arthur Fadden, the acting Prime Minister, told the people of Australia that despite the heroism of the new Anzacs, 'there is no ground for hoping that the fighting in Greece can, or will, take any turn to our advantage. We are now seeing the last stages of a most gallant rearguard action.'[16]

Ralph Honner was in charge of the 19th Brigade's rearguard, consisting of a mixed bag of five infantry companies, several machine-gunners and a few artillery pieces. Whenever the line buckled, he reinforced it from his reserve and then pulled his men back to a second and then a third line of defence. An ancient Greek peasant armed with a rifle even older than himself approached one decimated platoon and asked if he could join. 'All right,' the platoon sergeant replied, 'we're not too crowded anyway.' Monty Woodhouse, a British intelligence officer who overheard the exchange, noted that Leonidas would have recognised a kindred spirit.[17]

At 5 pm, the rest of the Australian, New Zealand and British nursing teams at Kifisia, a group totalling 160, set off by truck for the harbour at Nauplion in the Peloponnese. Bomb craters, dead horses, donkeys and vehicles filled with Greek refugees blocked the road. As they passed, the Greeks, seemingly oblivious to the destruction that had been wreaked on their economy – and the starvation that awaited them – waved and cheered and shouted, 'Thias Kalos!' (Goodbye and good luck.)

Shortly after crossing the Corinth Canal, enemy aircraft appeared and machine-gunned the convoy. One of the trucks carrying 19 New Zealand nurses overturned, injuring four of them. 'Our orders were when the front car gave the warning of an aerial attack we were to jump out of the trucks and scatter on either side of the road,' Mabel Johnson says.

> We were just past an aerodrome when the alarm came and we scattered in a barley field. We saw the planes fighting and had guns firing all around us. We also heard shrapnel falling and something whistled past me. I was lying face down in my best suit and eight-guinea overcoat, flat on the ground with, of course, my treasured tin hat on my head.[18]

When darkness fell, the nurses resumed their journey. It was bitterly cold but there was no moon and no sign of the Luftwaffe.

At Nauplion, ships were burning all around the harbour and the nurses were loaded aboard high-prowed Greek fishing caiques and taken out to *Voyager*, which was lying offshore with *Stuart*, *Phoebe* and *Glenearn*. As the nurses climbed up the scrambling nets, one of *Voyager*'s ratings whispered to the destroyer's gunnery officer, 'Look, sir, they're *women!*' Mabel writes:

> We climbed over the rails in black night, first passing our luggage to sailors who got the shock of their lives to find we were women – the crew had no idea what troops they were getting. One English sister fell between the two ships but one of the marvellous crew dived down and held her up. He placed a rope around her shoulders and she was pulled on board.

The hero of the hour was Ordinary Seaman Cyril Webb. 'His action,' writes *Voyager*'s skipper, Captain James 'Copper' Morrow, 'probably saved the sister's life as she was weighed down with equipment and there was a grave danger of them both being crushed between the ships.'

Embarkation was completed around 4 am on 25 April and the ships sailed for Suda Bay with 6685 personnel, including Marianne, a blonde dancer from Maxim's restaurant.[19] At midday, the Stukas appeared. Some of the nurses took cover in the destroyer's galley. As the cook hurried to his battle station, he urged them, 'Keep an eye on the peas, girls.' Other nurses were more adventurous. 'We were zig-zagging madly, with our anti-aircraft gun running hot,' Sister Margaret Barnard writes. 'Most of us were on the deck watching and barracking and giving directions [to the gun crew].'[20] The attack failed to damage Voyager and she reached Crete safely at 4 pm.

The New Zealand commanders were extremely upset when they heard Blamey had departed – 'hooked it', in the words of Colonel Stewart. 'Had Blamey appeared among the troops on the beaches,' he said, 'it would have been a great morale booster.'[21] But that wasn't Blamey's style; as Norman Carlyon could testify, he cared little for the opinion of his troops. Yet by leaving Greece and taking his son with him, he had demonstrated a lack of faith in the evacuation at a time when confidence was paramount.

Sydney Rowell noted that nothing more was ever heard about 'the headquarters for the Western Desert', confirming his belief that it was a fabrication to justify Blamey's departure from Greece.[22] It wasn't until Blamey had checked into the Cecil Hotel in Alexandria and been reunited with his wife that he read about his new post in a newspaper she had brought with her from Cairo.[23]

'The British acknowledged the spectacular fighting which had been done by Australians and New Zealanders in Greece by appointing as second in command in the entire Middle East the Australian commander, Lieutenant-General Sir Thomas Blamey,' Time magazine informed Americans on 5 May.

Like most Australians, Tom Blamey is a weather-beaten, hearty fellow. He was born on a farm at Wagga Wagga, NSW. He did the outdoor things – hunting, shooting, riding, hockey, soccer, rugby, lacrosse – until he was all gristle. He joined the Army, fought Turkey, emerged as Chief of Staff of the AIF, then retired to versatile successes, as a police commissioner, businessman, radio commentator.

One month before World War II broke out he bought a little seaside home, got married and prepared to go off into the wilds for a honeymoon. He never went. He was called up to command the entire Australian Infantry Force. Australians call the second AIF 'Blamey's Mob'. Tom Blamey says he doesn't mind; he's 'proud to be associated with such a mob'.

At Thermopylae, Ralph Honner had kept the Germans at bay until 9 pm on the 24th. At that hour, he withdrew three of his companies and boarded them into trucks and then, as they drove off into the darkness, leapfrogged the remaining two companies back along the road from corner to corner, with a couple of Bren-carriers protecting the rear until every man had been taken on board. 'This officer is the best company commander I have known in this or the last war,' Colonel Louch said in his citation recommending Honner for the Military Cross.[24]

In the early hours of Anzac Day, Iven Mackay – immaculately dressed but with his hair and neck coated with dirt – handed over his responsibilities to the indomitable Tubby Allen and flew to Crete with nine of his staff, convinced that the Greek campaign had been an 'extraordinary disaster on which we should never have embarked'. Although exhausted after travelling the length of Greece with his men, he was waiting on the dockside at Suda Bay to meet the first troopships.[25]

That day, Freyberg sent his divisional staff off to Crete with Brigadier Jimmy Hargest's 5th Brigade in the cruisers *Calcutta* and *Perth* and the troopship *Glengyle*, but retained a tiny battle headquarters to supervise the evacuation of the remainder of his division.[26]

Throughout Anzac Day, George Vasey, Ivan Dougherty and Ralph Honner rested with the 19th Brigade under the olive trees around Megara. After nightfall, they were conducted by Charles Spry, now a major, down to two jetties. Carrying little more than their .303s, submachine guns, Bren-guns and anti-tank rifles, they were ferried out to the transport *Thurland Castle*, the cruiser *Coventry* and the destroyers *Havock*, *Hasty*, *Decoy*, *Waterhen* and *Vendetta*, and stowed on the decks like so much cargo.

Matron Katie Best and her stay-behind nurses had continued treating patients at the Ekali hospital until receiving General Blamey's order that all Australian nurses must leave Greece. 'They were brought out despite protests that they wished to stay and nurse our wounded,' says Lieutenant-Colonel Leslie Le Souef, commander of the 2/7th Field Ambulance which was also evacuated from Megara that night.[27]

Meanwhile, Keith Hooper and the 2/6th Battalion had just reached the Corinth Canal in trucks. A Company was ordered to hold the north side of the bridge and B Company the south bank. Early on 26 April, German paratroops descended on the canal, overwhelmed the defenders and cut the only road linking British forces with the Peloponnese. 'The bridge was mined and the Germans shelled it and blew it up themselves,' Hooper says. 'Consequently, half their force was on one side of the canal and half on the other but they were both large enough to overcome our fellows. The Corinth Canal was the first time we had had parachutists turned on us and they captured a third of my battalion.'[28] Having suffered many casualties, A Company surrendered but B Company succeeded in fighting its way clear.[29]

The 4th New Zealand Brigade had been holding the area north of Athens and was now cut off. Just as they prepared to counter-attack the Germans on the canal, Brigadier Puttick received orders to divert his men to Rafina and Port Rafti south of the Greek capital. Holding off advanced enemy units with the help of the 2/3rd Field Regiment, they were evacuated from those points the following night.

General Wilson had left Athens on 25 April and was ensconced with W Force headquarters in an olive grove in the village of Miloi on the Gulf of Nauplion in the Peloponnese. One of Wilson's aides circulated a rumour among the Greek high command at the Grande Bretagne Hotel that Wilson planned to stay to the very end 'and then take to the hills in disguise'.[30] Wilson had no such plan. Instead, the plan was for him and 54 other senior officers to fly to Crete in one of the Sunderlands on 26 April, while the lower ranks among his entourage followed by destroyer.

General Freyberg joined Wilson at his al fresco HQ on the 26th. 'Well, Bernard,' Wilson said, 'I hand over Greece to you.'[31] Then he walked down to the pier at Miloi where he was informed by his chief of staff, 'a fairly excitable' Brigadier Sandy Galloway, that the Sunderland had been indefinitely delayed. Galloway wanted to know what his commander-in-chief would like to do. 'I will do,' Jumbo replied, 'what many soldiers have done before me – I will sit on my kit and wait.'[32]

During the waiting, Group Captain Pelly found himself 'badgered by pongos of all ranks' for a place in the flying boat. 'I told them to shut up,' he says, 'and had the hell of a row with one general – an ass called Heywood, a real pongo, red-faced and eye-glassed.' General Heywood was given a seat on the plane but then tried to smuggle a heavy suitcase on board. After 'an ugly scene', Pelly removed the case and the Sunderland departed on the evening of the 26th minus all luggage.[33] Jumbo Wilson's kit and Heywood's suitcase were put on a Crete-bound caique which was sunk the next day with the loss of all cargo.[34]

On the night of 26 April, Vice-Admiral Pridham-Wippell took the cruisers *Orion* and *Perth* to join four destroyers and two transports at Nauplion, while Hec Waller in *Stuart* was detached to nearby Tolos Bay. Waller began embarking troops from the Tolos beach at 11.15 pm and, when he could take no more, steamed to Nauplion and transferred them to *Orion*. He had radioed ahead asking Pridham-Wippell for the help of a cruiser and at 1 am on the 27th he returned to Tolos with *Perth*.[35] G. Hermon Gill, Australia's official naval historian, comments, 'It was due to Waller's foresight in these operations that a far larger number was evacuated than otherwise would have been possible.'[36]

Les Cook and his party had stayed under cover outside the town of Argos until nightfall and then made their way to Tolos Bay. 'I threw my Boys anti-tank rifle over a cliff,' he says.

> We got the wounded into flat-bottomed landing barges early in the night. The blokes all crowded on board to go out to where the ships were anchored but there was a sandbar 30 metres offshore. As soon as the barges were loaded, they sat down on the sandbar and wouldn't move. All night long those of us who were still on the beach were out in the water pushing the barges over the sandbar.
>
> The ships had to leave well before dawn to be out of the range of the bombers. It was just about cracking daylight and *Perth* had stayed behind to pick up the last lot when we got into the barge but it wouldn't go over the bar. An officer started ordering people to get off but we could see that if we did we'd probably be left behind and taken prisoner.
>
> There was a lot of reluctance, so this officer pulled out his revolver and said, 'I'll shoot the first man who doesn't get off the boat.' All around him, you could hear rifle bolts open and close and then there was silence. It was a tense moment. The only sound was the idling throb of the engine. Then a young English midshipman who looked about 14 piped up in this very Oxford accent, 'I think it would be a good idea, sir, if you were to get off first and show the men an example.' That broke the

spell. We jumped off and pushed the thing over the bar and some got back on and some didn't ...[37]

On board *Perth*, Chief Petty Officer Bob Bland had worked through the night baking four batches of bread so that every evacuee could be given plenty of fresh bread and butter and jam – the thing they craved most after a diet of cold bully beef and biscuits.[38]

One of those who was left behind was Signalman Norm Simper, a short, compact Victorian whose father had been one of the first Anzacs. 'I was clambering on board the barge – hard work with greatcoat, rifle and waterlogged boots – when there was a call from shore to collect a badly wounded infantryman,' he says.

I went back with three others, all of them much taller than me, and we struggled to get the stretcher out to the barge. The waves were breaking over my head and I had to grab a breath between waves, but we shoved the stretcher on board and I was about to climb on when I saw this bloke standing on the stern waving a pistol in a mad panic. I called him a coward, told him I was an Anzac like my father and waded back to shore.[39]

Further south at Kalamata, the 16th and 17th Brigades had been assembled for evacuation. Tubby Allen, the senior officer at Kalamata, ordered his provosts to shoot anyone who fired a shot or lit a fire. The troops were so well hidden that when the destroyer *Hero* moored at the quayside at 9.25 pm on 26 April, her captain, Commander H.W. Biggs, thought the place was deserted.

Once contact had been established, *Hero's* sailors rigged up lights at the harbour entrance to assist loading. Then *Hero*, *Hereward* and *Defender* ferried 6800 troops in a steady stream from the quays to the transports *Dilwarra*, *City of London* and *Costa Rica*.[40] The remaining soldiers – some 7000 in number –

were assured that the ships would be back the following night to pick them up.

Keith Hooper was among the survivors of the 2/6th Battalion who found themselves on board the *Costa Rica* with members of the 2/1st, 2/7th and 2/8th Battalions. At 2.40 pm on Sunday 27 April, the 30-year-old vessel was approaching the coast of Crete when two bombs from a flight of three dive-bombers exploded close to the port side; one bomb smashed the propeller and the other split her sides near the engine room; she stopped dead in the water and began to sink. The escorting destroyers *Defender*, *Hereward* and *Hero* came alongside one at a time and rescued 2600 troops, with the loss of just one man who misjudged the swell as he jumped from *Costa Rica* on to the deck of *Defender* and was crushed between the two ships.[41]

'I was with my carrier crew Bill Ward and John McCombe and we got into a lifeboat on the port side of *Costa Rica* and rowed over to *Hero*,' Hooper says.

> Instead of coming in on the leeward side, we went round to the rough side. We were going up and the destroyer was going down. The fellows in the destroyer were shouting, 'Next time you come up, grab the gunnels.' That's how we got aboard. I started to cry like anything from post-traumatic stress – I couldn't stop it. The *Hero* took us to Crete and dropped us off there.[42]

Hero, *Hereward* and *Defender* then joined Captain Sir Philip Bowyer-Smyth's Force B with the cruisers *Perth* and *Phoebe* and the destroyers *Decoy*, *Hasty* and *Nubian* to evacuate the 7000 troops, including a large number of New Zealand reinforcements, still awaiting rescue at Kalamata. Learning that there was an additional group of 1500 Yugoslav refugees there, Pridham-Wippell added the destroyers *Kandahar*, *Kingston* and *Kimberley* to the operation.[43]

At 5 pm on 28 April, a 300-strong enemy column armed

with machine guns and two 6-inch guns entered Kalamata and advanced as far as the quay, where they captured Captain W. C. Clark-Hall, the naval officer in charge of the evacuation. Ordered to take cover, Sergeant Jack Hinton of the 20th New Zealand Battalion shouted, 'To hell with this! Who'll follow me?' He dashed towards a German machine-gun post and wiped out its crew with two grenades.

Groups of New Zealand and Australian infantry rallied around Hinton in a counter-attack with bayonets, forcing the German troops manning the first 6-inch gun to take shelter in two houses. Yelling to his fellow Anzacs to charge, Hinton smashed his way into the first house and killed the gun crew with his bayonet. He repeated this performance in the second house, while his companions engaged the rest of the German force.[44]

At 7.30 that night, Force B was 30 kilometres south of Kalamata when Bowyer-Smyth detached *Hero* to make contact with the army ashore. As Commander Biggs approached the port, tracer fire lit the night sky, so he anchored close to the beach to the east of the town to see what was happening. At 8.45 pm, the commanding officer at Kalamata, Brigadier Leonard Parrington, ordered his signallers to alert *Hero* that a battle was in progress. From the breakwater, the message was flashed by signal lamp: 'Boche in town'.

According to the official New Zealand historian, the signal added that an attempt to recapture the quay was already in progress and this information was passed to Bowyer-Smyth.[45] However, Hermon Gill reports that Biggs' signal to his commander made no mention of a counter-attack, simply saying, 'Harbour occupied by Germans. British troops to south-east of town.'[46]

Bowyer-Smyth was 16 kilometres from Kalamata when he received this signal at 9.10 pm. Tracer fire and 'big explosions' could be observed on shore, Bowyer-Smyth wrote four days later in a report to explain his actions.

As soon as I saw these explosions I realised that during embarkation Force B would be in an extremely hazardous tactical position in the event of attack from seaward. Ships would be silhouetted against explosions and fires on shore, would be embayed and unable to scatter, and there was no covering force in the offing. Taranto was only 12 hours steaming away and with the information the enemy obviously had such an attack was far from improbable.[47]

Bowyer-Smyth decided that 'the forces under my command constituted a substantial part of the light forces of the Mediterranean Fleet whose loss would be in the nature of a calamity, particularly in view of recent cruiser losses'. He therefore decided 'that the number that could be got away did not warrant the substantial risk to an important force'.

The responsibility for losing ships under such circumstances rested not with *Perth*'s skipper but with Pridham-Wippell, who had already decided that the risk was acceptable in order to evacuate the troops. However, at 9.29 pm, when Force B was less than 10 kilometres from Kalamata and without asking Biggs to clarify the position ashore, Bowyer-Smyth reversed course and withdrew his ships. By then, the quay was back in Allied hands and the emergency at Kalamata was over. Thanks to Jack Hinton, a force of 800 New Zealanders, 380 Australians and 300 members of the 4th Hussars had killed 41 Germans, wounded more than 60, taken between 80 and 90 prisoners and put the rest to flight.

Biggs learned that the coast was clear when he landed Lieutenant-Commander R. F. G. Elsworth on the quayside with orders to find Parrington and report back. At 9.30 pm, Elsworth reported that the beach was suitable for embarkation and Biggs signalled Bowyer-Smyth: 'Troops collecting on beach east of town. All firing ceased in town. Consider evacuation possible from beach.'

Owing to a defect in *Hero*'s radio transmitter, this signal was not passed to *Perth* until 10.11 pm. By then, Bowyer-Smyth was 30 kilometres south of Kalamata and had no intention of returning. Biggs sent two more signals saying that he was sending boats ashore, that the Germans had only light artillery and that a number of troops could be embarked from beaches south-east of the town. 'But the decision had been made by then,' Bowyer-Smyth writes, 'and they did not in any event alter the arguments on which I had based it.'[48]

Admiral Cunningham's biographer, Lieutenant-Commander John Winton of the Royal Navy, was inclined to overlook Bowyer-Smyth's actions. 'Misunderstandings such as happened at Kalamata were excusable,' he says, 'indeed it is surprising there were not more.'[49] Cunningham, however, was less forgiving. 'The senior officer in the ships sent there heard that the town and harbour were in enemy hands and abandoned the operation,' he wrote in his memoirs. 'It was an unfortunate decision … I was told later that a fine counter-attack by some mixed units had driven the Germans out of Kalamata.'[50]

As things were, the boats from *Hero* and the other three destroyers *Kandahar*, *Kingston* and *Kimberley*, could find just 332 troops on the beaches and after taking them on board set sail for Crete at 2.30 am on 29 April. In a last-ditch attempt to repair the damage to the navy's reputation, Cunningham dispatched three destroyers to the Kalamata area that night, but they could locate just 202 troops – in the interval, Brigadier Parrington had ordered all Allied troops to surrender when a much larger German force reached Kalamata earlier in the day. Jack Hinton and his companions had held the two German 6-inch guns until they were overwhelmed. Hinton was shot through the lower abdomen and taken prisoner. For his heroism, he was awarded the Victoria Cross.

The 7000 prisoners at Kalamata included 2000 Palestinian and Cypriot members of labour battalions and the 1500 Yugoslav refugees. 'The navy paid very heavily for getting us out of Greece,' says Les Cook, who was grateful to Bowyer-Smyth for staying behind to pick him up at Tolos the previous night. 'You can't keep on sending ships in and losing them.' But Bowyer-Smyth's actions were not forgotten. Cunningham moved him to a shore posting in October 1941 and replaced him in *Perth* with Hardover Hec Waller.

By 28 April, General Freyberg and his battle headquarters had reached Monemvasia, a rocky promontory with beaches on either side. At midday, he was joined on the jetty by Tom Baillie-Grohman, who had been sailing along the coast in a small launch looking for stragglers. Late that night, the destroyers *Isis* and *Griffin* arrived. 'This is the Royal Navy,' a voice shouted through a loudhailer. 'If there are any British or Allied troops ashore, announce your formation and the name of your commander.'

Freyberg stepped forward and answered in his squeaky voice, 'We have approximately seventeen hundred all ranks, principally New Zealand infantry with elements of British and Australian. Major-General Freyberg is in command. I am Freyberg.'

'As I am not certain of your identity,' the voice replied, 'I must warn you that all guns of this force are loaded and trained upon you. At the least suggestion of foul play, we shall fire.'[51]

Once Freyberg's identity had been established, the 6th New Zealand Brigade were ferried out to the destroyers in small boats and landing craft.[52] Then at 1 am on the 29th the cruiser *Ajax* and the destroyers *Havock* and *Hotspur* joined the evacuation. The gun crews had made special slings to hoist army stretchers from the rocking boats.[53] After the wounded had been loaded, Baillie-Grohman opened his dispatch case and took out a bottle of champagne. 'I think the time has come for a drink,' he said. The men enjoyed a well-earned mug of bubbly against a background of wrecked and burning trucks while the remaining soldiers were ferried out to the ships.

At 3.10 am, when every soldier had been boarded, Baillie-Grohman said to Freyberg, 'Come on, let's go.' They chugged out to *Ajax* in a landing craft and then jumped on to a scrambling net and clambered on board the cruiser. At 4 am, 'the Great St Bernard', as Wilson called him, sailed away from Greece, having earned a fine reputation as a commander who was prepared to sacrifice himself for the sake of his men.[54]

Lieutenant Jo Gullett and D Company of the 2/6th Battalion climbed wearily on to *Hotspur* and flopped down in the officers' wardroom. They were the last formation out of Greece.[55]

The hoisting of the swastika over the Acropolis on 27 April 1941 was proof that German armed forces had driven Britain out of continental Europe for the second time in two years. As Blamey had warned, defeat provided the Germans with a propaganda coup that arguably inflicted more damage on Britain's prestige than cancellation of Operation Lustre would have done. 'The Greek expedition hadn't a dog's chance from the start,' he admitted to Lieutenant-General Vernon Sturdee, Australia's chief of general staff. 'The Greek plan was a bad one and our plan to support them was equally bad.'[56]

Wavell wrote the epitaph for the Greek expedition when he declared in his dispatch that 'the whole expedition was something in the nature of a gamble, [but] the dice were loaded against it from the first'. Mystifyingly, he added, 'It was not really such a forlorn hope from the military point of view as it may seem from its results.'[57]

Air Marshal Pelly saw it differently. 'Metaxas, had he lived, would never have allowed us to send a totally inadequate army into Greece and just play into German hands,' he writes. 'We've spoiled the successful little war the Greeks were having [with the Italians], messed up the country and had another gallant evacuation, losing every piece of materiel we put into the country and risking Egypt into the bargain.'[58]

Churchill's cherished wish that his support for Greece would win favour with the Americans proved groundless. The State Department remained mute throughout the German invasion, apparently impervious to the plight of its own diplomats. 'I would never have thought it possible to work faithfully for anyone for eight years,' Link MacVeagh lamented, 'and then be so thoroughly ignored with all my people in trouble as I have been by Uncle Sam.'[59]

According to Admiral Pridham-Wippell, his ships plucked 50,662 British and Commonwealth troops from Greek beaches and quaysides. About 14,000 men, including 2030 Australians, 1614 New Zealanders and 6500 Britons, were left behind and went into captivity or escaped into the hills where they joined guerrilla bands of Greek partisans. Four British troopships and two destroyers had been sunk by aircraft, with the loss of 500 troops and 600 sailors.[60] A further 320 Australians, 291 New Zealanders, 256 Britons and 36 Palestinians and Cypriots had been killed in the fighting and the hospitals in Crete, Palestine and Egypt were full of wounded, many of whom would never fight again.

One of the wounded was Lieutenant Michael Clarke, who had been hit on the nose by shell fragments in a Stuka attack during the final stages of the evacuation. Eight of his comrades in the 2/3rd Field Regiment were dead and 12 severely wounded. After fighting off a strong German attack, the regiment had destroyed its remaining guns and embarked in the cruiser *Ajax* from Port Rafti on the night of 27 April.

Michael's wound was dressed and, as the sick bay was full of wounded, he was placed in the commander's day cabin – *Ajax*'s skipper, Captain Desmond McCarthy, slept on a camp stretcher in a little log hut on the bridge and his commander also had a sea cabin aloft. Stripping off his bloodstained shirt and singlet, Michael immersed himself in his first bath for five weeks and then crawled naked between the sheets and was soon asleep. He records in his diary:

Monday 28 April, 0700 hours: Woken by a sailor shaking me. My nose had bled on to the pillow, but I felt fine. Sat up to see two girls dressed in dark blue overalls standing beside the open cabin door. Short black hair and attractive, though nervous.

'Sorry to disturb you, sir, but Captain's orders,' said the sailor. 'I got to shove these two stowaways in here. 'Fraid you'll have to evacuate, sir, but have a shave first.' The girls turned their backs as I crossed to the bathroom.

I put on clean socks, underwear and shirt, packed my gear, and found the girls huddled together in the bed, a blanket drawn up to their chins, big brown eyes fixed on me apprehensively. I bowed to them and went off in search of breakfast.

On the foredeck, Clarke moved among his men and encouraged them to shave; he found that their esprit de corps was terrific. 'Half young Mick's bleeding luck!' someone remarked. 'He spent the night sharing the captain's bunk with two Greek sheilas. Didn't know which way to turn!'

At 10 am on the 28th, *Ajax* sailed into Suda Bay. The Greek campaign had been a nightmare – in Hitler's words 'one of the most famous strategical blunders of this war'[61] – but for the Anzacs the worst was yet to come. Over the airwaves, the Nazi propagandist Lord Haw-Haw taunted them that they had landed on the 'Isle of Doom'.

CHAPTER 14

Isle of Doom

George Vasey arrived at Suda Bay, courtesy of the 'Grey Funnel Line' (alias the Royal Navy) on 26 April 1941. He found General Mackay and the 6th Division headquarters were already there, along with 5000 bedraggled, hungry and poorly armed Anzac troops. But he was thankful. 'You know, padre,' Vasey said to one of the chaplains, 'those bastards might have beaten us. Without God's help we would not be here.'[1]

The bombed-out wreckage of a dozen ships littered the channel, which was cloaked in a thick curtain of black smoke carried on the west wind from a burning oil tanker off Kalami Point. Crippled and beached, her rear turret awash, the cruiser *York*, sunk by exploding Italian motorboats on 25 March, made a sorry sight in the shallows but her anti-aircraft batteries had been taken ashore and blazed away at enemy planes bombing the waterfront.[2]

In the last sunny days of April 1941, thousands of Anzacs struggled across the Aegean in anything that would float. Men stripped of everything except their rifles swarmed ashore at

Suda Bay, some so keen to get there they dived overboard from their ships.[3]

At 10 am on 29 April, Jo Gullett arrived in HMS *Hotspur* in the middle of an air-raid alert. The anchorage was crowded with ships and *Hotspur* drew alongside a merchantman tied up at the stone quay. The men scrambled on board her but just as they were about to go ashore, a stick of bombs burst on the quayside. The captain ordered the gangplank raised and the ship cast off. 'I'm sorry, soldiers,' he shouted from the bridge, 'but if I stay tied up I'll be sunk for sure. I'm going to sea.' 'And that,' Gullett says, 'was all I saw of Crete.'[4]

Norm Simper, who had been left behind at Tolos Bay, took ten days to make the crossing to Crete, switching from a rowboat, to a skiff to a schooner. Starving and dishevelled, he landed at Kastelli at the western end of the island, 'a frightful sight with thick whiskers'. Scrounging a meal of bread and cheese from a cafe, he and his companions went to a barber's shop and looked in the mirror. 'I had to put my hand up to check one of them was me,' Simper says. He was given a lift along the coast road through Maleme and Canea to Suda Bay, a distance of 40 kilometres, where he was reunited with his signals unit. 'I was given a singlet and a pair of underpants,' he says. 'I had half a blanket and I slept for the next 14 hours.'[5]

Suda Bay had been formed between the great mass of the Akrotiri Peninsula and the north coast of Crete. The anchorage extended for eight kilometres along the arm of the bay and was surrounded on three sides by wooded hills and mountain ridges, with the fishing village of Suda at its western extremity. The wharf had no crane or any other cargo-handling appliance and ships were extremely vulnerable to air attack. Moored at the quayside or anchored in the bay, they were at the mercy of enemy aircraft which swooped over the hills, dropped their bombs and disappeared behind the ridges before the anti-aircraft gunners could get them in their sights.[6] 'There was no warning of their arrival, apart from the screeching of a pet monkey on one of the ships,' says Roy Roberts, a rating in HMAS *Perth*. 'The monkey could hear them coming.'[7]

The labour corps at Suda docks, mostly young British shipping clerks without any military experience, had taken such a hammering from German planes that they refused to work any longer. Major Alex Torr of the 2/1st Australian Field Company was put in charge of unloading and called for volunteers. He assembled a mixed group of Cypriot labourers and Australian engineers and gunners. Torr told them to 'dive over the side if your ship is hit'. His stevedores maintained a phenomenal work rate throughout the campaign despite constant harassment from German fighters and bombers. Their best effort was to retrieve a dozen Bren-carriers from the deck of a sunken ship.[8]

The British garrison in Crete was known as Creforce and its commander, Major-General Eric Weston of the Royal Marines, had taken charge as recently as 26 April. When the evacuation of Greece seemed imminent, his quartermaster had asked GHQ Middle East for tents, clothing and blankets for 30,000 men but very few of these supplies had been received. Weston's meagre resources were stretched to breaking point when a further 20,000 men were landed at Suda between 25 and 28 April.

A red-tabbed British officer met the men as they disembarked and ordered them to place all weapons, apart from rifles and side arms, in a pile on the quayside. Ralph Honner of the 2/11th Battalion stepped ashore from the *Thurland Castle* 'with only the clothes I wore and my battle equipment: pistol, binoculars, respirator, compass, ammo, about a week's rations and a Bren-gun'.[9] The chances of anyone relieving Honner of his Bren-gun were nil, and although the vast majority of Anzacs disobeyed the order, military police succeeded in confiscating dozens of machine guns and mortars, many of which remained under lock and key in the armoury.

At the end of the quay, New Zealanders were directed to the right and Australians to the left. Trooper Harry Spencer, who arrived in the *Calcutta* after an eventful trip during which he loaded ammunition for one of the 3.7-inch guns, took the right-hand fork. One of the tree-lined thoroughfares leading off the main road to Canea had been named Tobruk Avenue and it contained several large storehouses. There was no sign of any food. Harry found two members of his unit sitting by a stream. 'I knew them very well and one of them said, "G'day – you got a toothbrush?" I said I had and we all cleaned our teeth. We laughed about that.'[10]

Michael Clarke collected half of B Troop and set off in search of a suitable place to camp. Behind the fishermen's stone cottages, some of which had taken direct hits from bombs, vineyards and olive groves rose in neat terraces up the slopes into the purple foothills of the snow-topped White Mountains. He marched his men east along the narrow coastal strip in the hot sun. They had no water, rations or hats.

> By mid-afternoon on the 28th, we reached a fast-running stream of icy cold water. We drank and filled our water bottles, and were ordered to bivouac. Parties were detailed to go into Kalives, the next village, in search of food. Roy Macartney of C Troop[11] and I selected an olive tree and lay down on the bare ground to sleep. We had one blanket each, no greatcoat or groundsheet. It was a bloody cold night and damned difficult to wrap oneself in one army blanket. We didn't get much sleep.[12]

The men were downhearted over events in Greece and were further demoralised when they learned that none of their mail had been delivered to Crete. Many hadn't received a letter from home since leaving Egypt in March. There was no pay staff or canteen, and medical supplies to treat the sick and wounded were scarce. Many troops had been separated from their officers and NCOs and discipline broke down when some units discovered *raki*, the fiery local spirit.[13] 'The discipline is fair on the whole,' Vasey reported to Sydney Rowell in Egypt, 'but there have been a few major incidents including an alleged murder.'[14]

Brigadier Brunskill, who had made the trip to Crete, 'cosseted by the crew in the captain's cabin of HMS *Isis*',[15] cast a jaundiced eye over the rag-tag army. 'For the first ten days at least,' he writes, 'there were a number of men at large, many armed with rifles, living as tramps in the hills and olive groves.'[16] Unlike Brunskill, who was staying in the Creforce mess, the 'tramps' had nowhere to go. Some camps had been set up but they were a long march from Suda Bay and difficult to find. The 2/4th Battalion was told its camp was 'two miles inland' but after marching for two hours it was nowhere to be seen. Inquiries revealed that the camp was 'another two miles around the next bend' but those directions also proved illusory. Thus the 'Crete mile' entered the battalion's vocabulary.[17]

Once the men had found their allotted sites, there were very few tents, the only cooking pots were old petrol tins and there were no knives, forks or spoons. Food was scarce, even when supplemented with locally purchased bread, eggs and oranges.[18] 'The ordinary soldier didn't know much about what was going on but we knew one thing for sure: we went hungry on Crete,' says Les Cook, who was with the signallers at Suda Bay.

> For entertainment, we listened to Lord Haw-Haw on German radio. He used to say, 'We know where you are – you're hiding under the olive trees behind Suda Bay. We don't want you to feel lonely, so we'll have a flight of Stukas over there at 8.15 in the morning.' You could set your watch by it.[19]

Starting his broadcast with the popular song 'Run Rabbit Run', Lord Haw-Haw informed the soldiers in his mocking nasal tones that there was a 'bomb for every olive tree' and a 'bullet for every blade of grass'. He called Crete 'the Island of Doomed Men'.[20]

Curiously, the only people who didn't seem to be listening to Lord Haw-Haw were the German Intelligence officers whose job was to estimate the size of the garrison on Crete, a task they singularly failed to accomplish.

The evacuation had mixed up many of the Anzac formations. Some troops were armed with Lee-Enfield rifles, Bren-guns and Vickers machine guns but their 25-pounders had been destroyed in Greece along with all their trucks, cars and Bren-carriers; other troops, including the survivors of the *Costa Rica*, had no weapons or even boots.

'There were 264 of us from the 6th Battalion and 100-odd from the 5th Battalion,' Keith Hooper says. 'We were formed into the 17th Brigade Composite Battalion and joined Cremor Force. Many of us had only the clothes we stood up in.'[21]

Cremor Force, numbering 2283 men and commanded by Colonel Bill Cremor, consisted of the 16th Brigade Composite Battalion (from the 2/2nd and 2/3rd Battalions) and the 17th Brigade Composite Battalion (from the 2/5th and 2/6th Battalions), plus the 2/2nd Field Regiment and 2/3rd Field Regiment.

The 2/7th Battalion had landed without just about all of its arms and kit but received an issue of towels, shorts, socks and soap at its camp two miles south of Kalives. The men were then re-armed with the rifles, Bren-guns and machine guns handed over by the two Australian artillery regiments 'because it was realised that the infantry were much more adept at handling these weapons'.[22]

In exchange, some of the gunners were equipped with 1918-vintage Springfield rifles from the United States, covered in protective grease and without slings. As one-third of his troops were unarmed, Bill Cremor named them 'His Majesty's Unarmed Forces on Crete'.

Mabel Johnson and the Australian nurses were driven eight kilometres west of Canea to the 7th British General Hospital, a tented hospital on a little promontory overlooking the Sea of

Crete. The nurses treated boatload after boatload of wounded from the fighting in Greece, as well as soldiers who had fallen ill with diarrhoea or dysentery from unsanitary conditions in the camps.

One of her patients was an old friend from Yeronga, 26-year-old Hubert Rigby. 'He was sick – not too bad, more a medical case, so don't alarm his family,' Mabel wrote to her parents in an undated letter. 'He thought it odd to see me take a broom and sweep the ward, although only after much protest from men who had worked almost to dropping point. We Australian nurses were very popular with the English orderlies – they thought us great sports.'

Says her daughter Sally Vickery, 'The patients adored my mother. They wrote poems to her and out of respect put on their singlets at dinnertime.'[23]

One exasperated digger wrote down his feelings in a poem entitled 'The Isle of Doom'. It reads in part:

Here I sit upon the Isle of Crete
Bludging on my blistered feet
Little wonder I've got the blues
With feet encased in great canoes

Khaki shorts instead of slacks
Living like a tribe of blacks
Except that blacks don't sit and brood
And wail throughout the day for food

The food was like the water – crook
I got fed up and slung the hook
I returned that day full of wine
And next day copped a fiver fine

My pay-book was behind the hell
When pay was called I said, 'Oh well,

They won't pay me, I'm sure of that'
But when they did I smelt a rat

Next day when no rations came
I realised their wily game
For sooner than sit down and die
We spend our pay on food supply

And now it looks like even betting
A man will soon become a Cretan
And spend his days in darkest gloom
On Adolf Hitler's Isle of Doom[24]

In command terms, Crete had been a revolving door. The garrison had had no fewer than seven commanders in seven months, none of whom had either the time or the resources to prepare the island against a German invasion.[25] Collectively, they had failed to arrange a proper reconnaissance of the terrain or to make any improvement in the roads and harbours or to clear space inland for an airstrip that would have afforded the RAF a measure of protection from the Luftwaffe.

Crete lies 160 kilometres south of the Greek mainland but was even closer to enemy airfields in the Dodecanese. Initially, Wavell intended to use the island merely as a transit camp, 'a receptacle', as Churchill had put it, 'of whatever can get there from Greece'. But to Hitler Crete had much greater significance as a vital element in his strategy to protect the Ploesti oilfields from Allied bombing and, at the same time, secure his southern flank for Operation Barbarossa. Its airfields could also be used to supply Rommel's Afrika Korps and to bomb the Anglo–Australian garrison at Tobruk.

On 21 April, General Kurt Student, commander of XI Air Corps, met Hitler in his armoured train *Amerika* in the Semmering Pass, Austria, from where the Führer was directing his Balkans campaign. Student assured Hitler that his paratroopers, assisted by other airborne units, could capture Crete. No island in the history of warfare had ever been taken other than by assault from the sea but the paras were Hitler's pride and joy, the embodiment of all of the virtues of Nordic manhood, and were expected to achieve great things. Hitler was obsessed with the vision of 'the sky black with bombers and from them, leaping into the smoke, the parachuting stormtroopers, each one grasping a submachine-gun'.[26]

Impressed with Student's idea, he ordered plans to be formulated for an airborne and seaborne attack on Crete. On Anzac Day, he signed Directive No 28, activating Operation Mercury for 'the occupation of the island of Crete in order to have a base for conducting the air war against England in the eastern Mediterranean'. There was one strict proviso: that Operation Mercury should not interfere with preparations for Barbarossa.

The German airwaves were soon running hot from airborne headquarters at Berlin–Tempelhof with Student's orders to the 7th Parachute Division's 11 camps throughout Prussia. These messages were intercepted by listening stations at Malta, Heliopolis and Sarafand in Palestine, and decrypted by Churchill's 'geese that laid the golden eggs' – his nickname for the Ultra staff at Bletchley Park.

On 28 April, he learned that the Germans had sufficient aircraft in the eastern Mediterranean to land from 3000 to 4000 paratroops or airborne troops on Crete in a first sortie, and that two to three sorties a day could be made from Greece and three or four from Rhodes.[27] This estimate was passed on to GHQ Cairo and Churchill followed up with a message of his own to Wavell: 'It seems clear from our information that a heavy airborne attack by German troops and bombers will soon be made on Crete. Let me know what forces you have in the island and what your plans are. It ought to be a fine opportunity for killing the parachute troops. The island must be stubbornly defended.'[28]

Wavell had done almost nothing to turn Crete into a defensive citadel and the navy was nowhere near converting Suda Bay into 'a second Scapa', as Churchill had wished, although 2200 members of General Weston's Mobile Naval Base Defence Organisation (MNBDO), a special unit trained to establish a naval base in any part of the world, were on their way from England with light and heavy anti-aircraft guns to boost its defences.

Wavell replied that in addition to the original garrison of three battalions of British troops and the existing anti-aircraft and coastal batteries, Crete now contained some 30,000 men evacuated from Greece. However, he was not convinced that Crete was the German target. 'It is just possible,' he added, 'that plan for attack on Crete may be cover for attack on Syria or Cyprus, and that real plan will only be disclosed even to [their] own troops at last moment.'[29]

Jumbo Wilson, bemoaning the loss of his luggage, received a cable from Wavell telling him that Crete was about to be attacked and that the troops evacuated from Greece must defend it until they could be replaced with fresh troops and repatriated to Egypt. Wavell added he was assuming that large-scale seaborne landings were improbable but that airborne landings were possible; that the RAF would not be able to provide additional aircraft for some time; and that reliable Greek troops on the island must be used as much as possible. Wilson was to consult Generals Weston and Mackay about the size of the forces required to man a permanent garrison.[30]

Having presided over one disaster, Jumbo Wilson was not about to be lumbered with another. As commanding officer of W Force, he had been a ready-made scapegoat for the Greek debacle. He was now in his 60th year, bald, overweight and slower-thinking than Wavell or Blamey. During the evacuation, he had remained 'calm and collected and kept a perfect grip on things the whole time'.[31] Cyrus Sulzberger, an American war correspondent who had covered the Greek campaign for the

HEROIC GUNNER: Lieutenant Michael Clarke joined the 2/3rd Field Regiment AIF in 1939 at the age of 24. He fought the Italians in the Western Desert and the Germans in Greece and Crete. He was left behind during the evacuation of Crete and spent almost four years as a prisoner of war. *Louise Morris collection*

HAPPINESS: Michael and his bride, Helen Lewis, daughter of BHP chief Essington Lewis, at St John's Church, Toorak in 1948. *Louise Morris collection*

RUGGED ANZAC: Sergeant Keith Hooper with his bride, Olive Short, on their wedding day in Cardiff in 1946. Keith was shot by a Messerschmitt on Crete on 31 May 1941 and captured. He was imprisoned in a POW camp for 'troublemakers' in Germany. He finally escaped at his sixth attempt in April 1945. *Keith Hooper collection*

IVEN'S ARMY: The 6th Division's senior commanders posed for this photograph in Egypt in December 1940. (Front row from left): Brigadier Arthur Allen, General Iven Mackay, Brigadier Horace Robertson; (back row from left): Colonel Frank Berryman, Brigadier Stanley Savige and Colonel George Vasey. *Australian War Memorial Negative Number 044266*

SHARP END: The 2/7th Battalion AIF practises bayonet drill prior to the Battle of Bardia in January 1941. *Australian War Memorial Negative Number 001947*

AUSTRALIAN PIMPERNEL: John Peck as a private in the 2/7th Battalion in 1941 and as Captain John Peck of the Special Operations Executive (SOE) with Brenda Bird on their wedding day in England on 6 January 1945. *Barbara Daniels collection*

ABOVE LEFT: DICTATORS: Hitler farewells Mussolini after their final meeting in 1943, during which the dictators reviewed the disastrous Axis campaigns in North Africa and Russia and planned the production of flying bombs to be used against Britain. *Australian War Memorial Negative Number P02018.203*

ABOVE RIGHT: DEDICATED: Australian Prime Minister Robert Menzies and British PM Winston Churchill stand shoulder to shoulder outside 10 Downing Street during Menzies' visit to London in March 1941 just before the Anzac Corps was reformed in Greece. *Australian War Memorial Negative Number 006414*

DESERT DUO: General Sir Archibald Wavell (left) congratulates Major-General Sir Iven Mackay on the 6th Division AIF's victory in the Battle of Tobruk in January 1941. *Australian War Memorial Negative Number 005633*

SUPER SKIPPER: Captain (later Vice Admiral) John Collins of HMAS *Sydney* flashes his trademark grin. Collins took on two Italian cruisers in the Battle of Cape Spada in July 1940. *Australian War Memorial Negative Number 007887*

ABLAZE: The dying moments of the Italian cruiser *Bartolomeo Colleoni*, destroyed in the Battle of Cape Spada. *Australian War Memorial Negative Number PO1103.005*

FIRST BLOOD: Heavily laden Australian troops charge towards the Italian defences at the start of the Battle of Bardia, January 1941. *Australian War Memorial Negative Number 069221*

SUDDEN DEATH: Troops of the 2/11th Battalion AIF examine an Italian gun-pit that was blasted by Allied artillery in the Battle of Tobruk, January 1941. The Italian gunners were the most ferocious fighters in the Italian Army. *Australian War Memorial Negative Number 005612*

NIGHTMARE: Ivor Hele's painting depicts the bloody scene in the trench at Post 11, Bardia, when two platoons of the 2/6th Battalion AIF, numbering just 43 men, attempted to take a position held by more than 300 Italians. In the centre, Sergeant Jo Gullett is being dragged to safety. *Australian War Memorial Negative Number ART27576*

SURVIVOR: Sergeant Jo Gullett, who was wounded three times in the attack on Post 11, talks to Robert Menzies during the Australian Prime Minister's visit to the Middle East in February 1941. Menzies was a close friend of Gullett's father, Sir Henry Gullett, who was one of three Federal ministers killed in a plane crash near Canberra in August 1940. *Australian War Memorial Negative Number 005769*

PARTHENON PALS: Sister Mabel Johnson of Queensland with a friend from the 2/6th Australian General Hospital outside the Acropolis in Athens after arriving to nurse Australian sick and wounded in March 1941. *Dr Sally Vickery collection*

ANGELS: Australian nursing sisters of the 2/6th General Hospital enjoy a meal at Canea on 26 April 1941 after their dangerous evacuation from Greece. The nurses were later sent to Egypt on General Freyberg's orders. *Australian War Memorial Negative Number 087661*

DESTROYER: HMAS *Stuart*, one of the 'Scrap Iron Flotilla' made famous by its skipper Captain Hector 'Hardover Hec' Waller in the Battle of the Mediterranean in 1940–41. *Australian War Memorial Negative Number 306647*

ABOVE LEFT: LEGEND: Captain Waller led HMAS *Stuart* to glory in the Battle of Matapan in March 1941. *Australian War Memorial Negative Number 005002/13*

ABOVE RIGHT: VALIANT: The great Australian cruiser HMAS *Perth*, which fought in the Mediterranean in 1940–41 and rescued hundreds of Anzac troops from Greece and Crete. Hec Waller took over as captain of *Perth* in October 1941 and went down with her when she was sunk by the Japanese in February 1942. *Australian War Memorial Negative Number 301166*

HEAVYWEIGHTS: General Sir Thomas Blamey (Australia), General Sir Maitland Wilson (Britain) and General Bernard Freyberg (New Zealand) during the doomed Allied campaign in Greece in March/April 1941. *Australian War Memorial Negative Number 128425*

'BLOODY GEORGE': Vasey took command of the 19th Brigade AIF in Greece in March 1941 and commanded Australian forces on Crete in May. He is pictured after arriving back in Egypt in June. *Australian War Memorial Negative Number 134868*

FROZEN: New Zealand troops of the 27th Machine Gun Battalion with their battered vehicle damaged in an enemy air attack in Greece, April 1941. *War History Collection, Alexander Turnbull Library, Wellington, New Zealand, reference no. DA-14389*

BLITZED: A Greek caique similar to the ones used by soldiers to escape from Greece in April 1941 and by the German Army to take troops to Crete the following month. *Author's collection*

BOMBED: The old Venetian harbour at Canea (now Chania). Many of the city's historic buildings were destroyed by German carpet-bombing in May 1941. *Author's collection*

ANZACS UNITED: An Australian and a New Zealander share their experiences after meeting up on Crete following evacuation from Greece in April 1941. *Australian War Memorial Negative Number 068591*

DEATH DIVE: German paratroopers jump from Ju-52s over Canea on 20 May 1941.
War History Collection, Alexander Turnbull Library, Wellington, New Zealand, reference no. DA-12638

UNDER ATTACK: General Bernard Freyberg (right), commander of Creforce, stands on the parapet of his headquarters in a quarry above Canea on the Akrotiri Peninsula to watch the German attack on Day 1 of the Battle of Crete. With him is his aide-de-camp Jack Griffiths, a former All Black. *War History Collection, Alexander Turnbull Library, Wellington, New Zealand, reference no. DA-01149*

TAKE-OFF: German paratroopers prepare to board a Ju-52 on the island of Milos on 20 May 1941. *Australian War Memorial Negative Number 069214*

HILL 107: New Zealand troops were dug in under olive trees at Maleme airfield. *Author's collection*

BELOW LEFT: KEY CROSSING: Airborne German troops captured the iron bridge over the Tavronitis Bridge after crash-landing their gliders in the dried-up riverbed. *Author's collection*

BELOW RIGHT: CASUALTY: One of the many German gliders that crashed on landing in Crete on 20 May. Two dead airborne troops can be seen beside it. *War History Collection, Alexander Turnbull Library, Wellington, New Zealand, reference no. DA-01156*

THE BATTLE OF RETIMO: Artist Vernon Jones recreates the battle in a vivid painting that shows German paratroopers landing among the Australian positions on the afternoon of 20 May 1941. The paras were killed or driven into the olive groves. Some managed to seize the crest of the vital ground on Hill A but were driven off the following morning. *Australian War Memorial Negative Number ART 27776*

GALATAS: The church and village square were the scene of a famous battle in which a scratch force of New Zealanders under Colonel Howard Kippenberger retook the village from German Mountain troops on 26 May 1941. *Author's collection*

WRECKED: Lieutenant Roy Farran's Mark VI light tank destroyed in the Battle of Galatas. *War History Collection, Alexander Turnbull Library, Wellington, New Zealand, reference no. DA-12645*

GETAWAY: The village of Sphakia on the south coast of Crete was the main evacuation point for Allied troops. Naval landing craft lifted them from the little horseshoe-shaped beach in the middle of the photograph. Most of the rearguard, including the 2/7th Battalion and the 2/3rd Field Regiment, were left behind. *Australian War Memorial Negative Number PO4067.005*

FREE: Jack Thomson of the 2/7th Battalion holds the Union Jack given to him by John Peck on Crete for his epic voyage to Egypt in an open boat. The flag is now in the Australian War Memorial. *Australian War Memorial Negative Number 023723*

SAFE: One of the Maoris wounded in the Battle of Crete is helped down the gangplank at Alexandria after his evacuation. *War History Collection, Alexander Turnbull Library, Wellington, New Zealand, reference no. DA-01618*

CRETE TODAY: Memorial shield at Retimo, Allied Bofors on Hill 107 and Anzac graves. *Author's collection*

REST IN PEACE: The Commonwealth War Cemetery at Suda Bay is the resting place of thousands of Australian, New Zealand and British soldiers killed in the Battle of Crete. In the background is the wharf where the troops came ashore from Greece under heavy German air attack in April 1941. *Author's collection*

New York Times, thought Wilson 'resolute, friendly, intelligent', and added, 'Poor man, he will never secure his fair place in history.'[32]

Iven Mackay and his staff were leaving for Egypt the following day, so Wilson consulted Eric Weston about the size of the existing garrison and the number of troops needed to hold the island against a combined sea and airborne attack. He was informed that the Black Watch Battalion was at Heraklion and the remainder of the 14th British Brigade in the Suda Bay area. The air force, commanded by Group Captain George Beamish, consisted of four depleted squadrons from Greece, with eight Blenheims, six Hurricanes and six Gladiators, and one squadron from Egypt with nine Blenheims. No. 805 Squadron of the Fleet Air Arm, which had performed valiantly in the Battle of Matapan, was still at Maleme with a large number of ground crew and other RAF personnel.[33]

The main fighting force would therefore have to come from the Anzacs: there were seven New Zealand battalions plus part of a machine-gun battalion and four Australian battalions plus a full machine-gun battalion and half of a fifth infantry battalion.[34]

Everything was in short supply. The storehouses contained limited quantities of food, clothing and arms for a garrison of one brigade totalling just 5000 men. Although stores were gradually being boosted to 90 days' supply for 30,000 men, the evacuees from Greece needed to be fed immediately, largely re-armed and clothed, and provided with vehicles, heavy weapons, ammunition and entrenching tools, few of which were available.

Wilson cabled Wavell that three brigade groups, each of four battalions, and one motor battalion distributed between the Suda Bay area and Heraklion would be required to prevent a successful German attack. He concluded: 'I consider that unless all three services are prepared to face the strain of maintaining adequate forces up to strength, the holding of the island is a dangerous commitment, and a decision on the matter must be taken at once.'

Considering the litany of problems which confronted him in North Africa, Iraq and Syria, this was the last thing Wavell wanted to hear. As a classics scholar, he was familiar with Crete's turbulent history and doom-laden mythology. Crete was the point at which Europe collided with the Middle East, an exotic synthesis of Byzantium, Islam and Orthodox Christianity. It was the birthplace of the painter El Greco and of Venizelos, the liberator of Crete from foreign rule. Zeus, king of the gods, had been born on Mount Ida. As the centre of the Minoan civilisation from 2600 BC to 1400 BC, it had been home to The Minotaur, the half-man, half-bull of Greek mythology who was trapped in the Labyrinth beneath King Minos' palace at Knossos. Daedalus, the builder of the Labyrinth, had fashioned wings of wax and feathers so that he and his son Icarus could escape from Crete, only for Icarus to fly too close to the sun and fall into the sea.

After the demise of the Minoans, wiped out by earthquakes and volcanic eruptions, the island had been conquered by the Romans and then the Byzantines. Following the fall of Constantinople to the Fourth Crusade in 1204, the Byzantine Empire was split up and Crete was sold to the Venetians, who ruled it for the next 400 years.[35]

They were replaced by the Ottoman Turks, who invaded Crete in 1669. The Greek War of Independence of 1821 ended Turkish rule over continental Greece but Britain refused to allow the unification of Greece and Crete. Instead, the island was handed over to Egypt until 1840 when Palmerston, fearing that a Turkish collapse would bring Russia into the Mediterranean, forced the Egyptians to give it back to the Turks.

In 1897, Eleftherios Venizelos, a young Cretan lawyer, joined a band of armed Christians on the Akrotiri Peninsula and defied all attempts at mediation by the great powers. The matter was resolved when the powers granted Crete a form of self-government, with Venizelos as Prime Minister. In the aftermath of the Balkan Wars, Turkish forces were finally expelled from the island and, on 1 December 1913, *enosis* – union with Greece – was achieved when Venizelos and King Constantine of Greece raised the Greek flag over Canea.[36]

While the north coast towns became more westernised with the arrival of Greek settlers, the traditional Cretan way of life, strong on hospitality and blood feuds, continued in the foothills and mountain valleys. According to a German briefing document completed on 31 March for the invasion of Greece, 'The Cretans are considered intelligent, hot-blooded, valorous, excitable as well as obstinate and difficult to govern. The agricultural population is accustomed to using arms, even in everyday life. Vendetta and abduction are still customary and criminality is high.'[37]

Cretan men wore a black head-cloth, embroidered jacket and waistcoat with dark breeches and high boots and were traditionally armed with guns and knives.[38] Because of the island's long history of invasion and earthquakes – sent in from the sea by the angry god Poseidon – the coast was considered 'unsatisfactory, potentially dangerous and un-Cretan'. Coast-dwellers were known as 'long-trousered men' and Cretans whispered that they had no souls and were not to be trusted.[39]

The Cretans' relationship with Athens was turbulent. They had never forgiven Constantine's son, the present George II, for giving his blessing to the Metaxas dictatorship in 1936, which had seen the persecution of Venizelist supporters in parliament and the purging of Venizelist officers in the army. On the second anniversary of the 4 August Decree which had put Metaxas in power, the Cretans had risen in revolt. Martial law was declared and the island occupied once again – this time by Greek soldiers and gendarmes. Metaxas ordered that the rebels be punished and the Cretan population disarmed.

Some weapons were handed over, but many were hidden away or buried.

Once British troops arrived in November 1940 to garrison the island, the flower of Cretan manhood – the Cretan V Division containing every male of military age – was dispatched to the mainland to fight the Italians in Albania. Noted for its superb marksmanship, the division had fought with great distinction but had been betrayed by the treacherous General Tsolacoglou. Cretan troops were now prisoners of war in Epirus and most of the Greek soldiers who had fled to Crete were poorly armed men in training units or young cadets.

On 28 April, the Greek Prime Minister, Emmanuel Tsouderos, and the Greek commander, General Achilles Skoulas, requested a meeting with Generals Wilson and Weston. Skoulas explained that he wished to continue the fight against the Nazis. His forces on Crete consisted of 2500 gendarmes, 7500 soldiers and 1000 reservists, organised into 11 battalions, none of which was well equipped. He asked that a British general be appointed to command all Allied forces on the island and that the Greek troops be armed with British weapons.[40] As British generals were in short supply, Colonel Guy Salisbury-Jones, formerly of the military mission to Greece, was selected for the task.

Meanwhile, Brigadier Jimmy Hargest of the 5th New Zealand Brigade had established his headquarters in a farmhouse near Platanias, a coastal village west of Canea. He received orders from Jumbo Wilson to be prepared to repel a German invasion. His four New Zealand battalions (the 21st, 22nd, 23rd and 28th) were deployed, in his words, to 'deny the advance of enemy landing parties from the west'.

As fate would have it, defence of the RAF's westernmost airfield at Maleme fell to the 22nd Battalion.[41] It was an experience the young New Zealanders and their commanding officer, 41-year-old Lieutenant-Colonel Leslie Andrew, would never forget. Andrew, a regular soldier, was tall and lean, with a stiff black moustache and grizzled hair. He had won a Victoria Cross as a corporal in the First World War. He was brave and conscientious and something of a disciplinarian. It hadn't taken long for the men to come up with a nickname for him. They called him 'February' because his automatic sentence when anyone broke the rules was '28 days' detention'.[42]

CHAPTER 15

Ultra's Secrets

At nine o'clock on the morning of 29 April, General Freyberg arrived in Suda Bay in the cruiser *Ajax* after what he describes as 'a hard time of great anxiety' in the Battle of Greece. Nine cars had been shot from under him and he had been terribly concerned about the fate of his men. Freyberg had no inkling that he was in for an even more testing experience in Crete, one that would have broken a lesser man. Pulling in to the wharf in *Ajax*'s launch, he looked smart in his red-braided cap, with his many medals pinned to his tunic. A photograph taken at the quayside shows him smiling and relaxed, the very model of the warrior general.

Tiny Freyberg went ashore with his chief of staff, Colonel Keith Stewart, and senior administrative officer, Lieutenant-Colonel William Gentry, to check on his 4th and 5th Brigades and arrange their passage to Alexandria. He then planned to take a plane to Egypt, where he would re-organise and re-equip his division. All went well: he discussed this plan with Jimmy Hargest and Edward Puttick, whose 4th Brigade had landed in Crete the previous day and was settling in around Canea. He also had no trouble arranging a lift for himself in a flying boat which was leaving for Egypt early the next morning. Freyberg went to bed that night believing that everything was in order and that he would soon be enjoying some well-earned leave in Cairo with his wife Barbara, who was flying out from London to join him.

Churchill, meanwhile, had discussed the question of who should command Creforce with Sir John Dill. 'I suggested to the CIGS that General Freyberg should be placed in command of Crete,' Churchill writes.

> Freyberg is so made that he will fight for King and country with an unconquerable heart anywhere he is ordered, and with whatever forces he is given by superior authorities, and he imparts his own invincible firmness of mind to all around him.[1]

When Freyberg stirred at seven o'clock on the morning of 30 April, he was handed a cable from GHQ Middle East instructing him to attend a conference at 11 am at General Wilson's headquarters in the village of Ay Marina near Platanias. He arrived with Keith Stewart to discover that General Weston, Sir Michael Palairet, General Heywood, Group Captain Beamish and Wilson's chief of staff, Brigadier Sandy Galloway, were among those present.

'We met in a small village between Maleme and Canea and set to work at 11.30,' Freyberg says in his report of the Battle of Crete. 'General Wavell had arrived by air and he looked drawn and tired and more weary than any of us.'

The meeting was held under an awning on the tiled, flat-topped roof of a seaside villa. Wavell took Wilson into one corner and had what Freyberg calls 'a heart-to-heart talk' with him. Wilson knew what was coming. His bold reply to Wavell that it would be impossible to hold Crete with the available forces had effectively disqualified him as commander of Creforce. Instead, Wavell had an unpleasant surprise for him. 'I want you to go to Jerusalem and relieve Baghdad,' he said. Wilson was astonished. Baghdad? 'I had no idea what had been happening outside Greece for the last three weeks,' he says.[2]

The question of Wilson's successor then arose. If Wavell intended to reinstate General Weston, his plans were disrupted when a cable from Sir John Dill, which had been relayed from Cairo to George Beamish's high-powered RAF radio station, was handed to him.[3] 'Would suggest Freyberg to succeed Weston in Crete,' Dill wrote. 'It need only be temporary command and Freyberg could collect later his scattered flock.' There was no mention of Churchill's preference for the New Zealander; indeed, Freyberg said later he was 'nominated by Whitehall by name to take over command of Crete', although he must have known by then that he was Churchill's personal choice.[4]

To Wavell, Dill's cable was a godsend. He called Freyberg over and, taking him by the arm, said, 'I want to tell you how well I think the New Zealand Division has done in Greece. I do not believe any other division would have carried out those withdrawals as well.'

Relations between Freyberg and Wavell had been strained ever since Wavell had tried to hijack New Zealand units in the Western Desert back in December and he was grateful for the commander-in-chief's words of praise. Wavell then informed Freyberg that he wanted him to take command of Creforce, adding that he considered Crete would be attacked by the Germans in the next few days.

For all his unflappability, Freyberg was taken aback. 'I told him that I wanted to get back to Egypt to concentrate the division and train and re-equip it and I added that my Government would never agree to the division being split permanently,' he says. 'He then said that he considered it my duty to remain and take on the job. I could do nothing but accept.'[5]

Having sorted out his command problem, Wavell sat down at a table with the other participants and the rooftop summit meeting got under way. 'We were told that Crete would be held,' Freyberg says. 'The scale of attack envisaged was five to six thousand airborne troops plus a possible seaborne attack. The primary objectives of this attack were considered to be Heraklion and Maleme aerodromes. Our object was to deny the enemy the use of Crete as an air and submarine base.'[6] General Weston chipped in that he considered a seaborne landing very probable and that, as far as he could see, the Royal Navy would not be able to prevent it.

In view of the controversy that has dogged events in Crete ever since, the circumstances surrounding Freyberg's appointment are crucial. One account insists that Wavell solicited General Dill's advice in response to a query from Churchill as to whether General Weston was the right man to hold Crete.[7] Weston was a Royal Marine officer and had had no active service as a land commander. Dill then discussed the matter with Churchill, who stated his preference for Freyberg. Wavell's biographer John Connell says that Dill 'had doubts about Weston's fitness for this difficult command' and suggested Freyberg – 'a proposal which Wavell instantly accepted'.[8]

However, it is abundantly clear from Dill's cable that he saw Freyberg as a 'temporary commander' who would shortly leave Crete to collect 'his scattered flock'. Yet both Dill and Wavell knew from Ultra decrypts that the Germans intended to invade the island within a matter of days and it seems most unlikely that they planned to parachute yet another senior commander on to the island to take charge. Barring death or injury, Freyberg was fated to be there for the duration of the conflict.

This was confirmed after the conference when Wavell and Freyberg walked into the garden of the villa for a private talk. Although he had only the haziest idea of Crete's resources, Bernard Freyberg echoed Wilson's opinion that there were not enough men on Crete to hold it and that they were inadequately armed for the task. Having witnessed the harmful effects of air attack on troop morale in Greece, he asked that the decision to defend the island be reconsidered if the RAF was unable to supply adequate air cover.

Wavell, slippery as ever, replied that the scale of the attack had possibly been exaggerated. He was confident the troops would be equal to the task and efforts would be made to obtain more fighter aircraft from England. In any event, he added, the troops on Crete could not be evacuated because there were not enough ships to take them away.[9]

At this point, Wavell told Freyberg that he would receive Ultra intelligence reports on German plans. He explained that Ultra was obtained by decrypting German radio transmissions using an Enigma machine identical to the ones used for encoding these messages. Wavell then gave Freyberg two specific orders to safeguard the Ultra secret and prevent the Germans from suspecting that their code had been broken. 'First, he was not to mention the existence of Ultra to anyone else on Crete,' Freyberg's biographer, his son Paul Freyberg, writes. 'Second, he was never to take any action as a result of what he learnt from Ultra *alone*.'[10]

As Freyberg understood it, Wavell was ordering him to find an alternative source before he implemented any of the Ultra information obtained via Enigma. It sounded like the equivalent of removing the blindfold and then ordering him to keep his eyes shut. Freyberg had never heard of Ultra and his initial difficulty in comprehending its meaning and usage is entirely understandable.

In fact, Freyberg's problems were only just beginning. He might have expected some assistance from General Weston, who had been appointed by Wavell to command British troops in the Suda Bay area. It was not forthcoming. On arriving at Creforce headquarters in Canea, Freyberg discovered that the place had been stripped bare apart from a few pencils and some chairs. Clearly miffed at Freyberg's appointment, Weston had decamped to Suda Bay and taken everything, including his staff, with him.

Freyberg had to create a corps staff for himself from his divisional staff and then find a new staff for the division, including a new commanding officer. In the role of chief of staff, he retained Colonel Stewart, while Brigadier Brunskill was named chief administrative officer/quartermaster and Colonel J. H. Frowen, of the 7th Medium Regiment, artillery commander. Brigadier Puttick – 'a talkative man apt to fuss over trifles'[11] – was promoted to acting major-general and given command of the New Zealand Division, with Colonel Gentry as his chief of staff. Colonel Kippenberger, the 44-year-old barrister who commanded the 20th Battalion, would replace Puttick as commander of the 4th Brigade until Brigadier Lindsay Inglis, who was in charge of New Zealand training in Egypt, could be flown to Crete.

Brunskill was horrified about his own appointment. 'I had not visualised Crete being attacked and I dreaded being stuck there,' he says. His beloved terrier Susie had been sent on to Alexandria and he wanted to be reunited with her. 'I asked Jumbo Wilson to get me a reprieve but he quoted the C-in-C's personal order.'[12] So once again Brunskill found himself in a position of power over the fate of Australian troops. In Greece, Weary Dunlop had clashed with him several times, once over his reluctance to provide a hospital train to evacuate Australian wounded from the front. Dunlop had also been appalled to hear Brunskill address the British deputy medical officer with the words, 'Get out, you little rat! Get out!'[13]

As Ultra liaison officer, Freyberg had the services of George Beamish, who had been receiving Ultra intelligence under its Middle East code name 'Orange Leonard' since 28 April in the hope that he might use the information to mount attacks on the growing German air menace from airfields in Greece and Rhodes.[14] As a fighter pilot, the 36-year-old Irishman was used to beating the odds and there was no tougher man on Crete: Beamish had won the RAF's heavyweight boxing championship in 1929 and then, in 1932, captained Ireland's championship-winning rugby team.[15] But with all the will in the world, he could make very little use of the information with the handful of serviceable aircraft at his disposal.

Then, at 4.15 pm on 1 May – the first day of Freyberg's command of Creforce – Beamish received confirmation via Ultra that Crete, and not Cyprus as Wavell thought possible, would definitely be the Germans' next target in the Mediterranean. Ultra informed him that orders had been given to the Luftwaffe that Suda Bay should no longer be mined nor Cretan airfields bombed so as not to hamper 'operations planned for the coming weeks'.[16]

Beamish passed this information to Freyberg later that day at Creforce's battle headquarters which had been established in an old quarry at the top of a winding road in the foothills of the Akrotiri Peninsula. The staff operated in dugouts and stone huts which blended in with the walls of the quarry, providing natural camouflage against air attack.[17] The position afforded Freyberg a panoramic view of Canea, with the old walled Venetian city and its battlemented castle protecting the harbour entrance. Looking south, the White Mountains formed an impregnable barrier as far as the eye could see, while the heavily timbered terrain between the mountains and the shoreline was hilly and pitted with ravines and watercourses. To the west, the coast swept in a gentle arc towards Maleme and the Rodopos Peninsula. Villages and farmhouses dotted the landscape and here and there the golden cupolas of Orthodox churches glinted in the sunlight.

Freyberg reviewed his options.

'The main defence problems which faced me in Crete were not clear to me at this stage,' he says.

I did not know anything about the geography or physical characteristics of the island. I knew less about the condition of the force I was to command. Neither was I aware of the serious situation with regard to maintenance and, finally, I had not learnt the real scale of attack which we were to be prepared to repel.[18]

Deciding that the sooner he 'introduced a little reality into the calculations for the defence of Crete the better', he cabled Wavell, who had returned to Cairo, restating his opinion that his forces were 'totally inadequate to meet attack envisaged'. He continued in the same vein. 'Unless fighter aircraft are greatly increased and naval forces made available to deal with seaborne attack I cannot hope to hold out with land forces alone, which as a result of campaign in Greece are now devoid of any artillery, have insufficient tools for digging, very little transport, and inadequate war reserves of equipment and ammunition. Force here can and will fight, but without full support from Navy and Air Force cannot hope to repel invasion.'

Freyberg argued that if naval and air support was unavailable, the decision to hold Crete should be reconsidered, and added that it was his duty to inform the New Zealand Government 'of situation in which greater part of my division is now placed'.[19]

In Wellington, Peter Fraser received a cable from Freyberg informing him of the parlous state of affairs on Crete. 'There is no evidence of naval forces capable of guaranteeing us against seaborne invasion and air forces in island consist of six Hurricanes and 17 obsolete aircraft,' he said. He recommended that Fraser 'bring pressure to bear on highest plane in London either to supply us with sufficient means to defend island or to review decision Crete must be held'. Fraser was so concerned by Freyberg's cable that he made arrangements to fly to Cairo to discuss the matter with Wavell at first-hand.

Freyberg's use of the terms 'seaborne attack' and 'seaborne invasion' show that he was thinking in terms of defending the beaches against a mass assault, rather than seeing such a landing as the enemy's way of reinforcing his airborne troops by sea *after* they had taken control of an airstrip and captured a section of coastline. The vital ground at the outset of the

Battle of Crete would be the airfields rather than the beaches. That these should be defended with all available means now seems elementary, but that was not clear to Freyberg or his commanders at the time.[20]

As no island had ever been captured other than from the sea, Freyberg's confusion is understandable.[21] Instead of correcting him, Wavell sought to pacify him by once again assuring him that the War Office estimate of the attacking forces had been exaggerated and that he would receive naval support, artillery and tools, while efforts were being made to provide increased air support. 'I am trying,' he added, 'to make arrangements to relieve New Zealand troops from Crete and am most anxious to re-form your division at earliest opportunity. But at moment my resources are stretched to limit.'[22]

Wavell must have known when he sent that cable that there was absolutely no chance of replacing the New Zealanders; indeed, he had already told Freyberg that there weren't enough ships for such an operation. On 2 May, Wavell cabled Dill that 'at least three brigade groups' and a 'considerable number of anti-aircraft units' were required to garrison the island. If he removed the two New Zealand brigades, he would have to replace them with two other brigades which simply didn't exist in the Middle East. And despite his promise to Freyberg, he told Dill, 'Air defence will always be a difficult problem.'[23]

Over the next few days, Freyberg toured the main points of his command, boosting troop morale and discussing their deployment with brigade and battalion commanders. Crete is 256 kilometres long and up to 56 kilometres wide and, in 1941, had a population of 400,000. All the main settlements are on the north coast, where the land slopes down from the mountain ranges via foothills and spurs to a narrow coastal plain. From west to east, the main towns are Kastelli, Canea (the capital), Suda, Retimo and Heraklion. In 1941, these were linked by the only metalled road on the island, while rough tracks spiralled out to the villages of the interior. Along the south coast, the mountainous spine dropped down to the sea and the only habitation was a few tiny fishing villages.

No one knew the sheer awkwardness and defensive difficulties of Crete better than Admiral Cunningham:

> All the bays and harbours are on the northern coast, an unfortunate factor for us as they could only be reached through the Kaso Straits at the east end of the island, and the Antikithera and Kithera Channels to the west, all of which were in easy range of enemy aerodromes. No port or real anchorage exists on the south coast, while the only country suitable for airfields is on the northern side. From the point of view of defence it would have suited us much better if the island could have been turned upside-down.[24]

Freyberg visited 4th New Zealand Brigade in the rough, hilly country around Galatas to the south-west of Canea. He warned Colonel Kippenberger that the attack was coming and that it would be 'tough going'.[25] He asked whether the men would fight; Kippenberger was 'very confident' that they would.[26]

Then on 3 May Freyberg divided the island into four main areas – Maleme and Galatas; Suda Bay at the eastern foot of the Akrotiri Peninsula; Retimo airfield, eight kilometres east of the town of Retimo; and, further east, Heraklion town and airfield. He then issued instructions to his commanders, Brigadier Puttick (Maleme–Galatas), General Weston (Suda Bay), Brigadier Vasey (Georgiopolis–Retimo) and Brigadier Brian Chappel (Heraklion).

The commanders at the airfields were to dispose one-third of their troops on or round the landing strips and two-thirds 'outside the area which will be attacked in the first instance'. The attack would probably take the form of intensive bombing and strafing of the airfields and its environs, a landing by paratroops to seize and clear the airfields, followed by the landing of troop-carrying aircraft. In addition, a seaborne attack might be made on beaches close to the airfields and Suda Bay.[27]

Churchill cabled Peter Fraser that every effort would be made to re-equip the New Zealand Division, particularly with artillery 'in which General Wavell is already strong'. He continued, 'Our information points to an airborne attack being delivered in the near future, with possibly an attempt at seaborne attack. The Navy will certainly do their utmost to prevent the latter, and it is unlikely to succeed on any large scale. So far as airborne attack is concerned, this ought to suit the New Zealanders down to the ground, for they will be able to come to close quarters, man to man, with the enemy, who will not have the advantage of tanks and artillery, on which he so largely relies.'[28]

The Australian Cabinet, hugely disconcerted over the losses incurred in the Greek campaign and fearful about the fate of its troops on Crete, consulted General Blamey in his new role of deputy commander-in-chief at Grey Pillars. If they expected some help from him, they were to be disappointed. As Wavell retained all of his powers of command and rarely delegated anything, Blamey's appointment had been nothing more than a gesture to keep the troublesome Menzies quiet. Blamey himself admitted, in a letter to Army Minister Percy Spender in June, 'I am rather a fifth wheel to the coach.'

In his reply to the Cabinet, Blamey simply followed the Wavell line that the island should not be abandoned to the Germans without offering the strongest resistance. The enemy was likely to use one airborne and one seaborne division, with one-third of an airborne division making the first attack. The troops required to defend the island were three infantry brigade groups, with coastal and harbour defences and a 'reasonable air force'. The forces available were the 14th British Brigade and troops from Greece who were adequate in numbers but had no artillery. He considered that the 16th British Brigade, together with more artillery and fighter squadrons, should be sent from

Egypt. 'Situation far from satisfactory,' he concluded, 'but everything possible being done to improve it.'[29]

Blamey then raised expectations at home by adding that most of the AIF troops would be withdrawn as soon as the 16th British Brigade arrived in Crete. Once again, this was pie in the sky: shipping simply did not exist to perform such a large turnaround and there was absolutely no chance of the Australians being relieved. Like the unfortunate Freyberg and his two New Zealand brigades, the Australian Anzacs were also there for the duration.[30]

Michael Clarke's regiment had been formed into an infantry battalion, with Horace Strutt in command. Clarke was made a platoon commander on the strength of his rifle and Lewis gun skills. His men were issued with .303 Lee-Enfield rifles, collected from other units, and a Lewis gun with five magazines. He took them on a route march through the hills like proper infantry. 'The men discovered a NAAFI in an old Turkish fort near the road to Suda,' he says. 'The supplies were for British troops only. Despite this stupid ban, they acquired several boxes of tinned fruit – probably during the siesta.'

Things were starting to look up. Bread, cheese, eggs and wine were available and there was an issue of blankets and groundsheets, although that was far from universal among the units of Creforce. 'Some of the gunners were running a two-up school in Kalives,' Clarke says. 'The Cretans are mad gamblers, betting up to 5000 drachma on a spin.'

The positive mood seems to have reached Bernard Freyberg, whom Peter Coats, Wavell's aide-de-camp, described as 'a man of quickly changing moods, easily depressed and as easily elated'. Freyberg experienced a remarkable change of heart, presumably after learning that he had been Churchill's choice to head Creforce. Forgetting his gloomy predictions, he cabled the British Prime Minister on 5 May, 'Cannot understand nervousness; am not in the least anxious about an airborne attack.'

> I have made my dispositions and feel that with the troops now at my disposal I can cope adequately. However, a combination of seaborne and airborne attack is different. If that comes before I can get the guns and transport here the situation will be difficult. Even so, provided the Navy can help, I trust that all will be well.[31]

It was clear from his message to Churchill that Freyberg had not appreciated that the main danger would come from the air and not the sea. The chiefs of staff in London were concerned. The following day they inquired of Wavell in Cairo, 'Please inquire from General Freyberg whether he is receiving Orange Leonard [Ultra] information from Cairo; if not please arrange to pass relevant OL information maintaining utmost security.'[32]

Yet Freyberg was right. Hitler himself had insisted on a seaborne component to Operation Mercury as an insurance policy in case the British had destroyed the runways at Crete's three airfields making it impossible to land the Mountain troops and heavy equipment.[33] At his meeting with General Student, he insisted on amphibious landings to support the air attack so that the invasion would not be 'standing on one leg'. Student had ignored this instruction in his planning. When Hitler discovered through one of his spies in Athens that it had been discarded, he sent a direct order to Student that the sea landings must be reinstated.

Student planned to make seaborne landings with two light ships groups consisting of dozens of caiques and a number of little steamers, escorted by two Italian light destroyers. As the Luftwaffe enjoyed total air superiority over the Aegean during the day, the Germans planned to send their armadas across in daylight, giving them a clear run to the invasion beaches. The first would land west of Maleme on Day 1 of the invasion and the second at Heraklion on Day 2. As it was, Freyberg had most of his troops guarding the coast and none at all in the one place it would matter: the west bank of the Tavronitis River overlooking Maleme airfield.

CHAPTER 16

Mercury Rising

General Kurt Student set up the headquarters of his XI Air Corps in the Grande Bretagne Hotel in Athens, so recently the habitat of General Heywood's failed military mission to save Greece from the Nazis' clutches.[1] With his indispensable chief of operations, Lieutenant-Colonel Heinrich Trettner, at his side he began to gather the Operation Mercury forces around him.

In great secrecy, thousands of Prussian glider and parachute troops of XI Air Corps arrived from Germany in lorries with their identification marks painted out. To avoid recognition, the paras were dressed in ordinary Luftwaffe uniforms devoid of badges and, in case of accident, they carried identity papers which made no mention of their unit. They were forbidden to send postcards or letters to their families, or to sing regimental songs.[2]

Despite their anonymity – or perhaps because of it – the paratroopers made their presence felt. Camped by the sea in captured British tents, they swam and sunbathed naked and swaggered through the streets stripped to the waist in tiny shorts, regardless of the blushes of Greek women. One

American aid worker complained they had turned his district into 'a German nudist colony'.[3]

Born on 12 May 1890, Student was the third of four sons of a minor member of the Prussian landed gentry. His boyhood ambition was to be a doctor but that was beyond his father's means so, aged 11, he was enrolled to receive free tuition at the Royal Prussian Military Cadet School at Potsdam. Commissioned as a lieutenant in 1911, he was serving in a light infantry battalion when, in 1913, he was offered the chance to train as a pilot despite little aptitude for mathematics and an aversion to heights.[4]

Student spent the First World War in the German air force, commanding a fighter squadron from October 1916 onwards and claiming six victories over French aircraft. In one dogfight, he was seriously wounded. After the war, he returned to his home in Prussia. As Germany was forbidden under the terms of the Treaty of Versailles to have an air force, prospects for the young veteran looked bleak. 'I had served an apprenticeship,' he says, 'only to discover that I had no sphere in which to practise my profession.'[5]

Student developed an interest in gliders (since gliding was exempt from the ban) and began to appreciate their military possibilities. Following Hitler's rise to power, the Luftwaffe was secretly re-established in the guise of the 'Central Flying School'. It was here that Student developed a close working relationship with Herman Goering, who appointed him head of training.

In March 1935, Hitler renounced the Treaty of Versailles, reintroduced conscription and brought the fledgling Luftwaffe out into the open. Student was appointed commander of the 7th Air Division and set about converting it into a parachute force. His interest in airborne operations dated from watching the manoeuvres of the Red Army Air Force in 1937 which included an impressive display by 1500 parachutists. Student realised that armed paratroopers could be launched en masse against suitable targets.

It was to his advantage that the Junkers-52 aircraft were being superseded as bombers. He grabbed as many of these lumbering, three-engined giants as he could and, by the time World War II broke out, had co-opted 242 of them into transport wings capable of lifting his entire division. To carry heavily armed troops, artillery and vehicles, he developed the DFS-230 glider to be towed behind the Ju-52s.[6] His division then won its spurs in the offensive of 10 May 1940, when paratroopers seized airfields and bridges in Holland and Belgium, and glider troops landed on top of the 'impregnable' Belgian fortress of Eban Emael and captured it.

With gimlet eyes and a cruel mouth, Student was a lone wolf among his Luftwaffe peers. It was ironic that he had been accidentally shot in the head by his own side during the Battle for Rotterdam. His life was saved by a Dutch surgeon and, although the wound incapacitated him for eight months and left him with a slow, drawling manner of speaking, it did nothing to quell his ambitions for his airborne troops. On the contrary, having survived two close shaves, he realised this might be his last chance of glory.

In January 1941, Goering appointed Student commanding officer of XI Air Corps, the newly formed command for the Luftwaffe's expanding airborne forces. Following the Luftwaffe's defeat in the Battle of Britain, the tubby *Reichsmarschall* needed a spectacular victory to inveigle his way back into favour. It was Goering who had placed his protégé in front of Hitler, although he secretly disavowed his grandiose scheme to make Crete a stepping stone in a German invasion of Suez. With his eye firmly fixed on the Barbarossa timetable, Hitler warned Student, 'In the interests of other operations, the attack should take place as quickly as possible. Every day earlier is a profit, every day later is a loss.'[7]

As expected, Hitler placed Goering in overall command of Operation Mercury but then, to his dismay, Student discovered that Goering had delegated that role to General Alexander

Lohr, commanding officer of the 4th Air Fleet in the Balkans. There were further disappointments. To eliminate anti-aircraft batteries on Crete and soften up the defending troops, Lohr chose the fighters and bombers of General Wolfram von Richthofen's VIII Air Corps but declined to place these forces under Student's command.

Student had also wanted the 22nd Airborne Division as his air-landing force but it was guarding the Romanian oilfields and, owing to Barbarossa commitments, transport was unavailable to bring it down to Greece in time for Operation Mercury. Instead, he was given the 5th Mountain Division of Field Marshal List's 12th Army, which was currently in reserve near Athens. Its commander, the bearded General Julius Ringel, was an Austrian like his boss General Lohr, and Student rightly feared that Lohr would favour his fellow countryman.

Ringel's alpine troops were mostly Austrians and Bavarians who had little time for the stolid Prussians of the parachute corps. They had enjoyed a good campaign against the Greek Army and considered themselves the *corps d'elite* of German infantry. There was friction on the streets of Athens whenever Ringel's soldiers bumped into Student's paratroops. For their part, the paras rightly regarded the infantrymen as novices in airborne warfare.[8]

Student planned to launch simultaneous attacks on all four main objectives – Canea and the three airfields – to prevent Freyberg from concentrating his reserves at any one point. Lohr didn't like this idea. By scattering his forces along the coast in small groups, Student risked being defeated everywhere. Lohr was adamant that the first thrust should be a massive assault on one spot to overcome enemy resistance and establish an unassailable bridgehead. He identified Maleme, the airfield nearest German air bases in Greece, as the vital ground. Its coastal position provided the perfect start-line from which to attack Canea and then seize Suda Bay for the landing of seaborne troops and heavy arms and equipment.[9]

Student was dismayed. The whole point of vertical warfare was to envelop the enemy in several places at the same time, whereas Lohr's plan would enable Freyberg to concentrate his reserves at the point of attack. He argued that as speed was of the essence in the capture of Crete, his plan should take precedence. Richthofen then weighed in with the opinion that even with 570 Stukas, Junkers 88s, Dorniers, Heinkels and Messerschmitts, VIII Air Corps could not possibly provide adequate air support for four simultaneous attacks in different parts of the island.

The Mercury commanders were hopelessly divided, so the issue was referred to Berlin, where Goering's staff opted for a hybrid scheme containing elements of both plans. Using the same aircraft in two waves, the first attack would be on Maleme airfield and Canea in the morning and then, in the afternoon, on the airfields at Retimo and Heraklion. After Lohr had assessed the gains, Ringel's Mountain troops would be landed at the most opportune spot.[10]

It was typical of Goering that this compromise actually achieved the worst of all possible worlds. For a start, it lacked the concentration of force that had made Lohr's plan so attractive and yet it eliminated Student's succession of quick, devastating blows. More importantly, it could only work if there was a smooth turnaround at the Greek airfields. Depending on how many Ju-52s, fighters and bombers had been lost over Maleme and Canea, the second wave would have to go into battle with fewer aircraft and without the advantage of surprise.

One further drawback was that, unlike the 22nd Airborne Division, General Ringel's Mountain troops had never flown before and would have to be trained in no time at all in some of the arts of their despised para rivals. When he read his orders, Ringel felt a chill creep down his spine, 'for it was clear that the operation so laconically and soberly described would be a suicidal adventure'.[11]

On 6 May, an Ultra decrypt revealed that preparations for

Operation Mercury would probably be completed by 17 May. In the first phase of the attack on Day 1, paratroopers of the 7th Air Division and corps troops of XI Air Corps in gliders would seize Maleme, Heraklion and Retimo airfields, enabling dive-bombers and fighters to occupy Maleme and Heraklion.

In the second phase on Day 2, the remainder of XI Air Corps and its headquarters would be landed. Once these gains had been achieved, three Mountain regiments from the 12th Army in the Balkans, armoured and anti-tank units, motorcyclists and supplies would be landed in an invasion fleet of Italian and German vessels, protected by Italian motor torpedo boats and other naval forces. The whole operation would be preceded by an air attack on RAF bases, army camps and anti-aircraft batteries.

On 7 May, the Director of Intelligence at the Air Ministry informed Creforce headquarters that 450 German troop-carrying aircraft were available for the German operation, rising to perhaps as many as 600. Up to 12,000 parachutists could be dropped on Day 1 if two sorties were made, and 4000 men and 400 tons of supplies might arrive on Day 2 in the air-landing operation.[12]

On 7 May, General Freyberg addressed the 2/3rd Field Regiment. 'He stood on a pile of rocks and we formed a square under the cover of the olive trees,' Michael Clarke says.

He told us that he was in command and we were relieved to hear that someone was. He praised us for our fine performance in Greece and the support given to NZ units at Porto Rafti. He also told us that we had to prepare to repel a seaborne landing. He said that arms would be in short supply and that we would have to improvise. Willie Smith asked me if I could whip up some bows and arrows.

Despite his upbeat message to Churchill, Freyberg's problems seemed to be multiplying. He signalled Wavell urging that 10,000 men who were without arms 'and with little or no employment other than getting into trouble with the civil population' should be evacuated. He made no effort to form these men into labour battalions to carry out vitally needed roadwork or to build an inland airfield, or to complete a road across the mountains to the south coast for the simple reason that there were no spare picks or shovels for them to use, let alone any earth-moving equipment.

There were also 14,000 Italian prisoners of war on the island who were banned under the Geneva Convention from carrying out works that would benefit the enemy. Freyberg wanted these men – poorly dressed and guarded by Greek soldiers – evacuated to POW camps in Egypt but although the officers were shipped off the other ranks remained on Crete, devouring valuable food along with his own useless mouths.

One of Freyberg's biggest headaches was the Greek Royal Family. Wavell had forgotten to mention when appointing him commander of Creforce that King George and several royal princesses, as well as the Greek Prime Minister and his Cabinet and their families were on Crete. The King had moved from the Villa Ariadne at Knossos to a villa near Canea, which was now officially the seat of the Greek Government. Freyberg, however, persuaded the King that the Royal Family should be evacuated to Egypt and the princesses and some of the other families departed.[13]

On 8 May, the King threw a cocktail party for Freyberg and his officers and the following day Freyberg reached an agreement with him that he and his government would depart on 14 May. Shortly afterwards, he received a cable from General Dill saying that the British War Cabinet strongly urged that the King and his ministers should stay in Crete, even if the island were attacked. The Foreign Office had advised that it would create a bad impression if he abandoned the last piece of unoccupied Greek territory, whereas his presence in Crete was having a beneficial effect on public opinion at home and in neutral countries.

Dill then placed Freyberg in an impossible position by declaring that neither the King nor the Greek political leaders were to be exposed to any undue risk and that *Freyberg* was to be the sole judge of what undue risk might be.[14] 'It seemed to me that in the circumstances the frontline – and Canea during the middle of May was certainly very much in the frontline – was not the right place for the King and the National Government,' Freyberg says. 'I did not see any reason to expose those important and gallant people to the risk of being killed or wounded or, far worse, captured.'

Nevertheless, Freyberg informed the King and Tsouderos that there was no reason for them to leave the island for the time being. He moved the royal party, along with General Heywood, Sir Michael Palairet and Lady Palairet, to a villa at Perivolia, a village just south of the capital, and ordered a platoon of the 18th Battalion under Lieutenant W. H. Ryan to form a royal bodyguard. Cairo was asked to have a warship or flying boat standing by to evacuate the King and his party if it became necessary. Jasper Blunt, the British military attaché, was put in charge of the whole group.

After attending the King's party on 8 May, George Vasey returned to his headquarters at Georgiopolis to find an angry letter from Colonel Cremor, known to his men as 'Old Bugger and Blast'. 'It has now been raining for nearly three hours,' he wrote.

> The troops under my command are without greatcoats and only about 12 per cent have a blanket. There are no waterproof capes at all. There are practically no medical supplies and I greatly fear both an epidemic and an outbreak of influenza or pneumonia.[15]

Cremor's complaints were passed to Creforce headquarters, which had ample supplies of clothing and blankets in its storehouses but no supplies were forthcoming. The attitude of the quartermaster's staff was 'completely incomprehensible' to AIF officers – but then they had never met Bruno Brunskill. Although Freyberg had visited all units and warned them that an air invasion was imminent, Brunskill's underlings carried on as though they were in Egypt and took a siesta from 1 pm to 5.30.[16] 'God knows who is in charge of supplies,' Michael Clarke wrote despairingly in his diary. 'Their main task is to guard them from the troops.'

It was only after the fighting had started that British and Greek troops, desperate for arms, ransacked the huge Venetian warehouses on Canea harbour and found British rifles and Italian machine guns which had not been distributed.[17]

There was further disquiet when the Australian veterans saw the fresh-faced Royal Marines who formed the advance party of the Mobile Naval Base Defence Organisation (MNBDO), the special unit trained to establish bases for the Royal Navy. The marines looked young and inexperienced and their officers had brought trunks, hat-boxes and a fine array of mess equipment to make life in this uncivilised post more tolerable.[18] The marines placed searchlights and light anti-aircraft guns in sand-bagged gun-pits around the shores of Suda Bay. Most of the lights were knocked out in moonlight bombing raids and the easily detected guns suffered the same fate.[19]

Despite the unwelcome attentions of the Luftwaffe, supply ships had continued to arrive in Crete's harbours, while fast warships stole in undetected by night to drop off vital supplies and personnel. In addition to the Royal Marines at Suda Bay, the 2/Leicesters arrived at Heraklion on 16 May and the 2/Argyll and Sutherland Highlanders three days later at Timbaki on the south coast.

The artillery pieces promised from Wavell's 'strong' Middle East stock turned out to consist of eight 3.7-inch howitzers and

39 elderly field guns, mainly French and Italian 75-mm and 100-mm pieces, minus their sights and with varying quantities of ammunition. Freyberg had to make do with these relics while more than 80 brand-new 25-pounders were left with reserve units in Egypt. Six heavy Fiat machine guns also arrived, but each one had a part missing and it was only by cannibalising four of the guns that two of them could be made to fire and then one could only fire single shots.[20]

On 9 May, four Italian 75s and some of the French guns were issued to Michael Clarke's regiment.

Horace Strutt and 'Old Bugger and Blast', Colonel Cremor, CO of 2/2nd Field Regiment, had called a high-level conference to discuss the allocation of the guns. They had supposedly been captured at Tobruk. Personally I rated them as Great War relics, or maybe some Greek uprising against the Turks last century. One box of shells read, 'Use by November 1916'. We were told that neither Strutt nor Cremor wanted the guns at any price, so they decided to toss for them. Strutt lost, so the French guns went to Ian Bessell-Browne and 6th Battery, while the four Italian guns were allocated to Dick Bale and 5th Battery. The Italian guns were dreadfully inferior to our lost 25 pounders. Their maximum range was only 7000 yards, compared to 12,500 (four miles as opposed to seven miles). The shells were terrible – five components had to be assembled. At least we had trucks of a sort to pull them.

The arrival of the guns enabled the men to quit 'the blasted composite infantry battalion'. The following day Colonel Strutt moved to the Georgiopolis area, south-east of Suda Bay, and B Troop followed him along the winding road through hills and ravines dotted with stunted palm trees and the occasional eucalypt. Between Suda and Vrissas the road darted inland towards stands of conifers flanking the White Mountains before winding its way north to the coast at Georgiopolis.

'We dug in and camouflaged the guns, three on flat ground near the beach and facing north out to sea, and the fourth on a hillock to the rear to give better elevation and hopefully a longer range,' Michael Clarke writes. 'We were told to cover sea and airborne landings and anti-tank defence. It felt that we were doing something useful for a change.'

The island's garrison now totalled 42,000 men, made up of 17,200 British, 11,000 Greeks, 7000 New Zealand and 6500 Australian troops. Although the British force was the largest, only 6400 of its total could be classified as combatants. As in Greece the Anzac component would do most of the fighting. Freyberg received an offer of help from an unlikely quarter when the convicts in Prison Valley wrote to him 'wholeheartedly putting ourselves under any service, dangerous or not, provided that the cause of our Allied effort is fulfilled'. Their offer was declined.[21]

On 11 May, Wavell sent Brigadier 'Chink' Dorman-Smith to Crete with the latest Ultra information, which Keith Stewart worked into an appreciation to be issued to all commanders down to battalion level. The one surviving copy of this document in Freyberg's possession shows that he now grasped the importance of the airfields. After outlining the German plan of attack, Stewart wrote, 'It will be noted that the entire plan is based on the capture of the aerodromes. If the aerodromes hold out, as they will, the whole plan will fail.' For good measure, he added that sea landings 'must not be overlooked; but they will be of secondary importance to those from the air'. In view of these comments, Freyberg's attitude in insisting on the bulk of his forces guarding the coast rather than the airfields becomes even more mystifying.[22]

At Georgiopolis, B Troop carried out a trial shoot with a gun aimed out to sea. 'There was much nervousness,' Michael Clarke says, 'as to whether the barrel might split open or the ancient crock blow itself up, so a long lanyard was attached to the trigger, the crew took cover, and Peter Cudmore pulled the lanyard. The gun fired okay but the round was a dud.'

Privately, Clarke wrote to his parents, 'My main desire now is to finish the war as soon as possible and return to Australia to take up farming in peace and quiet. Certain it is that I shall escape from the army as soon as peace is achieved and never again surrender my freedom of movement and action. When one sees the ancient cities of Greece lying in ruins, one realises the frightful destructiveness of war and the utter futility of it.'[23]

On 14 May, 16 battle-weary Mark VIB light tanks of the 3rd Hussars and six heavy Matilda tanks of 7th Royal Tank Regiment arrived at Suda Bay. It took a week to retrieve the light tanks after their transport ship took a direct hit and sank in shallow water. The Matildas were distributed two each to the Maleme, Retimo and Heraklion sectors. One tank made it only as far as Georgiopolis before breaking down. A ball race had been cut through, probably by saboteurs in Alexandria.

Paddy Leigh Fermor and Michael Forrester, two of the evacuees from the military mission to Greece, moved into a cottage overlooking Hospital Peninsula with Prince Peter, the King's cousin. During the day, the Prince went snorkelling in the crystal-clear waters of the little bay and at night, over Cretan specialties prepared by Marcos the cook, the three men discussed the likely timing of the German invasion. 'It was thought the invasion would take place on the 18th or on one of the next two days,' Forrester says. 'No one could pinpoint the source of the information but it stemmed, of course, from Ultra. Bearing that in mind, it's surprising how widely that piece of information was circulated.'[24]

One of the sources seems to have been Freyberg himself. On Saturday 17 May, he visited the 21st Battalion on Vineyard Ridge south of Maleme and, according to the unit's historian, announced 'the likely date for the attack. It was expected to come on Monday [20 May].'[25]

Thanks to Ultra, Freyberg was bang up to date. General Student had assembled a fleet of just over 500 Ju-52s on seven hastily prepared airfields in southern Greece but much to his chagrin a shortage of aviation fuel forced him to postpone Operation Mercury until 20 May to allow an oil tanker to sail down the Adriatic coast to Patras in Greece.[26]

That Saturday, while Freyberg was inspecting his troops, Student briefed his regimental and battalion commanders in the Grande Bretagne's 'hermetically sealed and shuttered' ballroom, where a huge map of Crete had been fastened to one wall.[27] The forces chosen to carry out Operation Mercury were divided into three groups: Group West under Major-General Eugen Meindl; Group Centre under Major-General Wilhelm Sussmann; and Group East under Lieutenant-General Julius Ringel. The groups were codenamed 'Komet', 'Mars' and 'Orion' respectively, and the landings were to be preceded by saturation bombing and strafing of troop and anti-aircraft gun positions.[28]

Group West (General Meindl): Two companies of the 1st Assault Regiment were to land in 27 gliders south of Maleme airfield to wipe out any gun positions that had survived the bombing, while nine more gliders carrying the headquarters' battle group landed on the bed of the Tavronitis River and captured its iron-girdered bridge. Within minutes of these landings, the regiment's main body – three battalions with more than 1850 troops – would be dropped by Ju-52s to capture the airfield, removing any obstacles from the runway and holding it open for airborne landings. Meindl would be reinforced by sea that afternoon by a battalion of Mountain troops landed on the beaches west of Maleme. Using captured transport such as civilian buses, he was to range as far west as Kastelli and, in the east, link up around Canea with Group Centre.[29]

Group Centre (General Sussmann): The 3rd Parachute Regiment (Reinforced) was to seize Canea and Suda to eliminate the main enemy headquarters, which was thought to be located in the capital, and dispose of any reserves which might be concentrated there. Two more companies of the 1st Assault

Regiment would land south and west of Canea and Suda Bay in 30 more gliders and suppress surviving guns. Five more gliders carrying Major-General Sussmann and his staff would follow with more airborne troops who, when reinforced by the 100th Mountain Regiment, would capture Canea, Suda village and Galatas. Eight hours after the first landings, the 2nd Parachute Regiment less one battalion was to capture Retimo town and airfield 50 kilometres east of Canea.

Group East (General Ringel): The three battalions of the 1st Parachute Regiment (Reinforced) and II Battalion of the 2nd Parachute Regiment were to seize Heraklion town and airfield, 65 kilometres east of Retimo. The runway would be held open for air-landed troops. Ringel's force would be reinforced by sea the following afternoon by a battalion of Mountain infantry. Student, however, denied Ringel the glory of going into action with his troops on Day 1. The initial assault on Heraklion would be led by Colonel Bruno Brauer of the 1st Parachute Regiment.[30]

The commanders were then briefed by Major Reinhardt of Student's intelligence staff. He stated that the British garrison on Crete consisted of no more than 5000 troops, with only 400 men at Heraklion and none at all at Retimo. All the New Zealanders and Australians from Greece had been evacuated to Egypt and there were no Greek troops on the island. Even by the notoriously low standards of German Intelligence, this was an incredibly inept performance.

Reinhardt further claimed that the Cretans were pro-Venizelist and therefore anti-Metaxas. He predicted that the Germans would receive an enthusiastic welcome. A pro-German fifth column would emerge uttering the password 'Major Bock'.[31] Indeed, Abwehr, the German secret service run by Admiral Wilhelm Canaris, had made an attempt to contact pacifist circles on the island but with little success.[32] However, Canaris told Student during a visit at the beginning of May that the island was weakly defended and that the population was willing to surrender without a fight.[33]

Like Reinhardt, Canaris had clearly failed to read the German appreciation of the Cretan character back in March which had concluded, 'In case of invasion account must be taken of obstinate resistance by the civilian population.'

German air reconnaissance was so poor that it had not only failed to locate Allied positions in the main areas of resistance but had designated the 7th General Hospital as a 'tented encampment'. The hospital consisted of three buildings – an officers' mess, a cookhouse and a storage hut – a number of marquees and an assortment of smaller tents. The roofs of the three buildings were painted with large Red Crosses and an even larger one was marked out in stones on the lawn between the mess and the sea. The marquees used as hospital wards were mostly grouped near the cookhouse and a large Red Cross banner was laid out on the ground among them.[34]

In the run-up to the invasion, eight bombs were dropped in the hospital area, killing four people and wounding four others; fortunately, 561 patients and the entire female nursing staff, including Mabel Johnson, had been evacuated in the hospital ship *Aba* on General Freyberg's orders on 15 May. 'The nurses were furious at being sent away when they knew that a battle was pending,' he says, 'but I could not agree to women being mixed up in the shambles that was about to commence.' The *Aba* was bombed and machine-gunned on her way to Alexandria and one person was killed and eight injured.[35]

On the evening of 18 May, German quartermasters provided the paratroopers with beer and brandy and the following day they got down to the serious business of cleaning their Schmeisser submachine guns, rifles and Spandau bipod machine guns. For the parachute drop, each man would wear a weatherproof padded overall, topped with a leather jerkin and a round crash helmet. He was issued with two days' rations, including chocolate, rusks, sugar, thirst-quenchers and Benzedrine tablets to combat tiredness. Every company had its own portable water-sterilising equipment and medical officers had tubes of blood for transfusions in the field. They would also carry supplies of a caffeine-sodium salicylate solution which could be injected to overcome extreme fatigue.[36]

Meanwhile, Freyberg had become quite bullish about his chances of holding the island. On 16 May, he sent the following cable to Wavell:

> I have completed plans for the defence of Crete and have just returned from a final tour of defences. I feel greatly encouraged by my visits. Everywhere all ranks are fit and morale is now high. All defences have been strengthened and positions wired as much as possible. We have 45 field guns in action with adequate ammunition dumped. Two infantry tanks are at each aerodrome. Carriers and transport still being unloaded and delivered. 2nd Battalion Leicesters have arrived and will make Heraklion stronger. I do not wish to seem over-confident but I feel that at least we will give an excellent account of ourselves. With help of Royal Navy I trust Crete will be held.

On the morning of 18 May, Patrick Leigh Fermor left Prince Peter's cottage to join Brigadier Chappel's staff at Heraklion as an intelligence officer. Michael Forrester, now promoted to captain, delivered some ammunition to the guns there and had dinner with his friend at a hotel in the town that night. 'I rose early next morning and saw a Henshall spotter aircraft flying slowly up the main street photographing everything,' Forrester says.

> It was sinister and foreboding. It flew with complete impunity because Brigadier Chappel had ordered no shooting at aircraft. It was this policy that led to the Germans suffering colossal

losses on the first day because they had no idea there were any anti-aircraft guns at Heraklion.

Forrester returned to the cottage that evening to discover from Marcos the cook that Prince Peter had joined the King at his villa near Perivolia.

That day, Churchill wrote to Freyberg:

> All our thoughts are with you in these fateful days. We are glad to hear of reinforcements which have reached you and strong dispositions you have made. We are sure that you and your brave troops will perform in deed[s] of lasting fame. Victory where you are would powerfully affect world situation. Navy will do its utmost.[37]

All defending troops were urged by Freyberg to launch swift counter-attacks – with the bayonet if necessary[38] – to reclaim any lost ground at the three airfields, of which Maleme was nominated as the most vital. The villages of Maleme and Pirgos were 15 kilometres west of Canea and the airfield was located a little further west between a sandy beach and the winding coast road. It consisted of nothing more than a runway and a tented RAF encampment between the east–west road and the Tavronitis River.

The runway ran parallel to the road and its western end almost reached the stony bed of the dried-up river. Here, the road curved around the southern edge of the RAF camp, past Kavkazia Hill, designated Hill 107, and over an iron bridge. The RAF had built a radar station, manned by 56 personnel, on high ground to the south of Hill 107. On the west bank of the river, a ridge commanded a view of the airfield from the west. This was the area that Freyberg had left unguarded.

Concerned about the gap in his defences, Brigadier Puttick suggested to Freyberg that the 1st Greek Regiment, stationed 25 kilometres west at the small port of Kastelli, should be moved on to the ridge. The permission of the Greek high command was secured but the move was cancelled because Freyberg thought it would be impossible for the Greeks to dig in before the Germans attacked.[39]

Freyberg later claimed that Wavell had forbidden him – in a letter dated 16 May which he destroyed after reading – to make any changes in his dispositions as to do so would jeopardise the security of Ultra. The greatest secret of the war was in his hands and, for that reason, he claimed his hands were tied. Freyberg's reasons for his lack of action do not stand up to scrutiny. Troops were on the move in many parts of the island, including Greek troops in Prison Valley and Australian units around Suda Bay. The Leicesters and Argylls had only just arrived on the island and were still moving into position. Moreover, most of the New Zealanders in the Maleme area were cleverly camouflaged in olive groves. To suggest that the German high command would make a connection between Ultra and the movement of a couple of hundred men at night into a position where they could hardly be seen from the air seems ludicrous. The acid test of Freyberg's explanation, of course, is in the action he took once the blow had fallen and Ultra was no longer an issue.

Colonel Andrew, commanding 22nd Battalion, was also concerned about the absence of any unified command at Maleme. The anti-aircraft armament at the airfield was controlled from the gun operations room at Canea; the Royal Marine gunners were responsible to General Weston; and the large numbers of RAF and Royal Navy personnel were under the control of their own senior commanders.

Brigadier Puttick had noticed the vulnerability of the guns during a visit to Andrew's battalion. In a note to Brigadier Hargest, he wrote: 'The AA guns at the aerodrome seem to me to be horribly exposed. Unless they are dug in and screened by bushes, etc., I'm afraid they won't last long.' Puttick spoke of raising the issue with Creforce or General Weston but, as in so many things, nothing was done.

On 19 May, the only aircraft on the island were four Hurricanes, three Gladiators and two Fulmars. That day, one of the Hurricanes was shot down over Maleme and the two Fulmars were destroyed on the ground. Freyberg told George Beamish that 'it would be painful to see these machines and their gallant young pilots shot down on the first morning'. With Churchill's agreement, the surviving aircraft were flown to Egypt.

Freyberg wanted to blow up the three runways but the Air Ministry insisted that the RAF intended to return to Crete as soon as possible. For that reason, all three fields had to be preserved. It still would have been a relatively simple matter for Freyberg to have blocked the runways with obstacles such as trees and boulders but he did nothing. 'Freyberg was not essentially a trained soldier,' Brigadier Brunskill opined. 'He was not even really an experienced peacetime soldier. He was put in a completely unfair position.'[40]

One man who did not share Freyberg's confidence that Crete would be held was Jimmy Hargest, a forlorn figure in baggy shorts and khaki sweater. 'I don't know what lies ahead,' he told Geoffrey Cox, the editor of the troops' newspaper *Crete News*, on the eve of battle. 'I know only that it produces in me a sensation I never knew in the last war. It is not fear. It is something quite different which I can only describe as dread.'[41]

Lieutenant Theo Stephanides, a doctor in the Royal Army Medical Corps, remembers a 'remarkably fine sunset that evening; the sun appeared to be sinking in a sea of blood'.[42]

CHAPTER 17

Icarus Descending

Crete's day of destiny – 20 May 1941, a Tuesday – dawned calm and clear. Through the early-morning light, the sound of cooks preparing breakfast reached the troops standing-to at Maleme airfield. A few minutes after 6 am, enemy bombers and fighters appeared overhead in greater numbers than ever before and attacked the airfield and surrounding hills, the built-up area of Canea, the anti-aircraft batteries and the road leading east and west. The daily 'hate', as the troops called these attacks, had begun.[1]

Exploding bombs showered the defenders with debris and great dust-clouds obscured the view of the anti-aircraft gunners. The airfield was defended by six mobile Bofors, four static Bofors, two 3-inch anti-aircraft guns and two 4-inch naval guns, some of which were knocked out by the Stukas before they could open fire. Unaware of Freyberg's decision to send the few remaining aircraft to Egypt, an Australian gunner manning a Bofors in a sand-bagged gun-pit on the airfield perimeter shouted to the hapless members of an RAF ground crew, 'Where's the bloody Air Force, you pommy bastards?'[2]

There was no braver man at Maleme than Squadron Leader Edward Howell – he had taken on 12 Messerschmitts in one of the last Hurricanes a few days earlier and shot down several – but he had no aircraft now and like everyone else he was obliged to seek shelter in a slit trench.

By seven o'clock, dozens of enemy bombers and fighters of von Richthofen's VIII Air Corps were bombing and strafing the areas that had been chosen for glider and parachute landings. Then, around half past seven, the planes departed and there was a lull. The troops climbed out of their trenches and ate their breakfast. Twenty minutes later, they were back under cover as the entire area occupied by the 5th Brigade's forward battalions came under an air attack even more ferocious than the first.

'The whole area was shrouded in thick choking dust,' Squadron Leader Howell says. 'We were covered in earth. Our eyes and mouths were full of grit. And still it went on.'³

Fifteen kilometres away at Creforce headquarters above Canea, General Freyberg was as stoical as ever. Earlier that morning, Monty Woodhouse had arrived at the quarry to deliver a message. The blitz had yet to start and Freyberg invited him to stay for breakfast on the veranda of his house overlooking the coast. 'The sky was exquisitely blue – a perfect summer's day,' Woodhouse says, 'but momentarily looking up, I was startled to see the sky full of gliders and parachutists. Freyberg did not let it spoil his breakfast. He looked up, grunted and remarked: "Well, they're on time!"'⁴

While the air attack was at its height, the first gliders swung in from the south-west over Maleme, their giant wings swishing through the air like evil birds of prey. They landed on the dry, rocky bed of the Tavronitis River, the dead ground that Freyberg had hesitated to protect for fear of exposing the Ultra secret. It was now his Achilles heel.

Freyberg walked out on to the hill at Creforce HQ to observe the German attack through his binoculars. The bombardment had cut all signal lines from Brigadier Puttick's headquarters south-west of Canea and Freyberg had heard nothing from that quarter for several hours. But he had the evidence of his own eyes to tell him that this was a most unusual battle. He admits he stood 'enthralled by the magnitude' of what he was witnessing.

> While we were still watching the bombers, we suddenly became aware of a strange sensation, a pulsation, a kind of throbbing in the air. Looking out to sea with my field glasses, I picked out hundreds of enemy transport planes, tier upon tier coming towards us. Here were the troop carriers with the loads we were expecting. We watched them circle counter-clockwise over Maleme aerodrome and then, when they were only two hundred feet above the ground, white specks suddenly appeared beneath them mixed with other colours as clouds of parachutists floated slowly to earth.[5]

It was still only a quarter past eight in the morning and these were just the first of 9530 parachute and glider troops to land on Crete that day.

Colonel Andrew, commander of the 22nd Battalion's 20 officers and 592 men, was a fighter at heart and his dander was up. Slightly wounded during the aerial bombardment at Maleme, he pulled a piece of shrapnel from his bleeding temple, cursed loudly and said, 'We'll go out and get these bastards when the bombing stops.'[6]

As the spearhead of his attack, General Meindl had sent in three groups of gliders carrying crack troops of the 1st Assault Regiment to silence the airfield's guns. The Luftwaffe tugs of Group West crossed the coast west of Maleme before releasing their gliders, which swung towards the airfield and skimmed low over the heads of the riflemen in A and B companies in their positions on and around Hill 107.[7]

The 14 gliders and 108 men of Lieutenant Wulf von Plessen's detachment came down in the broad estuary of the Tavronitis River a few hundred metres north of the iron bridge. The Germans expected an easy victory; they had no idea that the garrison contained an entire battalion of fit, young New Zealand troops to whom, in the words of one, 'action came as a relief – almost a grim joy – after cowering under cover for a fortnight of air raids'.[8]

The pilots touched down in the sand and shingle but could not stop their heavily laden craft from skidding into boulders or crashing into olive trees. There were many casualties. The New Zealanders dug in on the brush-strewn east bank of the Tavronitis and the slopes of Hill 107 were unable to see what was happening owing to the dense foliage and deep riverbanks but they could tell from the rending of wood and metal that some of the gliders had come to grief. One glider strayed as far away as the beach near Platanias, where its crew was killed by the Maoris of 28th Battalion.

Most of the gliders, however, landed around the airfield and their heavily armed troops – ten to each glider, including the pilot who was expected to fight as well – jumped out, formed up and went into action.[9] Plessen led his men towards the gun-pits at the western end of the airstrip and must have been surprised to discover that the gunners there had rifles but no ammunition. They were easily overcome.

The German commander then tried to cross the runway to reach the guns near the RAF camp on the south side of the airfield but encountered strong opposition from Captain Stan Johnson's C Company deployed around the perimeter and along the east–west road. Plessen was killed trying to link up with one of the other two German commanders, Major Walter Koch, whose detachment of 102 men in 15 gliders had landed on Hill 107 and along the riverbed.[10]

Two of Koch's gliders had crashed almost on top of the trench sheltering one of the RAF ground crew, Aircraftman

Marcel 'Lucky' Comeau of 33 Squadron. As the door of the nearest plane flew open, he was confronted by a German soldier in full battledress. Comeau 'fired and shot him at almost point-blank range. He fell backwards on to a second glider-trooper now standing behind him.' Comeau fired again and the second German 'spun round and collapsed, his body blocking the doorway'.[11]

Comeau's rifle then jammed and he ran up the hill, pursued by Koch's detachment which ran straight into the concentrated fire of Captain S. Hanton's A Company. Many of the German troops were killed and Koch himself was severely wounded in the neck.[12] The rest of his men retreated towards the iron bridge, where the nine gliders of the third commander, Major Franz Braun, had come down. Braun hadn't quite made it on to the battlefield himself – he was shot through the head and killed by a burst of machine-gun fire while still inside his glider – but his 72-strong detachment seized the bridge intact and overran a machine-gun post on the east bank.[13]

This attack forced the right wing of D Company, wedged between Hill 107 and the Tavronitis River at the iron bridge, to fall back behind an irrigation canal at the base of the hill. Quickly recovering, the New Zealanders kept the Germans at bay with heavy fire. Their commander, Captain Tom Campbell, suggested to the Royal Marines manning the two 4-inch naval guns on Hill 107 that their weapons might be turned on the enemy but this 'was rejected on the ground that the guns were sited for targets at sea'.

At 8.20 am, the air around Maleme, Galatas and Prison Valley reverberated with the sound of lumbering Ju-52s bearing thousands of paratroopers of Group West and Group Centre to their drop zones. Suddenly, the sky was filled with coloured parachutes that fell to earth like pieces of a broken rainbow – white for paratroopers, violet or pink for their officers, and red, green or yellow for weapon canisters, equipment and medical supplies.

Among the first to jump were three battalions of the 1st Assault Regiment – a total of 1850 troops – who were tasked with capturing Maleme airfield. The Ju-52s approached at a height of just 100 metres, too low for the surviving anti-aircraft batteries to hit but easy targets for the rifle companies and Bofors guns on the fringes of the runway. 'They were sitting ducks,' a sergeant of the Royal Marines said afterwards. 'You could actually see the shot breaking up the aircraft and the bodies falling out like potato sacks.'[14]

As we have seen, the guns in the key position on the west of the runway had been put out of action by Plessen's men but the Bofors still intact on the perimeter, fearful of giving their positions away, remained silent. It was left to the New Zealand infantry, armed with rifles and light machine guns, to defend the vital ground as hundreds of paras, firing their Schmeissers through the swirling dust, came down on the terraced vineyards and olive groves on the south side of the airfield. Others crashed through the roofs of houses in Pirgos and Maleme villages. Within minutes, dozens of silk canopies were draped over thickets of bamboo or dangled from telegraph wires. Michalis Doulakis, a villager at Maleme, recalls his uncle clubbing a paratrooper to death with his walking stick while the man was still entangled in his parachute harness.

On Hill 107, Captain Hanton ordered A Company to hold its fire until the paratroopers were 30 or 40 metres off the ground and then aim at their boots as their descent was deceptively swift. Only 22 paras landed alive in Hanton's area and those were quickly dispatched by bayonet. Hanton recalls seeing 'dozens of corpses on the ground or in the trees'. His men eagerly grabbed German stores – 'canisters of gear, food, motorcycles and even warm coffee from Hun flasks'.[15]

To the south-west of Pirgos, paratroopers overran one platoon of the 22nd Battalion's Headquarters Company, which was fighting as a rifle company. The platoon had been armed with just eight rifles and two bayonets and had no chance against a force armed with Spandau machine guns and grenades. The entire position was in danger of being overrun but the company commander, Lieutenant G.G. Beaven, rallied his men and beat off a series of fierce attacks. The bombing had severed all field telephone lines to battalion headquarters and Beavan's only means of reporting his predicament to Colonel Andrew was by runner.[16]

At 9 am, Freyberg dispatched an urgent signal to Wavell in Cairo: 'Attack started. Troops landed by parachute and glider. Estimate approximately 500 parachutists south-west of Canea. Approximately 50 troop-carrying aircraft. More now approaching. Situation obscure.'[17] Freyberg had no idea how many paratroop divisions were available to the German commanders; in fact, Student had just one such division among his total force of 22,750 assault troops. And it was suffering appalling losses.[18]

Anthony Madden, whose transport unit had been incorporated in the New Zealand Composite Battalion commanded by Major H. M. Lewis, was on guard duty on a ridge near Platanias. 'I was having breakfast of toast, marmalade and tea when the attack started,' he says.

> The fighters came in first and started strafing us. I kept my head down but some of our chaps got it down in the valley. They strafed us for half an hour or so to soften us up – it might have been longer but time didn't seem to mean much – and then the troop-carriers came in fairly low. The paratroopers tumbled out and their chutes opened straight away. A lot of them copped it on the way down in the first few minutes.[19]

These were probably the paras of II Battalion of the Assault Regiment, who had landed on the rising ground south of the Maleme–Platanias road believing it to be free of enemy troops. Instead, they found themselves in the middle of Brigadier

Hargest's reserve, the 21st and 23rd Battalions, who promptly killed two-thirds of them.

'Suddenly, they came among us,' Captain Carl Watson, commanding the 23rd's A Company, says. 'I was watching the 21st Battalion area and a pair of feet appeared through a nearby olive tree. They were right on top of us. Around me rifles were cracking. I had a Tommy gun and it was just like duck-shooting.'[20]

With all of their officers dead, the remaining paras in this group were unable to launch their intended attack on the airfield from the east or to make their way towards Canea to join up with Group Centre. They had no alternative but to locate as many canisters as they could and dig in. Many of the paras stripped off their suffocating jumpsuits to escape the burning heat of the rising sun.

Colonel Andrew had set up his battalion headquarters in a trench on the south slope of Hill 107. He had a radio set – a No 18 with fading batteries – but his companies had neither receivers nor transmitters. Clouds of smoke and dust also prevented his signallers from making visual contact with his units and his runners encountered pockets of German troops and were never seen again.

Anticipating such an eventuality, Brigadier Hargest had called a conference with Andrew, Lieutenant-Colonel John Allen of the 21st Battalion and Lieutenant-Colonel David Leckie of the 23rd in Maleme's little white stucco courthouse on 11 May so that, in his words, the defence 'would be properly co-ordinated and confusion avoided when an actual attack takes place'. If one of the commanders needed assistance and all other means of communication failed, he could summon help by firing white-green-white Very flares into the sky.[21]

Although Andrew had no way of assessing the progress of the fighting, his men had actually won the first gruelling round in the

Battle of Crete but conditions were grim. The heat in the trenches was intense. Water bottles had run dry and there was nothing to wash away the stench of cordite or the smoke and dust clogging eyes, throats and lungs. The eight Vickers machine guns deployed among his companies had almost run out of ammunition. And now a new menace was developing in the undefended ground to the west, where glider troops had clambered on to the fateful ridge beyond the Tavronitis River. At 8.30 am, they were joined by parachutists from Captain Walther Gericke's IV Battalion, who landed unopposed in the vineyards, olive groves and ravines west of the river. Armed with heavy weapons, including mortars, anti-tank guns and mountain howitzers, they were capable of doing serious damage to the New Zealand defenders.

General Meindl, in his 50th year, had jumped with this group and was now in command of all German forces in the Maleme area. His units had been separated from the start and he had difficulty reuniting them. From his position on the west bank of the Tavronitis, he had no more idea than Colonel Andrew about what was happening all over the battlefield, but he quickly saw that his best chance was to exploit the capture of the iron bridge and develop an attack that would take Hill 107 from the north-west.[22]

Meindl then made a near-fatal mistake: he waved a signal flag in the direction of where Koch was supposed to be and was promptly shot through the hand by a New Zealand sniper. The general was so startled that he rose to his feet and was seriously wounded in the chest by a burst of machine-gun fire.[23] As he was carried to the regimental aid station, he gave the order for Captain Gericke to go into action. Reinforced by one company of Major Edgar Stenzler's II Battalion – which had landed even further west – the Germans advanced across the river, dodging from pylon to pylon of the iron bridge.

Their first objective was the RAF camp on the east side. Here, RAF and Fleet Air Arm personnel, 'a motley collection', had been armed with rifles to defend the area but had dispersed for breakfast and had then been scattered by the bombing.

According to one of their number, 'We didn't know where our own people were; we didn't know where the enemy were; many people had no rifles. Many people had rifles and no ammunition.'[24]

Squadron Leader Howell rounded up some of these men and deployed them among the New Zealanders. The Germans, meanwhile, had captured the RAF operations office, where they found a set of top-secret codebooks and Freyberg's order of battle revealing the strength of his forces. Returning to the camp with the intention of destroying the codebooks, Howell was shot and left for dead in a pool of blood. 'I craved for water as I had never craved for anything,' he says. 'I was alone and dying from loss of blood and thirst. It was a race to see which won. I only desired the race to end.'[25]

At 10 am, Colonel Andrew's signallers succeeded in getting his temperamental radio set to work. He reported to Jimmy Hargest at brigade HQ in his farmhouse near Platanias that hundreds of German troops had landed in the riverbed and further west. While Andrew was making his report, three Germans who had taken a number of prisoners around the RAF camp were forcing them up the hill as a screen. 'Very soon a large party of around 40 men appeared with hands above their heads, many terror-stricken, all yelling and pleading with us not to shoot at the enemy but to let them come on or they would be shot in the back,' Sergeant Frank Twigg says. 'The party included RAF men and some members of our battalion.'[26]

One of the prisoners was Gordon Dillon, a provost sergeant. 'When any defences were seen, the Jerries just took one or two of us and pushed us ahead,' he says. 'The Jerry doing it put a Luger in your back and just pointed. It was easy to understand.'

When the New Zealanders realised that the prisoners were being used as human shields, there were cries of 'shame' and although the Germans kept close behind their captives, 'some damn good shots picked the three Jerries off'. This was the signal for firing from both flanks. 'In a moment nothing but an untidy row of dead bodies remained . . . [but] over half the prisoners were also dead.'[27]

Meanwhile, Group Centre was faring no better than General Meindl's Group West in its mission to seize Canea and Suda. At 4.30 that morning, Major-General Wilhelm Sussmann, invoking the spirit of Mars – the Roman god of war after whom his group had been named – flew into battle in one of Student's flimsy gliders.

As his tug plane crossed the Bay of Athens, the glider carrying Sussmann and six members of his staff was overtaken by a faster Heinkel He-III bomber on its way to pulverise the island's defences. Buffeted by the bomber's slipstream, the glider bucked violently, snapping the towing cable. As the pilot struggled to regain control, the wings broke off and the fuselage spiralled down to crash on the little island of Aegina. Everybody on board was killed.[28] Even before he had landed in Crete, command of Centre Group had passed to the senior surviving officer, Colonel Richard Heidrich, commander of the 3rd Parachute Regiment.

Two glider detachments from the 1st Assault Regiment had been allocated to Centre Group to prepare the way for the arrival of Heidrich's paratroopers. At 8.15, Lieutenant Alfred Genz, with 90 men in nine gliders, flew over Canea with the intention of suppressing the guns at Mournies, south of the capital, and seizing the nearby radio station. The guns, however, blew two of the gliders out of the air and a third was hit as it landed, killing most of the crew.

Genz and his remaining 50 men overran a troop of anti-aircraft gunners at a crossroads on the Canea–Mournies road. All but seven of the garrison were said to have been shot. One survivor claims that the 180 gunners had only a dozen rifles among them and were overwhelmed by just ten men who then 'lined up their unarmed adversaries and shot them to death against the sandbags'.[29]

Genz advanced towards the radio station but found his way blocked by members of the Rangers Battalion, backed by the Bren-carriers of the Welch Regiment, the strongest element of the Canea garrison. With his force now reduced to 34 men, he dug in to await the arrival of Heidrich's paratroopers.[30]

The second glider detachment – 150 men in 15 gliders under Captain Gustav Altmann – was supposed to have knocked out the guns on the Akrotiri Peninsula. However, Altmann's pilots mistook that vast outcrop of rock and forest for the Rodopos Peninsula and were almost over Retimo before they discovered their mistake. Turning back towards the target, the gliders ran into heavy anti-aircraft flak. Several crashed short of their landing zones and others broke up when they hit the rocky crest of the peninsula. One group captured a gun emplacement near the tomb of the venerated Eleftherios Venizelos only to discover it was a dummy.[31] It was some hours before General Student learned that Sussmann, Plessen and Braun were dead, that Meindl and Koch had been wounded and that his invasion was balanced on a knife-edge.

CHAPTER 18

Hospital Horror

The Canea–Galatas–Prison Valley sector was the province of the newly formed 10th New Zealand Brigade, containing all the 'odds and sods' of the New Zealand Expeditionary Force. Following Brigadier Inglis' arrival from Egypt to take over the 4th Brigade, Colonel Howard Kippenberger had been placed in charge of these improvised units, in which 'battledress' usually meant a steel helmet and a pair of shorts.

The 10th Brigade, ranging from the Divisional Cavalry (minus their armoured cars) to artillerymen, drivers, cooks and the stalwart members of the Divisional Petrol Company all fighting as infantry, plus the 2300-strong 6th and 8th Greek Battalions, had replaced the 4th Brigade around Galatas, while that brigade had gone into reserve near Canea.

Kippenberger disposed most of his forces around Galatas and positioned the rest along a road running south-west from Canea to the village of Alikianou eight kilometres away. The Aghia prison was located halfway along this road and, a further kilometre on, there was a reservoir and powerhouse. Here, Kippenberger placed the 194-strong Divisional Cavalry, now known as 'Russell Force' after its commanding officer, Major John Russell. Russell organised his men into three squadrons and settled down to defend the north and west sides of the reservoir opposite Pink Hill which, along with three other mounds, Cemetery Hill, Wheat Hill and Ruin Hill, controlled the approaches to Galatas. Pink Hill had been named by Kippenberger after the pink dwelling on its crest which had become his battle headquarters. Its defenders were the Petrol Company under their inspirational, Irish-born commander Captain Sean McDonagh.[1]

That morning, Kippenberger had been in his two-storey villa at Galatas when a fighter roared down the main street shooting up everything in its path. He hurriedly finished shaving and looked out of the window. There were some aircraft swooping over the road to Canea but 'nothing appeared imminent' so he sat down to breakfast under the trees in his garden near the village square. He was grumbling that his daily bowl of porridge hadn't been properly cooked when four gliders passed silently overhead. Leaping to his feet, Kippenberger shouted, 'Stand to your arms!' and dashed upstairs for his rifle and binoculars.[2]

At 8.30 am, Colonel Heidrich's parachute troops began landing at various points in Kippenberger's sector, although not necessarily the correct ones. Major Ludwig Heilmann's III Battalion missed its dropping zone to the east of Galatas and was immediately in trouble. 'The moment we left the planes,' Lieutenant Karl Neuhoff says, 'we were met with extremely heavy small-arms fire. From my aircraft we suffered particularly heavy casualties and only three men reached the ground unhurt. Those who had jumped first, nearer to Galatas, were practically all killed.'[3]

Heilmann's 12th Company landed with I Battalion near the low white rectangular buildings of the civilian prison at Aghia, while Headquarters and 9th Companies touched down south-east of Galatas. Here, they encountered the 6th Greek Battalion armed with just three rounds per man. A large supply of ammunition had arrived some days earlier but their colonel had refused to issue it to his troops. In a matter of minutes, the Greeks were put to flight and their ammunition dump seized. The Germans then fought their way up Cemetery Hill, a treeless mound in front of Galatas, in what was to be the most significant German success of the morning.

Over on the coast, Michael Forrester was shaving when he looked north 'and there approaching over the sea was a simply vast concentration of aircraft moving directly towards the island on a very wide front. Very soon there were parachutes dropping on every side of where I was looking, particularly on the British military hospital.'

At 9.30 am, the 10th Company of III Battalion, commanded by Lieutenant Nagele, stormed the area marked as 'tented encampment' on all Operation Mercury maps. Some of the tents on Hospital Peninsula had been set ablaze during the bombing and others were riddled with machine-gun fire. 'They strafed up and down our lines for two hours,' says Lance Corporal Allan Robinson of the 6th New Zealand Field Ambulance which was located across a clearing from the hospital at the Galatas turn-off. 'To say that I was scared would be an understatement.'[4] Patients who could walk hobbled to slit trenches, while some of the bed-ridden were wounded by gunfire or shrapnel.

To his dismay, Nagele discovered that rather than a military barracks he had captured a hospital full of sick and wounded. 'We were all herded out of the trenches by paratroopers and were marched to the roadway where we were made to sit down with our hands on our heads,' says Alf Creed, a New Zealand driver who was being treated for scabies. 'When the Jerry had rounded us up, he tried to ask questions, first in French, then in every language but English. One dag called out, "Ask in good down-under language, Heine," and was promptly knocked about by another German. I don't think he knew what was said but reacted to our laughter.'[5]

The patients were then lined up in fours and marched over to the 6th Field Ambulance. As they arrived, several paratroopers opened fire on some trees from which a sniper had just shot one of their men. At that moment, Lieutenant-Colonel John Plimmer, the unit's military surgeon, rose out of one of the slit trenches. He had been wounded and his arm was in a sling so he moved awkwardly. As Creed watched, one of the Germans opened fire and shot the doctor.[6] Allan Robinson, who also witnessed the shooting, says, 'I'd just got out of the slit trench, hands on my head, when the next thing I heard was bang! Crack! A shot. [Dr Plimmer] had put his arm down to help himself out and they must have thought that he was reaching for his pistol and they shot him. He just went back into the slit trench. He didn't die straight away. We tried to comfort him but he died.'[7]

Meanwhile, most of Major Friedrich von der Heydte's I Battalion touched down safely in an undefended area around the jail in Prison Valley. Its aristocratic commander had the indignity of being dumped in a tree at the edge of the Alikianou reservoir. Disentangling himself, Baron von der Heydte went in search of his men, who failed to recognise him and fired several shots which, fortunately for him, missed. Von der Heydte then set off along Prison Valley to attack the hills to the east, which would take him through Perivolia to Mournies, where Genz's men were dug in awaiting reinforcement.[8]

At the same time, Lieutenant Roy Farran of the 3rd Hussars was heading towards Galatas in his light tank, one of the 'battered, ancient hulks' from the desert which had no cooling system for its guns and no radio. Coming under fire from snipers hidden in an olive grove, the 20-year-old machine-gunned three Germans and when five more parachutists came out with their hands up he hesitated only briefly. 'I was not in any mood to be taken in by any German tricks,' he says. 'I ordered the gunner to fire. Three dropped dead, but two others managed to limp away into the trees. I do not think that I would make a practice of shooting prisoners, but Crete was different, and in the heat of the moment I had not had time to think.'[9]

Back on the coast, Michael Forrester armed himself with a rifle and fought his way across the Canea–Maleme road, where he joined up with the Composite Battalion of Kippenberger's 10th Brigade. The New Zealanders were keyed up, having just wiped out a group of paratroopers who had landed north of Galatas. The siege at the hospital, however, was still in progress. Once during the morning, a carrier from the 18th Battalion appeared but was unable to work out what was happening and turned back to report to Brigadier Inglis at 4th Brigade headquarters.

Not long afterwards, a tank rumbled on to the scene. This was Roy Farran's Mark VI, which he had driven out to the hospital in search of water to cool the red-hot barrels of his machine guns. Farran knew nothing about the seizure of the hospital but learned from a wounded New Zealand soldier, 'The bastards shot up the tents in the hospital. Nothing's too bad for those bastards. Do what you can, chum.'

In the event, Farran could do little to help, but the very sight of armour was enough to panic Lieutenant Nagele. Rounding up 500 patients, many barefoot and in their pyjamas, he marched them down the road towards Galatas with the intention of linking up with elements of Group Centre in Prison Valley. Lance Corporal Robinson says the patients were told they were 'going to be used as a shield to go into some of the lines held by the New Zealanders'.[10]

Further south, Lieutenant Neuhoff had been ordered to capture Galatas to open up the road to Canea from the south. At 10 am, he launched an attack on its main bastion, Pink Hill. Hundreds of paratroopers were landing all over the valley as Kippenberger climbed up the hill to his battle headquarters, which had been left unguarded. Arriving breathless, he was about to enter the gap in the cactus hedge in front of the pink house when a burst of machine-gun fire trimmed the cactus on either side of him but somehow missed his body. He jumped sideways and rolled down the bank, twisting his ankle. Whimpering a little, he climbed up to the back of the house, saw his man through a window and shot him through the head. 'The silly fellow was still watching the gap in the hedge,' he says.[11]

Lieutenant Neuhoff got halfway up Pink Hill with his 7th Company without opposition. 'Suddenly, we ran into heavy and very accurate rifle and machine-gun fire,' he says. 'The enemy had held their fire with great discipline and had allowed us to approach well within range before opening up.'[12] The Petrol Company fought with great tenacity, killing or wounding half of the attacking force at a cost of 35 casualties to themselves, including Captain McDonagh, who was shot through the heart by a German machine-gunner.[13]

By now, Colonel Heidrich, the commander of Group Centre, had landed in Prison Valley. Realising the importance of the Galatas heights, he sent three companies under Major Heilmann towards the sounds of battle on Pink Hill to press the attack against the Petrol Company.[14]

At Maleme shortly after 10 am, Colonel Andrew set off from his entrenched battalion HQ to see the situation for himself. He made a valiant effort to reach Headquarters Company at Pirgos but was driven back by heavy mortar fire. He then tried to get through to B Company (Captain Ken Crarer) on the eastern side of Hill 107, with the same result.[15]

At 10.55, he returned to battalion headquarters, where he reported to Hargest that he had no communication with his companies. He asked whether the nearest battalion – David Leckie's 23rd Battalion at Dhaskaliana, one kilometre east of Pirgos – could contact his men there. In response, Leckie sent one platoon towards the village which discovered that Beaven's men were firing at every movement. Unable to make contact, the platoon returned to its company lines but no message was sent to Andrew to say that the Pirgos position was being rigorously defended. Andrew therefore concluded that his men had been overrun.[16]

Meanwhile, the 11th Company of Heilmann's III Battalion had landed around Perivolia. Many of his paras were dispatched by the defenders or by Cretan civilians armed with axes and spades. None of the Cretans seemed to have heard of the mysterious 'Major Bock'. The Germans complained bitterly to their officers that they had to fight bands of *francs-tireurs* – irregular combatants – as well as the British garrison.[17] The survivors concentrated around Perivolia and later linked up with von der Heydte's I Battalion.[18]

As he had said himself, Freyberg had known the exact date of the German invasion but he seems to have forgotten that he was personally responsible for assessing the risk this might pose to the King. With enemy activity all around Perivolia, that risk was now very great. Indeed, King George narrowly escaped capture when 40 German paratroopers dropped near his garden. The Germans had no idea that the King and his Prime Minister were in residence in the smart villa, now known at Creforce HQ as 'The King's House'.

Lieutenant Ryan, leader of the royal bodyguard, hustled the King out of the house and with Tsouderos, Jasper Blunt, Prince Peter, General Heywood and the rest of the party headed for the White Mountains with the aim of reaching the south coast. Their departure was so abrupt that the King left behind private papers which alerted the Germans to his presence on Crete.

At one point, the royal party was pinned down by rifle fire from a detachment of Cretan volunteers. Prince Peter shouted at them in Greek to cease fire but the Cretans replied, 'Germans also speak Greek and wear Greek uniforms.' Fortunately, they recognised their King and he passed safely through their lines. The party was picked up by the destroyers *Decoy* and *Hero* on the night of 22/23 May and taken to Alexandria.

Further west at Kastelli, the 1st Greek Regiment – which

should have been defending the west bank of the Tavronitis River – was heavily engaged with an advance force of 72 paratroopers. Lieutenant Peter Murbe had been ordered to land east of the little port to secure the area for the landing of the II Battalion of the Assault Regiment.[19]

Major Geoff Bedding, the senior New Zealand adviser to the Greek Regiment, had formed his raw recruits into two battalions and it was one of these poorly armed formations that took on the Germans. Hearing the sound of gunfire, Cretan villagers, carrying whatever weapons came to hand, rallied to the assistance of their compatriots. With little thought of their own survival, they fell upon the Germans, knifing and clubbing them to death.[20]

The surviving paras ran for their lives into a farmhouse and opened fire through the windows with machine guns. Major Bedding advised the Greek soldiers, now armed with captured weapons, to besiege the property and let hunger and thirst force the enemy out. The Cretans, however, stormed the farmhouse and overwhelmed the defenders by sheer force of numbers. The Germans had machine guns that could fire at the rate of 300 rounds a minute, five different types of grenade and 2000 rounds of tracer and armour-piercing ammunition per man, yet they were, 'in the space of a few hours, defeated by the valour of those whose soil they had attacked'.[21]

By the time Bedding was able to bring the killing to an end, Murbe and 53 of his men had been slaughtered. The survivors were driven in the school bus to the Kastelli police station, where they were incarcerated for their own protection.[22]

The Cretans would pay a high price for their reckless courage. When the Germans overran the Kastelli area on 27 May, they found the bodies of paratroopers who had been knifed or clubbed to death. Assuming they had been tortured and the bodies mutilated, more than 200 Kastelli men were lined up and shot.

*

At the Hotel Grand Bretagne, General Student was receiving only sporadic reports from Crete but he concluded from these that his men had taken control of Maleme airfield. 'My early impressions were that the start of the operation was favourable,' he says. Von Richthofen had reported – wrongly – that his morning bombardment had destroyed the defences at Maleme and Galatas, while the Luftwaffe pilots falsely claimed that the paratroopers had been dropped in the correct zones with little opposition.[23]

Student ordered Captain Albert Snowadzki, head of his airfield service company, to fly to Maleme in a Ju-52 to clear the runway for the landing of the 5th Mountain Division. When he reached Maleme, Snowadzki spotted a large swastika flag laid out on the western perimeter of the airfield. Assuming the airfield was in German hands, he ordered the pilot to land but as the Ju-52 touched down it was hit by rifle and machine-gun fire from three sides. Streams of tracer ripped into the fuselage and shattered the Perspex windscreen. Snowadzki's pilot hastily opened throttle and the badly damaged aircraft lurched into the air and returned to Greece.[24]

Meanwhile, the hostages from the 7th General Hospital had been herded over rough, broken country by the paratroopers of Heilmann's 10th Company. The temperature had risen steadily throughout the morning and many of the patients were thirsty and distressed. At times, the column came under sniper fire, although it was impossible to tell who was doing the shooting. The straggling line of prisoners travelled more than a kilometre without finding any sign of the battalion of parachutists whom Lieutenant Nagele hoped to join. In fact, those troops had descended in the lines of the 19th New Zealand Battalion and had either been killed or driven off southwards.[25]

In the early afternoon, the column halted at the top of a hill from which the paratroopers could look down on Prison Valley for signs of their comrades. They took up positions to the left and right of a low stone wall, while the prisoners collapsed on the ground. Soon afterwards, a New Zealand patrol from the 19th Battalion was seen making its way through a plantation of olive trees. One of the New Zealanders was heard to say, 'There are no bloody Huns down here.'

Keeping their guns trained on their captives, the Germans allowed the patrol to pass unhindered and the patients' hopes sank. Minutes later, however, the New Zealanders retraced their steps and this time one of them fired a random shot. A nervous Luftwaffe pilot, who had been a patient in the hospital after his aircraft was shot down, returned fire.

The New Zealand patrol deployed for action and began exchanging fire with the Germans. 'They started firing straight through us,' Allan Robinson says. 'The 19th Battalion had a Bren-gun [which they] put on a fixed trace and fired. I got behind a decent-sized olive tree and bits of bark [were] flying around.'[26] Inevitably, some of the patients were hit. The New Zealanders only realised that hundreds of wounded were present when the patients started directing their fire towards the paratroopers. 'I cannot praise too highly,' said a British officer among the patients, 'the way in which the New Zealand troops developed their attack with the utmost regard for our safety.'

Some of the New Zealanders outflanked the wall, while their marksmen picked off the paratroopers one by one until only two remained. Working in from the rear, Greek troops finished them off.[27] German losses were very heavy: most of the company who had attacked the hospital had been killed in the course of the day's fighting. Allied estimates put the number at nearly 200.[28]

After the war, an inquiry was held by the New Zealand Army to investigate claims that the Germans had used hospital patients as a screen. 'Apart from a few cases of bad behaviour which can be explained as due to the nervous excitability of individuals,' the inquiry report says, 'the paratroops do not seem to have behaved themselves worse than might be expected of worried men in an awkward position, not sure where the defenders were or where they were themselves.'

Presumably, the cold-blooded murder of Colonel Plimmer was one of the cases of 'bad behaviour'.[29] The Germans, the report continued, did not push their captors ahead of them, but moved them as a column surrounded by guards. Nobody seems to have asked why the Germans had found it necessary to remove the patients from the hospital in the first place.

By now, the barrage laid down with mortars and howitzers by General Meindl's men on the Tavronitis ridge was blowing great divots out of Hill 107 and causing consternation among the forward platoons of Colonel Andrew's A Company. Some were forced to move back even beyond battalion headquarters on the south slope.

At this point, a mystery arises over the evidence of Major H. H. Thomason of the 23rd Battalion. 'Colonel Andrew came to our Battalion headquarters in person and asked for help,' he says.

> He was first guided to me by one of my men. I knew Les Andrew well, he and I were good friends. He was very shaken and disturbed and I personally took him down to Battalion headquarters. I don't know the outcome of his visit except that his request was not granted. This took place fairly early in the afternoon. I cannot state the exact time.[30]

There had been bad blood between the 22nd and 23rd Battalions in the past, 'an odd hostility towards one another which sprang from old antipathies between earlier commanders'.[31] Nevertheless, it seems inconceivable that Colonel Leckie rejected a personal plea from a fellow officer who had risked his life to make it. Whatever the truth of that strange incident, Andrew was back at his HQ at 2.55 pm, when he reported to

Hargest that 'position was fairly serious as enemy had penetrated his headquarters'; at 3.50, 'left flank had given way but position was believed to be in hand'.

Andrew appealed for a counter-attack to relieve the pressure. Hargest, however, maintained that the 23rd Battalion was engaged in heavy fighting and could not be detached. In fact, the 23rd's area had been cleared of paratroopers since 11.40 that morning.[32]

Hargest simply did not know, or perhaps understand, what was happening to the units in his brigade. His headquarters was eight kilometres from the airfield and had been chosen to enable him to deal with an amphibious landing as well as the airborne attack. Despite his 'properly co-ordinated defence', he had already signalled Leckie at 2.25, 'Will not call on you for counter-attacking unless position very serious. So far everything is in hand and reports from other units satisfactory.' One wonders by what stretch of the imagination Hargest could have interpreted Andrew's increasingly frantic messages as 'satisfactory'. The embattled commander at Maleme was left to fight on alone.[33]

As a last desperate measure, Andrew fired off his white-green-white Very flares to summon help and sent in his two Matilda tanks, accompanied by his own small infantry reserve and a group of armed RAF men – a total of 26 men – to try to halt the surge across the river. Captain Johnson of C Company asked one of the tank commanders how he could communicate with him. He was told to press a bell at the back of the tank and the commander would open his turret. 'When the counter-attack started, contact was attempted with the tank crews,' Johnson says. 'Nobody answered the bell.'[34]

The commander of one tank turned back after discovering his turret wouldn't traverse and that he'd taken the wrong ammunition into battle. The second tank made its way as far as the riverbed, where it headed for the iron bridge and crushed a mortar crew dug in under one of the pylons. Fired on from three directions without noticeable effect, the Matilda carried on for another 300 metres but then became stranded on some rocks and had to be abandoned.[35]

So far, Group Centre had failed to take any of its objectives except the futile capture of the 'tented encampment'. The British garrison at Perivolia and Mournies, which had repulsed Lieutenant Genz's assault, had been reinforced by the 2/8th Battalion (Major Arthur Key) from Brigadier Vasey's force at Georgiopolis.[36]

Sensing that the Germans were vulnerable, Howard Kippenberger asked Puttick for permission to mount a strong counter-attack to recapture the prison and clear Prison Valley of German troops. Inglis was also planning a thrust along Prison Valley to dispose of Heidrich's force and then swing right through the hills to eliminate Group West.[37]

It was a simple plan and there was no shortage of manpower to achieve it. During the day, Freyberg had placed three additional battalions – the 18th, 19th and 20th – under Puttick's command and these troops were all available. But Puttick, like Hargest and Freyberg, believed implicitly that he faced a grave threat from an amphibious landing. After prevaricating for some hours and then consulting Freyberg, he refused to authorise Kippenberger and Inglis' plans. The Germans were left to re-group and recover.

Colonel Andrew was having exactly the same trouble getting Jimmy Hargest to send help from the 21st and 23rd Battalions. He had had no response to his Very signals which the 23rd Battalion's observers must have missed in the dust and smoke rising over Maleme.[38] Andrew now assumed that his Headquarters Company at Pirgos, C Company around the airfield, and D Company nearest the river, had been wiped out. He feared that A and B Companies would meet the same fate when the Messerschmitts and the Stukas launched their dawn attacks as a prelude to a massive attack by the paratroopers gathering on the west side of the airfield.

According to the war diary of 5th Brigade headquarters, Andrew spoke to Brigadier Hargest at 6 pm and informed him of the failure of his tank attack. He requested permission to withdraw his men from Hill 107 to join B Company on its tree-lined ridge to the east of the hill. Over the crackling airwaves, Hargest replied, 'Well, if you must, you must.'[39] With those six words, he virtually signed Crete's death warrant. Only the strongest possible show of force could now prevent the enemy from flying troops and supplies into Maleme airfield.

PART IV

Wrath of Zeus

CHAPTER 19

Barbaric Beauty

At 9 am on 20 May, Lieutenant-Colonel Ian Campbell, commander of Retimo Force, saw 14 Ju-52s, each towing a glider, approach the ancient Venetian town. Campbell's positions stretched in a ten-kilometre arc along the coast from Retimo to the airfield and on to the little village of Stavromenos. Just as his men steeled themselves for an airborne attack, the aircraft veered west towards Canea and Maleme. Campbell had no anti-aircraft guns at all and there was nothing he could do except wait for his turn to be attacked.

The gliders were those of Captain Gustav Altmann's detachment that had overshot the Akrotiri Peninsula and, although Campbell had no way of knowing it, their appearance in his sector signified that General Student's plan for his attacks on Retimo and Heraklion was running late. The German commander had allowed just three hours for his aircraft to turn around on the Greek airfields for the second wave of attacks and everything had gone wrong.

Quite apart from the dozens of aircraft that had failed to return or had been damaged or had broken down, the dust clouds over his rudimentary airstrips were thicker than ever. Fire engines had been brought in to hose down the runways but the water simply evaporated in the 40-degree heat. Many damaged aircraft had crashed on landing, creating dangerous obstacles, and refuelling had taken longer than had been anticipated. Paratroopers waiting to board the Ju-52s were ordered to strip down to their shorts and manhandle 40-gallon fuel drums over to their aircraft.[1]

The second wave finally reached Retimo at 4 pm when 20 Dorniers and Messerschmitt ME-110s bombed and machine-gunned the area round the airfield in advance of the landing by the 2nd Parachute Regiment (less one battalion), commanded by Colonel Alfred Sturm. Campbell's policy of passive air defence coupled with effective camouflage during earlier raids now paid off. The air-crews of von Richthofen's strike force had virtually no idea where the troops or their guns were located.

The airfield was eight kilometres east of Retimo, sitting on a coastal shelf 100 metres from a shingle beach. Overlooking the runway was a narrow ridge running parallel to the sea, with Hill A at the eastern end and Hill B at the western end. Campbell's headquarters were on Hill D, which dominated the area from the south.

The terrain was thickly covered with olive groves and terraced vineyards and rutted with dry gullies in one of which Campbell concealed two Matilda tanks of the 7th Royal Tank Regiment. He placed his own battalion, the 2/1st, supported by artillery and machine guns, on Hill A and Major Ray Sandover's 2/11th Battalion, similarly supported, on Hill B. The infantry were seeded with two machine-gun platoons of the 2/1st Machine Gun Battalion, elements of Major Ian Bessell-Browne's 6th Battery of the 2/3rd Field Regiment, and one section of the 2/8th Field Company, making a grand total of 1300 men.

The Australians had plenty of small arms but ammunition was limited; there were only five rounds for each anti-tank rifle, 80 bombs for each of the four 3-inch mortars and 16 belts of ammunition for each of the four Vickers machine guns.[2] Bessell-Browne's 90 gunners were equipped with four 100-mm Italian guns and four 75-mm guns with no sights.

Campbell also had 2300 Greek soldiers of the 4th and 5th Battalions. The 4th was dug in along the ridge connecting the two hills and the 5th was held in reserve in the valley to the rear. He left the defence of Retimo, a town of 10,000 people, to 800 well-disciplined and well-armed Cretan gendarmes, commanded by Major Christos Tsiphakis.[3]

The Luftwaffe's softening-up attack had wounded only a couple of men but it unsettled some of the Greek recruits in the 4th Battalion. There were signs of panic in the ranks and men started to withdraw up the ridge. Campbell sent in a number of Australian NCOs to lead them back into line, where they acquitted themselves well in the ensuing battle.

Every man was alert and ready when, at 4.30 pm, 24 Ju-52s chugged in from the sea to the east of Hill A, the vital ground overlooking the eastern end of the airfield. They turned west, flying parallel to the coast at heights of 30 to 60 metres, each one disgorging a dozen paratroopers and dropping their weapons canisters east and west of the airfield. 'Such was the sheer barbaric beauty of the scene that, for a moment, all firing ceased as men gazed silently up at the sight,' the 2/1st historian recalls.[4]

The troop-carriers kept coming until a total of 161 were counted in the space of 35 minutes. The troops' wonderment quickly passed and they opened up with every available weapon from anti-aircraft guns to revolvers. Nine aircraft were destroyed, most of them crashing in flames near the coastal village of Perivolia on the outskirts of Retimo (to avoid confusion with the town of the same name south of Canea, this village will henceforth be referred to as Perivolia II). Other planes were on fire as they flew back over the sea, one trailing a string of entangled paratroopers.[5] 'As Ian Campbell had instructed us, we hit them in the planes, we hit them in the air and if they reached the ground we hit them in the arse,' says Lieutenant Noel Craig, who was dug in with his platoon on the slopes of Hill A close to the airstrip.

From his gun-pit at Georgiopolis, 23 kilometres west of Retimo, Michael Clarke saw a vast force of bombers and fighters fly in over the Suda–Canea–Maleme area, while a second armada flew across the sea towards Retimo. 'We could see parachutists floating down to our east,' he says. 'Our own guns pointed uselessly out to sea. We sheltered under the trees as heavy bombers flew overhead. The Germans had no interest in our area. They were concentrating on capturing the airfields at Maleme and Retimo.'

Some paratroopers dropped into the sea and drowned; many of those who fell on the rocky terraces were injured. Lew Lind, a gunner on Hill B, saw paras firing submachine guns clamped between their knees. Many were shot dead and folded like clasp-knives when they hit the ground.[6] A dozen men suffered a horrendous death when they came down in a large canebrake and were impaled on shafts of bamboo.[7]

Only two companies of Major Hans Kroh's battle group landed in the right place – in front of Campbell's positions on Hill A – while the main group came down two kilometres to the east at an abandoned olive-oil factory at Stavromenos. Kroh gathered his men together and, after linking up with his other two companies in the vines and terraces around Hill A, attacked the closely defended area held by Captain Doug Channell's A Company.

Some of these paratroopers had actually landed on top of one platoon of infantry, the 6th Battery's 75-mm French guns and two Vickers machine guns killing many of the crews. Removing their breech-blocks, the surviving gunners retreated up the ridge to 6th Battery headquarters, where they held out with three pistols and a few captured German weapons until a concerted German attack at 9 pm swept them aside. Further west, most of the crews of the other two machine guns were killed in a series of fierce clashes but three isolated infantry posts held out on the northern slopes of Hill A, while the rest of Channell's company was still intact across the neck of the hill.[8]

At 5.15 pm, Campbell mounted a rapid counter-attack to prevent the Germans from advancing west of Hill A. He deployed two platoons (Lieutenants Noel Craig and Vince Kiely) from his reserve company and sent in his two Matilda tanks, which advanced down a gully named Wadi Pigi. The tanks were supposed to swing right across the airfield and then along the road to attack the Germans east of Hill A but one became trapped in a drain on the north side of the airfield and the other, after passing east of Hill A and firing a few shots, plunged into a gully three metres deep. Both crews were captured by German paras.[9]

Colonel Sturm's HQ detachment of 200 men landed in front of the 2/11th's wired area on Hill B. Many were killed or wounded; indeed, not a single member from one batch of 12 who came down between two sections on the left of the 2/11th touched the ground alive. Others had the good fortune to land among the vineyards north of the 2/11th and were able to scramble for cover among the vines and huts.[10] Sturm, who had led the successful attack on the Corinth Canal, found refuge in dead ground at the foot of Hill B with a few survivors but with Australian gunfire covering either side he was unable to move. He had no radio and no way of getting one, even though several were dropped in that area when Student failed to hear from him.

Captain Ralph Honner, commanding C Company on the left of Hill B, described the German assault as 'a spectacle that might have belonged to a war between the planets'.[11] He estimated that as many as 500 paratroopers had moved westward towards the coastal village of Platanes beyond the range of his machine guns. Ray Sandover ordered a quick northward advance along his whole line to eliminate this threat before dark. By nightfall, however, the Australians had not reached the main road at all points and the enemy had disappeared into the vineyards.

That evening, Campbell radioed General Freyberg for reinforcements and also issued orders for two attacks at dawn the next morning. The 2/1st would drive the enemy off Hill A and the 2/11th would clear them from the low ground between Hill B and the sea. Each Australian battalion would be assisted by one Greek battalion, which would strike north against the southern flank of the German force opposing each Australian battalion. At midnight, Freyberg replied to Campbell's entreaty, regretting his inability to send reinforcements and wishing him luck.

Meanwhile, Major Sandover had withdrawn his companies within the wire for the night. He sent out patrols to prevent the Germans moving towards Retimo. By 10.30 pm, the 2/11th had captured 84 prisoners and a mass of arms and ammunition.[12]

At Georgiopolis, the 5th Battery felt it was missing out on the action. 'Willie Smith was in a fuming rage all day, waiting for orders to move,' Michael Clarke says.

> Colonel Strutt had been appointed CRA [Commander Royal Artillery] for the whole island, and was away God knows where. Heavy fighting could be heard both east and west, and we saw fresh waves of parachutists jumping out of planes and gliders. At dusk, the planes disappeared but firing continued all night in the distance. A message arrived that a German flotilla was at sea and was expected to land on our beach.

All through the morning of 20 May, Brigadier Brian Chappel, commander of Heraklion Force, received no word from Creforce headquarters that the western end of the island was under attack to airborne and parachute troops. After breakfast, the off-duty staff left Chappel's HQ, located in a quarry similar to General Freyberg's, and went about their business. The colonel of the Leicesters headed for Heraklion to have a bath and one of the intelligence officers, a keen botanist, went in search of wild flowers. Dusty Rhodes of the 2/4th Battalion borrowed Bill Andrews' pants, the only respectable pair in his section, to go into town to buy a few extras to supplement his ration.[13]

The first Brigadier Chappel heard of the drops on Maleme and Prison Valley was in a radio message at 2.30 pm. Some time later, the warning 'super red' – that the pre-invasion bombardment was about to start – was flashed to Chappel from the radar station on a ridge two kilometres to the south-east of the airfield. At 4 pm, von Richthofen's Stuka dive-bombers and Messerschmitt-110s attacked the town and by 4.34 the whole area was being bombed and machine-gunned.[14]

At five o'clock, the bombardment ceased and smoke and dust gradually began to subside. Then one of the infantrymen yelled, 'Parachutists!' Coming in low from the north, the Ju-52s' first target was Heraklion itself. The troops watched transfixed as flight after flight came over the dusty, smoking town and paratroopers tumbled from their bellies. One officer in Ivan Dougherty's B Company remarked, 'Good God, they're just like hens laying eggs.'[15]

Group East was the biggest force that Student had put into the field that day, an indication of the importance he attached to Heraklion's airfield and port. It consisted of the 1st Parachute Regiment reinforced by the II Battalion of the 2nd Parachute Regiment and a machine-gun battalion. German Intelligence had estimated the garrison at just 400 men. In fact, Brigadier Chappel had three battalions of the 14th British Brigade as well as one Australian battalion – the 2/4th, which had emerged from Greece 500 strong and had since been reinforced – an artillery regiment armed as infantry and three Greek battalions. He had 14 anti-aircraft guns and a dozen Bofors, as well as six light tanks and two Matildas. He assigned the town and harbour to the Greeks, concentrating the rest of his forces around the airfield in the shape of a horseshoe with its open end facing the coast.

The western sector was assigned to the gunners of the 7th

Medium Regiment, supported by the Leicesters and the Yorks and Lancasters. The centre was occupied by the Australians dug in on two smooth twin hills called 'the Charlies' overlooking the runways. The eastern sector was held by the Black Watch on a rocky outcrop called East Hill, which dominated the airfield and the coastal road. The Leicesters had been ordered to counter-attack any paratroopers landing on the airfield or between the Charlies and the low ground in front of them.[16]

As the first troop-carriers came within range, Chappel's artillerymen opened fire with their 3-inch guns and Bofors. The Bofors were well camouflaged and had hardly been touched by von Richthofen's bombardment. Norm Johnstone and Dick Parry of the 2/4th A Company described the carnage inflicted on the enemy:

> Nine troop-carriers came straight at us. We watched red streaks of tracer shells carry upwards. The first plane was hit squarely on the nose and, bursting into flames, crashed on the shore. The next plane also caught fire and crashed in front of us before any paratroops had succeeded in jumping. The third was hit and caught fire but blew up. The men jumped, blazing fiercely, but not one parachute opened; they dropped like stones. The fourth plane burst into flames, the men jumped and most of their 'chutes opened but the flames from the burning plane seemed to reach down and I saw puffs of smoke as each parachute burned and the poor devils hurtled to their deaths. The fifth plane had its tail shot off and crash-landed just to our left; the troops jumped at about fifty feet and all were killed. The sixth plane dropped its men but was hit and almost crashed on us, passing over our heads with a bare six feet to spare and crashed fifty yards away. The rest of those planes were brought down on our right, so not one escaped.[17]

Captain Burckhardt's II Battalion of the 1st Parachute Regiment dropped in two groups east and west of the airfield, both of which were almost annihilated. Most of the western group, under Captain Dunz, were killed or wounded in the air. The remainder landed around the airfield or just west of it on a broad meadow known as 'Buttercup Field', exactly where Chappel had expected them. Two tanks rumbled on to the field, machine guns blazing. The commander of one tank waited for a group of paratroops to land and then crushed them beneath the tracks of his machine. About 20 Germans sought refuge in a barley field which was set on fire and they were mowed down as they escaped from the flames.

In less than half an hour, II Battalion had suffered more than 300 dead and 100 wounded. All that remained were a few riflemen who rallied around Captain Burckhardt at the foot of the ridge where the radar station was positioned.

Things were not much better in Heraklion itself, where the population of 36,000 inhabitants had awaited this moment with a certain amount of macabre relish. III Battalion, under Major Karl-Lothar Schulz, suffered heavy casualties from anti-aircraft fire south-west of the town. Schulz was the only survivor among the men in his aircraft, which exploded just after he had jumped. Other units landed without mishap but fell into the hands of Cretan irregulars, who killed them with knives, axes and spades.

Major Gerhard Schirmer and two companies of the II Battalion of the 2nd Parachute Regiment had an easier descent west of Heraklion, where they blocked the coastal road.[18] Schulz collected Schirmer's men and other survivors and tried to break into the walled Old Town through the north and west gates. The Germans met fierce resistance from the Greek police under Captain Kalaphotakis and further groups of armed civilians.[19]

Among those who participated in the street battles were John Pendlebury, a one-eyed British archaeologist recruited by SOE to train Cretan guerrillas, and one of his guerrilla chieftains, Captain Satanas. They were visiting the town when the invasion began and joined in the fighting. Pendlebury's arms included a swordstick which he thought would be the ideal weapon for stabbing paratroopers.[20]

The Greeks had limited supplies of ammunition and small groups of paratroopers fought their way through the narrow dog-legged streets without any chance of establishing a bridgehead. The ferocity of the resistance had taken Schulz by surprise and he broke off the action and withdrew to the southern fringes of Heraklion to re-group his men.[21]

Shortly before 8 pm, Colonel Bruno Brauer landed with Major Erich Walther's I Battalion of the 1st Parachute Regiment near the radio station at Gurnes, five kilometres east of the airfield. The radio station was quickly taken and Brauer, knowing nothing about the catastrophe that had befallen the other battalions, signalled Athens that the operation was going 'as smooth as silk'. Expecting to find the airfield in German hands, he assembled a platoon under Lieutenant Count Blucher and set off in that direction.

Chappel, however, had ordered a counter-attack by the Leicesters' carrier platoon and a platoon of the Yorks and Lancs to clear Buttercup Field. By the time Brauer arrived at the airfield, the operation was almost complete. It took him some time to realise that the few snipers operating from the perimeter represented the sum total of Burckhardt's II Battalion.

Brauer's next report – shortly after midnight – informed Student that the attack on Heraklion had failed dismally with heavy losses. It was now clear to Student that none of the Cretan airfields was in German hands and that the loss of life in every drop zone had been horrendous. A total of 1856 paratroopers had been killed and that figure would exceed 2000 when the mortally wounded were taken into account.[22] Student had only a small reserve of 550 parachutists who could be dropped the next day and his staff officers were urging him to prepare plans to call off the invasion.

Matters came to a head when a furious General Lohr demanded an urgent decision from Student about what he intended to do. With the fate of his men – and his career – twisting in the wind, Student planned a bold stroke that would, if it succeeded, tip the balance of the battle in his favour.

He ordered one of his staff officers, Captain Oskar Kleye, to fly to Maleme in a Ju-52 at first light and attempt a landing. If the airfield was still under fire, he would lose a plane and a brave officer, but the mission would establish one way or another whether reinforcements could be landed with some chance of success. Student then had the greatest piece of luck of the entire campaign, the kind of good fortune – grotesque in its consequences for Creforce – that snatches victory from the jaws of defeat.

Colonel Andrew's latest entreaty had stirred Hargest into ordering A Company of the 23rd Battalion (Captain Carl Watson) and B Company of the 28th Maori Battalion (Captain Rangi Royal) to go to his assistance. However, it would take time for the two companies to arrive. When the 114-strong Maori contingent set off at 7 pm, it faced a march of more than 12 kilometres. Andrew was informed that these units – the very minimum he could have expected – were on their way. 'From the gist of the message,' he said later, 'I expected the companies almost immediately.'[23]

Yet his orders to Captain Hanton of A Company do not reflect that belief; instead, it is clear that he had already decided to re-group his battalion around the B Company ridge. Hanton was informed that reinforcements were expected but wouldn't arrive until 9 pm and at that hour A Company was to pull back to the regimental aid post behind Hill 107 and await orders for a further withdrawal at midnight. Hanton was astonished to receive the order 'as things were not bad with me'.[24]

At 7.25 pm, Andrew's last recorded message reached brigade headquarters in which he '… asked for immediate assistance and reported their casualties as heavy'. As time passed, Andrew's anxieties increased. Although he didn't know it, the Germans had established a weak presence on the western edge of the airfield and were encroaching on Hill 107.

By 9 pm, no reinforcements had reached Maleme and darkness had enveloped the battlefield. Andrew's radio was working again and he told Hargest that he 'would have to withdraw to B Company ridge'. There is no trace of this conversation in the 5th Brigade log but it was etched on Andrew's memory and he recalled it after the war for the official New Zealand historian. What is undisputed is that he began pulling men off Hill 107 and the eastern perimeter of the airfield and consolidating them around B Company.[25]

Just a few minutes later, the first reinforcements – Captain Watson's A Company from 23rd Battalion – arrived on the ridge and made contact with Andrew. He sent them up to the trenches on Hill 107 with orders to hold on until the Maoris showed up. The Maoris, however, were running behind schedule – they had taken a wrong turning in the dark and run into a German patrol.

'Two paratroopers got up from the ground and surrendered,' Private Arthur Midwood, a 21-year-old private of B Company, says.

> We thought everything was all right and were about to make them prisoners. We didn't know there was a whole mob of them there. Next thing, they dropped down on the ground and the firing started. It was in a bushy area where they could get out of sight. I copped a bullet in the chest that came out the back of my armpit. My mates charged in with bayonets.[26]

Yelling 'Surrender be buggered', the Maori charge accounted for 24 Germans. 'Those Maoris not actually engaged assisted with hakas,' the battalion's historian records.[27]

Meanwhile, Andrew had realised that at daybreak his new position would be vulnerable to enemy fire from the unoccupied parts of Hill 107. He made the fateful decision to abandon the airfield altogether and fall back behind the 23rd Battalion at Dhaskaliana. Soon after 10 pm, he ordered a full withdrawal of his battalion, with Captain Watson's company acting as rearguard.[28]

When the Maoris arrived at the airfield, they were halted by barbed wire around the perimeter. Captain Royal asked a shadowy figure behind the wire if he belonged to 22nd Battalion and was answered with a grenade which slightly wounded one man. The company began to deploy for action 'but its destination, a low ridge where trees could be seen against the skyline, was clearly in enemy hands and the troops, though reluctant to depart without a fight, were withdrawn'.[29]

At 2 am, the Maoris caught up with Colonel Andrew on the Pirgos road and reported what they had seen at Maleme. Had Andrew turned back and retraced his steps, he would have found that C and D Companies were still active and that the only German troops at the western end of the airfield capable of fighting were a disorganised group of 57 men who were short of food and ammunition. A counter-attack by the New Zealand troops would have stood a very good chance of dislodging them.

After almost 24 hours of combat, however, Andrew was no longer capable of rational thought. 'You are damn lucky to be alive,' he told Captain Royal and then ordered him to return to his unit.

More positive action might have been expected from Colonel Leckie when Andrew reached 23rd Battalion's headquarters. Indeed, Leckie summoned Colonel Allen, who had taken over from Polly Macky as commanding officer of the 21st Battalion, to a meeting with Andrew. There was still time for the two fresh battalions to march to Maleme, re-occupy Hill 107 and push the Germans back across the Tavronitis River. Ignoring Freyberg's orders for rapid counter-attacks to retrieve lost ground, they decided to remain in their existing positions and do nothing.[30]

At 5 am, Andrew, now travelling in a Bren carrier, reached

Hargest's headquarters near Platanias. The brigadier told him
to fit his battalion into the New Zealand line with the 21st and
23rd Battalions. He did not criticise Andrew's withdrawal or
attempt to rectify the situation at Maleme. Indeed, he wrote
in his diary, 'The infantry seemed cheerful except 22nd, which
was badly knocked about. I sent the 23rd to their assistance, but
Andrew decided to fall back a little off the prominent feature
above the aerodrome.'[31]

At midnight, General Freyberg sent Wavell a terse summary
of the day's events:

> Today has been a hard one. We have been pressed. So far I
> think we hold Maleme, Heraklion and Retimo Aerodromes
> and the two harbours. Margin by which we hold them is a bare
> one and it would be wrong of me to paint optimistic picture.
> Fighting has been very heavy and we have killed large numbers
> of Germans. Communications are most difficult. Scale of air
> attacks upon troops has been severe. Everybody here realises
> vital issue and we will fight it out.[32]

Astonishingly, Freyberg made no requests for additional
assistance, not even for radio sets to overcome his 'most
difficult' communications problem which had left him ill-
informed about the fighting throughout the day and which, at
the time he was sending his cable, was largely responsible for
the disaster unfolding at Maleme.

Given up for dead, Captain Campbell of D Company discovered
that Andrew had withdrawn when he led a party to battalion
headquarters on the south side of Hill 107 to obtain water and
ammunition and found it abandoned. His company had been
reduced to about 40 men but they were still inflicting casualties
on the enemy. According to Campbell, 'the surviving men were
in excellent heart in spite of their losses. They had *not* had

enough. They were first-rate in every particular way, and were as aggressive as when action was first joined.'[33]

At 3 am, he pulled his men out of their positions beside the river, with each platoon heading off in a different direction. One moved south and then east into the hills; another headed south beside the river and was captured; the third went eastward and reached the 5th Brigade's rear battalions.[34]

C Company, similarly written off by their battalion commander, had been badly mauled but was still full of fight. Captain Johnson tried until 4.20 am to get in touch with battalion headquarters without success. At first light, as Captain Kleye prepared to take off on his death-defying mission to Maleme, Johnson ordered his men to remove their boots, hang them around their necks and creep past the enemy.

Terrified of an Allied counter-attack under the cover of darkness, the Germans had tried to stay awake but were so exhausted that even Benzedrine tablets had ceased working. The only sound emanating from their foxholes as C Company slipped past were the discordant grunts of men snoring.[35]

CHAPTER 20

Losing Maleme

At 7 am on 21 May, the Ju-52 carrying General Student's airborne emissary Captain Kleye circled Maleme airfield like a lone hawk and then came in to land. A platoon of machine guns opened fire but the plane touched down on the western edge of the airfield and, after a briefing from the German commander, took off again without being hit. After a sleepless night, Student was elated when he received Kleye's radio signal that aircraft could land on the far side of the airfield with a good chance of success.

Switching his main attack from Heraklion to Maleme, Student ordered the Luftwaffe to fly the 5th Mountain Division to Maleme in transport planes. The pilots were instructed to crash-land anywhere in that vicinity so long as they got their troops and supplies on the ground.[1]

Student said later that the night of 20/21 May had been critical for the German command. 'I had to make a momentous decision,' he said.

I decided to use the mass of parachute reserves, still at my disposal, for the final capture of Maleme airfield. If the enemy had made an organised counter-attack during this night or on the morning of 21 May, he would probably have succeeded in routing the much-battered and exhausted remains of the Assault Regiment – especially as these were badly handicapped by the shortage of ammunition. But the New Zealanders made only isolated counter-attacks.[2]

It was not until later that morning that General Freyberg learned of Colonel Andrew's withdrawal from Maleme. To soften the blow, Freyberg's staff informed him that the airfield was still covered by artillery, mortar and machine-gun fire and could not be used by the enemy to fly in reinforcements and supplies.[3]

Bombing and strafing, however, had disabled the remaining gun batteries on the perimeter and scores of weary Royal Artillery and Royal Marine gunners were drifting away from the airfield and heading east towards 5th Brigade's lines. The only guns which could now bring fire on to the airfield – albeit indirectly – were the two English 3.7-inch howitzers, three Italian 75-mm guns and four French 75s of the 27th Battery with the 21st and 23rd Battalions at Vineyard Ridge and Dhaskaliana.[4]

Freyberg must have been baffled about what had happened during the night. He had issued specific orders to his commanders that lost ground must be speedily regained through counter-attacks. Why hadn't Puttick and Hargest taken that action at the time? And what were they doing about it now?

Since dawn, the remnants of the Assault Regiment, numbering about 1000 men, had occupied Hill 107 and formed a line on the eastern edge of the airfield. Von Richthofen's Stukas and Messerschmitts then blitzed targets all around Maleme to clear a path for the Ju-52s bringing in General Julius Ringel's

Mountain troops. They also attacked the radar station south of the hill, inflicting casualties on its RAF staff, who were forced to abandon their posts.[5]

Soon afterwards, a section of Ju-52s appeared overhead with desperately needed ammunition for the Assault Regiment. The planes were spotted by observers of the 27th Battery and an intense barrage forced them to veer away from the airfield. The formation leader, Uffz Grunert, brought his plane down safely on the rock-strewn beach to the west, but the second aircraft was raked with machine-gun fire and then blew up when a mortar bomb set off its cargo of ammunition.[6]

At 8.10 am, despite the fire of the 27th's nine guns and a platoon of machine guns, the first transport landed unscathed on Maleme airfield, unloaded its cases of ammunition and took off again. At 9 am, reinforcements arrived when an anti-tank company was dropped by parachute near the Tavronitis River and moved over the iron bridge to join the troops at the airfield. By 11 am, the eastern edge of the airfield was secure. Re-armed and reinforced, Meindl's battered force then moved forward to occupy the abandoned villages of Maleme and Pirgos. It was all going Student's way.[7]

At 11.15 am, Puttick accepted a proposal from Hargest that a counter-attack should be made on the airfield by the Maoris of the 28th Battalion and the 20th Battalion of the 4th Brigade under the cover of darkness that night, when the troops could move forward without being strafed. Had Hargest gone anywhere near the front, he would have realised that the Germans were becoming more powerful by the hour and that it would take more than two battalions to overwhelm them. The fact that his plan for a night attack would give the enemy a whole day to increase their grip on the airfield and fly in reinforcements seems to have been accepted without reference to Creforce headquarters.

Freyberg's relationship with Puttick and Hargest was described as 'delicate' and even in this hour of crisis he handled them with kid gloves. He must have realised that the German attack on the airfield meant that Ultra would no longer be compromised if he moved large numbers of reinforcements into that area. But instead of ordering fresh troops to attack the west bank of the Tavronitis – the one he had left unguarded specifically to protect Ultra – he allowed Hargest to proceed at a snail's pace with his plan for a limited attack.

None of Creforce's commanders had fought in a battle like this before – no one had – and their hesitation is perhaps understandable. Like many World War I commanders, Puttick and Hargest believed the best defence lay in strong, wired-in positions, whereas the Battle of Crete demanded aggressive patrolling and instant response by a well-organised mobile reserve.

Freyberg later admitted,

> I should have realised that some of my commanders were too old for the hand-to-hand fighting and were not likely to stand up to the strain of an all-out battle of the nature that eventually developed around the Maleme airfield and its eastern approaches. I should have replaced the old-age group with younger men who, as a rule, although less experienced as fighting soldiers, stood up much better to the physical and mental strain of a long and bitter series of battles.[8]

Freyberg thought, on reflection, that he ought to have led the counter-attack himself.[9] So what had prevented him from doing so?

All through the crucial day of 21 May Freyberg's attention was fixed on what he considered to be the true menace in the German attack: the seaborne landings. Earlier that day, he had misread an Ultra signal saying it was 'reliably reported that among operations planned for 21 May is air landing two Mountain battalions and attack Canea. Landing from echelon of small ships depending on situation at sea.' Believing a great fleet was bearing down on him from the Aegean, he interpreted this message to mean that Canea was in imminent danger of an assault from the sea.

Even though the naval officer-in-charge at Suda Bay, Captain Anthony Morse, assured him that the Royal Navy would deal with any threat from that quarter, Freyberg issued the following order to his commanders, 'Reliable information. Early seaborne attack in area Canea likely. New Zealand Division remains responsible coast from west to Kladiso River. Welch Battalion forthwith to stiffen existing defences from Kladiso to Halepa.'

The idea of enemy warships storming the narrow entrance to Canea's old Venetian harbour and landing troops on the quayside was patently absurd – the Germans had no battle fleet in the Mediterranean and the Italian Fleet showed no signs of wanting a repeat of Matapan. Also, the notion that a contested landing might be made on one of the beaches on the rocky foreshore around Canea presupposed that Admiral Karlgeorg Schuster, the Kriegsmarine officer in charge of the seaborne component of Operation Mercury, had motorised barges or assault ships at his disposal when it was known from intelligence sources that he possessed none of these craft.

Moreover, Freyberg had seen an operations order, found on the body of a dead German officer, which revealed that the first light ships group would land its troops on the undefended section of coast west of Maleme. The 'attack Canea' section of the Ultra message referred to the Mountain troops mentioned in the same sentence and/or the paratroopers in Prison Valley who had been tasked from the very beginning of the invasion with capturing the capital.[10]

Eyes glued to his binoculars, Freyberg scanned the northern horizon for any sign of enemy ships. There were none but he kept the main body of his defence force waiting uselessly on the coast when three or four battalions could have reclaimed Maleme airfield. The only fresh troops on the airfield were half of Student's final reserve of 550 paratroopers, who had been dropped there under the command of Colonel Bernhard Ramcke. Ramcke took over command of all German troops in Group West from the stricken General Meindl, who was flown to Athens that afternoon.

Student then decided that the final batch of 250 parachutists should land further east in the enemy's rear. In their lines between Pirgos and Platanias, the Maoris were preparing for that night's counter-attack. They couldn't believe their eyes when paratroopers started raining down on them again. Leaping out of their trenches, 'the Maori boys fell upon the enemy with fixed bayonets in a terrible skirmish, wiping out every invader'.[11]

At 1 pm, the first Ju-52s arrived at Maleme with Ringel's Mountain troops. One of the troop-carriers burst into flames from a direct hit, while others were deliberately crashed to get the troops down. Soon, the airfield resembled a junkyard of broken undercarriages, smashed fuselages and torn-off wings; several planes were on fire and wounded men were crawling from the wreckage. Major Snowadzki's airfield service company landed safely and went to work amid the chaos, using a captured Bren-carrier to tow wrecked machines off the runway. Other transports landed on the riverbed or on the beaches to the west.[12]

'We had made a miscalculation,' Freyberg later admitted.

It had not been considered feasible for aircraft to land in the river-bed west of the Maleme aerodrome. But during the morning troop-carriers began to crash-land there and also on the beaches west of the aerodrome. These landings continued under constant shell-fire from nine field guns and despite this observed fire, which destroyed numbers of the enemy planes, it went on regardless of loss of machines or life.[13]

By 5 pm that night, the Battle of Crete had taken a decisive turn against the defending forces.

All this time, the source of Freyberg's main concern – Admiral Schuster's armada of little ships – was heading across the Aegean. After loading Mountain troops, gunners, weapons, pack animals and supplies at Piraeus, the ships had re-grouped on the island of Milos, 140 kilometres from Crete, with the intention of crossing the last stretch of water during daylight hours while von Richthofen's fighters and bombers kept the Royal Navy at bay.

The first light ships group had been scheduled to reach the beaches west of Maleme on the first day but the British fleet had been considered too active for it to sail. Now that convoy, comprising 25 caiques and two little steamers escorted by the Italian light destroyer *Lupo*, was to land its 2300 troops of the III Battalion of the 100th (Reichenhall) Mountain Regiment at Maleme on the evening of 21 May, while the second convoy of 38 caiques, escorted by the destroyer *Sagittario*, was to take 4000 troops of the II Battalion of the 85th Mountain Regiment to Heraklion the following evening. Heavy guns and tanks would follow in a third convoy of steamships.[14]

During the 21st, British naval forces waited south of Crete to resume their aggressive patrols along the north coast. The ships had been bombed continuously from 9.50 am and at 12.50 pm the destroyer *Juno*, close to *Perth*, had been hit by three bombs. Her magazine had exploded and she had broken in half and sunk in less than two minutes with the loss of 121 lives. The cruiser *Ajax* had also been damaged by near misses.

Signals intelligence had identified the first convoy and the course it was taking from Milos to Maleme. Following his usual procedure to protect Ultra, Admiral Cunningham sent a Maryland aircraft on a reconnaissance flight to 'discover' the ships at sea. As night fell, the Luftwaffe went home, but the convoy was still at sea. Many of the caiques relied on sail-power and the wind had failed during the day. Cunningham ordered three of his forces back into the Aegean to hunt them down.[15]

Late that afternoon, Freyberg held a conference with Puttick, Vasey and Inglis, among others, to consider, in the words of his son, 'how to regain control of the landing grounds on and around Maleme airfield'.[16] Freyberg outlined Hargest's plan under which three light tanks would attack along the road, with the Maoris on the left and the 20th Battalion on the right between the road and the beach.

The troops would form up 350 metres west of the Platanias River at 11.30 and set off at 1 am. The first objective would be Pirgos, followed by the airfield on the right and the Tavronitis River on the left. Then, in the morning, the 21st Battalion would move from Vineyard Ridge on the extreme southern flank and re-occupy Hill 107.[17]

Brigadier Vasey listened in astonishment when he heard that the 20th Battalion would not leave its position on the Kladiso River on the western outskirts of Canea until it had been replaced by an Australian unit – the 2/7th Battalion – which would have to travel 30 kilometres from Georgiopolis in borrowed transport.[18] To make sure that the 20th did not leave its positions on the coast until it had been relieved, it was to be moved west in the same vehicles.

As Vasey's 2/1st and 2/11th Battalions were cut off at Retimo with some of his gunners and the 2/8th Battalion was under General Weston's command at Perivolia, the loss of the 2/7th meant that the only troops now under his orders were the 2/7th Field Ambulance and a detachment of engineers. Vasey protested strongly. 'I went and saw General Freyberg,' he says.

The latter regretted the tactical necessity which compelled him to withdraw these various AIF units from my command. I pointed out that my HQ was capable of controlling a sector of the battlefront and that I would be glad to be given an area in which I might concentrate and employ the 7 and 8 Battalions.[19]

Freyberg, however, was reluctant to overrule Puttick and Hargest. He told Vasey he was sticking to the counter-attack plan as announced. It was not until the conference ended that Colonel Walker, the 2/7th's commanding officer, learned from Vasey that his battalion was moving west to relieve the 20th Battalion. He sent his intelligence officer, Lieutenant Henry Lunn, back to Georgiopolis to pass on the orders to his second-in-command, Major Henry Marshall, while he travelled to the Kladiso River with Brigadier Inglis to reconnoitre the new area. The road was congested and traffic was stopped several times by air attacks.

On the way, Walker made it plain to Inglis that he did not like the idea of bringing forward his battalion at night in borrowed trucks in time to relieve another battalion which was to make an attack the same night. Inglis snapped that 'a well-trained battalion could carry out such an operation in an hour'.[20]

Later that evening, Freyberg ordered B Troop of the 2/3rd Field Regiment and a section of the 106th Royal Horse Artillery to join the New Zealand Division in shelling the airfield prior to the troops going in. He also requested aircraft from Egypt to bomb the area from midnight until 2.30 am.

B Troop had been sitting around its gun-pits at Georgiopolis all day waiting for just such an order. 'Willie Smith was fretting and fuming,' Michael Clarke says. 'We had no information as to the situation in Retimo or Maleme but could see that heavy bombing was taking place over Suda and Canea and a parachute drop was in progress in the hills to our south-west. We felt utterly frustrated.'

At seven o'clock, Smith returned from a meeting with Colonel Strutt and ordered the troop to pack up quickly and get the guns on the road. In less than an hour, they were on the move along the winding track through the hills to Stilos, south of Suda. Progress was slow. The road was blocked with transport and one of the ammunition trucks lost a wheel in a shellhole and had to be repaired. It was 11.30 pm before they reached Stilos, where they were ordered to be in position overlooking Maleme airfield before dawn to support the counter-attack.

Meanwhile, frantic efforts had been made to shift the 2/7th to Kladiso River. The transport had arrived a few trucks at a time from a number of different sources. Unnerved by the bombing, the drivers had stopped and taken shelter every time they heard aircraft approaching. 'I hoped to get away at 5 pm and speeded things up,' says Henry Marshall.

> We whizzed down the road and passed the food dump and breathed again. Then we turned a corner and found half a dozen planes above with the obvious intention of attacking us somewhere. I stopped the column until I was sure [Captain John] Savige with A Company had caught up and then we sailed on. It was rather exhilarating. The planes had now obviously got on to us, but the road was winding along a valley and there were few straight stretches. The planes cruised about those straight stretches waiting for us. Twice I watched a plane single us out, bank and turn to machine-gun us along the straight and I told the driver to crack it up. It then became a race to the curve. We streaked along and I hoped the battalion was following.[21]

At Suda, Marshall left Lieutenant Lunn to bring on the three rear companies, while he continued with the two leading companies, arriving at the 20th Battalion's camp at 8 pm. Colonel Jim Burrows, the 20th's commanding officer, rang Puttick's headquarters to see whether he could set off for the start-line at once. To Puttick, however, the coastal defences were sacrosanct and Burrows was ordered to wait until the whole of the Australian battalion was in position before moving out.

*

At 11.30 pm, Rear-Admiral Irvine Glennie's Force D of the cruisers *Dido*, *Orion* and *Ajax*, and four destroyers, *Janus*, *Kimberley*, *Hasty* and *Hereward*, closed on the first light ships group 30 kilometres north of Canea. *Dido*'s skipper, Captain H.W. McCall, caught *Lupo* in the beam of his searchlight as she was approaching Cape Spada at just five knots.

The Italian captain, Commander Francesco Mimbelli, was steaming towards the British ships but instead of veering away he maintained course and fired two torpedoes, both of which missed. *Dido* scored two hits on the little destroyer and *Ajax* blasted her with a broadside at close range. *Lupo* was hit by 18 6-inch rounds and suffered many casualties. Making smoke to protect the caiques, she charged through the British line and took off into the darkness.[22]

In the caiques, German soldiers stood up and began waving handkerchiefs and white towels in surrender. McCall gave the order to open fire but, according to a yeoman of signals on the bridge, the commander protested that firing on unarmed caiques would be murder. The captain pushed him aside and shouted the order down the speaking-tube himself, 'Guns, open fire!' The ship's light armament of Oerlikons, pom-poms and Hotchkisses raked the little ships.[23]

'Suddenly,' wrote Geoffrey Cox, who was at Creforce headquarters, 'on the horizon away to the north came the flash and thunder of guns, and the dull red glow of burning vessels.' Freyberg – 'bouncing up and down', according to intelligence officer David Hunt – watched the battle through his binoculars with excitement mingled with relief.[24] 'It has been a great responsibility,' he told Keith Stewart. 'A great responsibility.'

The Royal Navy fired on the enemy convoy for two and a half hours, sinking or setting fire to one of the steamers and a dozen caiques. Hundreds of German troops were thrown into the sea, but many were later recovered by the enemy's air-sea rescue service and the death toll of 327 was surprisingly light. Many of the caiques escaped. One became separated from the convoy and actually made it to Cape Spada with its full complement of three officers and 110 men.

Hearing about the attack on the first convoy, Admiral Schuster ordered the second little ships group to turn back to Milos. Admiral Edward King's C Force, including HMAS *Perth*, caught up with it and sank a couple of ships before it could reach port but when the Luftwaffe showed up King withdrew, much to the fury of Admiral Cunningham, who pointed out that the safest place for his force would have been among the enemy ships.

At midnight, during the early stages of the sea battle, Brigadier Hargest had gone down to the schoolhouse at Platanias to meet the chiefs of his attacking battalions. Colonel George Dittmer of the 28th Battalion was there but there was no sign of 20th Battalion CO Jim Burrows, so Hargest watched the fires and gun-flashes illuminating the night sky and waited.

At the same time, B Troop was driving west through Canea bound for Maleme. Heavy bombing had set the town alight and flames leaped from many buildings; out to sea, the gunners could see the flashes of naval gunfire. They drove along the coast road in the dark, dodging bomb craters and barely able to see the verges. 'We stopped at Platanias and found the village in ruins,' Michael Clarke says. 'The Kiwis gave our guns a warm welcome and pushed aside wrecked ammo trucks to clear the road. Then we carried on through Gerani towards Maleme.'

The 20th Battalion was not relieved by the 2/7th until shortly after 11.30 pm and, as a result, its two leading companies did not reach the start-line until 2.45 am on 22 May. When the attacking force finally moved off at 3.30, it was running two and a half hours late, the Maoris had been standing around for four hours and only three hours of darkness remained.[25]

Nevertheless, Roy Farran's three light tanks rumbled down the road towards Pirgos and the 20th Battalion advanced through rough country between the road and the beach. Encountering German paratroopers among the vineyards and farmhouses, the New Zealanders went straight into action. Lieutenant Charles Upham, who won the first of his two Victoria Crosses during this battle, says, 'The amount of MG fire was never equalled. Fortunately, a lot of it was high and the tracer bullets enabled us to pick our way up and throw in grenades. We had heavy casualties but the Germans had much heavier. They were unprepared. Some were without trousers, some had no boots on.'[26]

On the left of the road, the Maoris made good progress and at daybreak were ahead of the 20th but then ran into strongly defended positions. Farran's leading tank was hit by a captured Bofors gun and disarmed and when all three tanks moved back behind a bend in the road his own tank broke down and could not continue. Farran refused to let the third tank go into battle unsupported. On the extreme right near the beach, D Company of the 20th Battalion, commanded by Lieutenant P. V. H. Maxwell, was the only one gaining ground; the rest of Burrows' companies were held up by fierce resistance round Pirgos and were still two kilometres short of the airfield. [27]

At 6 am, the trucks of B Troop bumped off the road and drove on to level ground overlooking the runway. 'Willie Smith and Peter Cudmore ran up the hill behind us to select an OP, while Roy Macartney [the 22-year-old newspaperman who had joined B Troop with some of his C Troop gunners] raced forward to select the gun positions,' Michael Clarke says. 'I could see the airfield about two miles west. It was littered with wrecked transport planes and gliders. The Germans were busy hauling the wrecks to the side of the strip.'

The four Italian 75s were manhandled over a stone wall and across a muddy field and were ready for action when transport planes bringing in two more Mountain battalions – the I/100th and I/85th – started to fly in low from the sea. From their hilltop OP, Smith and Cudmore had a grandstand view. They timed the interval between the planes passing the last in-shore wave and taxiing to a halt, and ordered fire accordingly. 'We were soon observing direct hits on the still-laden planes,' Michael Clarke says. 'Others were missed and we could see Germans jumping out of them and rushing to the far side of the airfield.'

The German ground troops picked up the gunners' position and opened fire with mortars and called up air strikes. Willie Smith could see the sun glinting on the shells fired by his troop, one shell passing between two low-flying Stukas whose pilots swerved violently to avoid it.

The men bringing up the ammunition to the guns crawled forward along a shallow ditch, lugging boxes containing ten shells each. The charges came separately in snow-white bags, packed in bundles of three or four inside shiny tins that flashed in the sunlight. The fuses and primers were in other boxes. At the guns, the ammo handlers faced the laborious process of sorting out the various components and preparing the shells for firing. Having no keys to set the fuses, they had to use fencing wire. The war diary recorded, 'Good shooting by B Troop on to Maleme aerodrome. Reported 27 troop-carriers (13 confirmed) destroyed by Troop guns.'

The New Zealanders on Hill 120 to the left poured machine-gun and mortar fire on to the airfield but nothing could stop the steady stream of Ju-52s. 'The Germans were losing hundreds of men but they kept coming,' Clarke says. 'If only our guns had been there the day before.'

By now, German fighters were strafing all of the Allied attacking positions. On the right, Lieutenant Maxwell's D Company fought its way through the northern part of Pirgos and reached a clearing near the airfield. Only the heavy fire of Colonel Ramcke's mortars and machine guns prevented it from making a frontal assault on the perimeter.

'From time to time, platoons hurried forward through our position, while wounded were carried back on stretchers improvised from rifles,' Clarke says. 'God alone knows why some of our blokes were not hit. Air attacks seemed to be almost continuous and we had no slit trenches.'

Maxwell, meanwhile, had sought cover from the Messer-schmitts in a bamboo thicket 100 metres from the eastern corner of the airfield. Having come further than any other unit, he then misread a signal and ordered his men all the way back to the start-line.[28]

At 7 am, the 21st Battalion advanced from Vineyard Ridge with the objective of occupying Hill 107 but after making good ground initially its attack ran into strong opposition and halted. During the afternoon, it became clear to Hargest that the main attack along the coast had failed. The New Zealanders were exhausted and began to withdraw under heavy enemy pressure.

Freyberg said later, 'One counter-attack to recapture the airfield with only two battalions of infantry went in too late and was badly planned. The weak artillery support did not help and the Air Force never turned up. The men did get a footing on the airfield but after dawn on 22 May the Luftwaffe came over and our forward troops were again heavily bombed and were driven back.'[29]

The Australians were bitter about the outcome. At one stage during the night, the 16th Composite Battalion at Suda Bay was informed that it would be taking part in the attack. The move was called off because of lack of transport, but its commander, Major Paul Cullen, says, 'there is no doubt that our 443 men of 16 Composite Battalion could have turned the tide at Maleme on which the whole campaign hinged'.[30]

The 2/7th Battalion had even more reason to be aggrieved. It had 580 men with a proven fighting record in Libya and although they had lost their kit and arms on the *Costa Rica* they had been re-equipped and re-armed. When word of the failure filtered down to John Peck and his mates Ken Huxtable, Steve Warner and Arnold Newnham, there was general agreement that they were being denied a fair chance to get at the enemy.

'At this stage, the 2/7th were a tried and disciplined unit who had never suffered a defeat in battle and were probably more experienced under air attack than any other unit in Crete,' the battalion's historians write. 'Furthermore, because they had suffered no great losses in Greece they were strong in numbers.' Certainly George Vasey and Theo Walker believed it would have been much better to attack with the 2/7th, 'thus avoiding the delay caused by the relief, and thus putting a fresher and more-experienced battalion into the fight'.[31]

At sundown, the air armada ceased landing at Maleme and the gunners were informed they would be supporting another big counter-attack to retake the airfield later that night. The men ate their rations and lay down on the ground to grab a couple of hours' sleep. Some of them had not closed their eyes for 36 hours.

Even as they dropped off, the Germans launched a new attack from the direction of Prison Valley towards Galatas that threatened to drive a wedge between the 4th and 5th Brigades on the coast. If they broke through, Freyberg's defences would be cut in half, with unimaginable slaughter.

CHAPTER 21

Holding Retimo

While Creforce came under increasing pressure in the west, Colonel Ian Campbell's star was rising in the east against the German forces known as Mars, but he had not achieved this position without a terrific fight. At the end of the first day's combat, the enemy had been split into two main groups, one on Hill A and the other around Perivolia II. At 5.25 am on 21 May, Campbell sent Captain Doug Channell with A Company, reinforced by five additional platoons, to reclaim Hill A, while Ray Sandover's 2/11th Battalion cleared the left flank around the village.[1]

Channell placed himself in the centre of the line and, with members of a Greek battalion on either flank, led his men over the top of the hill. At the same time, Major Kroh ordered the Germans to attack from the other side of the hill. The two forces clashed head-on. Under heavy machine-gun fire, the Australians hit the ground and blazed back with their .303s and Bren-guns. The enemy replied with a mortar barrage. In the unequal contest, Channell and one of his officers, Lieutenant Walter Delves, and a number of other ranks were wounded.

A Company was driven back to a line on the western edge of the neck of the hill.[2]

At 6 am, as arranged, Captain Boyd Moriarty arrived with D Company and the carrier platoon, fighting as infantry, to lend a hand if needed. He was informed by Delves, who was bleeding from a head wound, that the attack had failed. Moriarty ordered him to 'get the hell out of it and get a bandage on his head'. He then telephoned battalion headquarters and reported that the position was 'very desperate'.[3]

Ian Campbell had been waiting for the call. He set off along a gully known as Wadi Bardia on the western side of Hill A with one of his remaining companies. Leaving a couple of platoons with Noel Craig in the gully, he reached Moriarty with the reinforcements. After a quick update, Campbell ordered Moriarty to combine the two forces and drive the enemy off the hill. While Moriarty organised his men into four groups, a German bomber dropped six bombs on the German frontline, killing 16 men.[4]

Taking advantage of the carnage, Moriarty attacked with tremendous dash and swept the Germans off Hill A, recapturing the 75s abandoned on the first day and netting 59 prisoners. Lieutenant Craig in Wadi Bardia then moved forward to the main road, forcing the Germans to fall back on to the beach and thence to the olive-oil factory at Stavromenos, where Kroh set up a strongpoint behind the solid stone walls.[5]

Thus the German force that had succeeded in occupying one of the heights overlooking the airfield had been driven off by a forceful and determined counter-attack. There were now only isolated pockets of paratroopers on the coastal plain between Hill A and Perivolia II. At the same time, the 2/11th Battalion cleared scattered groups of Germans from around the base of Hill B and took several prisoners. One of them was Colonel Sturm, who had been trapped on the dead ground at the base of the hill. The Australians also found an operational order on the body of one of Sturm's officers.

Ray Sandover, who spoke German, translated the document, which revealed that two battalions of German troops totalling 1500 men had been dropped on Retimo. It was imperative to discover whether reinforcements would be flown in, so he interrogated the German commander. 'I had a very unpleasant interview with Sturm,' Sandover says.

> He was far older than I was and he couldn't talk English and I could talk German. I had his operation order which he didn't like and he'd lost his brush-and-comb set and he was a very frightened man. And he didn't like me at all! He wasn't very co-operative. He wanted to see whose operation order I had and I wouldn't show him. Because, of course, you are not allowed to take an operation order into battle.[6]

Another officer let slip that the Germans 'do not reinforce failure', thus providing the answer that no more paratroopers were on their way.[7]

That night, with the airfield and the heights secure once more, Colonel Campbell signalled Freyberg's headquarters that the situation at Retimo was well in hand. Two groups of Germans remained to be dealt with: one around the olive-oil factory blocking the road to Heraklion and the other at Perivolia II on the road to Retimo. Campbell ordered Ralph Honner's C Company of the 2/11th to thrust west towards the village first thing in the morning, while two companies of the 2/1st struck east towards the factory.

At Heraklion on the morning of 21 May, all the signs told Brigadier Chappel that Group East's attack had failed. Despite the presence of a small enemy party dug in on the southern edge of the town and a larger one east of the airfield, many German units had been destroyed before they could be organised into a coherent attacking force. British, Australian and Greek casualties had been light.

Colonel Brauer, the Group East commander, ordered his easternmost force, supported by light guns, to attack the Black Watch on East Hill and infiltrate the eastern end of the airfield with the aim of achieving his main objective. This force ran into a barrage of artillery and small-arms fire and was stopped in its tracks.

Ivan Dougherty's 2/4th Battalion attacked selected targets with mortars and machine guns, while patrols flushed out snipers and pockets of Germans in the battalion area. Three or four Germans took cover in the undefended Greek barracks. When the building was rushed by the Australians, two dead Germans and a German uniform were found inside. As there were British stores inside the building, it was assumed that at least one of the Germans had escaped wearing a British uniform.[8]

Brauer's message – that the airfield was to take priority over everything else – had not reached Major Schulz, commander of III Battalion, who renewed his attack on the town. He was denied entry by the Greek defenders, who had re-armed themselves with captured German weapons. As darkness fell, the Greeks, reinforced by a platoon of the Leicesters and one from the Yorks and Lancs, counter-attacked and drove almost all of the Germans back to their start-line.[9]

Student, however, had not given up on Heraklion. At 5.05 pm, the Germans received reinforcements when 11 troop-carriers dropped men near the East Wadi. Brauer now had enough fresh troops to attempt one final assault on the fortress.

Overnight, the Australians salvaged German equipment from the West Wadi and lined their trenches with silk parachute canopies, which were found to make comfortable beds. German arms and ammunition increased the unit's firepower considerably, while a number of weapons were handed over to the Greeks.

One of the prizes was a copy of a codebook giving the ground-to-air signals to be used by the enemy for air-drops. Captain Cecil Rolfe of C Company had also obtained a German

Very pistol and cartridges, so Dougherty decided to try out one of the signals in the hope of deceiving the enemy. Late on the afternoon of 22 May, he saw seven enemy aircraft approaching the coast. As the planes came closer, he ordered Rolfe to fire the pistol.

The pilots changed course and headed towards C Company. Rolfe then fired again. To the Australians' delight, canisters began raining down on them, providing an astonishing array of items ranging from machine guns, a radio tuned to the German wavelength and mortars with baseplates to a motorcycle and sidecar, chairs and tables, a tent and much food and ammunition. 'To everyone's amazement,' says the battalion's historian, 'two German fighter aircraft gave the troops protection, evidently thinking in the fading light that they were Germans.'[10]

Back at Retimo on 22 May, the Australians under Captain Boyd Moriarty besieging the olive-oil factory found the Germans strongly entrenched inside the thick-walled buildings. There had been no sign of resistance on the way to the factory until the two Bren-carriers came within range of an anti-tank gun which destroyed both lightly armoured vehicles and killed Corporal John Kelly, one of the commanders.

Colonel Campbell arrived on the scene to find his men in a line running north–south about 140–230 metres in front of the factory and the 4th Greek Battalion on the spurs immediately south of the factory enclave. Both groups were under heavy fire and sustaining casualties. Campbell studied the factory buildings from C Company's right flank, then consulted Captain Moriarty, who was with D Company on the road 180 metres south-west of the factory. Moriarty had contacted the Greeks to the south of the factory enclave. They were mostly conscripts with only a few weeks' service and were for the most part poorly clad and armed with old-fashioned rifles and very little ammunition. Moriarty thought they were of doubtful military value.[11]

At 8.40, Campbell signalled Captain George Killey on Hill A for artillery fire on the factory from 9.55 to 10.10, while C and D Companies were given orders to rush the buildings at 10.12 if the bombardment proved successful. At 8.50, the troops heard the sound of approaching aircraft and feared the worst when six troop-carriers approached from the Aegean. The embattled Germans, who had no radios, fired white and red flares from the factory to indicate their presence. A great cheer went up from the Australian ranks as dozens of canisters rained down by parachute and came to rest in no-man's-land outside the factory complex.

Having made his plans, Campbell returned to his headquarters on Hill D, leaving Captain Moriarty in charge. From his position behind a forked tree, Moriarty called down artillery fire on a group of Germans who suddenly appeared on the beach to the north of the factory. This barrage scattered the group and the guns then swung their fire on to the factory buildings. Moriarty raised his head to observe the result and was shot dead.[12]

When the bombardment lifted, it was clear that the walls of the factory had not been breached. Nevertheless, the attack went ahead as planned. The moment the Australians stood up to charge, machine guns opened fire and great gaps appeared in their line. In scenes reminiscent of the First World War, C Company's 15 Platoon, closest to the beach, lost ten of its 25 men in as many seconds: Lieutenant Vince Kiely went down, along with his platoon sergeant Frank Cahill, two section commanders, the brothers Len and Neville Power, and Privates R. Humphries, Les Sammons, 'Dutchy' Holland, Tom Wallace, Bill Scott and David Mills. Humphries and Sammons later died of their wounds.

The remnants of this platoon got within 40 metres of the factory, 'but under fire, the momentum slackened, stopped and then rolled back', the unit's historian says. 'The survivors went to ground wherever they could find some sort of cover.'[13] For hours, the wounded lay under the blazing sun in the open or in a field of low crops, with bullets whipping in both directions a few metres above their heads. Several attempts were made by stretcher parties to rescue them, but each attempt was driven back by fire from the factory. Private C. J. 'Boots' Maxwell of 15 Platoon, who had survived the attack, volunteered to lead the stretcher-bearers and was mortally wounded trying to rescue his mates.[14]

Eventually, the German fire died down and parties showing the Red Cross were allowed to retrieve the wounded. Campbell now learned that Captain Moriarty had been killed and that Lieutenant Brian Savage, his second-in-command, had been wounded. He hurried across to the factory, accompanied by Lieutenants Dick Mann of A Company and Albert Herron of B Company, each company reduced by casualties to just 30 all ranks.

Campbell had sent his second-in-command, Major George Hooper, to liaise with the Greeks. He told Campbell that, according to his interpreter, the Greek commander was 'most anxious' to attack the factory. Campbell reconnoitred the factory approaches and decided to launch a converging attack, with the Australians attacking the front from the western wadi and the Greeks coming in from the east. The troops would be supported by Killey's artillery, a captured German mortar and volleys of small-arms fire.

It was now 1 pm and Campbell scheduled the attack for six o'clock to give the Greeks plenty of notice. The Greeks were to attack with 200 men, the Australians under Lieutenant Mann with 40. Lieutenant Herron would take charge of the mortar barrage, while the remaining Greeks and Australians covered the attack with small-arms fire from the spurs.

At 5.40, Campbell moved to the northern point of the spur, from which his voice would carry to the attackers. Five minutes later, the field guns and mortar opened fire, while rifle and Bren-gun fire was poured into holes that appeared in the walls. The 40 Australians led by Lieutenant Mann then rushed forward.

At the same time, Major Hooper tapped his interpreter on the shoulder and the interpreter tapped the Greek commander, who fired his pistol in the air and urged the troops in front of him, with well-aimed kicks, to move forward. All the other Greek officers then fired their pistols and kicked the troops and the battalion advanced in two long lines.

'All went well for perhaps 180 metres or so,' Hooper says, 'when firing from the attacking 2/1st Battalion and from the factory itself was heard and the Greeks began to lose momentum. Just after this, a few shots fired in our direction caused all the Greeks to go to ground and there they stayed.'[15]

The Australians suffered heavy losses and were forced to take cover behind a low bank 36 metres from the walls. Knowing that, without the Greeks, his men would be overwhelmed even if they got into the factory, Campbell shouted to Lieutenant Mann to stand still until the Greeks attacked. But Mann had been badly wounded and Corporal Norman Thompson replied that he was now in command of the few remaining men. He would wait as directed.

When darkness fell, the Australians were able to withdraw without further loss. Campbell sent his two companies back to their original positions overlooking the airfield, leaving the Greeks to contain the Germans in the factory.[16]

Meanwhile, Ralph Honner set off with C Company of the 2/11th to eliminate the Germans in the rear of his battalion and then sweep towards the coast. The main German force in this area was commanded by Captain Wiedemann, whose advance towards Retimo had been stopped by the Greek gendarmerie and some Cretan irregulars. Wiedemann had ordered his men to occupy the Church of Saint George at Perivolia II and also to take up positions in the next village of Platanes.

According to Honner, the first enemy that C Company encountered in the olive groves were blond Teutons turned black by two days of death under the hot sun. At the village of Cesmes, the only inhabitant was an old blind woman who had been left behind when her neighbours fled to Retimo. 'We could not imagine what agonies of fear and uncertainty she had suffered as Cesmes was bombed and machine-gunned on the invasion day, then shot at by us with the Germans firing beside her, and again bombed on this third day of her lonely terror,' Honner writes. The Australians placed food and water beside her, milked her goat and then tethered it within reach.[17]

Heading towards the coast, C Company discovered that the Germans had pulled out of Platanes. They also found hundreds of parachutes in the area where Honner had seen a large number of paratroopers descend on Day 1. 'We had captured their signalling code and now laid folded white parachutes on the road, forming a signal calling for bombs on the Perivolia stronghold, 1600 metres away,' he says. German aircraft circling overhead obeyed the order.

The diarist of the 5th Mountain Division recorded that 'reports from various sources that weapons and supplies were being dropped in the wrong places led to the definite conclusion that the Greeks and British were using swastika flags taken from dead or captured paratroops for deception purposes, and thus causing our aircraft to drop supplies in the wrong places or make false reports'.[18]

Honner advanced without opposition as far as a wadi outside Platanes, where he came under fire from some fortified houses on a small ridge. Supported by two mortars, one of them captured, his men successfully stormed the houses with a loss of one man killed and two wounded. Honner was then recalled to meet Ray Sandover at Platanes. C Company, now fewer than 100 strong, was ordered to advance down the road, break through the enemy's defences and capture Perivolia II.[19]

The difficulty and the danger were all too plain to Honner's seasoned eye. His men were already under fire from Wiedemann's heavily armed group in buildings and behind stone walls at

Perivolia II and the terrain between the houses and the village sloped downwards and lacked any foliage, making it easy for the enemy to spot his advance. The main German force was holed up in the Church of Saint George, which was surrounded by a stone wall and which overlooked the open ground.

By now, it was late afternoon. Fortuitously, Honner was joined by Captain David Jackson's B Company of the 2/11th, enabling him to plan a leap-frogging attack in the darkness with both companies between the road and the coast, using some shallow ditches as cover. As the light faded, Jackson advanced to the second of these ditches without incurring casualties. Honner was following with his own company when Major Sandover arrived at his shoulder.

Sandover informed him the 5th Greek Battalion – with whom the 2/11th had earlier exchanged friendly fire – was about to attack the church and he was anxious to avoid a similar incident in the dark. Sandover also doubted whether Honner's frontal attack had much chance of success, given the Germans' strong positions and the open ground ahead. He ordered the two companies to remain where they were and dig in. Later that night, the Australians heard noisy sounds of battle around Perivolia II but the Greeks withdrew after what Honner described as 'a brief raid' and the Germans remained in their heavily fortified positions.[20]

Meanwhile, an astonishing bond had developed between the medical services of the Australian and German forces in the Retimo sector. Early on 22 May, during its advance to the olive-oil factory, 15 Platoon of C Company captured a building east of the airfield which the Germans were using as a regimental aid post. Lieutenant Vince Kiely was met at the door by a German medical officer who indicated the scores of wounded Germans in every room. He said that when each man was admitted, he was disarmed and his weapons joined a pile outside in the yard. 'Much impressed by this prime example of military rectitude,' the unit's historian writes, 'Kiely rejoined his platoon and continued the advance.'

The following day, the medical officer of the 2/1st Battalion arranged with the senior German medical officer that the Germans should move their wounded from the aid post to the Australian dressing station in the valley near Adhele. Thereafter, Australian and German medical officers and orderlies worked side by side treating the wounded from both armies. 'Here, wounded Germans and Australians, ranged along the walls regardless of nationality, forgot enmity in a new brotherhood of suffering.' Lieutenant Kiely was now one of the patients taking advantage of this unlikely set-up.[21]

On 23 May, Ian Campbell received a signal from General Freyberg: 'You have done magnificently.' Freyberg also told him that a motorised company of the 1/Rangers was on its way from Canea to clear the road from Retimo to Perivolia II. Meanwhile, the Greeks promised Ray Sandover that they would drive the Germans from Saint George's Church that day.

Greatly heartened by these developments, the West Australians dug in east of the village shelled the church with a captured anti-tank gun and forced the Germans to abandon it, but the Greek battalion failed to capitalise on this success and the enemy were given time to establish themselves in other parts of the village.

In retaliation, 50 German aircraft attacked the area between that village and Platanes for five hours that afternoon. Jackson's company, nearest the Germans, escaped with nine casualties but Honner's and the mortar platoon next to them lost three men killed and 27 wounded.[22] Honner would never forget 'the furnace-odour of the hot metal of cannon shells and incendiary bullets'. Trees sheltering the wounded burst into flames and stretcher cases had to be dragged to safety from the enveloping flames.[23]

At sunset, the Germans on the ground attacked from Perivolia II, but ran into Bren-gun fire from Honner's forward positions and were beaten off. 'Our forward troops,' wrote an Australian, 'stood up and shot them down like rabbits.' Honner's company was then replaced by Captain Don McCaskill's A Company, which prepared to attack with Jackson's company as soon as the Rangers appeared. Unbeknown to either commander, the Rangers' commanding officer decided that his weapons – Bren-guns and one two-pounder anti-tank gun – would have no effect on the German strongholds and telephoned Freyberg's headquarters asking whether in the circumstances he should attack. He was ordered to do so.

While the Australians were still waiting to hear from them, the Rangers attacked on their own at dawn on 24 May. A number of their men were killed and wounded and the survivors climbed into their trucks and returned to Canea.[24]

General Student planned to join his forces in Crete on Day 3 of the battle – Thursday 22 May – but the slaughter of the elite parachute division had seriously damaged his reputation among the Nazi hierarchy. 'The great losses of the parachute regiment on the 20th of May disturbed Hitler and Goering very much,' he says. 'They thought that I was still suffering from my head injuries and did not possess the proper qualifications of a leading commander.'[25]

At this rate, the paras would be wiped out and the Barbarossa timetable deeply compromised. Goering ordered General Julius Ringel, commander of the 5th Mountain Division, to take command of all troops on the island. Student would remain in Athens, pending developments.

Yet Student's gamble to concentrate his efforts on Maleme had been the correct decision. And it was paying off. With every passing hour, the size and strength of Group West increased as planeload after planeload landed at Maleme with troops, munitions and transport. By the time General Freyberg reacted to the failure of the first counter-attack, it was five o'clock in the afternoon and a new menace was looming.

The previous day Colonel Heidrich, commander of the 3rd Parachute Regiment, had deployed the remnants of four battalions across a five-kilometre front in Prison Valley stretching from Daratsos to Alikianou. Heartened by an air-drop of 300 canisters, his men prepared themselves for the inevitable onslaught. When no attack had been launched by the morning of 22 May, Heidrich realised that the New Zealanders on the heights of Galatas were waiting for *him* to attack *them*.[26]

Although close to breaking point from stress and lack of sleep, Heidrich planned a two-pronged attack. To develop an attack on Canea – his main objective – he must first take Pink Hill and then Galatas. He decided that Major Helmut Derpa of his II Battalion would capture Pink Hill, while Major Heilmann of III Battalion headed north with 150 men to take the tiny village of Stalos. Here, a spur of the foothills ran all the way to the coast. It was the perfect spot to set up a roadblock cutting the road at Ay Marina and thus severing communications between the 4th and 5th Brigades.

Heidrich summoned Derpa to his headquarters inside the Aghia civilian prison to receive his orders. Derpa listened intently. He had seen the majority of his paratroopers killed during their fatal descent into Prison Valley on Day 1, some even drowning in the reservoir, and many more had been cut down by the drivers, fitters and engineers of the Petrol Company during the first assault on Pink Hill. When Heidrich finished speaking, Derpa expressed his doubts about the plan. Heidrich flew into a rage and accused him of cowardice. 'Deeply hurt, the sensitive and chivalrous battalion commander turned pale,' says Major von der Heydte, who was present.

Even from his tightly pressed lips, all the blood seemed to have been drained. After a momentary pause, he saluted. 'It is not a question of my own life, sir,' he said. 'I am considering the lives of the soldiers for whom I am responsible. My own life I would give gladly.'[27]

In the meantime, Kippenberger had not been idle. He had sent out patrols to test the Germans' strength and had then strengthened his own defences. Russell Force, which had withdrawn from its position at the reservoir on Day 1, was placed south-east of the Prison–Galatas road to support the Petrol Company under their new commander, Captain Harold Rowe. Major Russell had sustained an injury when he stumbled and fell on a bamboo stake during the withdrawal. A sliver of bamboo had speared his thigh and although in great pain he refused to leave the battlefield.

'John Russell was a lovely man and a great commander,' says Harry Spencer, who was a runner for the Divisional Cavalry. 'I was lucky – there was a ditch running up along the side of Pink Hill to headquarters and I could go most of the way under cover.'

One of the main problems – a constant complaint from frontline troops in all areas of the island – was the lack of food, or rather the lack of transport for B Echelon to carry it forward. 'There wasn't much to eat – mostly we lived on oranges and biscuits made into a sort of porridge,' Spencer says. 'I had to take a message to John Russell early one morning. He said, "Did you have breakfast?" I said, "What's that?" He had a bit of bully beef in the bottom of a tin and he shared it with me. I never forgot that.'[28]

At this late stage, Freyberg realised he had no alternative but to launch one big effort to recapture Maleme airfield. Brigadier Inglis' 4th Brigade (the 18th and 2/7th Battalions) would mount the attack, with the support of the 5th Brigade. Puttick was summoned to Creforce HQ to hear Freyberg's decision.

Freyberg then signalled Cairo that he had now committed most of his troops and was running short of some munitions.

He urged Wavell to reinforce the garrison with a fresh infantry brigade. And he warned that if his second counter-attack failed, he would have no alternative but to retreat to a shorter line.[29]

Absorbed with other matters, the Gabardine Swine at Middle East HQ had virtually no idea of Freyberg's difficulties, which somehow absolved them from the responsibility of providing solutions. And that applied to some extent to Wavell. He replied to Freyberg that he would send a force of commandos and, in the meantime, suggested that Freyberg move the Argylls from the south coast to Heraklion and then shuffle everyone westward. Chappel's troops at Heraklion would go to Retimo and Campbell's troops at Retimo would reinforce Canea.

Freyberg patiently explained that lack of transport and the distances involved made such moves impractical, especially as the road was blocked in several places by German troops.

When Puttick returned to divisional HQ from the quarry, he learned that Kippenberger's patrols had revealed 'considerable enemy movement' in Prison Valley and that the coastal road between 4th and 5th New Zealand Brigades 'was commanded by an enemy detachment' with a machine gun.[30] Puttick then went to see Inglis at 4th Brigade HQ, where he learned there had been a strong attack against Galatas and that movement in the hills north-west of Prison Valley 'indicated the probability of important enemy forces attempting to cut the Canea–Maleme road behind or east of the 5 Brigade'.[31]

Puttick was in a quandary. If he proceeded with the counter-attack, there was a danger that the 5th Brigade would be cut off. If he called it off, Britain and her Allies could kiss goodbye to Crete. It was a momentous decision and any support he might have expected from Hargest was not forthcoming. Hargest claimed that his troops were 'considerably exhausted and certainly not fit to make a further attack', an opinion that was to be disproved many times over the next few days.[32]

At eight o'clock that evening, General Ringel reached Maleme with a heavy fighter escort. His instructions from his fellow Austrian General Lohr were to secure the airfield, clear Suda Bay, relieve the paratroopers at Retimo, make contact with Heraklion and occupy the whole island, in that order. Ringel's first impressions could not have been good. He was forced to land on the beach because the airfield was still subjected to shellfire, and 12 British bombers – the force that Freyberg had ordered for the first counter-attack – had just bombed the crowded airfield and set six transports ablaze.

Ringel's first objective was to secure Maleme and capture Canea. He organised his forces into three battle groups: the first (Major Schatte with an engineer battalion) would protect Maleme from the west and south; the second (Colonel Ramcke and including most of the surviving parachute troops) would attack Canea from the west; and the third (Colonel Willibald Utz and the 100th Mountain Regiment) would envelop the defenders east of Maleme by outflanking the New Zealand positions on Vineyard Ridge and silencing the guns shelling the airfield.

Ringel's plan was to connect Group West with Group Centre by a sudden thrust along the coast road, while at the same time swinging in through the hills to Prison Valley. For the time being, he was happy to await the outcome of Colonel Heidrich's two bold moves that were already in progress.[33]

CHAPTER 22

Battle of Galatas

At seven o'clock that night, with two hours of daylight remaining, Major Derpa advanced up the prison road on a front of 700 metres against Pink Hill. The defenders had been blasted by heavy mortar fire and strafed from the air. Following their earlier brushes with the paras, the Petrol Company almost relished the chance of another skirmish. No one appreciated the New Zealanders' marksmanship and fighting spirit more than Helmut Derpa; considering his clash with Heidrich, it was somehow fitting that he was one of their first victims that night. Mortally wounded, he was carried from the battlefield and died the next day from a stomach wound.

But the New Zealanders were taking heavy casualties themselves and after losing 50 men Rowe pulled back 500 metres, enabling the Germans to mount two machine guns in cottages on the crest of the hill 400 metres below the walls of Galatas. Kippenberger realised that his whole brigade would be endangered if the Germans consolidated this position. He ordered Lieutenant MacLean's Composite Battalion reserve of 25 men to counter-attack from the right. Then he moved to

Wheat Hill with Lieutenant Bill Carson, a double All-Black (rugby and cricket), with the intention of sending Carson's equally small force, known as 'Carson's Rangers', in from the left. Kippenberger doubted that these forces would be sufficiently strong to dislodge the Germans, but help was at hand from an unexpected quarter.

The previous day, Kippenberger's brigade major, Captain Brian Bassett, had rounded up 200 Greek members of the 6th Battalion which had been overrun in Prison Valley and 'put them under a hero, Captain Forrester, a young blond Englishman (Queen's Regiment) who had trickled in the night before to liaise and report back. He nonchalantly forgot about reporting back in person until our scrap there finished a week later.'[1]

Forrester was in fact following orders from Guy Salisbury-Jones, whom he had contacted at Creforce HQ by field telephone on the first night of the battle and who instructed him to liaise with the Greek troops around Galatas. With Bassett's blessing, he had set up a training ground, protected by Russell Force, and for the past 36 hours he had been putting the Greeks through some basic military exercises.

To control their movements on the battlefield, Forrester instigated a system of whistle signals – one blast: standby; two: move; three: deploy; four: charge. He also suggested through an interpreter that as they dashed into battle they should give the war cry of Greece's Evzone troops, 'Aiera!'

Forrester noticed that a number of Cretan villagers, both men and women, were paying attention to his commands.[2] When the German advance started, he did not wait for orders. 'Communication being what it was with the Divisional Cavalry,' he says, 'I felt I required no orders because I'd already been briefed generally and I thought the time had come for action.'[3]

At the same time, Major Russell had taken Sergeant-Major Garth Seccombe around the outskirts of the village to see if

Russell Force could participate in the counter-attack. 'There were quite a few Greeks among us,' Harry Spencer says, 'and John ordered my friend Garth Seccombe to try to clean up Pink Hill with them.'[4]

Kippenberger was waiting for Bill Carson to line his men up on Wheat Hill before giving the order to charge when 'a most infernal uproar' broke out across the valley.[5]

'There came a terrific clamour from behind,' says Arthur Pope, one of Carson's Rangers.

> Out of the trees came Captain Forrester of the Buffs, clad in shorts, a long yellow army jersey reaching down almost to the bottom of the shorts, brass polished and gleaming, web belt in place and waving his revolver in his right hand. He was tall, thin-faced, with no tin hat – the very opposite of a soldier hero; as if he had just stepped on to the parade ground. He looked like a Wodehouse character. It was a most inspiring sight. Forrester was at the head of a crowd of disorderly Greeks, including women; one Greek had a shotgun with a serrated edge bread knife tied on like a bayonet, others had ancient weapons – all sorts. Without hesitation this uncouth group, with Forrester right out in front, went over the top of the parapet and headlong at the crest of the hill.[6]

Kippenberger had never seen anything like it. 'Over an open space in the trees near Galatas came running, bounding and yelling like Red Indians, about a hundred Greeks and villagers including women and children, led by Michael Forrester 20 yards ahead,' he says. 'It was too much for the Germans. They turned and ran without hesitation.'[7]

Meanwhile, Garth Seccombe had led his band of Greeks, which now included a number of Galatas residents including the village policeman, along the road to find the best point of attack. Lacking a system of whistle blasts to control them, he simply gave the order to charge and dashed up the hill. Nobody

BATTLE OF GALATAS   337

followed. The Greeks were arguing among themselves about the best thing to do. Seccombe 'repeated this performance four or five times until the whole situation was becoming quite farcical'.[8]

Then all of a sudden, with eyes rolling and bloodthirsty cries, the Greeks surged after him brandishing rifles, Tommy-guns, carving knives and bayonets. 'They killed all the Germans on the hill,' Harry Spencer says. 'Garth was nominated for the Victoria Cross but got the Distinguished Conduct Medal instead.' Between them, the two Greek forces had cleared Pink Hill and temporarily removed the threat to Galatas. Captain Rowe reported to Kippenberger: 'Div Pet are, and will remain, in their original positions.'[9]

Just before 11 o'clock that night, Michael Clarke was awakened by New Zealand troops of the 18th Battalion moving quietly through B Troop's position. They told him the attack on Maleme would begin about 1 am. Then Willie Smith rang on a field telephone to say he had been called to a meeting with Colonel Strutt and that the attack had been put back to three o'clock.

When Captain Smith reached Strutt's headquarters, he was astonished to receive orders to withdraw his guns and take up a new position near Ay Marina. He arrived back at B Troop in a fury. 'The bastards have called off the counter-attack,' he told the gunners. 'We've received bloody orders to bloody withdraw.'

'We were bitterly disappointed – yet another withdrawal when the situation seemed to be under control,' says Michael Clarke, remembering the Greek fiasco. What could have gone wrong?

The short answer was that Puttick had decided that the risk was too great. He figured that the counter-attack was unlikely to succeed against the heavily reinforced German force at

Maleme, while Brigadier Inglis would almost certainly find the road behind him cut by Heidrich's forces moving north-west through Stalos. Barely two hours after Freyberg had given orders for the New Zealand Division to eject the enemy from Maleme, Puttick decided that such an action would be too dangerous.[10] Around 7 pm, he rang Creforce HQ and recommended the withdrawal of the entire 5th Brigade to a new line in front of Platanias.

Freyberg did not contest his divisional commander's wishes, even though he must have known that such a withdrawal was an acceptance of the fact that Crete had been lost. He sent his chief of staff, Brigadier Stewart, to Puttick's HQ with authority to make a final decision.[11] From the beginning of his command of Creforce, Freyberg had been intent on re-gathering his 'scattered flock', as Dill had called the New Zealand Division, and the thought of six battalions being cut off at Maleme and forced to surrender would have meant the destruction of that division. For Bernard Freyberg, that was too high a price to pay.[12]

At 10 pm, Puttick confirmed his decision to withdraw at a meeting with Keith Stewart: the 5th Brigade would abandon all ground to the west of Platanias and pull back to a new line around the village.[13] The new orders were completed at 12.15 am on 23 May and biked to Jimmy Hargest. Just before dawn, he briefed his battalion commanders, except Colonel Dittmer who missed the meeting, on Puttick's decision. On hearing the news, Colonel Leckie's reaction was, 'What! Have they tossed it in?' He felt the 5th Brigade 'had made a mess of them the day before' and the morning of 23 May 'was so quiet and peaceful with not even a plane in the sky'.

When George Dittmer learned that the 23rd Battalion on his right was about to withdraw and that the Maoris were to provide the rearguard, he exploded. 'I went extremely rude about being left in such a manner but had little time to go into the reason for it,' he says. 'I knew that the enemy would see other units going over high ground to the east and then 28 Battalion would catch it.'[14]

B Troop continued to blast Maleme until 5 am and then started to manhandle its guns back across the field to the road. An hour later, Heilmann's 150 men reached Stalos, just inland from Ay Marina, without encountering any opposition. When the gunners reached their new position in front of Ay Marina at 9 am, they were sniped at from their rear. The Germans at Stalos were engaged by a strong patrol of the New Zealand Army Service Corps, which killed 15 of them. Then it was attacked from the north-east by a platoon of the 18th Battalion. All but one of its posts were knocked out before the platoon was recalled by the company commander, who was under the impression that the heights were held by a much larger force of Germans.[15]

By 10 am, all of the 5th Brigade's units were in position on the Platanias Line. The Maori Battalion, which arrived with the Germans hot on the heels of their rearguard, occupied its former position; the 23rd faced north on the high ground between the Maoris and Ay Marina; the depleted 21st and 22nd and the New Zealand Engineers faced north linking the 23rd Battalion with the 4th Brigade. Although the walking wounded in the 23rd Battalion's regimental aid post were evacuated, Leckie had left behind 60 stretcher cases in the care of his medical officer, Captain R. S. Stewart, and a handful of orderlies.[16]

The 27th Battery, which had provided the 5th Brigade's main support during the long battle, had extricated just two of its guns – French 75s – but added to the firepower of his own regiment Colonel Strutt had eight 75s, two Bofors and two two-pounders. These batteries laid down an accurate barrage on the advancing Germans and, after a stirring artillery duel, put their light guns out of action.[17] Roy Macartney spent most of the day chasing up ammunition for B Troop, which was well camouflaged beneath some trees out of sight of the roaming fighters.

At 11 am, Puttick met Freyberg. They agreed that the 5th Brigade should move into reserve that night; Inglis of the 4th Brigade would take over the units of 10th Brigade and command the right of a new frontline. The left would be formed by Vasey's 19th Brigade, which would take command of the 2/7th and 2/8th Battalions, just as Vasey had previously suggested to Freyberg, plus the 2nd Greek Battalion. This force would go into the line slightly west of Perivolia.

After dark, B Troop hooked up its guns and, alerted by Colonel Strutt that it was to move to a new position, waited by the roadside for further orders. At 10.30, Willie Smith informed them of their next destination: Galatas.

On 23 May, as billowing clouds of black smoke from the burning ships in Suda Bay settled over Freyberg's headquarters, he received a cable from Churchill. 'The whole world,' the Prime Minister wrote, 'watches your splendid battle on which great things turn.'[18] Freyberg was the first to admit things were anything but splendid. 'Rapidly deteriorating' were the words he later used to describe the situation at that time.[19]

In the late afternoon, the II Battalion of the 85th Mountain Regiment began an outflanking movement from Maleme to cut the battered New Zealand battalions off from Galatas. As agreed with Freyberg, Puttick and Hargest pulled the 5th Brigade into reserve beyond Galatas and Daratsos. The move was made overnight and by the morning of 24 May the frontline ran in an arc from Galatas to the sea. The Composite Battalion, which had been manning the northern end of this sector since the first day, was relieved by the 400-strong 18th Battalion of Inglis' 4th Brigade. 'It was heartening,' Kippenberger says, 'to see them come in – looking very efficient and battle-worthy – in painful contrast with the columns of clumps in which my unfortunate quasi-infantry got about.'[20]

According to Kippenberger, the day had started 'ominously

quiet', with the 18th and 19th Battalions on either side of
Russell Force and the Petrol Company holding the crucial
central section of the line. Everyone expected an attack
but Heidrich's troops were exhausted and running low on
ammunition. Indeed, Ringel's plan was for the Mountain troops
advancing from Maleme to link up with von der Heydte's
force in Prison Valley and Heilmann's men at Stalos to assault
Galatas from both southern and western flanks.

Big things, decisive things, were happening all over
Group West. That afternoon, von Richthofen's bombers set
about carpet-bombing Canea, forcing Freyberg to move his
headquarters to a safer spot, a camouflaged tent off the Suda–
Heraklion road. Early the following morning, Sunday 25 May,
General Student landed at Maleme to retrieve his shattered
reputation from among the burning debris of his once-proud
XI Air Corps. Looking old and shrunken, a mere shadow of the
martinet who had launched Operation Mercury, he reported
to Ringel's headquarters. He had been sent so that Goering
could claim Crete as a Luftwaffe victory but it had been made
painfully clear to him that Ringel was in charge of the battle.

At the same time, Radio Berlin – which had been ominously
silent about Crete until Goebbels could be assured of success –
suddenly announced Germany's invasion of the island. As the
men of the 3rd Parachute Regiment in Prison Valley listened to
the good news, von der Heydte received a message by runner
that contact had been made with the Mountain troops. After
much bloodshed and a great deal of anxiety, Group West had
finally met up with Group Centre.[21]

B Troop of the 2/3rd Field Regiment had sited its four Italian
75s in a dry wadi just east of the road between Galatas and the
coast. Shortly after dawn, they opened fire on the enemy. At
7.30 am, the Messerschmitts located the gun-pits and strafed
them every few minutes. By mid-morning the air attacks had
become so severe that the crews were reduced to two or three
men while the rest took cover.

A short distance away on Kippenberger's western flank, the 18th Battalion was bombed and strafed as a prelude to an assault by Ramcke's paratroopers and part of Colonel Utz's 100th Mountain Regiment. At 4 pm, Lieutenant-Colonel John Gray reported that he was 'warmly engaged'. Gray had neglected to occupy Ruin Hill and was paying a high price. In fact, his entire line stretching from the coast down to Wheat Hill was subjected to the most concerted enemy attack of the entire battle. According to Kippenberger, 'the crackle of musketry swelled to a roar, heavily punctuated by mortar bursts'.[22]

Kippenberger went forward to get a view of the action around Wheat Hill, where six mortar shells per minute were exploding on one company sector alone. 'In a hollow, nearly covered by undergrowth,' he wrote, 'I came upon a party of women and children huddled together like little birds. They looked at me silently, with black, terrified eyes.'[23]

At 6 pm, the 18th Battalion's line broke under pressure from Colonel Ramcke's paras, suddenly revitalised by the presence of their great rivals, the Mountain troops. Kippenberger ordered Gray to launch an immediate counter-attack with his reserve, consisting of Headquarters Company plus a mixed group consisting of 'the padre, clerks, batmen, everyone who could carry a rifle'.

The attack failed. Kippenberger then summoned a 120-strong contingent of the 20th Battalion who had been sent as reinforcements by Brigadier Inglis. Moving forward, they discovered that the Composite Battalion had cracked under the mortar barrage. 'Back, back!' some of its members were shouting. 'They're coming through in thousands.'[24] 'Already there was a trickle of stragglers,' says the official New Zealand historian.[25] There would soon be many more.

At the southern end of the 18th Battalion's line, Kippenberger had refused two requests from A Company holding Wheat Hill to withdraw. In the late afternoon, they could no longer hold on and the position was abandoned, exposing Major Lynch's C

Company in the centre of the line and forcing it to fall back. The Germans pushed through the gap and occupied Galatas.

Suddenly, Kippenberger found himself surrounded by a stream of running men, 'many of them on the verge of panic'. He strode among them shouting the most famous words of the Battle of Crete, 'Stand for New Zealand! Stand for New Zealand! Stand every man who is a soldier! Stand every man who is a soldier!'[26]

With the help of Sergeant-Major George Andrews of the 18th Battalion and Johnny Sullivan, the intelligence sergeant of the 20th, Kippenberger placed groups of men under the control of any officer or NCO who happened to be at hand. He then ordered them across the valley to a ridge west of Daratsos where he could see a white church gleaming in the evening sun. In that position, they would cover the right of the 19th Battalion's line and be able to offer some protection to Russell Force and the Petrol Company, which had been cut off on the south-west corner of Galatas. John Gray and the remnants of the 18th Battalion were sent over to join them.[27]

At his new headquarters, Freyberg wrote to Wavell:

Today has been one of great anxiety to me here. The enemy carried out one small attack last night and this afternoon he attacked with little success. This evening at 1700 hours bombers and ground strafers came over and bombed our forward troops and then his ground troops launched an attack. It is still in progress and I am awaiting news. Later. I have heard from Puttick that the line has gone and we are trying to stabilise. I don't know if they will be able to. I am apprehensive. I will send messages as I can later.[28]

At midday, Willie Smith reported that New Zealand infantry detachments were retiring past his observation post. An hour later, a German machine gun opened up from a rocky hillock. The bullets zipped low over the gunners' heads and slammed into a tree trunk shielding Michael Clarke. Gunner Dasher Dean, armed with a rifle, offered to stalk the machine-gunner. 'I gave this idea my warm blessing,' Clarke says. 'He ran off cheerfully – an undisciplined type, forever in hot water over some crime. He didn't seem to realise that German bullets were dangerous.'

Dasher Dean reappeared an hour later. He had forced the machine gun to move to a new position but had taken a bullet in his backside. He was sent off to the regimental aid post and took no further part in the battle.

In mid-afternoon, the air attacks over Galatas tapered off while the Germans concentrated their bombardment of Canea. But enemy troops were getting closer to the guns. Gunner Noel Brown sighted Germans advancing down a slope 600 metres away. B Troop fired a salvo and they went to ground. Then 200 members of the Maori Battalion appeared in a wadi to the gunners' left. They performed a spirited *haka*, waved and shouted to the gunners, then charged in open formation across the dry riverbed and up the stony slope into the olive trees. The Germans fled.

The next arrivals in the left-hand wadi were a group of Cretan civilians, mostly dressed in Sunday church attire of black trousers and white shirts. 'Some wore fierce moustaches and they ranged in age from greyheads to mere youths,' Michael Clarke says.

They were brandishing long-barrelled rifles, shotguns and ancient pistols, and halted to listen to a dramatic exhortation from their mayor, who was dressed in a black suit and a black beret, and wore his bright blue official sash diagonally across his chest. Their leader was a very tall black-robed priest with a thick black beard reaching to his waist. He was shouting, and waving a huge scythe whose blade caught the sun's rays. He and the mayor led a noisy charge up the slope and disappeared from our view.

At 4.30 pm, a retiring party of New Zealand infantry informed Willie Smith that they were the last unit in the line. In the absence of any orders from Inglis' headquarters, every spare gunner armed himself with a rifle, while the guns fired at the enemy over open sights.

The New Zealand official historian writes:

The Australian troop had done good work all day bringing down fire on the right flank. Eventually the enemy aircraft located them and gave them special attention but the guns kept on firing. They were still firing over open sights with their four Italian 75s when the Germans reached the outskirts of Galatas. At point-blank range, with each gun firing on its own commander's orders, they did a great deal to save the situation.[29]

Meanwhile, Brigadier Inglis had sent further reinforcements to Galatas consisting of two companies of the 23rd Battalion, the 4th Brigade band, a Pioneer platoon and the New Zealanders' concert party, all armed as infantry. Kippenberger knew that it was essential to drive the Germans out of Galatas and reclaim the village, otherwise the road to Canea would be wide open. 'It was no use trying to patch the line any more,' he says. 'Obviously we must hit or everything would crumble away.'

Kippenberger was assembling his force along a stone wall at the bottom of a hill leading up to Galatas when, in the fading light, Roy Farran trundled up with two light tanks of the 3rd Hussars and offered to help. Kippenberger asked him to go into the village and have a look round. Farran fought his way in and returned under heavy fire to report, 'The place is stiff with Jerries.' Kippenberger asked him if he would lead the counter-attack and he agreed.[30]

Men started appearing from everywhere. Captain Michael
Forrester, carrying a rifle and bayonet (but minus his Greeks,
who had fought magnificently but had been scattered and
killed), Bill Carson and his surviving Carson's Rangers, a
number of Maoris and stragglers from various units all took
their place along the wall until the force had swollen to 300.
Colonel Gray, warned in advance by Kippenberger's batman,
led the remnants of the 18th Battalion from the Daratsos ridge
to join the fray.[31]

'Everyone looked tense and grim,' says Lieutenant Sandy
Thomas of the 23rd Battalion, 'and I wondered if they were
feeling as afraid as I, whether their throats were as dry, their
stomachs feeling now frozen, now fluid. I hoped that I appeared
as cool as they. It occurred to me suddenly that this was going to
be the biggest moment of my life.'[32]

As Farran's tanks took off up the hill towards Galatas, 'the
Maoris began their *haka* war chant and everyone took it up,'
says Michael Forrester. 'The noise was incredible.' At 8.10 pm,
Kippenberger gave the signal and his men charged up the
hill after the tanks. 'Instantly there was the most startling
clamour, audible all over the field,' Kippenberger says. 'Scores of
automatics and rifles being fired at once, the crunch of grenades,
screams and yells – the uproar swelled and sank, swelled again
to a terrifying crescendo.'[33]

Women and children who had crept back into the village
fled down the road; a terrified old woman clung desperately to
Kippenberger's arm. By now, Farran's tank had travelled the
200 metres to the village square on the summit of the hill, but
there his tank was hit by an anti-tank grenade and he was badly
wounded. After ensuring that his crew had escaped, Farran sat
at the roadside shouting, 'Good show New Zealand, jolly good
show, come on New Zealand.'[34]

With the second tank still active, the attacking force
swarmed into the village square, dominated by a massive
Orthodox church with twin bell towers. The troops charged

at the Germans with their 18-inch Gallipoli bayonets, while others hurled grenades. The enemy had not had time to form up and was ill-prepared for such a frenzied assault. A German seized one of the cooks by the throat and swung him around as a shield against the bayonets but was smashed across the head with the butt of a rifle.[35]

Bullets ripped across the façade of the church and ricocheted off the hull of Farran's tank (one panel of which now forms a side gate in Galatas). Most of the Germans in the houses opposite the square panicked and fled, although one German stayed long enough to throw a grenade from the rooftops while another opened fire with a Spandau. Sandy Thomas was wounded by the grenade and then shot in the thigh. As he went down, one of his men rallied his platoon with the cry, 'Come on, you blokes, let's get stuck into the bastards and be done with it.'[36]

Having retreated, the Germans shelled the village with mortars and Kippenberger ordered his force to withdraw. The attack had achieved his purpose and he did not want to inflict further loss of life on his brave little band. He shepherded them back to the Daratsos ridge, where they found that the remnants of Russell Force and the Petrol Company – all that remained of his 10th Brigade – had been able to extricate themselves from Pink Hill. The seriously wounded, Farran and Thomas included, had to be left behind at Galatas amid the carnage in the village square.

Right at the end of the battle, Major Thomason had arrived on the scene with the other companies of 23rd Battalion and deployed them around the village in case the enemy counter-attacked. Heidrich, however, decided to wait until daylight, when he could bring artillery and aircraft to bear.[37]

After six days of defeat and humiliating retreat, 'Kip's charge' restored a lot of pride and boosted morale in the ranks and those who had taken part were the envy of their mates. Like the resolute defenders of Pink Hill, it showed that, given an opportunity, the New Zealanders were more than a match for the enemy.

CHAPTER 23

On 42nd Street

At 8.30 pm on 25 May, while the battle to retake Galatas was still raging, Willie Smith received orders for B Troop to pack up and join the 19th Brigade near Perivolia. The guns were pulled out singly, while Bombardier Donald Philps, firing over open sights with the last gun, kept the enemy at bay. During the move, one gun fell over the low parapet of a bombed bridge and had to be abandoned. Late that night, B Troop reached 'The King's House' and set up its guns in the garden.

By then, Colonel Kippenberger had joined Brigadier Inglis and most of his battalion commanders in his command post, a tarpaulin-covered hole in the ground near the Galatas turn-off. Inglis was anxious to use the 28th Battalion in a night attack to drive the Germans out of Galatas and its environs.

'Can you do it?' Inglis asked George Dittmer.

'I'll give it a go,' the Maoris' commander replied.

At that moment, Bill Gentry, Puttick's chief of staff, lowered himself into the hole. Given the details of the plan, he had no hesitation in vetoing it. Quite apart from the problems involved in such a difficult night manoeuvre, the Maoris were the division's last intact battalion and if they were used tonight there would be no chance of holding the line against a renewed German assault in the morning.

'There was no further argument,' Kippenberger says. 'It was quickly decided that Galatas must be abandoned and everyone brought back to the Daratsos Line before morning.'[1]

At 1 am on 26 May, the 4th Brigade withdrew through the 5th Brigade to a line linking up with Brigadier Vasey's two Australian battalions and B Troop's gunners at the eastern end of Prison Valley in front of Perivolia. In the morning, Puttick and Hargest met Vasey. 'Tall good-looking soldierly type,' Hargest noted in his diary. 'He was to be my comrade for one week and a good one. He said his troops were fresh and had not been engaged and could hang on indefinitely.'[2]

None of the commanders knew that at 9.30 that morning, after conferring with Captain Morse and Group Captain Beamish, General Freyberg had cabled the following to Middle East HQ:

I regret to have to report that in my opinion the limit of endurance has been reached by the troops under my command here at Suda Bay. No matter what decision is taken by the Commanders-in-Chief, from a military point of view our position here is hopeless. A small ill-equipped and immobile force such as ours cannot stand up against the concentrated bombing that we have been faced with during the last seven days. I feel that I should tell you that from an administrative point of view the difficulties of extricating this force in full are now insuperable. Provided a decision is reached at once a certain proportion of the force might be embarked. Once this sector has been reduced the reduction of Retimo and Heraklion by the same methods will only be a matter of time. The troops we have with the exception of the Welch Regiment and the Commandos are past any offensive action. If you decide in view of whole Middle East position that hours help we will carry on. I would have to consider how this would be best achieved. Suda Bay may be under fire within twenty-four hours. Further, casualties have been heavy, and we have lost the majority of our immobile guns.[3]

All day long, Freyberg waited for a reply to his uncompromising cable, all the more powerful because of its lack of rhetoric or excuse-making. He did not receive one. Wavell had to discuss the question of evacuation with his fellow commanders-in-chief and, at the same time, refer it to the chiefs of staff in London. Sir John Dill would then place it before Churchill, who had great hopes that the garrison might hold out.

John Peck and his mates did not feel that they were past it – in fact, the 2/7th's historian writes that on that day 'the battalion's tail was up' – and George Vasey was confident his line would hold for the next 48 hours.[4] But from first light on 26 May the troops were bombed and strafed and at 10.30 Mountain troops attacked the left flank of the Australian line at its junction with the 2nd Greek Battalion. This pressure eventually created a gap which forced the 2/8th Battalion to pull back, thus leaving the 2/7th's flank hanging in thin air. Any movement was difficult; German machine guns hidden in orchards raked the roads and olive groves. But when the enemy's attack was intensified in the afternoon Vasey ordered both battalions to fall back and join the marines in their position at Mournies.[5]

At 'The King's House', B Troop had spent most of the morning demolishing a garden wall near the stables to improve their field of fire. There was no sign of enemy activity and – inexplicably, considering the battle taking place on the Australian line – the gunners received no calls for fire, so they passed a restful afternoon asleep. As they snoozed, Vasey's situation became increasingly critical, while the bombing of Canea became ever more violent.

Dr Theo Stephanides, who was nursing patients in a makeshift aid post on the outskirts of the doomed city, says,

The whole landscape was erupting earth, smoke and flame, and all our ack-ack guns had been silenced except for an occasional shot from a couple of dogged Bofors near Suda. In Canea, only the harbour front was left unharmed, because it would soon be useful. Thirteen Venetian palaces from the 15th and 16th centuries were destroyed ... [villagers] gathered in stunned silence watching the holocaust and I could sense that to them it was like the end of the world. Canea was the only town that many of them had ever known. It was their joy and their pride, and it was now crumbling to smoke and cinders before their very eyes. Some of the men had tears streaming down their faces and others shook their fists and cursed the Germans.[6]

Two of John Peck's mates, Steve Warner and Arnold Newnham, had been killed by bombs in their trenches. 'Of Steve we had found nothing,' he says. 'We put Arnold's dirt-covered but unmarked body in a groundsheet and placed it in a nearby vineyard for later burial.'

At 5 pm, Vasey conferred with Hargest and Puttick and it was agreed that withdrawal was unavoidable owing to the threat to the Australians' left flank.[7] That night, the 5th and 19th Brigades pulled out. The troops tramped past the smouldering ruins of Canea to take up new positions in 42nd Street, a sunken dirt track running south-west from the head of Suda Bay to the foothills of the Malaxa escarpment. It would be the scene of an action that would go down as one of the most amazing in the new Anzacs' battle history.

The reason Bernard Freyberg had not heard from Middle East HQ on the 26th was that General Wavell and Air Marshal Tedder (who had replaced Arthur Longmore at the beginning of May) had gone to Alexandria to discuss the fate of Creforce with Admiral Cunningham on board *Warspite*. General Blamey and Peter Fraser, the Prime Minister of New Zealand, were also present.

After reading Freyberg's gloomy prognosis, the joint planning staffs in Cairo had prepared a paper which accepted that the troops in Crete were defeated, disorganised and running short of supplies. The RAF had lost many aircraft and could not operate effectively over Crete. The navy had lost a large part of its operational force, sunk or damaged, in a series of disasters, starting on 22 May when the cruisers *Gloucester* and *Fiji* and the destroyer *Greyhound* had been sunk.

In the middle of that terrible day Cunningham had signalled his ships, 'Stick it out. Navy must not let Army down. No enemy forces must reach Crete by sea.' By nightfall, the battleships *Warspite* and *Valiant* and cruisers *Naiad* and *Carlisle* had also been damaged. The following day, the destroyers *Kashmir* and *Kelly* went to the bottom. Taking all of this into account, the planners recommended that the commanders-in-chief order Freyberg to surrender.[8]

Wavell spoke first. He said that the remainder of the fleet might well be lost if they tried to evacuate the soldiers from Crete. If the fleet were lost, the Allies would lose control of the eastern Mediterranean, the Germans would reach Syria and then take the Persian oilfields. Without Persian oil, Wavell feared we could not win the war. It would take three years, he said, to build a new fleet.[9]

Blamey and Fraser felt they had no alternative but to join Wavell and Tedder in agreeing to accept the unanimous advice of their staffs. The only dissenting voice was Cunningham's. He spoke last and his words shone like a beacon through the prevailing darkness:

> It has always been the duty of the Navy to take the Army overseas to battle and, if the Army fail, to bring them back again. If we now break with that tradition, ever afterwards when soldiers go overseas they will tend to look over their

shoulders instead of relying on the Navy. You have said, General, that it will take three years to build a new fleet. I will tell you that it will take three hundred years to build a new tradition. If, gentlemen, you now order the Army in Crete to surrender, the fleet will still go there to bring off the Marines.

None of the army or air force planners had considered the loyalty of the navy towards the Royal Marines. Those 'fresh-faced English lads' proved to be Cunningham's ace in the hole – and the saviours of Creforce. 'My view was perfectly clear,' he said later. 'I needed no persuasion. It was impossible to abandon the troops in Crete. Our naval tradition would never survive such an action. Whatever the risks, whatever our losses, the remaining ships of the fleet would make an all-out effort to bring away the Army.'[10]

Late that night, Wavell replied to Freyberg's cable. It was not the answer he had hoped for; indeed, Wavell told him that the longer Crete could hold out the better. He came up with another crackpot idea: that the Suda–Maleme force retire to Retimo and hold the eastern part of the island. At 1 am on 27 May, Freyberg informed Wavell that Retimo had almost run out of food and ammunition; all guns in the Maleme–Suda sector had been lost; and Creforce could survive only if food was landed at once.[11]

Then Churchill signalled Freyberg direct, 'Your glorious defence commands admiration in every land. We know enemy is hard pressed. All aid in our power is being sent.' To the commanders-in-chief, Churchill cabled, 'Victory in Crete essential at this turning-point in the war. Keep hurling in all aid you can.'

Help had in fact been sent but very little had got through the Luftwaffe blockade. Earlier that day, Glenroy, with 1000 members of the Queen's Regiment on board, caught fire after being bombed on her way to disembark the troops at Timbaki. She was forced to return to Alexandria, as were two merchant ships loaded with supplies. Later that night, however, the destroyers *Hero* and HMAS *Nizam* (Lieutenant-Commander Max Clark) and the fast minelayer *Abdiel* slipped into Suda Bay with 80 tonnes of supplies and 750 commandos, commanded by Colonel Robert Laycock and including the novelist Evelyn Waugh as intelligence officer. 'Layforce' were the last reinforcements to reach Crete. The ships departed with 930 walking wounded and hundreds of base troops who were of no further use.

The dirt track dubbed '42nd Street' took its name from the 42nd Field Company of the Royal Engineers which had bivouacked there in late 1940. It is also true that the name had been inspired by the Ruby Keeler film *42nd Street*, winner of the Oscar for best picture in 1933. From the northern end of 'the Street', it was possible to see the quay at Suda Bay. Freyberg visited the Australians that night and noted that they seemed 'absolutely confident'. Then he watched the destroyers being unloaded down on the wharf.[12]

Puttick and Vasey had been placed under the commander of the Suda Bay sector, General Weston. He was not at 42nd Street when they arrived, so they deployed the troops themselves. The 2/8th was placed astride the main road, with the tightly packed 2/7th, 21st, 28th, 19th and 22nd Battalions looking out from the cover of an earth bank through a dense olive grove towards a creek.

The sudden withdrawal of the two brigades had left the 1/Welch, 1/Rangers and Northumberland Hussars stranded in Canea. The British units fought bravely against a large enemy force of paratroopers and Mountain troops but had taken a terrible beating and were now retiring in tatters through the Anzac line.[13]

From early morning on 27 May, the Germans bombed the Anzacs and raked their trenches with machine-gun fire. At

10 am, George Dittmer told Colonels Walker and Allen that if the enemy came to close quarters his battalion would open fire and then charge. Walker and Allen agreed that their battalions would do the same. The opportunity arose at 11 am when the Anzacs saw 400 Germans advancing down the Suda Bay road.

The 2/7th Battalion had two companies in position up front and Major Walter Miller, commanding C Company on the right, sent forward a patrol under Lieutenant Beverley McGeoch to keep the enemy under observation, while he suggested to Captain St Elmo Nelson, commanding D Company on his left, that he join the attack. He also dispatched a runner to Colonel Walker, who replied that both C and D Companies should attack after allowing the Germans to come very close.[14]

'When this order went out, it seemed to lift the tension that had been hanging over us for the past few days,' Walker's batman, Private Harold Passey, says. 'The time had come when we were going to show Jerry a few tricks.'[15]

No one knows for certain who charged first but the effect was electrifying. The Maoris, with the 19th Battalion on their left and the 21st on their right, jumped into action as soon as they heard a shouted command from their section commanders. At the same time, McGeoch's patrol discovered a large number of Mountain troops raiding an abandoned storage depot.[16] The Germans, members of Colonel Maximilian Jais' 141st Mountain Regiment, were just 50 metres through the trees, so close that the Australians could hear them talking. 'I saw a German soldier stand up in clear view,' says Reg Saunders, an Aboriginal member of the patrol. 'He was my first sure kill. I can remember feeling just for a moment that it was just like shooting a kangaroo.'[17]

Major Miller was on his way forward to join Lieutenant McGeoch when the firing began. He signalled C Company forward and, as they arrived, Mick Baxter, a submachine-gunner, stood up with his gun and said, 'Jesus, I can't see a bloody thing from here.' Then he walked straight into the Germans' machine-gun fire but the shots missed. He started to trot, then to run hard, firing from the hip as he went. 'It was then we charged – more to save Mick, I suppose, than anything else,' says Reg Saunders.[18]

The Germans were taken by surprise and started running for cover. St Elmo Nelson dashed forward, waving D Company to follow him and shouting, 'Get into them!' 'Someone gave a rousing yell and everyone took it up,' says the unit's historian. 'They were charging along shouting at the top of their voices. They ran, they stumbled, they got up again and ran onwards. Everyone was in it.' Nelson was hit in the shoulder and bowled over but Lieutenant Steve Bernard continued to lead the charge even after being wounded himself.[19]

John Peck does not remember anyone giving the order – 'it was a spontaneous thing' – but he was soon engaged with the enemy.

> They didn't just turn and run, they fought back. You have to be ferocious, 'Come on, you bastards! Let's have a go at you!' I got a bayonet through my arm. Hand-to-hand combat was very frightening. You know without a shadow of a doubt that if you make a fraction of a mistake, then you're dead. The German knew it and I knew it. It wasn't a question of, 'Put up your hands'. No quarter was asked or given. You're dead or you're alive, and if you're alive you move on to the next one. He was fairly big, bigger than me, and he got me through the arm but he was dead very soon afterwards. The German bayonets were nowhere near as long as ours – ours were 18 inches long. I never felt anything, not even relief.[20]

To the left, the Australians could hear the Maoris wreaking havoc among the Germans. Waving a bamboo pole and carrying a revolver, Captain Royal led B Company in a charge against enemy machine guns firing at a range of 150 metres. Captain

Scott's C Company deployed across the battalion front in 42nd Street and charged, while A Company moved around each flank of the battalion to get at the Germans. 'A few stray Greek soldiers added their Hellenic yells to the blood-curdling din,' the Maoris' historian says. 'Section after section of the enemy was overrun as the Maoris fanned out and swept around them and then went in for the kill.'[21]

After being bayoneted in the arm, John Peck carried on with the attack oblivious to the pain. 'You go on – you shoot and you stab and then they run,' he says.

> They ran and we kept running after them. We were absolutely exhausted – we'd gone from a gallop right down to a crawl. If we'd suddenly struck a fresh batch of troops we would have been dead. We were called back. The commanders were shit-scared because their troops were scattered everywhere. We were called back to where we had started and we weren't very pleased about it. We wanted to keep them on the run.[22]

The coup de grace was administered by Lieutenant Wilson Bolton of the 2/1st Machine-gun Battalion, who arrived with a Vickers machine gun and fired on the fleeing enemy. The Maoris estimated the dead on their front at more than 80. The Australians said that 200 Germans had been killed and three taken prisoner. In the charge, the 2/7th lost 10 killed and 28 wounded; and there were 14 Maori casualties.[23] 'Russ Barker got a bayonet in the chest,' John Peck says, 'so we took it in turns to carry him back but when we got back he was dead. He died because one of the bullets flying at us had hit him instead.'

Colonel Dittmer later wrote,

> After heavy enemy mortar fire also MMG fire the enemy was seen in undergrowth just the other side of 42nd Street. The 28th and at least some other units opened fire, then the front companies of 28 Bn under shouted orders of the

company commanders leapt up and dashed across the road and commenced to mix things. Very soon afterwards the 2/7 Australian, and about the same time the 21st, moved forward. From where I was with the reserve company I could see what happened. The 28 Battalion thought the 2/7 Australian Battalion a really great unit and does not wish to deprive the 2/7 of any credit that is its due.[24]

Like Bardia and Tobruk, the 'Charge at 42nd Street' had taught Peck that mateship was the driving force behind any successful unit. 'The thing that makes people fight – and fight hard – is their comradeship, their pride. They would rather die than let their mates down. Mateship is a closer thing than matrimony.'

By 2.30 that afternoon, the Germans hit back with mortar and machine-gun fire. Hundreds could be seen moving round the hills to the south in an attempt to encircle the Anzac positions. At 3.50 pm, Wavell signalled Freyberg authorising the evacuation of Crete. It would take place mainly at a little fishing village called Sphakia.[25]

CHAPTER 24

Road to Sphakia

Arthur Midwood, the Maori private who had been shot in the chest on Day 1, had been patched up by torchlight and then sent to some caves in a hillside near Canea with other wounded. The caves were being used as an air-raid shelter as well as a hospital. As the sounds of battle came closer on 27 May, one of the orderlies told the patients, 'We're going to be overrun in half an hour's time, so you'll be prisoners of war.'

The man returned a few minutes later and said, 'Those of you who think they can walk out of here are welcome to go.'

Midwood did not have to be told twice. His arm was in a sling but he still had his army boots and he could still walk. 'That was for me,' he says. 'I wasn't sticking around to become a POW. I finished up at Suda Bay that night but there was a fight going on, so I moved on.'[1]

Midwood joined the human tide of men and vehicles moving slowly along the coast road towards Kalives. Someone told him that the army was being picked up at Sphakia. He had no idea where that was, or how far, so he just kept walking. The distance between Suda and Sphakia was 48 kilometres over a steep, rutted, half-made road, across the high plateau of Askifou and up through a pass in the White Mountains.

The road ended in a series of hairpin bends and stopped at the edge of an escarpment. There was a 150-metre drop down to the village, with the beach further below. The only way to reach the beach was along a precipitous goat track covered in loose stones. For a fit man with a supply of food and water, the trek would have been a daunting prospect; for a wounded man with one arm in a sling and no provisions or medication, it seemed impossible.

The plan for embarkation was that the 20,000 troops in the Maleme–Suda Bay and Retimo sectors would travel overland to the south coast and embark from the beaches at Sphakia and Plakias, while those in the Heraklion area would be taken from that port. Embarkation would start on the night of 28/29 May and the ships would sail by 3 am to get as far as possible from enemy air bases by daylight.[2]

Word was conveyed to all commanders in the Suda area and to Brian Chappel at Heraklion, but there was a problem with Colonel Campbell at Retimo. He had no ciphers and such an important message could not be sent in clear. Earlier that day, it had been arranged that Lieutenant Robert Haig should ferry ten tons of desperately needed rations from the storehouses at Suda Bay to Retimo by sea. Freyberg told an officer to get Haig to pass on the order to embark to Campbell. Haig had already set off and did not receive the message. Freyberg then asked Cairo to drop it by aircraft; unbeknown to him, the Hurricane carrying it was shot down and Campbell remained in ignorance of the evacuation.

Meanwhile, B Troop had been ordered to pull out of 'The King's House' and proceed towards Suda, then south-east through the hills to Vrises. Major M. A. Bull of the New Zealand Divisional Artillery borrowed one of the troop's trucks containing their signals equipment and rations. He told Willie Smith to post guides at road junctions and he would pick them up and overtake the troop to give it instructions for a new position. Next day, there was no sign of Major Bull or the truck. Smith learned from a passing New Zealand gunner that Bull had ordered his own gunners to destroy their guns and make for Sphakia. B Troop's vehicle had also been destroyed.

This meant that Willie Smith's two surviving 75s were now the only artillery pieces between Suda and Sphakia and, though short of ammunition and minus their rations and signalling gear, they were bound to be part of the rearguard. Having been in action continuously since 21 May, the gunners badly needed a rest, but there was no chance of that now.

Meanwhile, Arthur Midwood trudged through the heat of the day towards Vrises. 'There was no one to help you,' he says. 'They were all looking after themselves.'[3]

With the Germans moving east in captured transport, Creforce headquarters left for Sphakia on the evening of 27 May. Freyberg's driver had decided to deny his car to the enemy by pushing it over the side of a bank so the general and Brigadier Stewart travelled in a commandeered vehicle whose radiator had been damaged by shrapnel. The car kept running out of water and would grind to a standstill every few miles. 'Never shall I forget the disorganisation and almost complete lack of control of the masses on the move as we made our way slowly through that endless stream of trudging men,' Freyberg says.[4]

General Weston, who was in command of the rearguard, had gone south to reconnoitre the road but found the route back to his headquarters blocked. At one point, he bumped into Evelyn Waugh, who was looking for Layforce's forward units.

'Who the hell are you and where are you going?' the general demanded.

Waugh told him.

'Where's Laycock?'

Waugh showed him his map.

'Don't you know better than to show a map? It's the best way of telling the enemy where headquarters are.'[5]

Neither Vasey nor Hargest heard from Weston that day but they discovered from Colonel Laycock that he had orders to act as rearguard on the road to Sphakia. This enabled Vasey and Hargest to extricate their forces from 42nd Street, with the 5th Brigade reaching Stilos that night, while the 19th Brigade dug in at nearby Neo Khorion.[6] 'The fact that the rearguard actions were effectively and successfully conducted was due mainly to the excellent co-operation between New Zealand and Australian brigadiers and Colonel Laycock,' Weston later wrote.

Freyberg, however, was making slow progress in his damaged car, which required a push from behind by one of the heavily laden trucks to get up hills. He later wrote about the long column stretching in front of him:

> There were units sticking together and marching with their weapons – units of one or other of the composite forces that had come out of the line – but in the main it was a disorganised rabble making its way doggedly and painfully to the south. There were thousands of unarmed troops including the Cypriots and Palestinians. Without leadership, without any sort of discipline, it is impossible to expect anything else of troops who have never been trained as fighting soldiers.
>
> Somehow or other the word Sphakia got out and many of these people had taken a flying start in any available transport they could steal. This transport was later abandoned at the end of the road above Sphakia, where it remained thus revealing to the enemy our line of evacuation.

At dawn on 28 May, the rearguard just beat the German spearhead to the foot of the road to Sphakia. If the enemy broke through, the entire evacuation operation would be in jeopardy. At 6 am, the Germans engaged a company of commandos and two Maori companies under Captain Rangi Royal. After a savage two-hour fight, they had surrounded them and were streaming towards the 5th Brigade at Stilos. The surviving commandos withdrew through the Maoris and at 12.30 Captain Royal and his troops fought their way back to their unit. At 6.30 that night, the German attack reached the 5th Brigade, where it was stopped in its tracks with the loss of some 50 killed or wounded.[7]

Sergeant Clive Hulme infiltrated enemy lines and stalked and shot German snipers from the rear – he was credited with killing 33 of them during the Battle of Crete before being seriously wounded. For his 'outstanding and inspiring qualities of leadership, initiative, skill, endurance and most conspicuous gallantry and devotion to duty', he was awarded the Victoria Cross.

As the 5th and 19th Brigades pulled back, B Troop was called into action to deal with a German machine gun which was preventing the 2/7th Battalion from retiring. This was done successfully. After dark, Willie Smith received orders to retire to a new site south of the village of Imbros about two-thirds of the way to Sphakia. All night, infantry straggled past the gunners as they slept beside their trucks. Theo Stephanides, who had set off from Canea wearing a pair of size 10 boots on his size 8½ feet, described the scene:

> I knew that I was taking part in a retreat; in fact I wondered if it should not be called more correctly a rout as, on all sides, men were hurrying along in disorder. Most of them had thrown away their rifles and a number had even discarded their tunics, as it was a hot day with the sun beating down from a clear sky.
>
> Nearly every yard of the road and of the ditches on either side was strewn with abandoned arms and accoutrements, blankets, gasmasks, packs, kitbags, sun-helmets, cases and containers of all shapes and sizes, tinned provisions and boxes of cartridges and hand grenades; now and then one ran across officers' valises and burst-open suitcases.[8]

Keith Hooper and his mates from the 2/6th Battalion at Suda Bay had stuck together as an orderly unit despite the constant presence of bombers and ground-strafing fighters which harassed the long, slow, defenceless column. 'I saw a most peculiar thing,' he says. 'I was going through a wood on the approach to the White Mountains and here was a group of fellows who had stopped to make a cup of tea. One was sitting there with a cup in his hand and another alongside him and a couple of others and they were all dead. They'd been killed by concussion from one of the bombs.'[9]

By now, Arthur Midwood was staggering up the steep slopes towards the mountain pass. He had drunk from the springs in the wooded area but couldn't remember eating anything and there was no water in these dry, limestone crags. 'I'd really had it,' he says. 'I was on my last legs.'[10]

Freyberg had reached the hills above Sphakia, where he set up his headquarters in three small caves on the west slope of a deep gully below the hairpin bends in the road. 'Twenty of us volunteered to fight a rearguard in front of the general's cave,' Harry Spencer says. 'We were pretty shot. Ian Bonifant's feet were bleeding and mine were blistered. There was a little stream outside the cave and I bathed my feet in it. Ian was an officer, so he went in to see the general, who was with John White (his aide de camp), and told him we were prepared to fight.' Freyberg thanked the men but said he had already made arrangements for the rearguard.[11]

Just as it was getting dark, Laycock and Waugh turned up. They found Freyberg saying goodbye to New Zealanders who were leaving that evening. Some had photographs of him which he signed. He gave Laycock and Waugh half a cup of sherry and a spoonful of beans. Waugh approached a one-eyed man with a quartermaster's flash on his uniform.

'When the enemy shows his head,' the man told him, 'hit him; drive him back.'

Waugh asked where he could find some food for the commandos, whereupon he was handed a wedge of Greek banknotes. 'Buy it,' the man said. 'Buy a caique.'

Waugh writes, 'I think this ass was called Brunskill.'[12]

Brunskill's version of this encounter omits any mention of his conversation with Waugh but confirms that he gave the commando chief the benefit of his advice on how to deal with the enemy. 'I happened to meet Laycock,' he writes, 'and ventured to suggest to him that the Germans must be kept at a distance by a show of force and small counter-offensives.' Laycock's reply is unrecorded.[13]

That night, Freyberg ordered John White to return to Alexandria with the first wave of evacuated troops, entrusting him with a short report on the Battle of Crete in case he did not make it himself. 'We have had a pretty rough time,' it said.

The bombing is what has beaten us, the strafing having turned us out of position after position. Bombs of a heavy calibre from heights of about 200 feet simply blew our people out of the ground. The actual parachute troops we annihilated and ordinary troops we knocked out in successful counter-attacks, only to be bombed out of our positions in the course of a few hours. We were bombed off Maleme aerodrome; we counter-attacked and retook it but the strafing of dive-bombers and extremely accurate heavy bombing and machine-gunning drove us from it. Troops are retiring to Sphakia through a covering position. It is extremely doubtful whether we will hold if the enemy concentrates his full air attack against it. The troops are frightfully battered and if we get away with 25 per cent of our original strength we shall be very lucky.

Freyberg's message would have struck a chord with many of the Australian troops on Crete. 'They felt, as did the New Zealanders, that they were better fighting soldiers than the Germans but had been given little opportunity to show what they could do,' the 2/7th Battalion's historian writes. 'Also, they felt they had been poorly disposed – the Australians often found themselves occupying lower ground than the enemy. And they had the feeling of being sold out, even exploited.'[14]

The evacuation began just after midnight that night – 28/29 May – when Captain S. H. T. Arliss, commander of the 7th Destroyer Flotilla in *Napier*, arrived with *Kelvin*, *Kandahar* and *Nizam*. Captain Morse had signalled Admiral Cunningham from Freyberg's cave that 'up to 1000 will be ready to embark'. Using whalers, the sailors ferried 744 troops out to the destroyers in three hours. The ships got away before dawn. They were attacked by Junkers Ju-88s and although *Nizam* was damaged by a near miss she maintained speed and the first evacuees reached Alexandria at 5 pm on 29 May.[15]

On reaching Cairo later that night, John White handed Freyberg's report to Wavell and then informed him that a direct order would be necessary to prise Freyberg off Crete. Wavell sent a personal order to him, 'You will return to Egypt first opportunity.' Even so, Freyberg did not leave immediately, because of the confused situation with regard to his troops.

Meanwhile, the 2/7th had reached Imbros at 3 am on 29 May and sheltered under a clump of trees. In the morning, they received their first food issue for two days – one tin of bully beef among six men and two biscuits per man – but there was plenty of water from a well for drinking and washing. While they were resting, the men learned from Captain Harry Halliday that they had lost the toss with the other fighting units and must fight the last rearguard action with the gunners of B Troop, the 2/8th Battalion and a detachment of Royal Marines.

Daybreak found the gunners waiting for the Germans in the last tenable position before Sphakia. They had placed their two 75s at the southern end of a narrow valley, with the mountain pass in front and the cliffs leading down to the sea some distance behind them. There were wooded hills on each side and late that morning the 2/7th Battalion moved into position in the hills on the left. All of B Troop's trucks had been sent off to help carry the wounded, while Willie Smith took his car in search of food and water.

It was a fine, warm morning and although there were no aircraft in sight, mobs of stragglers hugged the woods to avoid the road and the open valley where they might be strafed. Colonel Le Souef, Michael Clarke's cousin, passed through with a group of wounded.

'Hello, what are you doing, Michael?' he called out.

'Just preparing a reception for the German advance guard,' Clarke replied.

The first Germans arrived in the afternoon on motorcycles. They roared into the valley with Spandaus cocked and ready to shoot up the infantry but quickly turned tail after a couple of shells exploded in their midst. The Germans then opened fire with mortars from the far side of the valley, causing little concern to the gunners. They shared what food they had with each other and a search party went out looking for water. A British truck had been abandoned some way up the road and it was found to contain tins of bully beef, M&V stew, beetroot and potatoes. 'We humped a good quantity back to the guns, opened the beetroot and potatoes, and drank the juice,' Clarke says. 'It tasted lousy but by God it was thirst-quenching.'

Willie Smith returned almost empty-handed from his own quest and after consuming a few mouthfuls of food went forward to see Theo Walker. Jimmy Hargest had placed a cordon of troops with fixed bayonets around the beach to control the mobs of stragglers. Smith told Walker he had received assurances from Freyberg's HQ that the gunners and the 2/7th Battalion would be allowed through the cordon to reach the ships. Hargest's attitude was summed up in an entry in his diary:

There were hundreds of loose members, members of non-fighting units and all sorts of people about – no formation, no order, no cohesion. It was a ghastly mess. Into all this I was hurtled with no knowledge of it and with my hands already full. My mind was fixed. I had 1100 troops – 950 of the brigade and 150 of the 20th Battalion. We had borne the burden and were going aboard as a brigade and none would stop us.[16]

By now, Arthur Midwood – originally one of Hargest's soldiers but now, through no fault of his own, a 'straggler' – had made it to the top of the escarpment. 'I had walked across Crete,' he says. 'The Germans were still bombing us and I was waiting under some olive trees for the dark. I thought I'd been hit again when a bit of hot shrapnel fell through the trees and dropped on my thigh.'[17]

Admiral King's force had set sail on 29 May not quite knowing what to expect when it reached Sphakia. Captain Morse had signalled Cunningham that up to 10,000 troops would be ready for evacuation that night. Freyberg, however, had already sent a message saying he thought no more than 2000 troops could be taken off owing to the chaos on the beach. The soldiers had to remain on the cliff-top, keeping out of sight to avoid the Luftwaffe, until they were called forward to embark. It had been discovered on the first lift that the boats could land in just one small section of the shingle beach and the only way of communicating how many troops were needed was by runners who were often delayed by the crush of bodies on the path. Cunningham concluded from these signals that 10,000 troops remained to be evacuated but only 2000 of them were in organised units.

He had attached the troopship *Glengyle*, capable of carrying 3000 men, with King's force in case Morse's figure was correct. The ships arrived off Crete at 11.30 pm and the main evacuation began with *Phoebe*, *Perth* and *Glengyle* anchored off Sphakia, while *Calcutta*, *Coventry* and the destroyers patrolled out to sea.[18] 'Embarkation proceeded swiftly,' writes the Australian naval historian, 'after some temporary slowness with walking wounded.'[19]

One of the walking wounded was Arthur Midwood. 'We walked down the hill to the beach,' he says. 'A landing craft came in and the front dropped down and we walked on board. It took us out to the *Glengyle*. Then I had to climb up this rope netting on the side of the boat. I had difficulty getting to the top because my arm was in a sling and I could only use one arm. I held on by the back of my head while I grabbed another rope. I got on board and crawled two metres across the deck and stayed there.'[20]

Theo Stephanides, who had been put in charge of a number of wounded on the cliff-top, found himself taken out to *Perth*, 'the very ship in which I had made the passage to Greece in March – rather a strange coincidence'. The wounded were taken to the sick bay. Stephanides went down to the wardroom where he was greeted by the padre and a couple of officers who remembered him from the previous trip. 'How grand, in fact how *thrilling*, it was to sit in a comfortable armchair and be able to relax! How wonderful too to be in a warm, pleasant, brightly lighted room, to sip the delicious cup of steaming cocoa which was immediately brought to us.'[21]

Once *Glengyle* and the cruisers had been loaded, the destroyers came in to embark their quotas. Altogether, 6000 men had been embarked by 3 am when King sailed for Alexandria. Cunningham sent Hec Waller in *Stuart* with *Jaguar* and *Defender* to provide extra protection. Waller met up with the force at dawn south of Gavdo Island and soon afterwards the Luftwaffe launched the first of three attacks.

After a good night's sleep, Theo Stephanides was reading a two-day-old copy of the *Egyptian Mail* when an 'air-raid red' warning was announced over the loudspeaker. At 9.30 am, a bomb hit *Perth* near the bridge, pierced the deck and exploded in A boiler room, killing two stokers, two cooks, two marines and seven soldiers. As the bomb fell, John Anderson of the 2/2nd Field Regiment, now promoted to captain, was watching through his binoculars from the deck of *Glengyle*. 'This bomb had lost its tailfin and tumbled over and over and deviated from the rest of the string of bombs,' he says.[22]

Perth's forward boiler was put out of action but she kept going. Although she suffered a couple of near misses throughout the day, she reached port thanks largely to a couple of RAF fighters which turned up at the right time and disrupted the Luftwaffe's attacks.[23]

Arthur Midwood, in *Glengyle*, was oblivious to the danger. 'I was so tired I didn't move until we reached Alexandria,' he says. 'I came to with two blokes, one on each side of me, carrying me off the boat. They had set up a first-aid post for the wounded. The first thing the doctor did was give me a big bowl of soup.'[24]

PART V

Anzac Heroes

CHAPTER 25

Deadly Exodus

At 6 am on 28 May, Admiral Bernard Rawlings in *Orion* set out for Heraklion with *Ajax*, *Dido*, *Decoy*, *Jackal*, *Imperial*, *Hotspur*, *Kimberley* and *Hereward*. High-level bombing, dive-bombing and torpedo attacks began at 5 pm when the ships entered the danger zone around the Kaso Straits. The gunners closed up for action and arrangements were made for dinner to be served at the guns, as the men would be at their stations all night long.[1]

At 7.30, *Imperial* had a near miss from a bomb. Although she appeared undamaged, her steering gear had been seriously weakened. Half an hour later, a bomb caused a fire in *Ajax*, 20 men were seriously wounded and she sustained some damage to her side. Rawlings couldn't afford to take 'lame ducks' with him on such a hazardous trip, so he signalled *Ajax*'s skipper, Captain Desmond McCarthy, 'Should I send you home?'

McCarthy replied in the affirmative and dropped out of the line as soon as darkness fell at 9 pm and the bombers withdrew to their bases at Scarpanto. 'The damage control people said it was serious, so I was of the opinion there was considerable damage from a bomb burst,' McCarthy says.

That ship had had more of a hammering than any of the other cruisers and we were getting anxiety neurosis: exhaustion and fear. It was a shocking thing. It isn't just being frightened – we're all frightened – it becomes a disease. I lost my commander to it and a couple of other officers and an awful lot of the lower deck had it. You know you can drive them up to a certain point but many were new to the navy and I wasn't sure how far I could drive them. So we went back. It turned out the damage done by the bomb was very little.[2]

At full speed, the rest of Rawlings' force arrived off Heraklion at 11.30 pm. *Hotspur*, which had transported the 2/4th Battalion there earlier that month, knew the harbour and led the way in. Not knowing whether the Germans had seized the town, all guns were manned as the destroyer moved slowly along the northern wall of the mole. Hugh Hodgkinson was relieved to see Australian troops marching towards the ship.

'We got alongside with the minimum of light and noise, no one raising his voice to shout, as the Germans were pretty close on the harbour,' he says, 'Now and then Very lights would go up round the town to show where the Huns were, but all the time our own men were slipping away from their lines and dropping back on the harbour mole.'[3]

Ivan Dougherty had heard about the evacuation of Heraklion Force from Brian Chappel just as the ships were setting out on their dangerous passage. The news that the battle was lost came as something of a surprise to him. The 4000-strong garrison was full of fight and the Germans had failed to take the airfield or the town despite days of carpet-bombing which had caused massive damage and driven civilians into the hills. However, munitions and food were running out and the navy could no longer keep them supplied. Once Suda Bay and Retimo were overrun, there was no realistic chance of withstanding a combined German onslaught.[4]

Heraklion itself, wrote Captain Paul Tomlinson, 'was one large stench of decomposing dead, debris from destroyed dwelling places, roads were wet and running from burst water pipes, hungry dogs were scavenging among the dead. There was a stench of sulphur, smouldering fires and pollution of broken sewers. Conditions were set for a major epidemic.'[5]

After damaging its vehicles, destroying stores and placing charges timed to explode the following morning in the petrol and ordnance dumps, the 2/4th set off company by company for the mole where the 14th Brigade was also assembling.[6] The embarkation went without a hitch, with destroyers coming in four at a time to ferry troops out to the cruisers. At 3 am, *Kimberley* and *Imperial* took the rearguard on board and half an hour later the force departed with the whole garrison (and four young Cretan women no one seemed to know anything about).

The ships were under way for just 25 minutes when *Imperial*'s steering gear failed as a result of the earlier near miss. Running out of control, she almost collided with *Kimberley* and then shot across *Orion*'s bows. Her skipper, Lieutenant-Commander Charles Kitkat, just had time to flash 'My rudder' to *Orion*'s bridge before he sped past.[7] The destroyer then lost power, fell astern and stopped.

With dawn due in two hours' time, Rawlings had to decide whether to wait in the hope that *Imperial* could be repaired or order her captain to abandon ship. He had little choice. It was imperative to keep the squadron together to fight off the Luftwaffe and as *Imperial* was carrying just 300 of the 4000 troops, it would have been foolhardy to risk the vast majority for the sake of one destroyer. *Hotspur*'s captain, Lieutenant-Commander Cecil Brown, received the order from the flagship, 'Take off crew and sink *Imperial*.'

Hotspur pulled alongside the stricken ship and the troops, mostly Australians and Black Watch, were urged to jump over as quickly as possible. Every ten minutes' delay put *Hotspur* eight kilometres further astern of the main force. By 4.45 am, the troops had been transferred and stored below deck. Brown then took *Hotspur* 750 metres away and ordered, 'Stand by to fire one torpedo starboard.'

The last thing Private Percy Webb of the 2/4th Battalion expected was to be torpedoed by his own side. On boarding *Imperial*, he had gone below and fallen into a deep sleep. He woke up to find the place strangely quiet; somehow he'd been overlooked in the scramble. As he was getting his bearings, a torpedo slammed into the ship.[8]

'There she was,' wrote Hugh Hodgkinson, 'a beautiful destroyer with engines, guns, torpedoes, everything, in perfect condition – lying utterly alone like some haunted thing. Then we saw a plume of blackness jump up amidships and a dull roar told us she had been hit. But she was made of good stuff. She heeled over and then righted low in the water. Her captain must have felt a glow of pride in her silent obstinacy.'[9]

Webb had been bombed and strafed for days at Heraklion but this was different. He clambered up on deck. *Hotspur* fired a second torpedo. 'With a shudder she turned over towards us, and disappeared into the black sea,' Hodgkinson says. 'We did not talk to her captain, as one does not talk to a man who has just lost his wife.'[10]

At the last minute, Webb had dived overboard and swum away from the ship. He found a raft floating among the wreckage and climbed on to it. Early on the morning of 30 May, he was washed ashore, taken into custody and handed over to the Germans.

Imperial was just the first in a series of cruel losses. Now loaded with 900 men, *Hotspur* set off to catch up with Rawlings' force. As dawn broke, every soldier who had a Bren-gun was mustered on the upper deck to add to the ship's firepower. Hodgkinson was scanning the skies through his binoculars when he spotted black shapes against the background of Kaso Island. 'It's the *Orion*,' he shouted. 'My God, they've come back for us!' Rawlings had in fact slowed down to wait for *Hotspur* and was only just turning south into the Kaso Straits.[11]

At 6 am, 100 German dive-bombers appeared. Half an hour later, the destroyer *Hereward* was hit by a bomb and veered off course towards the coast of Crete. Her guns, some of them manned by Australian anti-aircraft gunners among the evacuees, were still blazing. The captain, Lieutenant-Commander James Munn, gave the order to abandon ship. Lieutenant Jim Mann of the 2/3rd Light Anti-Aircraft Regiment saw that his men had something to keep them afloat. He was one of the last to leave the ship and by then all floating material had been taken. The former Rhodes scholar and Melbourne barrister was drowned.[12]

The survivors were strafed by a Stuka until an Italian Red Cross plane circled around them, keeping the Stuka away. Italian motor torpedo boats fished them out of the water and took them to Scarpanto as prisoners of war.

At 7.30 am, *Orion* was dive-bombed and her bridge raked with machine-gun fire, mortally wounding her skipper, Captain G.R.B. Back, who died two hours later. Admiral Rawlings himself was wounded. Then it was *Dido's* turn. At 8.15, a bomb hit her forward gun turret and exploded between decks. Bill Andrews of the 2/4th recalls that the loudspeakers were playing a popular tune, 'It's a Hap-hap-happy Day', when 'everything turned red and black. I couldn't breathe and I remember little or nothing else until Reg Angel grabbed me and carted me on deck, [otherwise] I would have roasted like so many poor fellows. We both went back down to help and the scene was shocking. Most of the members of our particular section were dead. Those surviving, with a few exceptions, were shockingly burnt.'[13]

At 10.45, a large bomb hit *Orion's* bridge, passed through the deck and exploded in the stokers' mess-deck, which was crowded with soldiers. *Orion* had nearly 1100 troops on board and there were very heavy casualties: 260 killed and 280 wounded.[14] The attacks continued until 3 pm. By then, the convoy had slowed down to keep *Orion* with it. She needed a tow when the ships reached Alexandria harbour at 8 pm on 29 May.

Admiral Cunningham signalled the convoy: 'I am extremely sorry that, after their magnificent record in Crete and your admirable arrangements for evacuation, there should have been so many casualties among your command in the last stage of the journey.' Brigadier Chappel acknowledged the message and expressed his command's regrets for the navy's own losses. He thanked Cunningham for the manner in which the navy had taken care of Heraklion Force.[15]

'I shall never forget the sight of those ships coming up harbour,' Cunningham said, 'the guns of their fore turrets awry; one or two broken off and pointing forlornly skyward, their upper decks crowded with troops, and the marks of their ordeal only too visible.'

He went on board *Orion*, where he found Rawlings 'cheerful but exhausted'. The ship was 'a terrible sight and the mess-deck a ghastly shambles'. Apart from the casualties in *Orion*, 103 officers and men out of 240 of the 2nd Black Watch were killed in *Dido*. Out of the 4000 troops embarked from Heraklion, 800 – one in five – had been killed, wounded or captured since leaving Crete. The death toll included 48 Australians of the 2/4th Battalion and 2/3rd Light Anti-Aircraft Regiment.[16]

John Hetherington, who met the convoy, reported in the Sydney *Sun*:

I saw today the end of one of the most gallant chapters of British History, when tired and bearded men, Australians, New Zealanders and Tommies, marched down the gangways of the warships in which they had been evacuated from Crete. I had seen these Australians fight winning battles in Libya, a losing battle in Greece, and today was their finest hour. They were flung from Greece by superior weight of men and superior weight of armaments but in courage – that indefinable thing these men call guts – they were never defeated. They are not defeated now. They don't know the meaning of defeat.

On Friday 30 May, the valley outside Sphakia was quiet and deserted until 9 am, when a German armoured car drove into the pass. 'Roy Macartney and I had a dispute as to which of our guns hit it first,' Michael Clarke says. 'By midday, we had shot up half a dozen light tanks.' The Germans sent in a patrol, which warily probed along the edge of the woods. John Peck's company was dug in at the roadside. 'We let them reach the road and rest awhile,' he writes.

> For a long five minutes they sat there, talking quietly and drinking from their water bottles. We stared from our slit trenches astride the road and prayed that our sparse camouflage would be good enough to draw the patrol into close contact.
> Suddenly, almost unexpectedly, they were on their feet and moving rapidly towards us. A few yards from our position the leader stopped. He seemed to sniff the air for danger. Suspicion gave way to certainty as he spotted something and yelled. Almost together, C Company opened fire. Six men fell to the first intensive volley and lay still in untidy bundles on the road.[17]

For the third lift at Sphakia, Captain Arliss in *Napier* took the destroyers *Nizam*, *Kelvin* and *Kandahar* with him on the night of 30–31 May. *Kandahar* developed a mechanical fault and was ordered back to Alexandria and *Kelvin* suffered near misses by bombs from three Ju-88s, which reduced her speed to 20 knots. Arliss ordered her to turn back as well. *Napier* and *Nizam* arrived off Sphakia at 12.30 am on 31 May. Using three landing craft which had been left behind on the previous trip, the two destroyers embarked 700 troops each and sailed again at 3 am, reaching Alexandria at 7 pm that evening. On the way back, Arliss signalled Cunningham that at least 6500 troops still remained to be evacuated from Sphakia.

Freyberg had already asked for one last lift to take the remaining troops off Sphakia on the night of 31 May–1 June. Wavell thought the navy had done everything in its power and was prepared to absolve it from further responsibility. Cunningham, however, agreed to extend the evacuation by 24 hours. At 6 am on 31 May, King sailed out of Alexandria with *Phoebe*, *Abdiel*, *Kimberley*, *Hotspur* and *Jackal* to carry out the final evacuation.

Having done all that was humanly possible for his men, Freyberg boarded one of two Sunderland flying boats that night after handing over command to General Weston. He arrived back in Alexandria at 3.30 on the morning of 31 May.[18] Bruno Brunskill hitched a lift in the second plane. '[Colonel Keith] Stewart and I and something like 60 of all ranks filled one aircraft to absolute capacity,' he writes, 'and thankfully sat drinking sweet tea till we landed at Alexandria in the small hours.'

Brunskill later penned a 12-point appreciation on why Freyberg had lost Crete and how he could have held it with the troops at his disposal. He neglected to mention that one of the troops' greatest bugbears during the fighting was extracting food, ammunition and weapons from the supply depots and warehouses under his control.[19]

At first light that day, the Germans launched mortar and machine-gun fire against the rearguard's position above Sphakia, making it difficult for B Troop to operate their guns. At 2 pm, German observers were seen on the hillside across the ravine to the gunners' right. Roy Macartney's gun was swung around, exposing the crew to machine-gun fire from the front. One round was enough to send the enemy scampering off the hill, but a few minutes later every member of Macartney's gun crew was wounded.

Meanwhile, in a message from Cairo, General Weston was alerted to the navy's final trip to Sphakia. At 7.40 pm, he left his HQ in the caves and climbed the hill to Vasey's headquarters, where he told the Australian commander to evacuate the troops still under his command – the 2/7th, B Troop of the 2/3rd Field Regiment and 19th Brigade headquarters. After issuing the orders, Vasey and his staff packed up and set off for the beach at 9 pm.

Willie Smith passed the order on to B Troop. They smashed the sights on their Italian guns and threw the breech blocks into the ravine. Michael Clarke had just a dozen shells left. Shouldering haversacks, mostly filled with tinned food, and picking up rifles, they set off on the long march down to the beach. Smith assured them that cabins had been reserved for them on a luxury liner and that Major Victor Burston, who was acting as beachmaster, would give them top priority. He also told them that guides had been posted on the route down from the cliffs. When they started to descend, however, there was no sign of them and they slid and slipped on the rough, narrow track.

Halfway down, they came to a little hollow in which Leslie Le Souef had gathered his wounded. 'We crossed to him and he asked for all the rations we could spare,' Clarke says. 'We took up a collection from our dozen men and I half-emptied my haversack. After exchanging a few sentences, we resumed our way down.'

Roy Macartney was in some distress from dysentery, which he attributed to the beetroot juice. Clarke took his rifle and slung it over his spare shoulder. 'Progress was even slower due to other men ahead on the steep narrow path and we were all getting pretty weary,' he says. 'I found carrying two rifles mighty tiring. It was hours before we emerged from the cliff and walked on to the beach.'[20]

King's force had arrived off Sphakia at 11.20 pm. The three landing craft were pressed into service again and the embarkation went so well that at one point the beach was actually empty of troops. This, however, caused a last-minute rush. The 2/8th Battalion, which had been attached to the 5th Brigade, had withdrawn from its positions in the Sphakia Gorge at 8.30 pm. 'The embarkation was carried out with the utmost speed and efficiency,' the unit's historian writes, 'although on two occasions stragglers attempted to break through but fell back when several shots were fired.' At 1.30 am on 1 June, the majority of the battalion's 203 surviving members embarked in *Phoebe* and the rest in *Jackal*.[21]

Vasey, who had to push past the stragglers himself, decided to wait on the beach to ensure the rest of his troops got through. There was no sign of them, so he sent two officers back to find them. Just before 2.30 am, one of the officers returned with the news that brigade HQ and Colonel Walker were on the beach. Vasey then boarded a naval launch with his staff and, as it pulled out, he saw the rest of his headquarters and the leading troops of the 2/7th board one of the landing craft.

From the top of the cliff, John Peck had seen the shadowy ships of the Royal Navy waiting off the coast. 'Exultantly, we realised we had made it,' he says. 'Soon we would be in those dim grey shapes sailing to freedom.' But something was wrong. The old army game of shuffleboard had started. The column would move forward three paces and stop. Then another three paces and stop. At this rate, they would not reach the barges before dawn.

'Then came the incredible news,' he says. 'Orders had been given to halt us where we stood. We had been promised a clear march to the boats and could not believe it.'

Colonel Walker, short, quiet and utterly fearless, went forward to sort things out while the men waited for ten interminable minutes. Then they were on their way again, but the delay had been fatal. 'We were now hopelessly entangled in a mass of milling, panic-stricken men,' Peck says. 'The word had gone around that this was the last night of the evacuation and these were the last boats the navy could send. Hundreds of stragglers who had been hiding in the caves above had come down determined to get away at any price and bugger the arrangements and controls for an ordered embarkation. Now it was every man for himself and now there was chaos.'

All of the stragglers were being turned back at the barges and the 2/7th's only hope lay in sticking together as a unit. Every hundred metres the column was stopped by the mobs and precious time was lost forcing a way through. 'It was nearly 3 am when we finally felt the wet shingle under our feet,' Peck says. 'One landing barge started loading the head of our column and some of HQ Company managed to squeeze on board. As it pulled out, a second barge moved in. Soon it would be our turn.'

Strangely, the second barge was not being loaded. A sudden commotion followed the naval beach officer as he came down the line of waiting men. Quietly, he broke the news, 'Sorry, lads, that's all for the *Skylark*.' At that moment, from out to sea, came confirmation that the evacuation was over: 'the sound of anchor chains through the hawse'. To the men on the beach, it must have seemed like a death rattle.[22]

Victor Burston had pluckily remained behind to tell B Troop the bad news. A total of 4050 troops had been lifted, but the last boat had gone and they had been left behind. On Wavell's instructions, General Weston had flown out in a Sunderland, leaving written orders to surrender to be handed to the most senior officer. A thousand of Weston's Royal Marines and most of Bob Laycock's commandos, although not Laycock or Evelyn Waugh, were among those facing captivity along with thousands of Australians and New Zealanders.

Sixteen months after George Vasey had arrived in Egypt with the advance party of the 2/6th Division, he stepped ashore from the cruiser *Dido* in Alexandria on the evening of 1 June 1941 with a profound sense of relief. It was only then that he discovered that Theo Walker – who had stepped off the barge at the last moment – most of his battalion and the gunners of B Troop were still on Crete.[23] Just two officers and 14 others ranks of the 2/7th Battalion had got away. 'It is a most regrettable thing,' Vasey wrote in his report on Crete, 'that a battalion which had been covering the beach and protecting the embarkation for 48 hours and which was then ordered to embark that night should have been prevented from doing so through lack of control of the area behind the beach.' To John Hetherington, he was more expressive. 'Crete,' he said, 'was a bloody balls-up from arsehole to breakfast time.'

CHAPTER 26

Abandoned

Stunned and exhausted, John Peck and his comrades in C Company's 15 Platoon peered through the gloom at the ships slowly steaming out to sea. The deep throb of their turbines echoed from the cliffs as the last chance of freedom slowly faded into the distance, leaving its wash on the wet black rocks of Sphakia beach. 'We wished them God speed,' he says. 'They would need it at dawn when the bombers found them on the open seas.'[1]

Colonel Walker addressed his battalion. He explained that they had missed their place in the queue despite cast-iron promises that the rearguard would be evacuated. As the senior commissioned officer, he had been ordered to contact the Germans at dawn to surrender all troops, but he would not stop them if they moved off before then.[2]

Peck became aware that the tumult around him was subsiding. Perversely, the news that the men were marooned had acted like a lightning rod to calm their fears and now they discussed their options: whether to fight on or surrender. While some wandered aimlessly up and down the little beach, the majority were determined to try anything rather than give in.

Grandiose schemes were put forward for holding back the enemy for yet another day in the hope that the navy would return the next night. The most resourceful organised themselves into fighting patrols and their enthusiasm caught the imagination of a substantial number of volunteers. Some sections prepared to move back up the cliffs.

On the same strip of shingle, Michael Clarke, almost at the end of his endurance, listened to the arguments percolating through the darkness. Vic Burston said that the regiment should surrender as an organised body in a dignified manner. Willie Smith disagreed and so did a number of other gunners. The angry discussion went on for some time, with a good deal of talk about the possibilities of finding boats that could be sailed to Egypt.

'My ears pricked up,' Michael Clarke writes, 'when Burston said that submarines might come inshore on the following night.'

> The signal to them was to be E E E in Morse code. This statement was met with much sarcasm. Everyone was feeling very bitter that the Royal Navy had abandoned us and they rejected the submarines as a fairy story. I got talking to the blokes lying near me. We decided to clear out while it was still dark and head along the coast to the west. I still had my small electric torch – maybe it could bring in a sub. I shook Roy Macartney awake, but he refused to move. He said, 'I'm plain buggered. Off you go and good luck.' So six of us got to our feet and strolled casually away, leaving the big group who were still arguing.

The gunners kept to the back of the beach until the cliffs came right down to the sea and they were forced to climb a mule track up to the cliff-top. By first light, Sphakia was out of sight and the sea was calm and empty of all craft as far as the eye could see. The group consisted of Clarke, a lance-bombardier called Reg and four gunners. Jack, a slim fellow, asked Clarke, 'Is it okay to have a drink?' Clarke nodded, but Reg protested it was important to conserve their water so none of them had a drink.

Back on the beach, gnawing hunger drove John Peck and his platoon from C Company in search of food and water. The few wells around Sphakia were almost dry and the few drops of muddy water they managed to haul up in empty meat tins did little to slake their thirst. The village itself was derelict and everything edible had been scrounged days ago. Hoping for miracles, the men climbed up to the caves. 'On the way we came across a group cutting up a newly slaughtered donkey and despite their protests, we hacked off some strips of warm red flesh,' Peck says. 'Joining the crowd around a small brush fire, we managed to half-roast a few pieces of the meat on the ends of our bayonets.'[3]

It was bright daylight when Peck's men reached the caves to find them crammed with men from almost every unit. The badly wounded, who had been carried up from the beach, were being treated by medical officers and orderlies. One of them was Colonel Le Souef. Although he was on George Vasey's list for evacuation, he had been rescuing some more wounded when the order had been given and could not be found. He had then been held up on the way to the boats and had been left behind. He accepted the situation calmly. There was work to do and he got on with it. His regimental cooks had boiled some of the donkey's carcass in a huge cauldron of seawater. Le Souef shouted to his exhausted troops, 'Fall out, stretcher bearers, for donkey soup.'[4]

For all their foraging, 15 Platoon could find only a few tins of bully beef and some hard biscuits. Warmed by the morning sun, they sat outside the caves and planned their next move. Having made one terrible forced march to Sphakia, they knew that the misery of the return journey to the north coast as prisoners of war under the Germans had to be avoided at all costs. The wells along the route were already dry and there were no food dumps. 'We had no intention of tamely waiting to be rounded up and shipped off to a prison camp for the duration of the war,' Peck says.

> We decided to stick together and travel up the west coast in search of a boat. If none could be found, we would at least hide up for a few days and watch for a chance to break through the German cordon to the mountains. If that failed, the bulk of the prisoners would have been moved by then and conditions for the return journey to Suda Bay might have improved for a smaller party. The decision made, we started down the slope towards the beach.

On the beach, the capitulation was now official and white flags of surrender dotted the shingle in the hope of avoiding the morning strafing. As Peck's group set off along the coast, a large landing craft packed with men pulled out from behind an outcrop of black rocks. One of those on board was Roy Macartney. He had recovered sufficiently to make his way along the beach, where he encountered some soldiers working on the abandoned barge. Together they managed to repair one of its two six-cylinder Chrysler engines and set sail among a fleet of little boats heading for Gavdo Island a few kilometres off the Cretan coast.[5]

A few minutes later a squadron of Stukas dived out of the sun, bombing and strafing everything on the water. The landing craft chugged on but the little boats had no chance. Only pitiful bits of wreckage remained to mark the watery graves of the occupants.

Towards evening, Peck's group, now eight strong, had a stroke of luck when two of their number, George McMillan and Jim Gorton, went swimming behind the rocky outcrop and found the sea cave where the barge had been kept during daylight hours. Bobbing at anchor was a dinghy which had been used by the barge crew. It could hold four people. According to the Australian War Memorial archive, McMillan and Gorton claimed two of the places on account of the fact they had found the dinghy. Sergeant Roy Doran, the only married man in the group, was nominated as the third man. The other five then cut a pack of cards to see who would get the final place. It went to Jack Thomson who drew the jack of spades.

'At dusk, we gave the four lucky ones a water bottle and half our rations,' John Peck says. 'I also gave them a small Union Jack I'd taken from the body of a British officer at Suda Bay to wave in case Allied aircraft went over. We wished them God speed and watched them disappear into the darkness.'[6]

In the vanishing twilight, Peck's group moved further along the coast towards Loutro. They could hear occasional gunfire from the beach area and kept a close lookout for German patrols. Their eyes strained out to sea for a signal from the Royal Navy.

Just before dark, Michael Clarke's party found a narrow goat track leading up to a rocky shelf, a good spot from which to signal the submarine. Reg asked, 'Does the sub send a boat or do we swim?'

'I think we swim,' Clarke replied.

Tom, a signaller, took the torch and flashed the E E E signal every half-hour from 11 pm until 4 am.

It was very quiet up there. They could just hear the waves lapping against the rocks far below. It was a long night and cool. Like Peck's men, the gunners peered out to sea every few minutes, hoping against hope for an answering signal.

*

At 10 pm on John Peck's part of the coast, a Sunderland flying boat landed and began cruising up and down. Peck had no torch and the sparse gorse bushes in that area refused to burn. The soldiers set about collecting bits of dried wood and twigs and all the paper in their possession to make a bonfire. Finally, they had a blaze going but the plane continued to motor up and down as though waiting for a particular signal. Suddenly, a German patrol opened up with machine-gun and rifle fire and the plane took off. As the sound of its engines faded away, Peck's heart sank. 'We waited in vain for it to come back,' he says.[7]

Michael Clarke's party hadn't seen the Sunderland or any other sign of a rescue craft. At 4.30 am, Reg suggested that they push on westwards in search of a better place. Tom led the way, having the best night vision. 'Comes from eating carrots,' he said. 'Some bloody vitamin.'

It was slow, stumbling progress in the dark.

The goat track led inland and they carried on in the hope of striking a house or village. Just on first light, the track forked and they took the left-hand fork which headed back towards the sea. At 7 am, they sighted an open space on top of the cliffs, with a stone bench which could be used as a lookout.

A plane flew low overhead and took a good look at them, so they lay down among the shrubbery beside the path and ate some of their rations for breakfast. The plane came back, then a couple of others showed up, presumably monitoring the round-up of prisoners on the beach by the Germans and looking for escapees. The men took a siesta until 3 pm when all was peaceful and quiet.

Reg said, 'I guess that I'd better take a recce to see if there's a path down to the beach.' Twenty minutes later he reappeared and reported that there was a good path down to a small beach 'as good a place as any for a sub to come in'.

*

Meanwhile, John Peck's group had moved further up the mountain and hidden among some rocks. German patrols were visible on the horizon but not near enough to worry them. With the little water and food they had, they knew they could not hide up for more than a day or two in this barren terrain. Choosing between a German POW camp and the Cretan mountains required little discussion: they would take their chances in the hills. Next morning at dawn, the six of them set out to re-cross the island and get back to Georgiopolis, their first defensive position in Crete.

They headed north through the mountains, travelling mostly by night and avoiding the road wherever possible. The few shepherds they met on the way gave them goat's milk and cheese, but their poor knowledge of any Cretan dialect made conversation impossible.

'It was weird passing through our old battlegrounds scrounging what we could among the litter of war,' Peck says. 'We found a little food and quite a few bodies. One of our main concerns was lack of cigarettes. We took unjustified risks walking along the road collecting the few butts which had been missed by the prisoners on their march back. Once or twice we were nearly caught as the odd German vehicle came along the road.'

At dusk on Michael Clarke's cliff-top lookout, a man with a large black dog came along from the west, heading for the bench. He sat down for a while, gazing out to sea. Then he got up and headed towards the fugitives. The dog found them and barked. He silenced it and walked over.

'Okay,' Reg said to Michael Clarke. 'This is where you practise your Greek, Italian, French, Arabic, or maybe even bloody German.'

Clarke knew no Greek and his salutations in other languages failed to elicit a response. Then the man said, 'Afstralos?' and indicated drinking and eating in sign language. The troops nodded eagerly. He told them to lie down and walked off.

After dark, the man returned with a big water flask and a large wooden platter of soft cheese. The men topped up their water bottles and shared out the cheese. The water was flavoured with retsina, a welcome addition. The man went off with his flask and platter and the troops moved over to the bench. Looking over the cliff, it seemed a long way down to the sea. They spent a second night signalling and peering into the darkness. It was very quiet and still, but cold.

At dawn, they returned to the shrubs, ate and drank, and went to sleep. It was a pleasantly warm day. The planes came over a couple of times, still searching for stragglers, and they had to remain under cover. And all the while their faith in the submarine wore a little thinner.

At the junction of the Canea–Retimo–Sphakia roads, John Peck's group trudged east into the mountains above Vrises to Klima, a little hollow in the foothills above Georgiopolis. Only one family lived there in a house near a large well and they invited the fugitives in to share what little food they had. Despite the soldiers' weariness and dirty appearance, it felt good to sit down at a table again. The wife had prepared potatoes and beans smothered in olive oil. For pudding, there was *misithra*, a dish of wheat boiled with sour milk. 'It tasted terrible but we were hungry enough to ask for more,' Peck says.

On their cliff-top, Michael Clarke's men were also fed when the Cretan came back at dusk with some bread and cheese. He was accompanied by a slim youth who spoke a very few words of English. He indicated that the soldiers should go with them to their village, but they shook their heads and returned with their meagre meal to the bench, thinking that the third night might be lucky. However, the torch battery got progressively weaker and finally packed up altogether by 3 am.

Clarke was listening to the men's opinions about the next move when the Cretan and the youth appeared out of the dark. The youth explained that a party of Germans was on its way along the cliffs from Sphakia, looking for fishing boats and stragglers. They had halted for the night only a couple of kilometres to the east.

The older Cretan urged the Australians to follow them to the village and they agreed. But first Michael Clarke hid his revolver and binoculars among some stones behind the bench, saying to Reg, 'You'll probably have to give evidence at a court of inquiry into my loss of the revolver. Luckily the binoculars are my own.'

The village had less than a dozen small houses. The men were taken to a washhouse behind the taverna and had a shave in cold water. Then they were taken into the taverna and given a table near the kitchen. An old woman produced Greek coffee, yoghurt, bread and cheese. Clarke offered to pay but the woman waved his money aside.

They then moved into a small back room, lay down on the floor and went to sleep. It was one o'clock in the afternoon when the youth wakened them and ushered them back into the taverna. Most of the half-dozen tables were occupied by villagers, all busily talking and eating lunch and they glanced towards the Australians and a few called out a greeting. The soldiers nodded and waved back and sat down at the rear-most table where they were served an excellent meal of onion soup, followed by veal with potatoes and gravy, with carafes of retsina. The youth stopped by to tell them that they should be ready to move out at dusk.

Some of the other guests departed, bidding them a grunted farewell and they were enjoying some bread and cheese and little cups of black coffee when there were exclamations of dismay. A truck had driven up to the door and half a dozen

Germans walked in. They sat down at an empty table near the entrance, laughing and joking.

'We were taken completely by surprise,' Clarke says. 'Our corner was fairly dark and I prayed that they would not notice us. The old woman hastened to serve them and for some five minutes they were busy trying to order their meal, all with high good humour.'

Then the fair young *oberleutnant* stood up to look around, saw Clarke's group sitting there and walked cheerfully over to their table. He and Clarke exchanged '*Gruss Gott*'s and the officer asked him whether he was enjoying Crete. Clarke replied that the weather was indeed beautiful. The enemy officer then said, 'Have you visited Austria, sir?'

'I have stayed in Vienna and have been skiing in Kitzbuhel.'

'Ah!' he exclaimed. 'I am from the Tyrol. The mountains are beautiful there!'

'I have also skied at Lech and Saint Anton in the Arlberg,' Clarke continued.

'Ah, I was a ski instructor at Saint Anton two years ago!' the man exclaimed. 'Allow me to ask you, sir, which unit are you with?'

'The artillery,' Clarke replied.

The officer peered at Clarke's shoulder insignia and straightened up, astounded. '*Mein Gott!*' he exclaimed. 'Can it be that you are Australian soldiers?'

'Yes, Herr Oberleutnant,' Clarke replied.

For a few moments, the man was speechless. Then he pulled himself together, saluted and said, 'I have to inform you, Herr Oberleutnant, that you and your men are the prisoners of the German Army.'

Clarke nodded, turned to his men and said, 'I tried to bluff him but it didn't work. He's taking us prisoners. He's Austrian, so let's hope that it won't be too bad.'

Clarke got to his feet but the Austrian waved him back to his chair. 'Finish your meal, sir,' he said. 'It may be your last good one for some time.'

'Thank you for your courtesy, Herr Oberleutnant,' Clarke said.

'We shall eat our dinner,' the Austrian said, 'but I regret that I must send my *feldwebel* to guard you. Please tell your men that the Australian soldiers fought very bravely. And allow me to congratulate you on your German speech, sir.'

He saluted and returned to his table. The *feldwebel* (equivalent to warrant officer) came over, saluted and said, '*Gruss Gott, Herr Oberleutnant,*' and sat down at the adjoining table, where he ate his meal.

Reg said he had never dreamed that being taken prisoner would be as civilised as this. Tom said, 'It's a good job you talk the lingo. I guess that's made it easier, like.'[8]

The Austrian officer sent over a bottle of ouzo and the Australians solemnly drank a toast to freedom. But in his heart Michael Clarke knew that they had just become 'kriegies', short for *Kriegesgefangenen*, the German word for prisoner of war.

Roy Macartney's landing craft, containing 137 men and powered most of the way by a sail of seven blankets tied together with bootlaces, reached the Egyptian coast 30 kilometres west of Sidi Barrani after an epic ten-day journey.[9]

When he had recovered from exposure and malnutrition, Roy wrote to Michael Clarke's mother in Melbourne: 'I have not seen nor heard of Michael since the last night of evacuation from Crete but I am pleased to be able to tell you that he had come through the fighting unscathed and was on the evacuation beach when I last saw him. I am afraid that this means he was probably taken a prisoner of war. I must say how sorry I am to have to tell you that Michael is probably still on Crete but I do hope it is some little consolation to you to know that he should be alive and well.'[10]

Michael and his gunners were among 3102 Australians and 1692 New Zealanders who faced four years in German prisoner-of-war camps. Since 20 May, 945 Australian and New Zealand troops had been killed in the fighting. As at Gallipoli, the valiant Anzac cause had ended in evacuation and defeat.

Despite the order to surrender, more than a thousand Allied troops were still at large on Crete. They would become famous as 'the evaders' and would soon be joined by hundreds of escapers who fled from the camps as soon as they got a chance.

CHAPTER 27

In Captivity

At Retimo, Colonel Campbell's only source of news of what was happening in the rest of Crete was the BBC. On the night of 28 May, it described Creforce's situation as 'extremely precarious'. The 41-year-old regular soldier from Sydney had shouldered his responsibilities with great aplomb. He had defended the airfield against desperate enemy lunges and had then taken the fight to them.

At 6 am on 30 May, Ralph Honner's 40-strong company was still blocking the road from Perivolia II. It reported that their position was under constant artillery and mortar fire and they could hear the sound of many motorcycles warming up. About 9.30, two tanks appeared, followed by 30 German motorcyclists and some light field guns.[1]

Lieutenant Haig, who had arrived in a lighter with three days' rations for Retimo Force, told Campbell that he had orders to march across country to Sphakia after making the delivery. As we have seen, all efforts to order Campbell to do the same had failed and without orders he refused to budge. Even so, Sphakia was a three-day hike away and there was now no chance of reaching it in time for the embarkation. His men had been on half rations for days and, with 450 German prisoners of war to feed, there was only enough food to last one more day.

Campbell had three options: to fight on, to take to the hills, or to surrender. His two Australian battalions had suffered serious casualties in the fighting and the Greek battalions under his command had drifted away from their positions. In the absence of any anti-tank guns, Campbell decided that he could hold the airfield for little more than an hour against German armour and then only at a high cost. However, he did not want to make for the mountains and ask Cretan villagers to feed his force. The Germans had dropped leaflets threatening to shoot anyone who helped them.

He later wrote, 'I considered that the loss of many brave men to be expected from any attempt to escape now, and the dangers and penalties to which we must expose the Cretan civilians were not warranted by the remote chance we now had of being evacuated from the south coast.'[2]

Having mulled over the options, Campbell told Ian Bessell-Browne that he intended to surrender. He then telephoned Ray Sandover at his battalion headquarters and told him that further resistance would result in a useless waste of lives and asked for his opinion. Sandover pointed out that if Retimo surrendered the Germans could advance eastwards and take the force at Heraklion by surprise. Having heard that day from a Greek officer that Heraklion had been evacuated and that a German force was in fact approaching Retimo from that direction, Campbell said that he thought 'the show had packed up there'. In that case, Sandover said, he proposed to tell his men to destroy their arms and make for the hills.

As they were talking, heavy fire was being exchanged between the enemy and Ralph Honner's company. When Honner reported to battalion HQ, Sandover was discussing the situation with his other company commanders. He told Honner that he was in favour of making for the hills and Honner agreed to go with him. Sandover instructed his officers to tell the men there was no chance of evacuation and that they had a choice between surrendering and heading for the hills. 'I am going myself,' he said. 'We'll think what to do when we get out of this.'[3]

The battalion area was now under heavy fire from the tanks. The German gunners were shouting, 'The game's up, Aussies!' Sandover left with a party of officers and other ranks. They halted in a gully behind some Greek soldiers. Here, others, including Honner, caught up. Honner wrote:

> My party must have been the last organised group to leave the battalion area. It included three men wounded in the morning fight and we were joined by Private R.H. Shreeve, wounded in the arm eight days earlier, who left the dressing station with his arm in a sling to be with us. When we caught up the main body I found I was the only man with a map – a Greek map and it was our standby for the next three months.[4]

At the airfield, the tanks had reached the runway. Private Algie Lind opened fire and killed three German infantry crouching behind the turrets. As Lind changed magazines, he watched in amazement as Colonel Campbell walked across the runway towards the Germans. The adjutant, Captain Ernest Lergessner, followed waving a dirty white towel. Moments later, a runner arrived at the trenches, shouting, 'Don't shoot! We've just surrendered.'[5]

Ray Sandover had distributed the regimental funds and shared a few packets of biscuits among his men. They set off in two groups, with him leading one and Honner the other. Someone said there would be boats at the fishing village of Ay Galini on the south coast. It seemed as good a destination as any.[6]

*

Back in Cairo, Chester Wilmot was furious about the loss of thousands of good soldiers, many of whom he had known personally, including his good friend Leslie Le Souef. The more survivors he talked to, the more he realised that they hadn't had a chance. There had been a chronic failure of planning and organisation, and the culprits were Wavell and the Gabardine Swine at Middle East GHQ. They had had seven months in which to create strong defensive positions on Crete and to arm the troops and they had utterly failed.

The RAF under Tedder had also let the troops down. Apart from one two-hour period when Maleme airfield was bombed, the RAF had been absent over the battlefield. It had given the men no respite from the bombing and machine-gunning which old soldiers described as 'fiercer than any land or aerial bombardment we've seen in this war or the last'.[7]

On 2 June, Wilmot wrote a devastating nine-page report entitled 'Critique on Crete' for the ABC in which he attacked Wavell for 'lack of foresight, a lack of planning and preparation'. He continued:

By 12 May, it was certain that an airborne invasion of Crete was being elaborately prepared in Greece. An RAF spokesman said the other day that by that date FAR [forward air reconnaissance] had reported German transport planes and gliders standing wingtip to wingtip on the 'dromes of southern Greece. Fighters and bombers were being massed for an air attack. We knew then that there would be an airborne invasion of unparalleled intensity and that we would have virtually no air protection for the troops. There was still time to rush arms across or to withdraw those who couldn't be armed. There was still time to make plans to evacuate the island smoothly if the enemy proved too strong.

But five days later [sic] – the day before the first parachute attack – the High Command in Crete and Cairo was confident that Crete could be held with the force and the equipment that was there and General Freyberg rejected the offer of another battalion from Egypt. It was thought that they could hold even though the RAF had already gone.[8]

Wilmot submitted 'Critique on Crete' to the censors. They censored the whole report. A couple of days later the reporter saw George Vasey, who told him:

> From the point of view of winning the war, the defence of Crete was a success – as a local operation it was a bloody failure. We cannot hope to stand up to the Germans until we have at least equality in the air. We had mortars but no baseplates; we had French 75s made in the USA but no sights for them; generally we had bugger-all except Bren-guns and rifles and they were no bloody good against them.[9]

Wavell read Wilmot's report and agreed to see him. He found the commander-in-chief in his office at Grey Pillars. He was much shorter than Wilmot had thought, with thin grey hair brushed straight back, a square, rugged jaw and a swarthy jowl. His left eye 'lurks deep in its socket with an eyelid drooping over it'. Pacing up and down with his hands behind his back, Wavell admitted that almost everything Wilmot had written was true, the criticism was fair and he accepted that a large part of the blame rested on his shoulders. 'I realise I should have foreseen the things you mention but I didn't,' he said, 'and those that I did foresee I couldn't do anything about because I didn't have the equipment.' However, he said, Wilmot's report could not be released because it would stir up trouble between Britain and the Dominions and it would give information of propaganda value to the enemy.[10]

Wilmot then expressed the feelings of many troops about the Gabardine Swine. 'The general opinion among Australian and New Zealand officers and men who come into contact with GHQ is that the British in Cairo are not taking the war seriously; are not working all-out, are not working as hard as the men in the frontline,' he told Wavell. 'It is amazing and appalling to Australians that this GHQ can close down completely from 1.30 to 5.30 every afternoon.'

Wilmot's words seemed to bemuse Wavell. It was as though it had never occurred to him that there might be some slackness at GHQ. He murmured that it was too hot to work in the afternoon and then promised to discuss the issue with General Blamey. He made a note on his pad. After Wilmot had left his office, he wrote a personal note 'to Commanders of Formations which served in Crete, and officers Commanding Units which served in Crete':

> I should like the following to be communicated to the troops who have returned from Crete.
>
> I thank you for the great courage and endurance with which you attempted the defence of the island of Crete. I am well aware of the difficulties under which you carried out your task and that it must have appeared to many of you that you had been asked to do the impossible, and that you were insufficiently equipped and supported. As Commander-in-Chief I accept the responsibility for what was done. It was for strategical reasons necessary to hold the island of Crete if this could reasonably be done.
>
> I was aware of the difficulties you would experience and the dangers you would undergo, and I sent you as much equipment as I could, a large proportion of which was unfortunately sunk before it reached you. I trusted to your courage and skill to hold the island, as you would undoubtedly have done, against the scale of attack I expected. The enemy were, however, able to launch a far greater weight of attack on the ground and in the air than I had considered likely, and were prepared to accept sacrifices on a very high scale. By your gallantry, you made them pay a heavy price for their success.
>
> Again I thank you, and assure you all that your sacrifices have not been in vain.

> You are aware of the courage and skill with which the Navy brought you back from Crete; I have, on your behalf, sent them a message of gratitude. You saw little of the RAF and may have thought yourselves deserted by them; I can assure you that, in circumstances of extreme difficulty, they did all they could do to come to your assistance, and suffered heavy casualties in doing so.

As promised, Wavell consulted Blamey about the lassitude at Grey Pillars. The Australian commander took the criticisms personally and let Wilmot know he deeply resented them.[11]

No one felt the obloquy of defeat more than Bernard Freyberg. He sat outside Wavell's office, 'a crushed Goliath, almost in tears'. Lindsay Inglis had flown to London and seen Churchill. After attacking the lack of preparation prior to 20 May, he had some harsh words to say about Freyberg's handling of the battle. 'There appears to have been no counter-attack of any kind in the Western sector until more than 36 hours after the airborne descents had begun,' Churchill wrote in a minute to General Ismay to be placed before the chiefs of staff. 'There was no attempt to form a mobile reserve of the best troops, be it only a couple of battalions. There was no attempt to obstruct the Maleme aerodrome, although General Freyberg knew he would have no Air in the battle. The whole conception seems to have been of static defence of positions, instead of the rapid extirpations at all costs of the airborne landing parties.'[12]

Jimmy Hargest also plunged the dagger into his old comrade. According to his biographer, Hargest 'must bear a large measure of responsibility for the loss of Maleme airfield and thus, ultimately, for the loss of the island'. Yet at a private meeting with Prime Minister Peter Fraser in Cairo he criticised Freyberg in terms that deeply wounded him when he found out.[13]

Edward Puttick, who had failed to ensure that Hargest counter-attacked to support the 22nd Battalion at Maleme, also saw Fraser in Cairo. It would not have helped the mood of the troops left behind in Crete to learn that Fraser offered him the position of chief of the general staff, a post he took up on 1 August 1941, or that Hargest received a bar to his DSO and a Greek Military Cross (first class) for his services in Greece and Crete.[14]

After the surrender at Retimo on 30 May, the Germans walked past the Australian trenches calling out, 'Come on, boys, Berlin wants to see you!' German prisoners, who had been penned up in B Echelon, arrived with the weapons of their guards. One Australian likened the atmosphere to 'the end of a hard-fought football match, with the Germans laughing and joking and taking souvenirs'.[15]

Colonel Campbell and the other officers were interrogated. In particular, the Germans wanted to know the whereabouts of the 2/7th Battalion which had taken a heavy toll of their comrades three days earlier in the bayonet charge at 42nd Street.[16] The Australians gave their name, rank and army number and refused to say anything else.

Once these formalities had been completed, the German commander told Campbell to assemble his troops on the road. A whistle blew and the 450 members of Retimo Force who had surrendered with their commander were ordered to fall in. The soldiers instinctively reached for their rifles before they remembered they had thrown them away.

At Retimo, the prisoners were confined to the local high school where they were fed on rice mixed with raisins. Then they were marched through Georgiopolis to Suda. Three days later they arrived at Maleme. The airfield had become a graveyard of wrecked aircraft and the prisoners were forced to help clear away the debris. Then they were flown to Greece in the same Ju-52s that had attacked them.[17]

Meanwhile, Ralph Honner's group of the 2/11th Battalion reached Ay Galini at 5 pm on 31 May and Ray Sandover's men turned up later that evening. Within 24 hours, some 600 troops – Australian, New Zealand and British – had arrived at Ay Galini in the hope of taking a boat across the Libyan Sea to Egypt. The men dispersed inland during the day to avoid detection from the air. At night, they repaired a broken-down landing craft which had been washed ashore from Sphakia.

The craft needed new batteries to start the motor so two Australians, Bill Mortimer and Basil Avery, walked along the beach to Timbaki and removed batteries from some Argyll trucks which had been abandoned there. Then Mortimer and two others, Tom Bedells and John Fitzhardinge, sailed a small craft back to Timbaki to buy provisions. Just as they were leaving, they were fired on by a German motorcycle patrol. Bedells was wounded in the hand, foot and face. Fitzhardinge and Mortimer pushed the boat into the water, towed it out to sea and brought Bedells back to Ay Galini.[18]

The landing craft was being levered into the water on 2 June when the Germans showed up again. They were driven off by heavy fire. At 8.30 that night, a total of 77 all-ranks, including the wounded Bedells, set sail for Egypt. The landing craft was intercepted by an Italian submarine whose commander removed most of the officers and then ordered the others to return to Crete. Once the submarine had dived, they turned again for Africa and three days later came ashore near the lines of the 2/7th Field Regiment at Mersa Matruh.[19]

Back at Ay Galini, Ralph Honner, knowing the Germans would soon be back in force, 'got my various section leaders to take tracings of my map, advised them on routes and districts, food & water and boat possibilities, sea-routes and winds'. They then slipped away from the main group. At midday on 6 May, the Germans returned and demanded that the troops on the beach surrender. Sandover, who was swimming with five of his officers in a nearby river, later wrote, 'Everyone was very hungry, cold and beginning to despair, some were bootless and nearly all chucked it in.' Sandover and the five other Australians set off after Ralph Honner into the hills.[20]

Keith Hooper of the 16th Brigade Composite Battalion had no say in whether he surrendered or went on the run with the hundreds of Anzac and British soldiers now scattered in dozens of locations all over the island. 'I was on a bit of a cliff-face when these two Messerschmitts came down and fired at me,' he says.

> Two things happened simultaneously. One of the bullets ricocheted off a rock and I was struck in the face. At the same time, I got a bullet in the leg that knocked me off the cliff. I fell three or four metres, landed on my head and was knocked unconscious. This was 31 May, the last day of the fighting. When I came to, it was the first of June. I'd been found by a group of Germans. By this time, Colonel Walker had surrendered and most of the troops were in the process of going into captivity. This German fellow gave me a British biscuit with bully beef on it and an orange. My ear was hanging off, I had a wound on my forehead and my nose and leg had been damaged but I'd been patched up.[21]

Still concussed, Hooper was taken to the 7th British General Hospital on its little headland. Some of the tents had been completely destroyed and others riddled with bullets. Leslie Le Souef had been placed in charge of the Allied wounded. Next to the hospital, a prisoner-of-war compound consisting of a few tents and barbed-wire fences had been set up under some olive trees. It was a dangerous place to be a prisoner: three British soldiers had already been killed and eight wounded when German guards fired at random into the camp.

Complaints from the camp's senior British officer, Major D.R.C. Boileau, were stone-walled with the statement that all of the shootings had been 'accidental'. Shortly afterwards, a guard sprayed a working party on the march with his submachine gun because one prisoner with dysentery was forced to stop by the roadside. Six men were shot in the back, four of whom died.

Colonel Le Souef kept a dossier of these incidents. One 'nuisance' prisoner was forced to run away from his captor and then shot down as an escaper. The shot failed to kill him, so his captor drew his revolver and fired at his head at point-blank range. The man was left for dead but he was taken to hospital where he survived – minus one eye. Le Souef examined two other men who survived the same treatment.[22]

Keith Hooper was lucky. He was flown to Athens in a Ju-52 and admitted to a prison hospital in a block of flats at Daphni. 'That's where I made my first attempt to escape,' he says. 'I went over the wall and landed beside a German sentry.'

Anzac and British prisoners were being transported to Salonica in cattle trucks en route to prison camps in Germany. In one place, the bridge over the river had been smashed by bombing and everybody had to leave one train, walk over a footbridge and board a train on the other side. 'Here was a good chance to escape, so I ducked under the train and headed for a stone wall,' Hooper says. 'As I climbed over it, a German popped up – he'd been taking a pee. He looked at me and grinned, and I looked at him and grinned and we walked back to the train together.'

Many prisoners testify to the fact that the Salonica transit camp was a dreadful, unsanitary place where they were starved and beaten. 'We came up against German soldiers who weren't frontline troops and they tried to knock us around,' Hooper says.

We were sleeping on concrete floors in summer uniform of shorts and shirt. It was cold and damp and we had very little to eat. We found an escape route along a sewer which ran from the centre of the camp to a cemetery across the road.

One night there was a mass escape attempt, which was bloody silly because the noise alerted the guards. Some got out but one of the Cypriot pioneers was overcome by the stench and collapsed in a bend in the sewer and blocked it.

People were still piling in when the guards came in. I was just about to go down and got a bayonet through my hand. A mate pulled me away and said, 'You'd better come or he'll shoot you.' My mate Ivan Dudley Welsh was one of the blokes they pulled out of the sewer. They bashed him around and he was still in the hospital when they sent us to Germany on 10 August 1941.[23]

Hooper ended up in Stalag 13C at Hammelburg near Frankfurt. All of the village's young men had been conscripted into the armed forces. 'When we got to Germany, we didn't know our rights for the first six months,' Hooper says. 'I was sent out on a working party from the camp and put to work for the local baker. Customers in the bakery asked me where I'd been captured. Immediately I said Crete, I got respect from them. Crete was the first time they'd almost been defeated and they respected that.'[24]

After several days of good food and rest at Klima, John Peck and his mates Harry Blake, Dave Pettigrew, Bill Legerwood and Jack O'Brien felt fit enough to take on the German Army again. 'A trickle of our boys was beginning to pass through Klima on their way to wilder and safer areas of central and eastern Crete,' he says. 'Although they were a bit envious seeing us so comfortably ensconced, they passed on after a good meal.'[25]

By this time, German patrols had started working their way into the hills and the Australians plotted their movements. They knew that sooner or later one of the patrols would reach Klima and rather than endanger the family they moved towards the coast on to a rocky hill called Daphne Corfu. There they camped among the rocks and organised themselves into an army unit again. A guard was posted with the binoculars to spot patrols and escape routes were charted.

The group split up and, for added security, found different bivouac positions scattered among the large rocks. Warning signals were arranged and a roster compiled for water-carrying, fuel-gathering and cooking. They reconnoitred the surrounding countryside and carried out intermittent surveillance on the few roads and many trails and tracks in the area.

Despite all of these precautions, Peck was the first to be captured. He walked into a patrol of Austrian troops who were drinking around a well in a deserted village. Peck was wearing civilian clothes and tried to bluff his way out of it but the Australian paybook in his pocket gave him away. The patrol took him back to their camp at Kalives. For the four-hour hike, his belt was removed and he had to march with his hands holding up his trousers. At first, the Austrians laughed at this but after an hour of climbing up and down hills with heavy packs and weapons they realised he was the lucky one. Finally, one soldier complained bitterly to the sergeant, so Peck's belt was returned and he had to shoulder the biggest pack containing the day's loot of *raki* and foodstuffs.

At Kalives, he was interrogated and warned that as he had been captured in civilian clothes he could be shot as a spy. His paybook saved his life. Instead, he was sent to the civilian prison at Canea.

Michael Clarke arrived in Salonica in a cattle truck late in the afternoon of 17 June 1941 and was marched to the transit camp. Ian Campbell and the 2/1st Battalion were already there. In the morning, the prisoners were given a ladle of thin lentil or barley soup, one-ninth of a loaf of brown bread and three-quarters of a Greek army biscuit. 'This diet was designed to starve us into submission,' Clarke says. 'Our commanding officer was Ian

Campbell. He did a fantastic job, very firm and effective.' Here and later in Germany, Campbell stood up for the prisoners, complained about the food and the bed-bugs, and demanded medical treatment for the sick.

Word reached the camp from Greek sympathisers that Hitler had invaded Russia. While massive German forces had indeed attacked the Red Army on a front extending from the Baltic to the Black Sea on 22 June, the rumours were too good to be true: the Russians had crossed the Bulgarian border, they were in Yugoslavia, they had cut the main line from the Balkans to Austria. 'We really thought we might be recaptured by the Russians arriving in Salonica,' Clarke says.

On 22 July, Clarke, Campbell, Willie Smith and hundreds of other Australian and British POWs were taken by cattle truck along that same rail line to Germany. After a nightmare seven-day journey, they arrived at Lubeck on the coast near Hamburg.

On the way to their camp, Stalag 10C, the prisoners were paraded down the main street of the town in front of schoolchildren and morning crowds of shoppers. 'We were unwashed, unshaven, in filthy clothes, carrying an odd assortment of bundles,' Clarke says. 'Under the circumstances, I felt proud of our effort. We kept in step and we held our heads up.'

CHAPTER 28

On the Run

The makeshift craft that beached on Egyptian shores brought the news that hundreds of Allied servicemen were still at liberty in Crete. Plans were made to rescue them through MI9, the organisation responsible for escape and evasion in enemy-occupied territory.[1] Since the shootout at Ay Galini, this had become immeasurably more difficult. Enemy patrols now scoured the coastline looking for fugitives and German agents dressed in British battledress were attempting to infiltrate the escape network.[2]

The first lift was organised by Commander Francis Pool, who landed with his Cretan guide Stratis Liparakis from the submarine HMS *Thrasher* in the Bay of Limni on 26 July. 'Skipper' Pool spoke fluent Greek and had been manager of the Imperial Airways flying-boat station at Spinalonga on the north coast. He was a member of SOE but had been seconded to MI9 to make this trip. His mission was twofold: to pick up soldiers who had gathered in the Preveli area and to meet Cretan Resistance leaders.[3]

Pool was met by three Australians who were sending signals out to sea in the hope of rescue. They took him to the nearby

Saint John's Monastery, which was built into the cliff-face at Preveli and consisted of upper and lower levels. The abbot, Father Agathangelos Lagouvardos, was conducting mass in the Church of John the Baptist in the lower monastery. After the service, Pool introduced himself. He said that the submarine would return on the night of 27/28 July to evacuate a number of Allied troops. Pool looked and spoke like a Greek and the abbot was initially suspicious that he might be a German spy.

Once Pool had convinced him of his bona fides, the abbot agreed that the troops could be marshalled at the monastery prior to embarkation, in fact some were already staying there. The following night, 70 soldiers were led down the long flight of stone steps to the beach. At 10.50 pm, *Thrasher* surfaced just 65 metres offshore and launched a Folboat canoe manned by two heavily armed commandos carrying 40 lifebelts and a line which was attached to the submarine.[4]

Some of the troops changed their minds when they realised that they would have to swim out to *Thrasher*. Voices were raised. More men hurriedly joined the group. With shouted farewells to Cretan friends, the first swimmers entered the water. 'The noise was most alarming and difficult to stop,' says *Thrasher*'s war patrol report. 'The skill of these men in forcing their heads underwater when they were properly dressed in lifebelts was remarkable.'

'I pulled myself along the rope to the sub,' Geoffrey Edwards, one of the Australians, says. 'Halfway out there the soldier in front of me panicked as he couldn't swim a stroke and he started splashing around and shouting out. A sailor quickly quietened him with a terrific punch to the jaw and then guided him along.'[5]

That night, 39 Australians, 20 British, three New Zealanders, 11 Greeks and five naval ratings, a total of 78, were rescued. Pool stayed ashore to meet Resistance groups and to organise a second lift the following month.

Meanwhile, Ray Sandover and Ralph Honner had moved their group from the coast to one of the limestone caves in the foothills around the village of Apodoulou in the Amari Valley. They befriended Costas Folukis, an English-speaking Greek, who provided them with regular food supplies.[6] Late in July, Sandover was invited by a local Cretan to meet a mysterious stranger. Fearing betrayal, he travelled by donkey for 11 hours to a small hut on the road back to Retimo. The stranger turned out to be Commander Pool, who informed him he was gathering evaders and escapers for another lift.

Pool was delighted to learn from Sandover that a group of 2/11th soldiers was in hiding within a couple of days' march of Preveli. He told Sandover that his party should report to Brother Dionysius at the monastery on 18 August. This they did and were informed at the monastery that the submarine would be there the following night. Down on the beach, they found that a crowd of troops – 'Commandos, New Zealanders, Cypriots, Aussies and many Greeks' – had arrived from different parts of the island. Sandover writes:

> Having discovered I was the senior [officer] and that there were 120 troops, I divided them into three parties and drew lots for priority. We were the last group. Staring out to sea, knowing that there were Germans about a mile away on each flank, I had little hope of being among the lucky ones. Suddenly the submarine loomed up in the darkness. She looked huge.[7]

Sandover swam out to meet a naval officer who paddled close to shore in a Folboat canoe. He asked how many men were ready for evacuation and was told 120. 'Keep them quiet or we'll go away,' he said. He would take 120 people but no Greeks. Sandover was in no position to argue and the loading proceeded. One Greek almost drowned when he swam out to the submarine and was prevented from boarding.

Sandover and Honner were both on board when HMS *Torbay* left Preveli for Alexandria early on 20 August. No two men had fought harder in the Allied cause on Crete or had greater success against the enemy. Among the 125 escapers were 62 New Zealanders who had broken out of the prisoner-of-war camp near Galatas. As *Torbay* sailed into Alexandria harbour, Sandover, in a dirty pair of shorts, was given the honour of standing on the bridge.[8]

Word of the evacuations – and the monks' role in them – reached the Germans. On 25 August, they raided the buildings of the lower monastery and arrested several monks. 'The Germans removed all the goods that were stocked there and the sheep and transported them to Retimo,' the monastery's history says. 'They destroyed the furniture and the vestments of the monks and caused serious damage to the buildings. Wine barrels, the jars in which the olive oil was stocked, tools, even kitchenware as well as the reception rooms and the accommodation for pilgrims and the monks themselves were destroyed.'

The abbot went into hiding and was later spirited away to Egypt, where he joined the Greek Army in the Middle East as a priest. Once they knew he was safe, the monks were free to accuse him of being pro-British and thus heap all the blame on him.

John Peck probably knew nothing about these dramatic events. He had been sentenced to 30 days' solitary confinement. On 5 August 1941, he had been driven from Kalives to Canea to serve his sentence in the civilian prison. But instead of a cell of his own, he was incarcerated in a dungeon with a number of Cretan prisoners. Most of the Cretans had committed criminal offences but some were political prisoners awaiting trial. The dungeon stank and the daily food ration was one small bread roll. Other meals had to be sent in by family members or friends from outside the prison.[9]

Luckily, some of the Cretans shared their food with him, but after four days of sponging he demanded to speak to the commandant on his morning rounds. 'To my surprise, he heard me out and said he would see what could be done about finishing my sentence at the prisoner-of-war camp,' Peck says. 'Three days later, I was moved to the prison camp next to the general hospital.'

On arrival, Peck was interrogated at camp headquarters and then allowed to write a letter to his stepmother. Astonishingly, it got through the censor. Dated 12 August 1941, it is today among his papers at the Australian War Memorial. It reads: 'I am now a prisoner of war in Crete. I am well. Huck was wounded here in the battle and I don't know what happened to him so would you write to his mother, Mrs Huxtable, 9 Lorac Avenue, Brighton? Most of my mates were killed in the battle and I am heartbroken.'[10]

Peck was placed in the camp 'cooler', a tiny open-air stockade. It was on slightly higher ground than the rest of the camp and afforded a good view of prisoner-of-war life. It was dinnertime and most of the prisoners were lined up at the far end of the camp collecting their rations. 'Some of the boys drifted down towards me and asked me all about myself,' Peck says. 'I did not know any of them but it felt good to be talking to friends again.' There was no shelter from the sun and Peck was soon burning with thirst. He asked a passing German guard for water. 'No water,' he said, 'and lie down. You are not allowed to stand up in the stockade.' After the German had gone, some of the other POWs returned with news of what had happened since the capitulation.

The 2/7th Battalion had passed through the camp on its way to captivity in Greece. The wounded had been flown to Athens together with most of the officers, but not Colonel Walker. He had escaped two days after surrendering but had been recaptured and was still on the island. The remainder of the camp expected to leave for Greece as soon as the Germans could obtain transport. 'I didn't like the sound of that,' Peck says. 'If I was to make a break, it would have to be soon.'

Nobody was allowed to get close to the stockade but the POWs promised to return with food and water that evening. Gradually the afternoon passed and a cool breeze came in from the sea. The camp quietened and Peck fell asleep. He was awakened by a twanging of the barbed wire and a voice whispered his name. 'It was the lads bringing me supplies,' he says. 'I ate and drank my fill as they talked and afterwards dozed and watched the stars for the rest of the night.'

When the sun came up next morning, the guard brought him his ration of a hunk of black bread and a mug of water. This had to last all day, so he placed them in the shade of a corner post and covered them with grass. Each hour it got hotter and brighter and by mid-morning he had drunk all the water. By midday, he felt on fire and risked calling to a passing prisoner: 'For God's sake, try and get me some water.' The man looked dubious. 'If I go near you, the guards outside the wire will shoot,' he said, 'but I will try and do something.'

Ten minutes later he returned with a water bottle. Keeping his distance, he took a quick look around and tried to toss it over the fence. The bottle hit the wire and bounced back. As it hit the ground, a burst of shots rang out. The POW dashed off at speed for the safety of the tents. Some of the prisoners in the tents were in the line of fire. There were shouts and screams, followed by cries for a doctor.

Very soon the main gate was thrown open and a detachment of guards came in at the double. The guard on the wire shouted an explanation to them and they split up, half going to the tents and half coming up to the stockade. The leader found the water bottle and, telling Peck he would be shot, pulled the cork and emptied the water on the ground.

The guard looked for identification on the water bottle and finding none trooped off to the tents to look for the thrower. Soon afterwards, the wounded were taken to the hospital. Peck lay down with a sinking heart. During the afternoon, the commander of the guards came over to question him about the

POW. 'I denied knowing him,' Peck says, 'so he ordered me to do three extra days in the cooler (what a misnomer) for my part in the affair.'

Towards evening, the camp was lined up in two ranks near the hospital entrance. Four men came out bearing a coffin draped with the Union Jack. 'I realised I was watching my first prison camp funeral and that it was probably through me that the victim had met his end,' Peck says. As the coffin passed by, he stood to attention with tears streaming down his face.

John Peck was released from the stockade before his time was up. One of the guards simply unlocked the chain around the wire gate and, jerking his thumb, said, 'Out!' Peck walked over to the main camp. 'Nobody seemed very interested in me, so I wandered up and down the line of tents looking for friends,' he says. 'Eventually I found them and the return of the prodigal son was toasted in Greek wine filched from the Germans. A space was cleared for me in one of the tents and I settled in as a fully fledged prisoner of war.'

Peck went across to the hospital to visit the men who had been wounded in the water-bottle incident. He was gratified to see that they were all right: two had flesh wounds and the third, who had been shot through the chest, was mending fast. The funeral was that of a sergeant who had been fatally wounded in an earlier incident while recovering a parcel of food thrown over the wire by Cretan civilians.

The whole episode made Peck determined to escape. Reconnaissance showed that the eastern side of the camp presented the best opportunity. It was sheltered with trees and the double apron of wire looked loose. Moreover, the guards seemed to patrol up and down the wire whenever it suited them. On the fourth day, he decided to make a break that night. He scrounged a new pair of boots and swapped all of his civilian clothes for a pair of khaki shorts – he planned to go out in just shorts and boots, with no shirt or socks to catch on the barbed wire.

He said goodbye to his friends. Three volunteered to keep watch on the sentries in the guard house and signal if any of them moved. At dusk, Peck moved over towards the wire with his hands in his pockets. Approaching a tripwire, he stepped over it and lay down close to the fence. He says:

> For a long minute, I lay there waiting for something to happen. Nothing did, so I scrambled through the barbed wire and lay down again between the two fences. Hours seemed to pass before I felt brave enough to raise my head. I could see nothing but shadowy blackness and the faint outline of the wire pressing all around me. Twisting my head, I looked up at the sky and was startled to see how bright it was. Rustling noises seemed to come from everywhere, especially from outside the wire.
>
> I kept making excuses to myself for not moving – the light, the wire, the noises. I wondered if it would not be better to go back and try again some other night. I knew then that I was funking it and that if I did not go now I never would. With that thought, I stood up and parted the last wires.

A sudden scuffling noise to his left made him drop back and crouch down like a trapped animal. The noise was coming closer and appeared to be between the fences. He waited for a shout of discovery and the accompanying shot. Straining his eyes, he could just make out a dim shape crawling towards him. The figure stopped a short distance in front. 'I sprang for where his throat should be,' Peck says. 'We grappled silently for a few moments and then our writhing bodies rolled on to a sandbag full of bottles and tins, making enough clatter to alert every guard in the camp.' Involuntarily, both men stopped struggling. Peck realised he had run into a night trader coming in with his loot.

'What the bloody hell do you think you're doing?' the man asked.

'Getting out, you silly bastard,' Peck whispered.

'I thought you were after my stuff,' he said. 'Now you have drawn the crabs and God help us.'

As Peck climbed through the outer fence, a machine gun opened up, the shots twanging off the wire above his head. In panic, he forced his way through the remaining strands, gashing his head and neck on the barbs. Once outside, he ran blindly, knocking into tree trunks and branches. The trees thinned out as he crossed the Canea–Maleme road. He made his way inland for a couple of hours until he was safe from pursuit at least until daylight. Crawling into a low clump of bushes near the Prison Valley road, he dozed off for as long as quaking limbs and the ever-present mosquitoes would allow.

At dawn, he crossed the road into an olive grove. 'I fixed my position by the heights of Cemetery Hill and Pink Hill near Galatas village,' he says. 'This area had been one of our battlegrounds during the fighting and most of the bomb craters and slit trenches still remained.' By eight o'clock in the morning, Peck reached the site of his platoon's last defensive position before withdrawing to 42nd Street. He got a vicarious thrill sitting in his old slit trench under an olive tree eating a bunch of grapes.

'For almost a year I was on the island,' Peck says. 'I met up with a New Zealander, Noel Dunne, and we stuck together. We met bands of Cretan *andartes* [fighters with the Cretan Resistance] and trained them in infantry weapons and tactics. Food and shelter were freely offered by Cretan mountain folk.' Among the many Cretans he encountered were the fiercely independent guerrilla leader Manoli Bandouvas and George Psychoundakis, who later became famous as 'the Cretan Runner' delivering messages for Patrick Leigh Fermor, Monty Woodhouse, the Tasmanian archaeologist Tom Dunbabin, and other SOE agents on Crete. He also guided escaped servicemen and evaders to embarkation points where Royal Navy rescue parties took them back to Egypt.

Just before Christmas, Peck missed the next lift through sickness. 'I'd been ill for quite some time with malaria,' he says.

'There was no quinine available so I was put in the invidious position of having to be carted about.' One of the people who helped him was George Psychoundakis, who doubted he would survive his illness. Peck's life was saved when a Cretan family at Timbaki fetched a doctor from Heraklion. He gave Peck one of the few available doses of quinine.[11] He was also treated by Captain Kiernan 'Skipper' Dorney, an Australian physician who was providing medical care for sick and wounded troops. But it wasn't until one of the SOE officers – possibly Monty Woodhouse who was chief liaison officer with the Cretan Resistance at the time – arranged an air-drop of supplies, clothing and medicines including quinine that he recovered.

On 15 April 1942, Woodhouse was replaced by the 31-year-old Tom Dunbabin, a graduate of Sydney University and a fellow of All Souls, Oxford. The tall, powerfully built, dark-haired Australian had been working at the British School of Archaeology in Athens when war broke out. Dressed more like a wharf labourer than a Cretan peasant, he had spent his first few days on Crete in a cave overlooking the sea and then, avoiding German patrols, headed into the Mount Ida district where he established a radio station and acquired some Cretan clothes. He found that the Germans had cracked down hard on evaders and escapers, and their accomplices.

'They made it a capital offence to harbour stragglers, and those who remained had to move out of houses and cafes into caves and holes,' he writes. 'A few of them were picked up by accident or treachery. Two or three died and were reverently buried. One army doctor who died was buried by the bishop with half the clergy of the diocese and a crowd of two or three thousand people ...'[12]

John Peck was fortunate that Noel Dunne had stayed behind on Crete to help look after him. Around this time – April 1942 – the two young Anzacs headed into the two eastern provinces controlled by the Italian Army after hearing rumours that a British submarine was due to make a lift from the northern coastal town of Sitia. The Italian commander, General Angelo Carta, a short, rotund royalist who had brought his mistress with him to Crete, had his headquarters at Neapolis near Heraklion. While life in the two eastern provinces of Sitia and Lasithi bore little resemblance to the idyll portrayed in *Captain Corelli's Mandolin*, it was less terrifying than in the German zone where the Nazis earned the undying enmity of the Cretan people with their policy of mass execution and village-burning.

The original order for reprisals and punitive expeditions against the civilian population for allegedly mutilating German soldiers was issued by General Student on 31 May 1941. By 9 September, 1135 Cretans had been executed in outbursts of retributive violence against *francs-tireurs* and hostages, the vast majority without appearing before a military tribunal or any other court. Judge R. Rudel, who investigated the mutilation allegations, could find only about 25 cases on the entire island, nearly all of which had almost certainly been perpetrated after death.

George Psychoundakis spoke for many Cretans when he wrote, 'The Germans proved themselves to be, in every way, utter barbarians. They were avenging, they said, their slain brothers-in-arms who now filled the whole island with graveyards. But how could they justify this vengeance for their slain companions who, along with them, had tried to drive us from our homes and dishonour and kill us, and settle in our stead? What did they expect us to do? Cross our hands and surrender?'[13]

In the hills en route to the rendezvous point, Peck and Dunne found a radio transmitter dropped by a British aircraft and hid it in a shepherd's hut. 'Next morning, we slept while the shepherd went in search of other parachutes,' Peck says. 'We were woken by the sound of feet on rocks and thought it was the shepherd but an Italian patrol entered the hut.' Peck and Dunne claimed to have left their identity papers in Heraklion. As they both spoke passable Greek, they might have got away with it if one of the Italians hadn't decided to souvenir a gaily woven blanket and found the radio underneath.

On 28 April they were handcuffed and taken to Italian headquarters at Neapolis for interrogation. Peck was struck across the face with a riding crop by an Italian officer when he claimed prisoner-of-war status under the Geneva Convention and refused to answer questions.[14]

The two Anzacs were transported to Rhodes chained to the mast of a caique. They were to stand trial on charges of spying but on 15 May 1942 'we overpowered a guard at Rhodes prison and got away at night'.[15] They escaped from the island with three Czech prisoners of war in a small boat. Heading for Turkey, the boat broke up in a storm. The Czechs were drowned. Peck and Dunne were picked up by an Italian destroyer which found them trying to swim to Turkey. They were returned to Rhodes.[16]

By now, Peck had escaped four times. 'If you're young, agile and foolish, you do things that older wiser men never do, and mostly you get away with it,' he says.[17] That month, he was sent to camp PG 57 at Gruppignano, near the Austrian border with Italy. The camp held a large number of Australian and New Zealand prisoners as well as British, Canadian, South African and Indian. Peck took the opportunity to learn Italian from his guards. 'They were very pleased when somebody tried to learn their language,' he says, 'and they really went out of their way to help you.'[18]

Peck remained in captivity for an entire year. In June 1943, he escaped again after being transferred to a work camp near Vercelli to labour in the ricefields. Peck and another escaper made it over the Alps as far as the Swiss border. 'We'd actually gone into Switzerland and all you could see was range after range of snow-covered mountains,' he says. 'We had no supplies and no way of surviving if we were lost there.'[19] They returned to the Italian side of the border and made the mistake of asking an Italian shepherd for food. He promised to fetch some but returned with the police. On 1 July, Peck was in solitary confinement at Vercelli prison as a punishment for escaping.

On 3 September 1943, the head of the Italian Government Marshal Badoglio – who had returned from his pheasant-shooting vacation to seize the premiership from Mussolini – surrendered unconditionally to the Allied forces under General Dwight D. Eisenhower following the Allied invasion of Sicily. King Victor Emmanuel and the Fascist Grand Council had secretly arrested Mussolini on 25 July and were holding him prisoner. The Italians agreed to fight alongside the Allies to expel the Germans from Italy. Badoglio pledged to hand over the Italian fleet and air force, and to secure Italy's airfields and ports against the Germans.[20]

News of the armistice triggered one of the most unfortunate episodes of the war when MI9, formed to rescue Allied soldiers trapped behind enemy lines, radioed secret messages to POWs in Italy through the BBC ordering them to remain in their camps to await liberation. With the country cut in half and German reinforcements pouring in, this was going to take months. Yet without informing Churchill or the British War Cabinet, MI9 issued Order P/W 87190 stating that 'officers commanding prison camps will ensure that prisoners of war remain within camp. Authority is granted to all officers commanding to take necessary disciplinary action to prevent individual prisoners of war attempting to rejoin their own units.'

This was completely contrary to Churchill's wishes. He was so keen for all POWs to be released after the Italian surrender that Article 3 of the armistice agreement stated, 'All prisoners or internees of the United Nations to be immediately turned over to the Allied commander-in-chief and none of these may now or at any time be evacuated to Germany.' Acting on MI9's instructions, however, British officers posted their own guards in some camps to prevent the men from leaving, even after the Italian guards had abandoned their posts. As a result, the Germans walked into dozens of camps and rounded up the POWs.

According to War Office records, more than 50,000 Allied soldiers were transported from Italian camps in cattle trucks to Germany and Poland during the summer of 1943. Thousands were either shot while trying to escape from the trains or died of disease and starvation in the camps over the next two winters.[21]

Some 20,000 other POWs, either ignorant of the MI9 order or simply determined to take their chances, had walked out from behind the barbed wire and were now on the loose in Italy. John Peck was among the fortunate ones – Italian looters raided the Vercelli jail and freed him from his cell. He decided to go back to Switzerland with as many POWs as he could round up. 'It was somewhat similar to Crete – our people had been dispersed everywhere and were being looked after by the Italian people,' he says. He gathered together a small group and guided them across the Alps to the Swiss border. Once they were safe, he hesitated.[22]

'I had pangs of conscience and decided that for me to go to Switzerland and freedom meant now abandoning all my friends who had no way of knowing which way to go and how to get there,' he says. 'So I decided to go back and get these people and take them to Switzerland. I started off an organisation with the Italians and made arrangements on the route for people to pick up and guide the prisoners.'[23]

Peck's stepmother Jean was surprised to receive a letter from him dated 21 November 1943 saying he was well and living at Vercelli. 'On the back of this letter,' he wrote, 'you will find a note from a very beautiful young girl who has been very good to me and once saved my life. Don't be alarmed, our friendship is purely platonic.'

Dear Madame,
I am an Italian girl and have been of assistance to your dear
Gianni who is in Italy. Your son is well and hopes for the finish
of the war. Asked to the house, John partook of the food and
wine and they did him much good. I hope you are well and very
trustfully greet you from my heart.
– Adelina

On his next trip to Switzerland, Peck was recruited into SOE by
John McCaffery, an affable Irishman who was known as 'Jock'.
McCaffery ran the SOE mission at the British Legation in the
Swiss capital of Berne. He worked closely with Allen Dulles,
who was station head of Wild Bill Donovan's Office of Strategic
Services (and later head of the CIA).[24]

Jock McCaffery asked Peck to work as a liaison officer among
several of the Italian partisan formations which were at each
other's throats. As Churchill viewed the Italian Resistance
as 'too republican, too left-wing and too communist', funds
from London were drying up and Peck's work would be more
important than ever.[25]

Peck was given the temporary commission of captain in
the British Army, outfitted and armed as such, given identity
papers and briefed on his role. He returned to Italy with the aim
of rescuing stranded POWs as a sort of Australian Pimpernel.
At the same time, he assisted the Italian Resistance in its
fight against the Germans and Fascist diehards. He joined a
partisan group led by Giuseppe Bacciagaluppi, head of the POW
assistance section of the Committee of National Liberation.

Donning a suit and a pair of spectacles, Peck disguised himself
as a businessman to travel around northern Italy supervising
Italian partisans in guiding Allied prisoners to safety.

I was always in fear because even if I did everything correctly
I could have been picked up just casually like everybody else

... But with prisoners who were normally much taller than local men [and who] normally had fair hair, spoke only English and had no knowledge of how and where they were going, they were [like] sheep led to the slaughter and in many cases this happened with inexperienced couriers and inexperienced guides.[26]

Peck kept a base at Luino north of Milan between Lake Maggiore and Lake Como near the Swiss border. On one journey there, he was escorting 19 POWs to safety on a train. Through exhaustion, he fell asleep. Waking up an hour later, he was alarmed to discover that his charges had disappeared. They were supposed to alight at the next stop but after searching the train without luck, Peck got off the train with the intention of retracing his steps. He was out of luck. There were no trains making the return journey that night. A German guard told him, 'You'd better go home.'

Peck replied, 'Well, I don't live here. I made a mistake about the train and I've got to go back.'

'Well, you can't stop on the station or you go to jail.'

'What can I do?'

'Try the hotel.'

His comrade interrupted, 'But he can't stay there. We occupy the hotel.'

The Germans sympathised with Peck's situation and, with the curfew about to start, agreed among themselves that he should stay in the hotel. One of them guided him there and he spent the night sleeping under the same roof as German troops. In the morning, he had breakfast in the same dining room and then went in search of his missing POWs. All of them had in fact left the train at the prearranged spot and he had somehow missed them on the train.

It was a close shave but there were even more dangerous times ahead. Peck's photograph, showing him in spectacles and business suit, was on wanted posters displayed all over northern Italy. Nevertheless, on 12 February 1944, Peck was back in Italy as part of a team of saboteurs to blow up a railway tunnel at Luino. 'The Germans had confiscated the coinage of Italy and were taking thousands of tons of it to Germany to turn into armaments,' he says. 'To avoid the bombing in the Brenner Pass, they were taking it by train through Switzerland. I received instructions from McCaffery to stop it.'[27]

On the night of the operation, Peck's group was betrayed to the Gestapo and 32 people were arrested. Peck had adopted the guise of a German officer for the raid and was dressed in a German uniform, a capital offence. During the arrest, he had most of his teeth knocked out. The Germans also stripped him naked. He was tortured by the Gestapo and sentenced to death by a military tribunal in Como.[28]

Pending execution, he was sent to San Vittore Gestapo prison in Milan. By coincidence, Bacciagaluppi had also been arrested and was in San Vittore. In order to get Peck outside the walls, he arranged for him to join a bomb-disposal squad digging out unexploded bombs. On 14 May 1944, the squad was assigned to work in the Lambrate railway marshalling yards, which were under constant air attack. Peck and his co-workers were gingerly digging around a bomb with picks and shovels when the siren signalled another air raid. 'The guards ran like hell and so did I – in the opposite direction,' Peck says. One of the guards took several potshots at him but missed. Once out on the familiar streets of Milan, Peck took the first tram to the station, caught a train to Intra and then headed into the Alps and crossed into Switzerland on 22 May.

On 27 June 1944, Peck wrote to his parents from Camp d'Internment Militaire, Wil. St Gallen, Switzerland:

At last I'm a free man again having arrived in this free country about a month ago after being through hell and high water in Italy since the armistice. At present I can't tell you anything about what happened to me then. We are not doing too badly in this little Swiss town, plenty of liberty, enough good food and a good bed in a private house. What a hell of a difference between this and Italy, Greece and Crete. The beer in Switzerland is not so bad but I prefer Foster's Lager.[29]

Despite internal rivalries and lack of funds, many POWs were repatriated through the Committee of National Liberation. Peck is credited with a part in taking 1500 Allied escapers over the Swiss border, an incredible feat for a soldier who was just 22 at the time.

CHAPTER 29

Belated Justice

For the Germans, Crete had been a Pyrrhic victory. Hitler had secured his southern flank and was able to use most of his Balkan divisions for his campaign of terror, torture and extermination in Russia. But his cherished parachute division had been destroyed. He was 'most displeased with the whole affair' and never again authorised an airborne assault. 'Crete proves that the days of the paratroopers are over,' he told General Student. 'The paratroop weapon depends on surprise – the surprise factor has now gone.'[1]

Hitler later recalled Student for one more important task. By an odd twist of fate, he ordered him to take command of an operation to free Mussolini, the man whose vanity had led to the invasion of Greece and the destruction of Student's paratrooper division on Crete. Mussolini was being held by Italian police at the Campo Imperatore Hotel at a ski resort high in the Apennines. On 12 September 1943, a detachment of Student's airborne troops crash-landed their gliders on the mountainside at Gran Sasso and overwhelmed the Italian force without a shot being fired.

Major Otto Skorzeny supposedly greeted Mussolini with the words, 'Duce, the Führer has sent me to set you free!' Mussolini replied, 'I knew that my friend would not forsake me.' He was returned to power in the Italian Social Republic, the German-occupied portion of Italy. Although Hitler's puppet, he had the satisfaction of executing five of the conspirators who had deposed him, including his son-in-law, Count Ciano.

Following the Italian armistice in September 1943, the Italian division commanded by General Carta on Crete was offered three choices: to fight with the Germans, to put down their arms and work as labourers, or to be interned. Most went behind the wire as German prisoners, but not their commander who was smuggled off the island to Egypt by Paddy Leigh Fermor. In the following months, dozens of Germans were killed in hit-and-run raids by ever-larger groups of vengeful, well-armed *andartes*.

In April 1944, Leigh Fermor and a small Anglo–Cretan group boldly kidnapped the German commander, Major-General Heinrich Kreipe, at gunpoint, marched him across the island and evacuated him to Egypt in a Special Boat Squadron motor launch. Leigh Fermor's exploits were the subject of Stanley Moss' book *Ill Met by Moonlight* which was filmed in 1957 with Dirk Bogarde as Leigh Fermor.

The mounting crisis in Italy forced Hitler to pull his troops out of Greece, abandoning the Crete garrison to its fate. Faced with thousands of Resistance fighters led by Manoli Bandouvas and other Cretan kapitans, German units gradually withdrew from Heraklion, Retimo and other strongpoints until they were concentrated in a tight ring inside Canea. As they retreated, the Germans inflicted further punishment on the population, burning down houses and shooting more than 1000 hostages, 'including many old women who were unable to flee from their villages'.[2]

*

After six unsuccessful attempts, Keith Hooper finally escaped from his prison camp, Stalag 383 at Hohenfels, on 13 April 1945 and made his way to the American lines, where he joined up with a group of Allied war correspondents. Before enlisting in the AIF, Hooper had been a reporter on the *Sun News-Pictorial*, sister paper of the Melbourne *Herald*, and he filed news reports on the final stages of the Battle of Germany to both papers. Repatriated to London on 8 May, he got a lift to Fleet Street and went to the *Herald* bureau in the Reuters building. There, the bureau chief Trevor Smith handed him a cheque for £100 in payment for his stories, and a cable from Sir Keith Murdoch, the *Herald & Weekly Times* boss, congratulating him on his release. He adjourned to Codger's pub to celebrate.

Keith took various jobs on provincial newspapers in the United Kingdom. While working on the *South Wales Echo* in Cardiff, he married Olive Lucille Short, who had been his pen pal while he was a POW. He later returned to Australia, where he had a successful newspaper career and also lectured at the University of Canberra. Married three times and surrounded by children and grandchildren, he entered his 90th year on 27 August 2009.

The last Australian soldier to be killed in Europe was Private Lawrence Saywell, a bespectacled 26-year-old Sydneysider who had been captured in the Battle of Crete. With three other POWs, Saywell escaped during a forced march to a prison camp in Bohemia in January 1945. Finding sanctuary in the village of Miretin, he joined the Czech Resistance and fought with the partisans against the Germans for four months.

On 8 May 1945, the day the war ended, he was picked up by an SS patrol and summarily executed with a bullet through the head. Lawrence Saywell is buried in the Evangelical Cemetery at Miretin. In November 1945, the Czech President awarded him the Czech Military Cross for 'his brave and eminent services to our State in the battle for liberation'. His medal is now in the Australian War Memorial collection.

John Peck, a man the Gestapo would dearly love to have killed, had been the newest private in the 2/7th Battalion when it went into action in Bardia in January 1941. He arrived in the United Kingdom on 4 November 1944 as a captain in the British Army. For his services to escaping POWs in Italy, he was awarded the Distinguished Conduct Medal.[3]

John fell in love with an English girl, Brenda Bird, and they were married on 6 January 1945. His commission was confirmed by the Australian Army, although at the lower rank of lieutenant.[4] Peck had sailed to the Middle East with the 6th Division in February 1940 in the *Empress of Japan*. When he left England five years later, he went back on the same ship, now renamed *Empress of Canada*. Arriving in Melbourne on 10 April 1945, the first mention of his extraordinary exploits appeared in *The Argus* the following day. It was only a short report. 'The war in Europe was still on,' he says, 'but Australia's attention was focused on Japan.'[5]

Peck returned to England to lead the Victorian contingent in the London Victory March following the end of the war in Europe. The father of six daughters, five of whom survived infancy, he stayed in England and worked for the English Electric Company in Stafford. In 1991, he went back to Crete for the 50th anniversary of the Battle of Crete. He was reunited with George Psychoundakis, the Cretan Runner, who had helped him when he was struck down with malaria. 'George was delighted to see he was still alive,' Peck's daughter Barbara Daniels says, 'as he had given him up for dead.'[6]

George Vasey emerged from Greece and Crete with a fine reputation as a fighting commander. Blamey thought he had done 'particularly well. Not only did he have to stand the brunt of Greece but he had a very trying time in Crete. He came out of it fresher than any other senior officer that came off that island.' He was awarded a bar to his DSO and the Greek Military Cross, First Class, for showing 'courage and self-sacrifice, fighting at the side of our troops'.

Major-General Vasey fought against the Japanese in Papua New Guinea as commander of the 6th and then the 7th Division for two years. In February 1944, he became ill and was evacuated to Australia. After recovering, he was given command of the 6th Division again in early 1945. On 5 March, he was flying to New Guinea to take up his command when his Hudson aircraft crashed into the sea off Cairns, killing all on board.

The following month Allied forces, including a revitalised New Zealand Division under Lieutenant-General Bernard Freyberg, closed on Mussolini's redoubt in northern Italy. The Duce attempted to slip across the Swiss border with his mistress Claretta Petacci. They were captured on the shores of Lake Como by Italian partisans on 27 April. The next day they were shot and their bodies hanged by their feet from the gantry of a Milanese petrol station.[7]

Adolf Hitler outlived his ally by just two days. Before committing suicide in his Berlin bunker on 30 April, he commented on the Crete debacle. 'The Italians had the courage to launch themselves into the useless campaign against Greece without asking us for advice and without even warning us,' he wrote. 'We were forced, against all our plans, to intervene in the Balkans, delaying in a catastrophic way our attack on Russia. *If the war had been conducted only by Germany and not by the Axis we would have been able to attack Russia by 15 May 1941.*'[8]

Keith Hooper had no doubts that Greece and Crete imposed a fatal delay on the Barbarossa timetable. 'It was to have taken place on 15 May when he was busy fighting us on Crete,' he says. 'He lost his parachute corps and he lost around 400 planes.

That delay saw three million German troops bogged down in a Russian winter and they never recovered.'[9]

Military historians concede that the destruction of Student's parachute division was a serious blow to the Wehrmacht at the start of the Russian campaign (even though some parachute units were dropped behind Soviet lines to seize bridges and cut communications). They argue that the one month's delay in Barbarossa was caused by bad weather in Russia rather than the Battle of Crete. Hitler for one didn't seem to think so.

One consequence of the Balkan campaign was that it convinced Stalin that Hitler would not attack Russia as late as June, with just weeks of combat weather remaining. The Soviet leader therefore doggedly ignored many warnings about his ally's true intentions, including one from Churchill based on Ultra decrypts. It is also indisputable that the Battle of Crete prevented the airborne invasion of Malta, the island that was absolutely vital to the success of the Allied war effort in the Mediterranean.

The German garrison on Crete finally surrendered in May 1945 on the orders of Grand Admiral Karl Donitz, who succeeded Hitler as Führer of the dying Reich. The Germans were permitted to retain their weapons for self-defence until British troops arrived from Greece to protect them from Cretan revenge.[10] Thoroughly demoralised but lugging kitbags stuffed with loot, the Germans evacuated Canea and pulled back behind a defensive cordon on the Akrotiri Peninsula. Thousands of Cretans swarmed into their capital in a spontaneous outburst of joy. Old blood feuds and new rivalries were temporarily forgotten as they drank, danced and sang to celebrate a great victory.

As the longest-serving prisoner at Stalag 7A, Michael Clarke was in charge of a party of 45 POWs of different nationalities when they landed at an RAF airfield in Buckinghamshire on 10 May 1945. 'Welcome to England,' a matronly woman greeted them. 'Please come inside to morning tea.' The POWs were led into a large galvanised-iron hut. Two long tables were spread with sandwiches and cakes, and a dozen women waited to serve them.

'What is the ration per man?' Michael Clarke asked.

'Please eat as much as you would like, sir,' one of the women replied.

One of the American prisoners in the party, Edward V. Parnell Jr, stepped forward. 'Before we do so, Mr Clarke, we all wish to thank you for your leadership.' He saluted and shook Clarke's hand. 'My eyes were brimming with tears,' he admits.[11]

Back in Australia, Michael married Helen Lewis, eldest daughter of the great BHP steelmaker, Essington Lewis, who had contributed greatly to Australia's war effort as director of munitions. After four years' captivity, he could not bear to be confined inside an office or a courtroom. He put his career as a barrister to one side and bought a property at Rochester in northern Victoria, where he farmed for 20 years and raised three daughters, Andrea, Louise and Rosemary. He served two terms in Victoria's Upper House and, when his seat was redistributed, decided to put his electoral office in Rochester to different use. At the age of 60, Michael Clarke began to practise law as a country solicitor.[12]

General Kurt Student was captured by British forces in Germany in April 1945. After interrogation in London, he was charged with eight offences relating to the actions of German forces during the Battle of Crete, including using prisoners of war as a screen at Maleme, forcing POWs to conduct prohibited work at Maleme airfield, bombing No. 7 General Hospital, using hospital patients as a screen at Galatas, and shooting POWs at Maleme and Galatas.

After a two-day hearing, Student was sentenced to five years' imprisonment by a British military tribunal but the sentence was not confirmed. Instead of going to prison he was admitted to hospital, supposedly dying from the effects of his old head wound.

In September 1947, the British refused to hand Student over to the Greeks who wanted to try him for war crimes committed against Cretan partisans. A total of 3474 men and women had been shot by Nazi firing squads during the occupation, mostly for assisting Allied escapers and evaders like John Peck. The following year, Student – Goering's protégé and a diehard Nazi who admired Hitler and everything he represented – was discharged from POW status and returned to Germany where he lived to the age of 88. To the Cretans, it must have seemed like very rough justice indeed.[13]

On 29 September 1945, Bernard Freyberg returned to Crete for a memorial service in honour of the fallen. The New Zealand Division had fought magnificently in the Western Desert and in the Battle for Italy, adding El Alamein and Monte Cassino, among other famous names, to its battle honours. Watty McEwan, who was with Freyberg's tactical headquarters as signalman from El Alamein to Florence, recalls 'an absolutely marvellous commander who always loved to be at the front'. Freyberg had learned some hard lessons in the Battle of Crete. 'His tactics were all about concentration of force and retaining mobility on the battlefield,' McEwan says.[14]

Freyberg paid a visit to the battlefield at Maleme. His thoughts as he walked across the strip of battered turf that had cost him victory can only be imagined. Churchill had asked him to perform a military miracle in Crete and he had done his best. Later, at the Commonwealth War Cemetery at Suda Bay, he made a moving tribute to the Allied dead buried there. 'History will do justice to the part they played,' he said. 'It will be belated justice. Gallantry in failure, no matter how great it may be, has tardy recognition.'[15] He could well have been speaking about himself.

APPENDIX A

Metric conversion table

Distances and altitudes in the narrative have been expressed, where practicable, in (rounded) metric units; but in quotations from other works, the original units have been retained.

The displacements of ships – expressed in tons – are not converted because of the difficulty of knowing whether long (UK) or short (US) tons are referred to. A similar difficulty applies in the difference between British and international knots in referring to a vessel's speed.

Metric equivalents in round figures:

1 inch equals 25 millimetres
1 foot equals 30 centimetres
1 yard equals 0.914 metre
1 mile equals 1.6 kilometres (one kilometre is 5/8th of a mile)
1 pound equals 0.45 kilograms
1 ounce equals 28 grams
1 long (UK) ton equals 1.016 tonnes
1 short (US) ton equals 0.907 tonne
1 acre equals 0.4 hectare

1 knot (distance in sea miles travelled in one hour) equals approximately 1.85 kilometres per hour

Naval guns:

15-inch equals 381 mm
8-inch equals 203 mm
6-inch equals 152 mm

APPENDIX B

Service ranks

1. Admiral of the Fleet is equivalent to a field-marshal in the army and to a marshal in the air force
2. Admiral equals general or air chief marshal
3. Vice-admiral equals lieutenant-general or air marshal
4. Rear-admiral equals major-general or air commodore
5. Commodore equals brigadier or air commodore
6. Captain equals colonel or group captain
7. Commander equals lieutenant-colonel or wing commander
8. Lieutenant-commander equals major or squadron leader
9. Lieutenant equals captain or flight lieutenant
10. Sub-lieutenant equals lieutenant or flying officer
11. Acting sub-lieutenant equals 2nd lieutenant or pilot officer

Commissioned officers are followed in the navy by warrant officers and midshipmen, who are equivalent to 1st class staff sergeant-majors in the army. Naval ratings are organised, among other branches, into seamen, sailmakers, signals, telegraphists, engine room artificer, armourers, shipwrights, joiners, blacksmiths, plumbers, painters, coopers, sick berth attendants, writers, ship's cooks, officers' cooks, officers' stewards and bandsmen:

1. Chief petty officer
2. Petty officer
3. Leading rating
4. Able-bodied rating
5. Ordinary rating

APPENDIX C

Place names

The spelling of place names in mainland Greece and Crete conforms mainly with those in use at the time (for example Retimo not Rethymno).

Anzac Fury	Modern spelling
Aliakmon River/Line	Aliakmonas
Canea	Hania/Chania
Domokos	Domokos
Edessa	Edhessa
Elasson	Elassona
Georgiopolis	Georgioupoli
Heraklion	Iraklio
Kalabaka	Kalambaka
Kifisia	Kifissia
Larisa	Larissa
Monastir	Bitolj/Bitola
Olympus, Mount/Line	Olympos
Platamon	Platamonas

Anzac Fury	Modern spelling
Salonica	Thessaloniki
Sphakia	Sfakia
Thebes	Thiva
Veria	Veroia
White Mountains	Lefka Ori

APPENDIX D

Casualties

These casualty figures have been compiled from a variety of military history sources and may not accord exactly with other such lists.

Libya, January 1941:

Australian figures: 241 dead, 790 wounded, 21 captured

Greece, April 1941:

Australian figures: 320 dead, 494 wounded, 2030 captured
New Zealand figures: 291 dead, 599 wounded, 1614 captured
British figures: 256 dead, 369 wounded, 6500 captured
Greek figures: More than 13,000 dead and 50,000 wounded

Crete, May–June 1941:

Australian figures: 274 dead, 507 wounded, 3102 captured
New Zealand figures: 671 dead, 967 wounded, 1692 captured
British figures: 791 dead, 268 wounded, 6576 captured
Greek figures: Dead and wounded unknown, 5255 captured

Royal Navy figures: 1828 dead, 183 wounded, 9 ships sunk and
  18 damaged
German figures: 2124 dead, 1917 missing, presumed dead (4041
  total dead and missing), 2640 wounded, 17 captured

REFERENCES AND NOTES

Introduction: Anzac Fury

1   Author's interview with Keith Horton Hooper, April 2009.
2   Ibid.
3   Patrick Leigh Fermor, Introduction to Psychoudakis, *The Cretan Runner*, p. 10.
4   Author's interview with Les Cook, May 2009.
5   Playfair, p. 83.
6   Wavell, 'Operations in the Middle East, 7 February 1941 to 15 July 1941', p. 3432.
7   Author's interview with Les Cook, May 2009.

Prologue: Lighting the Fuse

1   International Military Tribunal, Nuremberg, p. 287; Hohne, p. 436.
2   Italian forces had swarmed across the Adriatic to invade Albania on Good Friday 1939, five months before the outbreak of World War II. On 13 April, the British Prime Minister Neville Chamberlain guaranteed the independence of Greece.
3   Two newsreels of Hitler's state visit to Florence, one German and the other Italian, can be viewed on www.youtube.com.
4   Iatrides, p. 267; Long, *The Six Years War*, pp. 50–1; Long, *Greece, Crete and Syria*, p. 113.
5   Engel, p. 88.

6   Ciano, *Ciano's Diary*, p. 297.
7   Calvocoressi, p. 168.
8   Engel, p. 88.
9   Kershaw, *Hitler*, p. 331.
10   von Below, p. 76.
11   Ciano, *Ciano's Diplomatic Papers*, p. 400.
12   'The Plague in Florence' had been looted from the sequestrated villa of the Jewish Landau-Finaly family in 1940.

Chapter 1: Sons of Anzac

1   Horner, *General Vasey's War*, p. 10.
2   Henry Nevinson, *The Times*, 27 March 1915.
3   From 7 December 1915, 105,000 men were evacuated from Gallipoli, starting at Suvla Bay and ending at Helles on 9 January 1916.
4   Bean, pp. 3–5.
5   Tel el Kabir was already rich in military history as the 1882 battlefield on which units of the rebellious Egyptian Army, commanded by Colonel Ahmed Bey Arabi, had been routed in their sleep by British forces under Lieutenant-General Garnet Wolseley.
6   'After "the war to end war" they seem to have been pretty successful in Paris at making a "Peace to end Peace,"' Wavell commented on the Versailles treaty that ended World War I. Fromkin, foreword.
7   John Peck interview, Imperial War Museum Sound Archive, 1996.
8   War Diary, HQ 6th Division, G Branch, AWM 52, 1/5/12.
9   Horner, *Blamey*, p. 69; Charlton, pp. 55–56. Born in Brooklyn, New York, of Anglo–Irish parents on 24 April 1906, William Joyce, known as Lord Haw-Haw for his 'Germany Calling' broadcasts that mocked the Allies' war effort, was hanged for high treason in Wandsworth Prison, South London, on 3 January 1946.
10   Hughes was a Gallipoli veteran who had done sterling work with the Imperial War Graves Commission between the wars in finding, identifying and burying Australian dead on the Turkish peninsula.
11   Lewin, *The Chief*, p. 14.
12   Genisse, p. 130.
13   Author's interview with Anne Robertson née Dove, January 2009.
14   Ziegler, p. 213. Lady Diana met Wavell in Singapore on 7 January 1942.
15   Schofield, p. 301.
16   Author's interview with Joan Bright Astley, April 2005. As Joan Bright, she met Wavell when she worked at the War Cabinet Office in Whitehall.
17   The Greater Egyptian Jerboa, a tough little rodent that lives in the Arabian desert, was chosen by Major-General Sir Michael O'Moore Creagh as the emblem of the 7th Armoured Division in Egypt. The Anglo–Australian forces in the 1941 Siege of Tobruk nicknamed themselves 'the Rats of Tobruk' after Lord Haw-Haw described them on Radio Berlin as being 'caught like rats in a trap'.

To confuse matters, a 1953 Hollywood movie entitled *The Desert Rats* actually concerned the adventures of 'the Rats of Tobruk'.

18 Chapman, p. 154.

19 Vasey to Rowell, 16 January 1940. Ambassador Lampson later denied this was the case but the facts seem clear.

20 When a British official explained to Farouk on the outbreak of war with Germany in September 1939 that it would be necessary to increase the size of British forces in Egypt, he had replied, 'Oh, all right, but when it's over, for God's sake, lay down the white man's burden and go!'

21 Cooper, p. 60. Royal hostility towards the Ambassador was not entirely unprovoked: Lampson made no secret of the fact that he thought Farouk a wastrel and referred to him dismissively as 'the boy'.

22 Wavell, *Allenby: Soldier and Statesman*, p. 172 *passim*; first published in two volumes as *Allenby: A Study in Greatness* (1943), and *Allenby in Egypt* (1944).

23 Long, *To Benghazi*, p. 71.

24 Ibid., p. 41.

25 Avon (Anthony Eden), p. 86. At Villers-Bretonneux in April 1918, the Australians halted the German Army's advance on Amiens, thus barring its way to Paris. At a conference in the early 1930s, Eden and Adolf Hitler discovered that they had probably fought on opposite sides of the trenches in the Ypres sector. At Suez, Eden was at the scene of the military disaster that would force his resignation as Prime Minister in 1956 when an Anglo–French force attempted to seize the canal following its nationalisation by President Gamal Abdul Nasser.

26 Long, *To Benghazi*, p. 72.

27 John Peck Papers, Australian War Memorial.

28 Peck Papers, AWM.

29 Wavell, *Speaking Generally*, p. 4.

30 Connell, p. 223.

31 McClymont, p. 24.

32 Churchill, *The Grand Alliance*, p. 242; Paul Freyberg, p. 147.

33 Blamey's first wife, Minnie Millard, the mother of his two sons Charles and Thomas, died in 1935. Their eldest son, Charles, had been killed in an RAAF flying accident in 1932.

Chapter 2: Best of Enemies

1 D. M. Horner, 'Blamey, Sir Thomas Albert (1884–1951)', *Australian Dictionary of Biography*, (ADB), Volume 13, Melbourne University Press, 1993, pp. 196–201.

2 Lavarack had dared to challenge the concept of the Singapore Strategy, which was supported by Shedden's mentor, Sir Maurice Hankey, secretary of the committee of imperial defence. Indeed, Shedden was known as 'the Pocket Hankey'. The Japanese capture of Singapore in February 1942 would prove that Lavarack had been right.

3 Long, *To Benghazi*, p. 46.

4 Long, *The Six Years War*, p. 22.

5   Long, *To Benghazi*, p. 101.

6   Gullett, *Not as a Duty Only*, p. 12. Sir Henry Gullett was one of three 'soldier ministers' killed in an air crash near Canberra on 13 August 1940. The other ministers were Jim Fairbairn, Minister for Air, and Geoffrey Street, Minister for the Army. The victims included the shrewd and experienced chief of the general staff, General Sir Brudenell White.

7   During World War I, Sir Robert Knox (1890–1973), although of military age, was an executive member of the Victorian central council of the Australian Red Cross Society and served as a commissioner in Egypt and France. Sir Robert Menzies was the subject of a swingeing attack by Sir Earle Page in the House of Representatives for allegedly dodging military service.

8   Extracts from Michael Clarke's diaries are published with permission of his daughter Louise Morris.

9   Michael Clarke Diaries, 27 May 1936.

10 Clarke, *My War*, p. 5.

11 After Australia beat England at The Oval in 1882, the *Sporting Times* published an obituary stating that English cricket had died and 'the body will be cremated and the ashes taken to Australia'. The English media dubbed the next English tour of Australia (1882–1883) as the quest to regain the Ashes. During that tour, the England team had lunch at 'Rupertswood', the property of Australia's first baronet Sir William Clarke, at Sunbury, Victoria. After lunch, Clarke suggested a social game between the English and a local side, made up largely of 'Rupertswood' staff. No one really kept score, but it was generally agreed that the English had won. At dinner that evening, Lady Clarke presented Ivo Bligh, the England captain, with a little pottery urn purported to contain the ashes of a burnt bail. This urn and its contents have since become the symbol of the Ashes contests between the two countries.

12 Michael Clarke archive, Tallarook.

13 Michael Clarke Diaries, 25 October 1939.

14 Clarke, *My War*, p. 11.

15 Prime Minister Savage died on 27 March 1940, just three weeks after receiving Menzies' cable.

16 *Documents Relating to New Zealand's Participation in the Second World War*, Volume II, 1951. Australia's population at the time was seven million and New Zealand's 1.6 million.

17 Horner, D. N., 'Lavarack, Sir John Dudley (1885–1957)', *Australian Dictionary of Biography*, Volume 15, Melbourne University Press, 2000, pp. 61–63.

18 Grey, *Australian Brass*, p. 78.

19 George Vasey to Jessie Vasey, 3 November 1940, NLA, MS 3782, Box 2, Folder 11.

20 Vasey to Jessie Vasey, 9 April 1940.

21 Braga, p. 87.

22 *Dictionary of New Zealand Biography*, Ministry for Culture and Heritage, Wellington, 1998, various entries.

23 Prime Minister Savage was suffering from the cancer which killed him in March 1940.

24 Hohne, p. 434.

25 Gooch, p. 5. Described by the *New York Times* as a 'noted revolutionist', Cipriani had been crippled by an Austrian bullet while fighting with Garibaldi for Italian independence in 1862. In 1897, he travelled to Greece with Garibaldi's son to fight against the Turks and was wounded once again in battle. However, the real saviour of Crete was the Cretan nationalist Eleftherios Venizelos, who fostered union with Greece – *enosis* – and later served as Prime Minister of the modern Greek state.

26 Cooper, p. 48.

27 Gooch, p. 132.

28 Duggan, p. 502, quoting Mussolini 2 October 1935, *Opera omnia*, Volume 27.

29 Duggan, p. 488, quoting Mussolini 9 October 1935.

30 Duggan, p. 503; Rory Carroll, 'Italy's bloody secret', *The Guardian*, 25 June 2001.

31 Duggan, p. 504.

32 Obituary of Robert Haggiag, *Daily Telegraph*, 25 March 2009. Haggiag later became a leading producer in the Italian and American film industries.

33 Gooch, p. 252.

34 Mosley, pp. 95–6.

35 Long, *To Benghazi*, p. 79.

36 Ebury, pp. 158–9, 164. In his unpublished memoirs, Brunskill claims to have had good working relations with the Australian Army but the evidence is heavily against him.

37 Anonymous nurse's diary entry, 22 April 1940, quoted in Bassett, p. 116.

38 Bassett, pp. 115–6.

39 Moorehead, *The Desert War*, p. 4.

40 Brune, p. 44.

41 Moorehead, *The Desert War*, p. 4.

Chapter 3: Whacko, Sydney!

1 During hostilities between 10 June 1940 and 8 September 1943, the Royal Italian Navy – Regia Marina – suffered 28,937 casualties and lost 13 cruisers, 42 destroyers, 41 minelayers, 3 corvettes, 84 submarines and many more lesser ships.

2 Gill, Volume I, pp. 156–7.

3 *Waterhen*, known to her crew as 'the Chook', sank off Libya on 30 June 1941 after being attacked by German bombers. She was the first RAN ship to be lost to enemy action during World War II.

4 Gill, Volume I, p. 137.

5 Waller's parents named him after General Hector Macdonald, who fought in the Boer War, and a nineteenth century ancestor, Admiral Laws.

6 *Stuart* was a Leader-class destroyer designed to lead a flotilla of V&W-class

destroyers. Launched in 1918, she had five 4.7-inch guns, one anti-aircraft gun, machine guns, torpedoes and depth charges.

7   The RANC was based at Osborne House until January 1915 while its permanent home was being built at Jervis Bay. Twenty-eight naval cadets, chosen from 137 applicants, began training in February 1913. The first captain of the college was Captain B. M. Chambers RN. During the Great Depression of the 1930s, financial strictures forced the college to move to Flinders Naval Depot, Victoria. The buildings served as a hotel until the college returned in 1958.

8   Author's interview with Mackenzie Gregory.

9   Ibid.

10 Collins, Vice-Admiral Sir John, p. 84.

11 Ibid., p. 85.

12 Ibid., p. 86.

13 Ibid., p. 86.

14 Gill, Volume I, p. 188.

15 Playfair, Volume I, p. 1.

16 Greene & Massignani, p. 85.

17 Long, *The Six Years War*, p. 43.

18 McGuire, p. 320.

19 Gill, Volume I, p. 195.

20 Collins, p. 88.

21 Hetherington: *Blamey: The Biography*, p. 81.

22 Carlyon, pp. 13–14.

23 Hetherington, *Blamey: The Biography*, p. 55.

24 Ibid., p. 55.

25 Reginald William Winchester 'Chester' Wilmot was born in Melbourne in April 1911. He was killed in a plane crash in the Mediterranean in January 1954. Wilmot to Bean, 14 August 1953, 3 DRL6673, 495.

26 Horner, *Blamey*, p. 143.

27 Carlyon, p. 12.

28 John Peck interview, Imperial War Museum Sound Archive, 1996.

29 Long, *To Benghazi*, p. 103.

30 Pack, quoting Commander Geoffrey Barnard, the fleet gunnery officer in *Warspite, The Battle of Matapan*, p. 34.

31 Foot, David, p. 204.

32 Michael Forrester interview, IWM Sound Archive, 2003.

33 Hetherington, *Blamey: Controversial Soldier*, p. 116.

34 Carlyon, p. 18.

Chapter 4: Spaghetti Western

1   Fraser, David, p. 215.

2   Ciano, *Ciano's Diary*, 9 September 1940.

3   Wilson, p. 55.

4   Wavell, 'Operations in the Middle East, August 1939 to November 1940', p. 3001.

5   Playfair, Volume I, p. 208.

6   Wavell, 'Operations in the Middle East, August 1939 to November 1940', London *Gazette*, p. 3001.

7   Ciano, *Ciano's Diary*, 17 September 2009.

8   Long, *The Six Years War*, p. 49.

9   Ciano, *Ciano's Diary*, 30 September 1940.

10 Gill, p. 285; Lewin, *The Chief*, p. 55.

11 *4th & 6th RMT*, p. 11.

12 Sir Richard O'Connor interview, Imperial War Museum Sound Archive, 1972; Baynes, p. 69.

13 Lewin, *The Chief*, p. 64.

14 Sir Richard O'Connor interview, Imperial War Museum Sound Archive, 1972.

15 On 28 June 1940, Balbo approached Tobruk airfield in his three-engined Savoia-Marchetti SM79 aircraft. He was coming in low against the sun when *San Giorgio*'s gunners, jumpy after their earlier experiences at the hands of the RAF, opened fire on his aircraft. The airfield's batteries followed suit and Balbo was shot down and killed.

16 Kershaw, *Fateful Choices*, p. 181.

17 Calvocoressi, p. 171.

18 Kershaw, *Fateful Choices*, p. 172.

19 Michael Forrester interview, Imperial War Museum Sound Archive, 2003.

20 Mott-Radclyffe, p. 52.

21 MacVeagh, p. 254.

22 Buckley, p. 22.

23 Churchill, *Their Finest Hour*, p. 472.

24 Gill, Volume 1, p. 226.

25 Ibid., p. 230.

26 Ciano, *Ciano's Diary*, 12 November 1940.

27 Iatrides, pp. 248, 257.

28 Reid, p. 118.

29 Mott-Radclyffe, p. 54.

30 Reid, p. 111.

31 Ibid., p. 108.

32 Ibid., p. 111.

33 Engel, p. 90.

34 United States Department of the Army, *The German Campaigns in the Balkan – Spring 1941*, p. 5.

35 Hunt, p. 14.

36 Connell, *Wavell: Soldier and Scholar*, p. 277, quoting 'Recollections' from the Wavell Papers.

37 Ibid., pp. 254–55.

38 Kennedy, p. 106. Churchill constantly mocked Wavell about the number of men under his command without taking into account the huge numbers of base and logistics troops needed to support an army in the field. Wavell sometimes had as many as three armies in action at the same time.

39 Menzies Diary, NLA, 14 April 1941.
40 Rhodes James, *Anthony Eden*, p. 249; Martin, p. 238.
41 Avon (Anthony Eden), p. 133.
42 Churchill, *Their Finest Hour*, p. 480.
43 Lewin, *The Chief*, p. 61.
44 Connell, *Scholar and Soldier*, p. 289.
45 Lewin, *The Chief*, p. 59.
46 Gill, Volume I, p. 287.
47 Baynes, p. 70.
48 Connell, p. 68.
49 Wilson, p. 49. The Kiwi drivers could make their way to any part of the desert using prismatic compasses. To prevent reflected sunlight giving them away to roaming Italian fighters, oil and sand were smeared on their windscreens, leaving only a small clear strip to see through. While they were driving, they heated tins of stew on their exhaust pipes for dinner.
50 For the sake of simplicity, many soldiers referred to the freezing winter winds that plagued them with vast quantities of sand and dust as the *khamsin* (Arabic: literally 'fifty'). This is actually a hot south-westerly wind that blows in from the Sahara for 50 days in spring between March and May. In winter, the cold, dry wind that, like the *khamsin* carries sand and dust, is known in Arabic as a *sharkiyya* or 'easterly', or in English as a 'sirocco'.
51 Playfair, Volume I, pp. 266–8.
52 Jackson, p. 43.
53 Stevens, p. 18.
54 McClymont, p. 64; *4th & 6th RMT*, p. 34.
55 Churchill, *Their Finest Hour*, p. 539.
56 Gill, Volume I, p. 287.
57 Ibid., p. 288.
58 Long, *To Benghazi*, p. 202.
59 *Lord Killearn's Diary*, 12 December 1940.
60 Goebbels, p. 214.
61 Ciano, *Ciano's Diary*, pp. 310, 312.
62 Mott-Radclyffe, p. 50.
63 Evans, Richard, p. 148.
64 Farrell, p. 339; Knox, p. 199. De Bono was executed by firing squad on Mussolini's orders in 1944 for plotting against him.
65 Halder, pp. 244–5.
66 von Manstein, pp. 152, 155.
67 Avon (Anthony Eden), p. 185; Knox, p. 241.
68 Farrell, p. 341.
69 Hohne, p. 436; Long, *To Benghazi*, p. 53; Beevor, p. 7; Calvocoressi, p. 167.
70 John Peck interview, Imperial War Museum Sound Archive, 1996.

Chapter 5: Baptism at Bardia

1   Bramall, p. 4.
2   Chapman, p. 168.
3   Lord Harding interview, Imperial War Museum Sound Archive, 1982.
4   Horner, *Blamey*, p. 159.
5   Rowell, p. 56.
6   Long, *To Benghazi*, p. 202.
7   Ibid., p. 202.
8   Pitt, p. 124.
9   'Smash way through modern Hindenburg Line', *The Age*, 7 January 1941.
10 Pitt, p. 148.
11 Jackson, p. 55.
12 'Early fall of Italian fort expected', *The Age*, 6 January 1941.
13 Jackson, p. 56; Long, *To Benghazi*, p. 149.
14 Long, *To Benghazi*, p. 154.
15 Russell, p. 198.
16 Long, *To Benghazi*, p. 155.
17 Barnett, *The Desert Generals*, p. 44.
18 Connell, *Scholar and Soldier*, p. 302.
19 McClymont, p. 70.
20 Playfair, Volume I, p. 281.
21 Chapman, p. 181.
22 Charlton, p. 45.
23 Long, *To Benghazi*, pp. 163–4.
24 Corporal Henry Rawson, quoted in Bramall, p. 7.
25 'Smash way through modern Hindenburg Line', *The Age*, 7 January 1941.
26 Bramall, p. 6.
27 Russell, p. 198.
28 Gullett, *Not as a Duty Only*, p. 30.
29 *Esprit de Corps*, 2/5 Bn history, p. 168.
30 Jackson, p. 48.
31 *The Fiery Phoenix*, 2/7 Bn history, p. 44; Long, *To Benghazi*, p. 178.
32 Gullett, Henry, *Not as a Duty Only*, p. 14.
33 Ibid., p. 2.
34 Ibid., p. 14.
35 Author's interview with Keith Horton Hooper, April 2009. The 2/6th Battalion lost 22 killed and 51 wounded in the two-day battle for Post II.
36 Long, *To Benghazi*, pp. 185–6.
37 Long, *The Six Years War*, p. 57.
38 Grey, *Australian Brass*, p. 83; Dean, p. 208.
39 Long, *The Six Years War*, p. 57.
40 Grey, *Australian Brass*, pp. 82–3.
41 Jackson, p. 59.
42 Brune, p. 52.

43 Russell, p. 204.
44 *Nothing over Us*, the 2/6 Bn history, p. 97; Long, *The Six Years War*, p. 59. Brigadier Arthur Godfrey was killed in action at El Alamein on 4 November 1942.
45 Long, *To Benghazi*, p. 198.
46 Moorehead, *The Desert War*, p. 114.
47 Ibid.
48 Connell, p. 302.
49 George Vasey to Jessie Vasey, 6 January 1941.
50 Wilmot, Chester, 'The Capture of Bardia', ABC, 14 January 1941.
51 Baynes, p. 105.
52 Chapman, p. 189.
53 John Peck interview, Imperial War Museum Sound Archive, 1996.

Chapter 6: Tobruk

1   Chapman, p. 198.
2   Grey, *Australian Brass*, p. 85.
3   Clarke, p. 93.
4   Chapman, pp. 160, 168.
5   Clarke, pp. 277–8.
6   Ibid., p. 281.
7   Chapman, p. 198.
8   Long, *The Six Years War*, p. 60.
9   Clarke, p. 285.
10 Pitt, p. 149.
11 Clarke, p. 285.
12 Long, *To Benghazi*, p. 215.
13 Author's interview with Keith Horton Hooper, April 2009.
14 Long, *The Six Years War*, p. 61.
15 Ibid., p. 62.
16 Clarke, p. 286.
17 Ibid., p. 287.
18 Le Souef, p. 76.
19 Ciano, *Ciano's Diary*, 22 January 1941.
20 Clarke, p. 289.
21 Michael Forrester interview, Imperial War Museum Sound Archive, 2003.
22 Papagos, General Alexander, pp. 310–11.
23 Mott-Radclyffe, p. 56.
24 Papagos, pp. 312–14.
25 Wavell, 'Operations in the Middle East, 7 February 1941 to 15 July 1941', p. 3423.
26 Ebury, p. 189.
27 Baynes, p. 109.
28 Field Marshal Lord Harding in his address at O'Connor's memorial service, 15 July 1981.

Chapter 7: Wily Wavell

1   Hetherington, *Blamey: The Biography*, p. 82.
2   Tedder to his wife, 5 February 1941, Tedder Papers.
3   Tedder to his wife, 10 May 1941, Tedder Papers.
4   Rhodes James, *Channon's Diary*, p. 290.
5   Moorhead, *The Desert War*, pp. 114–15.
6   Ranfurly, Hermione, p. 78. Hermione dates the lunch with Menzies as 7 February, whereas Menzies and the Ambassador correctly record it as taking place on 6 February.
7   Menzies, *Afternoon Light*, p. 26.
8   Obituary, *Daily Telegraph*, 13 February 2001.
9   Menzies Diary, 8 February 1941.
10   Fraser, p. 215.
11   Barnett, *The Desert Generals*, pp. 59–60.
12   Sir Richard O'Connor interview, Imperial War Museum Sound Archive, 1972.
13   Wavell, 'Operations in the Middle East, 7 February 1941 to 15 July 1941'.
14   Hohne, p. 443; Kennedy, p. 85.
15   Menzies Diary, 10 February 1941.
16   Barnett, *The Desert Generals*, p. 46.
17   Long, *The Six Years War*, p. 64.
18   Long, *Greece, Crete and Syria*, p. 8.
19   Wilson declined to use his first name, Henry, to avoid confusion with his uncle, Lieutenant-General Sir Henry Maitland Wilson, commander of XII Corps in Salonica in World War I.
20   Wilson, p. 60.
21   Hetherington, *Blamey: Controversial Soldier*, p. 175.
22   Menzies Diary, 12 February 1941.
23   Ibid., 13 February 1941.
24   Horner, *Blamey*, p. 168.
25   Blamey to Minister for the Army, 12 March 1941, AA A5954/1/528/1; Wavell, 'The British Expedition to Greece, 1941', pp. 178–9.
26   Blamey to Minister for the Army, 12 March 1941, AA A5954/1/528/1.
27   Clarke, pp. 309–10.
28   Freyberg's comments on Long's Narrative, AWM 67, 8/26.
29   McClymont, *To Greece*, p. 94.
30   Ibid. By early 1941, the AIF consisted of the following forces: 6th Division (16th, 17th, 19th Brigades), 7th Division (18th, 21st, 25th Brigades), 8th Division (22nd, 23rd, 27th Brigades) and 9th Division (20th, 24th, 26th Brigades).
31   Coombes, p. 92.
32   Sydney Rowell would later describe Charles Spry as 'one of the outstanding officers in the Australian Army. He combines a high standard of professional attainment with equally high personal characteristics and with what is almost a burning zeal to lift the status of the Army as a whole and its general efficiency and well-being in particular'. Rowell, VCGS Sydney, Annual Confidential Report – Officers, 19.07.49.

Chapter 8: Eden's Odyssey

1 Churchill, *The Grand Alliance*, p. 63.

2 Parkinson, p. 193.

3 Wavell, 'The British Expedition to Greece, 1941', p. 179; Rhodes James, p. 249; Martin, p. 323.

4 Wilson, p. 65.

5 Lewin, *The Chief*, p. 57.

6 Paul Freyberg, p. 247.

7 After the war, General O'Connor commented, 'I don't really know why he ever became a field marshal.' (Baynes, p. 108). General Freyberg attributed the promotion to his sympathetic treatment of Churchill's 'imprudent intervention' in Cos and Leros later in the war. (Paul Freyberg, p. 247).

8 de Guingand, *Generals at War*, p. 27.

9 Ibid., p. 27.

10 Wavell had responded to Shearer's report by quoting General Wolfe's axiom that 'war is an option of difficulties'. Ironically, Shearer was sacked and his replacement was Freddie de Guingand.

11 de Guingand, *Generals at War*, p. 23; Mott-Radclyffe, p. 60.

12 de Guingand, *Generals at War*, p. 28.

13 Ibid., p. 29.

14 Ibid., p. 22.

15 Menzies Diary, 23 February 1941.

16 Long, *Greece, Crete and Syria*, p. 1.

17 Kennedy, p. 85.

18 Parkinson, p. 196.

19 Menzies Diary, 24 February 1941.

20 Parkinson, p. 196.

21 Menzies to Wilmot, 2 December 1948, Wilmot Papers; Parkinson, p. 196.

22 British War Cabinet Minutes, 24 February 1941, PRO, CAB 65/21/26; Martin, *Robert Menzies*, p. 325.

23 Dilks, p. 358. Italics in the original.

24 Menzies to Fadden, 25 February 1941, and Fadden to Menzies, 26 February 1941, DAFP, Volume IV, pp. 452–5; Martin, *Robert Menzies*, pp. 325–6.

25 Long, *Greece, Crete and Syria*, p. 15.

26 Ibid., p. 15.

27 Churchill, *The Grand Alliance*, p. 69; PRO Cab 65/21, 32.

28 The Turks delayed their declaration of war until February 1945 when Germany was virtually defeated.

29 Kennedy, p. 86; Churchill, *The Grand Alliance*, p. 86.

30 Papagos, p. 317.

31 *London Gazette*, 14 March 1941. Richard Cullen had been killed in action ten days earlier on 4 March 1941. By then, his tally of enemy aircraft had risen to 13.

32 Buckley, p. 22.

33 Higham, p. 143.

34 Buckley, p. 23.

35 Avon (Anthony Eden), p. 211.

36 Lincoln MacVeagh Diary, 3 March 1941; Letter MacVeagh to Roosevelt, 8 March 1941, Iatrides, p. 312.

37 Avon (Anthony Eden), p. 213.

38 Parkinson, p. 201.

39 Wavell, 'Operations in the Middle East, 7 February 1941 to 15 July 1941', 3 July 1946, p. 3426; author's italics.

40 Long, *Greece, Crete and Syria*, p. 23.

41 Eden and Chief of Imperial General Staff to Churchill, 5 March 1940, PRO CAB 65122/17–18.

42 John Colville Diary, 5 March 1941, Colville Papers, Churchill Archives Centre, UK.

43 Churchill to Eden, 5 March 1941, PRO CAB 65/18/13; Churchill, *The Grand Alliance*, p. 90.

44 War Cabinet Minutes, Eden to Churchill, 6 March 1941, PRO CAB 65/22/23ff.

45 Menzies Diary, 5 March 1941.

46 Martin & Hardy (eds), p. 146; Menzies Diary, 5 and 6 March; Parkinson, pp. 205–6.

47 War Cabinet Minutes, 7 March 1941, PRO CAB 65/18/19; Churchill, *The Grand Alliance*, pp. 92–3.

48 Kennedy, p. 87.

49 Alanbrooke, p. 141. Alanbrooke's post-war note to his diary entry for 17 February 1941.

50 Wilson, p. 72. Wavell, 'Operations in the Middle East, 7 February 1941 to 15 July 1941', p. 3426.

51 Long, *Greece, Crete and Syria*, p. 33.

52 Wilson, p. 74.

53 Michael Forrester interview, Imperial War Museum Sound Archive, 2003.

54 Wilson, p. 84.

55 Author's interview with Miriam Dillon, née Preston, January 2009.

56 Michael Forrester interview, Imperial War Museum Sound Archive, 2003.

57 Hetherington, *Blamey: The Biography*, p. 132.

58 Semmler (ed.), *The War Diaries of Kenneth Slessor*, p. 202.

59 PRO CAB 65/22, 58; Churchill, *The Grand Alliance*, p. 93.

60 Lincoln MacVeagh diary entry 11 February 1941, Iatrides, p. 298.

61 Archer, p. 161.

62 Churchill, *The Grand Alliance*, p. 93.

63 Blamey to Minister for the Army, 12 March 1941, AA A5954/1/528/1.

64 Hetherington, *Blamey: Controversial Soldier*, p. 134.

65 Long, *Greece, Crete and Syria*, p. 17.

66 Menzies to Fadden, 8 March 1941, DAFP, Volume IV, pp. 484–6.

67 Ibid.

68 Horner, *Blamey*, p. 46.

69 Author's interview with Anthony Madden, October 2009. Many of the trucks were new 30-hundredweight, six-cylinder Chevrolets provided by the United States through the Lend-Lease scheme under which the United States would become an 'arsenal of democracy' that provided huge quantities of weapons, ships, aircraft and transport owned and paid for by the US Government and leased to the United Kingdom and her Allies.

70 Semmler (ed.), *The War Diaries of Kenneth Slessor*, p. 206.

71 Blamey to Acting Prime Minister, 14 February 1941, CRS A5954, 551/3.

72 Hetherington, *Blamey: The Biography*, p. 89.

73 Carlyon, p. 22.

74 Vasey to his wife, 30 March 1941, Vasey Papers, NLA.

75 Slessor, Kenneth, official Australian correspondent, Athens, 'Blamey and the King of Greece', Athens, 1 April 1941 in Semmler (ed.), *The War Despatches of Kenneth Slessor*, p. 141. To Slessor's fury, this quote appeared in the Melbourne *Argus* as 'his dad had always admired them'.

76 *4th & 6th RMT*, p. 50.

77 'General Statement on Situation in Greece as at 28 March 1941', Blamey Papers, AWM, 1/2a (vii); Rowell, p. 67; Horner, *Blamey*, p. 184.

78 Paul Freyberg, p. 247; Rowell to Long, 20 January 1947, AWM 67, 3/338, part 2.

79 Paul Freyberg, p. 248.

80 Major-General Sir Keith Stewart to Ivan Chapman 15 August 1968, Chapman Papers, AWM; Hinsley, pp. 406–409.

81 'General Statement on Situation in Greece as at 28 March 1941', Blamey Papers, AWM, 1/2a (vii); Horner, *Blamey*, p. 186.

82 Churchill, *The Grand Alliance*, pp. 142–3; Beevor, p. 33.

83 Churchill, *The Grand Alliance*, p. 144.

84 Parkinson, p. 213.

85 Playfair, Volume I, p. 315; Gill, Volume I, p. 299.

86 Hinsley, Volume I, p. 403.

Chapter 9: Wild Waller

1 During a stirring seven-month tour of duty, HMAS *Sydney* had been one of the most active and adventurous ships in the Mediterranean Fleet, so much so that Cunningham had nicknamed her 'the Stormy Petrel'. *Sydney* was sunk by the German raider *Kormoran* off Shark Bay, Western Australia, on 19 November 1941 with the loss of all 645 hands, including her new commander, Captain Joseph Burnett.

2 Gill, Volume I, p. 293.

3 The mines were globular or pear-shaped, some one metre in diameter, containing batteries and 350 lbs. of guncotton, trinitrotoluene (TNT) or amatol. On the upper surface were five or more leaden horns five inches long, each holding a glass tube containing a chemical mixture. Contact with a ship fractured the horn

and smashed the glass tube; the released liquid then energised the mine's battery, which fired the detonator.

4   McKie, *Proud Echo*, p. 29.
5   McGuire, p. 179.
6   From *The Chronicle of HMAS Stuart*, printed and circulated in the ship and quoted in McGuire, p. 180.
7   Pack, *The Battle of Matapan*, p. 31.
8   Winton, p. 142.
9   Ibid., p. 150; Wingate, pp. 161–2.
10 Roskill, p. 429.
11 Cunningham, p. 263; Long, *The Six Years War*, p. 69.
12 Seth, p. 107.
13 Gill, Volume I, p. 315.
14 Bragadin, p. 93.
15 Wingate, p. 178.
16 Cunningham, pp. 267–8; Gill, Volume I, p. 313.
17 Seth, p. 118.
18 Gill, Volume I, p. 316; Winton, p. 167.
19 Seth, p. 152.
20 Ibid., p. 125.
21 Richard Green interview, Imperial War Museum Sound Archive, 1976.
22 Ruge, p. 147.
23 Gill, Volume I, p. 137.

Chapter 10: Fire and Ice
1   Collier, p. 75.
2   Carlyon, p. 39.
3   Paul Freyberg, p. 249.
4   The *Leibstandarte* was given the title of 'Adolf Hitler' because of its long service as Hitler's palace bodyguard (as opposed to his military bodyguard under Rommel). The SS (*Schutzstaffel*: protective squadron) was a 'racially pure' Aryan force under the command of Heinrich Himmler who turned the SS into a ruthless machine dedicated to Hitler's protection. *Leibstandarte* is an archaic German term meaning the personal bodyguard of a military leader; Waffen SS means 'armed SS'. The SS committed many of the most infamous war crimes of World War II.
5   *White over Green*, p. 111.
6   Brunskill, G. S., unpublished manuscript, IWM; Horner, *High Command*, pp. 86–7.
7   Heckstall-Smith and Baillie-Grohman, p. 44.
8   Ibid., p. 47.
9   Simpson, p. 91.
10 Brunskill, G. S., unpublished manuscript, IWM.
11 Long, *Greece, Crete and Syria*, pp. 40–41.

12 Ebury, p. 213.

13 Wavell to Churchill 27 March 1941, in Parkinson, p. 212.

14 Long, *Greece, Crete and Syria*, p. 70.

15 *White over Green*, p. 111.

16 Horner, *High Command*, p. 96. 1st Armoured Brigade consisted of the 3rd Royal Tank Regiment, the 4th Hussars, 1/Rangers Battalion, 2nd Royal Horse Artillery and the Northumberland Hussars (102nd Anti-Tank Regiment). The 3rd RTR had 52 cruiser tanks and the Hussars 52 light tanks.

17 *Purple over Green*, p. 91.

18 Long, *Greece, Crete and Syria*, p. 43.

19 Kurowski, Franz, 'Dietrich and Manteuffel', in Correlli Barnett (ed.), *Hitler's Generals*. Following the failure of the *Leibstandarte* SS Adolf Hitler Division, then part of the 6th SS Panzer Army, commanded by General Dietrich, to stem the Red Army's advance through Hungary in March 1944, Hitler ordered the *Leibstandarte* to tear his name off their armbands. Dietrich responded by sending back his decorations including Iron Cross with Oak Leaf, Swords and Diamonds. (Shulman, pp. 344–5).

20 Adrian Gilbert, p. 6. Although wounded, 15 Warwicks survived the massacre. They were treated by a passing Wehrmacht unit and sent to prisoner-of-war camps where they revealed details of the atrocity.

21 Long, *Greece, Crete and Syria*, pp. 53–5.

22 Dick Parry, quoted in *White over Green*, p. 113.

23 Buckley, p. 56.

24 Clarke, p. 338. According to the official historian Gavin Long, all of the artillery was south of Vevi. However, Michael Clarke revisited the area in 1989 when members of the Greek Army took him to the site occupied by the 2/5th Battery in 1941.

25 Clarke, p. 338.

26 McClymont, p. 169.

27 Ibid., p. 167. Wilson was later accused of being naïve in the handling of his armoured force. In fact, he knew all too well about the frailties of tanks. In February 1940, the A9s of the 6th Royal Tank Regiment in Egypt were brand new and had not been run in, but Wilson's headquarters insisted that they should take part in a large-scale exercise, with the result that almost every one seized up.

28 McClymont, p. 192.

29 Mott-Radclyffe, p. 73.

30 Author's interview with Harry Spencer, October 2009.

31 McClymont, pp. 195–6.

32 United States Department of the Army, 'The German Campaigns in the Balkans Spring 1941', p. 91.

33 Long, *Greece, Crete and Syria*, p. 54.

34 Clarke, p. 340.

35 Long, *Greece, Crete and Syria*, p. 53.

36   Lincoln MacVeagh Diary 10 April 1941 in Iatrides.
37   Long, *Greece, Crete and Syria*, pp. 55–6; Clarke, p. 340.
38   *White over Green*, p. 114.
39   Hetherington, *Controversial Soldier*, p. 58.
40   Hetherington, *Blamey: The Biography*, pp. 98–9.
41   McClymont, p. 222.
42   Long, *Greece, Crete and Syria*, p. 70.
43   McClymont, p. 224.

Chapter 11: Anzacs Again
1   Author's interview with Keith Horton Hooper, April 2009.
2   Semmler (ed.), *War Despatches*, p. 147.
3   Long, *Greece, Crete and Syria*, p. 58.
4   *White over Green*, p. 119.
5   Long, *Greece, Crete and Syria*, p. 60.
6   'A Letter from the Front – No. 2', 16 April 1941 in McDonald, *Chester Wilmot Reports*.
7   Long, *Greece, Crete and Syria*, p. 73.
8   *Purple over Green*, p. 93.
9   Barter, *Far Above Battle*, p. 88.
10   Long, *Greece, Crete and Syria*, p. 58.
11   Horner, *General Vasey's War*, pp. 95–6; Long, *The Six Years War*, p. 70.
12   Clarke, p. 341.
13   Ibid., p. 341.
14   *4th & 6th RMT*, pp. 54–5.
15   Long, *Greece, Crete and Syria*, p. 61.
16   Horner, *Vasey's War*, pp. 96, 98.
17   *Purple over Green*, p. 93.
18   Department of Veteran Affairs, p. 6.
19   *Purple over Green*, p. 95.
20   Dick Parry, quoted in *White over Green*, p. 122.
21   Buckley, p. 61.
22   Long, *Greece, Crete and Syria*, p. 69; *Time* magazine, 5 May 1941.
23   Major-General Sir Keith Stewart interview, *Weekly New Zealand News*, 24 April 1967.
24   *Purple over Green*, p. 94.
25   Buckley, p. 73; Long, *The Six Years War*, p. 71.
26   *20 Battalion*, p. 53.
27   *19 Battalion*, p. 78.
28   Long, *Greece, Crete and Syria*, p. 87.
29   *19 Battalion*, p. 82.
30   Clarke, p. 345.
31   Freyberg, p. 252.
32   *Time* magazine, 5 May 1941.

Chapter 12: Thermopylae

1   Winton, p. 182.
2   Churchill, p. 201.
3   de Guingand, *Generals at War*, p. 36.
4   *20 Battalion*, p. 56.
5   Rowell to Long, 20 January 1947, AWM 67, 3/338, part 2.
6   Rowell to Long, Ibid.
7   *21 Battalion*, p. 60.
8   Long, *Greece, Crete and Syria*, pp. 95–6.
9   Horner, *Blamey*, p. 197.
10 Chapman, p. 226.
11 Long, *Greece, Crete and Syria*, p. 129.
12 Rowell to Long, 20 January 1947, AWM 67, 3/338, part 2; undated notes of interview with Wilson, Wavell Papers, IWM.
13 Churchill, *The Grand Alliance*, p. 201. Author's italics.
14 War Cabinet Minutes, 24 April 1941, PRO CAB 65/22/135. Menzies Diary, 24 April 1941, NLA.
15 Heckstall-Smith & Baillie-Grohman, p. 79.
16 Long, *The Six Years War*, p. 73.
17 Pelly, Air Chief Marshal Claude, Letter, 3/4 May 1941, Pelly Papers, IWM.
18 Ibid.
19 Marcel Comeau of 33 Squadron, quoted in Shores, p. 265.
20 *War Dance*, p. 139.
21 Clarke, p. 347.
22 Ibid., p. 348.
23 Pelly, Air Chief Marshal Claude, Letter, 3/4 May 1941, Pelly Papers, IWM.
24 Author's interview with Keith Hooper, April 2009.
25 Horner, *General Vasey's War*, p. 106.
26 Author's interview with Les Cook, May 2009.
27 Mott-Radclyffe, p. 77.
28 Coats, p. 98.
29 Connell, pp. 416–418.
30 Mussolini complained to Hitler who ordered the surrender terms to be cancelled. The Italian General Alberto Ferrero took the formal surrender alongside General Alfred Jodl, head of the German high command, in Salonica two days later.
31 Connell, p. 418.
32 Lincoln MacVeagh Diary, 21 April 1941, in Iatrides.
33 de Guingand, *Generals at War*, p. 39.
34 Menzies Diary, 19 April 1941.
35 Beresford-Peirse's battle wagon at Keren was a luxurious motor coach captured from an Italian corps commander at Sidi Barrani; Rankin, p. 196.
36 Cable 62369, Dill to Wavell, 19 April 1941, OW 216/120, PRO.
37 Cable 0/58696, Wavell to Dill, 22 April 1941, War Telegrams, Middle East I, PRO.

38 K. A. L. Best, 'Report of matron 5th Australian General Hospital', 18 May, 1941, quoted in Bassett, p. 123. Colonel Kay was killed on 26 April 1941 while evacuating 400 wounded from the 2/5th AGH at Piraeus.

39 Author's interview with Keith Horton Hooper, April 2009.

40 *Action Front, 2/2 Field Regiment history*, p. 108. This quote is actually by the poet Simonedes, who paid tribute to Leonidas and his 300 Spartans: 'Tell in Lakedaimon [Sparta], passerby, that here obedient to their word we lie.'

Chapter 13: Retreat to Crete

1 Horner, *High Command*, p. 89.

2 Rowell to Long, 20 January 1947, AWM 67, 3/338, part 2. While Colonel C. M. L. Elliott of Blamey's headquarters staff corroborated Rowell's version of events in Greece, Norman Carlyon claimed that he had never seen Blamey 'fearful or abnormally troubled'.

3 Beevor, p. 44.

4 Lincoln MacVeagh Diary, 25 April 1941, in Iatrides.

5 Mott-Radclyffe, p. 80. After escaping from Crete, Heywood was sidelined to India, where he died in an air crash in 1943.

6 Heckstall-Smith & Baillie-Grohman, p. 78.

7 Chapman, p. 230.

8 Hetherington, *Controversial Soldier*, p. 157.

9 Norman Carlyon thought that Blamey's decision to take his son was motivated by the fact that his first-born had been killed in a plane crash in 1933 and 'young Tom' was now his only son.

10 Chapman, p. 230.

11 Frederick Shedden's 'B' Diary, recounting a conversation with Bridgeford at a post-war dinner; CRS A5954, box 15, NAA.

12 Author's interview with Les Cook, May 2009.

13 Paul Freyberg, p. 258; Chapman, p. 231. According to General Freyberg, 'The court upheld my action and gave me an unsolicited testimonial.'

14 Long, *The Six Years War*, p. 74.

15 Churchill to Roosevelt, 24 April 1941, Kimball, p. 175.

16 Chapman, p. 229.

17 Woodhouse, p. 12.

18 Mabel Johnson letter to her family May 1941.

19 Gill, Volume I, pp. 321–2; Shores, p. 291.

20 Margaret Barnard diary entry 25 April 1941, quoted in Bassett, p. 124.

21 Horner, *High Command*, p. 91.

22 Rowell, p. 81.

23 Blamey returned to Australia in March 1942 and was appointed commander of land forces. During the Battle of Papua, he destroyed the careers of Sydney Rowell, Tubby Allen and Cyril Clowes, and banned ABC correspondent Chester Wilmot from the battlefield for expressing in public his suspicions that Blamey had engaged in corrupt conduct in the Middle East. (*Australian Dictionary of Biography*, Volume 16, Melbourne University Press, 2002, pp. 561–2.)

24   Brune, p. 90.
25   Chapman, pp. 232, 234.
26   Cox, p. 16.
27   Long, *Greece, Crete and Syria*, pp. 163–4; Le Souef, p. 108.
28   Author's interview with Keith Horton Hooper, April 2009. There are several versions of how the bridge came to be destroyed. The Germans claim that the explosion was caused by one of the charges which hadn't been deactivated by their engineers. Another version is that a British soldier set off the charge with a rifle shot.
29   Gullett, *Not as a Duty Only*, pp. 57–58.
30   Lincoln MacVeagh Diary, 24 April 1941, in Iatrides.
31   Paul Freyberg, p. 261.
32   Michael Forrester interview, Imperial War Museum Sound Archive, 2003.
33   Pelly, Air Chief Marshal Claude, Letter, 3/4 May 1941, Pelly Papers, Imperial War Museum.
34   Beevor, p. 49.
35   Long, *Greece, Crete and Syria*, p. 170.
36   Gill, Volume I, p. 325.
37   Author's interview with Les Cook, May 2009.
38   *Australian Dictionary of Biography*, Volume 17, Melbourne University Press, 2009, pp. 113–114.
39   Author's interview with Norman Simper, August 2009.
40   Gill, Volume I, p. 326.
41   *White over Green*, p. 143.
42   Author's interview with Keith Horton Hooper, April 2009.
43   Gill, Volume I, p. 329.
44   Sergeant John Daniel Hinton's Victoria Cross Citation, quoted in *20 Battalion*, p. 620.
45   McClymont, pp. 458–9.
46   Gill, Volume I, p. 330.
47   Ibid., p. 330.
48   Ibid., p. 330.
49   Winton, p. 186.
50   Cunningham, p. 356.
51   Gullett, *Not as a Duty Only*, pp. 60–61.
52   Hodgkinson, p. 96.
53   Ibid., p. 90.
54   Long, *Greece, Crete and Syria*, p. 179; Churchill to Peter Fraser, 14 December 1940, *Churchill Papers*, p. 1235. Oddly, Ned Herring did not agree. 'He was constantly coming to our headquarters and seemed a bit astray,' he told Iven Mackay's biographer Ivan Chapman. 'He was rattled in Greece.' Herring's comments were made after the war when the knives were out for Freyberg.
55   Gullett, *Not as a Duty Only*, p. 61.
56   Letter Blamey to Sturdee, 26 June 1941, Blamey Papers 5A.

57 Wavell, 'Operations in the Middle East, 7 February 1941 to 15 July 1941', p. 3432.
58 Pelly, Air Chief Marshal Claude, Letter, 3/4 May 1941, Pelly Papers, IWM.
59 Lincoln MacVeagh Diary, 24 April 1941, in Iatrides.
60 Long, *The Six Years War*, p. 74.
61 D'Este, p. 595.

Chapter 14: Isle of Doom

1   Horner, *Vasey's War*, p. 114.
2   *Action Front*, p. 132. The British submarine HMS *Rover* was moored alongside *York* to supply electrical power for her anti-aircraft guns but on 24 April 1941 the submarine was severely damaged by an air attack. *York* was also damaged by further air attacks and any attempt to salvage her was abandoned. She was wrecked by demolition charges on 22 May 1941.
3   Alan Clark, p. 22.
4   Gullett, *Not as a Duty Only*, p. 62.
5   Author's interview with Norm Simper, August 2009. The signalmen were taken off Crete in the Greek fishing boat *Lesbos* on 10 May.
6   Gill, Volume I, pp. 231–2.
7   Department of Veteran Affairs, p. 28.
8   *Action Front*, p. 125; Buckley, p. 168.
9   Brune, p. 119.
10 Author's interview with Harry Spencer, October 2009.
11 Roy Macartney was a journalist on the Melbourne *Argus*. During the war, he contributed a series of popular articles to his newspaper under the byline 'Subaltern'.
12 Clarke, p. 359.
13 Alan Clark, p. 22.
14 Vasey to Rowell, 12 May 1941, item 225/1/1, AWM 54.
15 Brunskill, unpublished manuscript, IWM.
16 Brunskill, 'The administrative aspect of the campaign in Crete'.
17 *White over Green*, p. 144.
18 Long, *Greece, Crete and Syria*, p. 207.
19 Author's interview with Les Cook, May 2009.
20 Stephanides, p. 45; Le Souef, p. 114.
21 Author's interview with Keith Horton Hooper, April 2009. The 17th Brigade Composite Battalion consisted of 20 officers and 367 other ranks.
22 *Action Front*, p. 124.
23 Author's interview with Sally Vickery, October 2008.
24 Attributed to O'Neill in *White over Green* and Boff Ryan in *War Dance*, p. 67. However, Jenny Rutherford says the poem was written by her father, John Joseph Walsh (VX44206).
25 The first commander, Brigadier O. H. Tidbury, was replaced by General M. D. Gambier-Parry on 8 January; Gambier-Parry left to take command of the 2nd Armoured Division in Libya (and was promptly captured by the Afrika

Korps); Lieutenant-Colonel C. H. Mather (52nd Light Anti-Aircraft Regiment) commanded from 2 to 19 February; Brigadier Sandy Galloway took over until 7 March when he was appointed General Wilson's chief of staff in Greece; Mather took over temporarily, then handed over to Brigadier B. H. Chappel from 21 March. Major-General E. C. Weston arrived on 21 April but did not assume command until 26 April.

26 Alan Clark, p. 44.
27 Churchill, *The Grand Alliance*, pp. 240–1.
28 Ibid., p. 241.
29 Long, *Greece, Crete and Syria*, p. 208.
30 Davin, p. 39; GHQ Middle East to Creforce, 28 April 1941.
31 Letter, 3/4 May 1941, Pelly Papers, IWM.
32 Sulzberger, p. 144.
33 Davin, p. 40; Long, *Greece, Crete and Syria*, p. 207.
34 Long, *Greece, Crete and Syria*, p. 210.
35 Boniface of Montferrat (c. 1150–1207), leader of the Fourth Crusade, founded a kingdom in Salonica and Crete, though he later sold Crete to the Venetians.
36 Kitromilides (ed.), p. 76.
37 'Military and Geographical Description of Greece', German High Command, 31 March 1941.
38 Beevor, pp. 63–4.
39 Pettifer, p. 76.
40 Long, *Greece, Crete and Syria*, p. 207.
41 Davin, p. 28.
42 *22 Battalion*, p. 2.

Chapter 15: Ultra's Secrets

1 Churchill, *The Grand Alliance*, pp. 241–2.
2 Wilson, p. 102.
3 Connell, *Scholar and Soldier*, p. 450.
4 Paul Freyberg, p. 267.
5 Davin, p. 40 quoting Freyberg's 'Report on the Battle of Crete to Minister of Defence', August 1941. Paul Freyberg (p. 267) prints almost identical quotes from his father, with the additional information that Wavell offered him a promotion to lieutenant-general which he turned down with the words, 'I insisted upon remaining a major-general as I did not require any inducement to do my duty.'
6 Freyberg, 'Report on the Battle for Crete', August 1941.
7 Barber and Tonkin-Covell, p. 7.
8 Connell, *Scholar and Soldier*, p. 450.
9 Long, *Greece, Crete and Syria*, pp. 208–9.
10 Paul Freyberg, pp. 268–9; Bennett, *Behind the Battle*, p. 79. Antony Beevor in his 1991 book, *Crete: The battle and the resistance*, says on pp. 88–89 that Wavell 'briefed Freyberg on "most secret sources" or "most reliable sources", as Ultra

intelligence was euphemistically termed, but he did not disclose exactly what this source was. He gave Freyberg the impression that the information came from a well-placed spy of the Secret Intelligence Service. Freyberg never doubted this cover story and failed to guess from the nature and presentation of the transcripts that the information came from signals intercepts.' This completely contradicts Paul Freyberg's account in his biography of his father. In the 2005 paperback edition, Beevor adds that Paul Freyberg 'claims that his father knew from the beginning what the true source was, but his version is unconvincing'. However, Paul Freyberg maintains (p. 268) 'my father told me definitely that Wavell explained to him at his garden briefing that Ultra involved the decrypting of German wireless transmissions, adding it soon became obvious from the contents and the timing of the Ultra signals (which started to flow to Crete towards the end of the first week of May 1941) that the information could not have been obtained by any other means in the time available. An example my father gave was advance warnings of enemy bombing attacks, which were carried out within a few hours of their being notified.' Indeed, General Freyberg said shortly after the war that he had received accurate information about Hitler's plans from 'War Office Intelligence and most secret *intercept* sources', indicating knowledge of the Ultra decrypts.

11 Cox, p. 57.
12 Brunskill, unpublished manuscript, IWM.
13 Ebury, p. 222.
14 Bennett, *Ultra and Mediterranean Strategy 1941–1945*, p. 53.
15 *Flight* magazine, 26 February 1948.
16 Orange Leonard 2155, 1615 hours 1.5.41; Bennett, *Ultra and Mediterranean Strategy 1941–1945*, p. 54; Freyberg received the most urgent Ultra reports as Orange Leonard signals direct from Bletchley Park, Hertfordshire, while others came from GHQ Cairo. Messages for Cairo and Crete were encoded on unbreakable 'one-time pads' and sent to the Combined Bureau Middle East at Heliopolis or direct to Group Captain Beamish in Canea. Freyberg was notified of all the most important German moves within a matter of hours. The word Ultra was never mentioned – the signals simply began, 'It is learned that …' or 'There is evidence that …'.
17 Cox, p. 59.
18 Long, *Greece, Crete and Syria*, p. 209.
19 Churchill, *The Grand Alliance*, p. 243.
20 Lewin, *Ultra Goes to War*, p. 158.
21 Bennett, *Behind the Battle*, p. 295.
22 Long, *Greece, Crete and Syria*, p. 209.
23 Churchill, *The Grand Alliance*, p. 244.
24 Cunningham, p. 358.
25 Kippenberger, p. 48.
26 Ibid., p. 48.
27 Long, *Greece, Crete and Syria*, p. 213.

28 Churchill, *The Grand Alliance*, p. 245.
29 Long, *Greece, Crete and Syria*, p. 210.
30 Ibid.
31 Churchill, *The Grand Alliance*, p. 246.
32 Ultra file OL 2166, PRO DEFE 3/894.
33 XI Air Corps, 'Operations Crete', Manuscripts Section, Imperial War Museum, p. 14.

Chapter 16: Mercury Rising

1 Barnett (ed.), *Hitler's Generals*, p. 471.
2 Buckley, p. 189; Laffin, *Greece, Crete and Syria*, p. 48; MacDonald, p. 65.
3 Archer, pp. 227–8.
4 Barnett (ed.), *Hitler's Generals*, p. 464.
5 Ibid., p. 464.
6 Ibid., p. 466.
7 MacDonald, p. 61.
8 Ibid., p. 68.
9 Ibid., p. 69.
10 Davin, p. 84.
11 Kuhn, p. 64.
12 Ibid., pp. 54–55.
13 Paul Freyberg, p. 293.
14 Davin, p. 37.
15 Horner, *General Vasey's War*, p. 113.
16 *Action Front*, p. 125.
17 Stewart, p. 159.
18 *Action Front*, p. 130.
19 Ibid., p. 132.
20 Shores, p. 339; *Action Front*, p. 138.
21 Lewin, *Ultra Goes to War*, p. 156.
22 Paul Freyberg, p. 284.
23 Michael Clarke letter, 10 May 1941.
24 Michael Forrester interview, Imperial War Museum Sound Archive, 2003.
25 *21 Battalion*, p. 83.
26 Shores, p. 336; Beevor, p. 78.
27 von der Heydte, p. 40.
28 Shores, p. 336; Beevor, pp. 79–80.
29 Davin, p. 89; Shores, p. 336; MacDonald, p. 79.
30 MacDonald, pp. 79–80; Buckley, pp. 181–182.
31 Beevor, p. 80.
32 Davin, p. 84. Admiral Canaris was executed in a concentration camp at Flossenburg on 9 April 1945 for conspiring to overthrow Hitler.
33 MacDonald, p. 77.
34 Davin, p. 475.

35   Paul Freyberg, p. 292. Sister Mabel Johnson set up a small advance hospital in the Western Desert to treat casualties from the Siege of Tobruk. She was mentioned in dispatches 'in recognition of gallant and distinguished services in the Middle East during the period 1 May 1942 and 22 October 1942'. Mabel returned to Australia in 1943 and on 19 January 1944 she married Flight-Lieutenant Douglas Aland, a fellow Queenslander who had fought in the Battle of Britain and whom she had met in the Middle East.
36   Shores, pp. 338–9.
37   Long, *Greece, Crete and Syria*, p. 220.
38   Le Souef, p. 116.
39   Cox, p. 66.
40   Simpson, p. 130.
41   Cox, p. 67.
42   Stephanides, p. 56.

Chapter 17: Icarus Descending
1   Davin, p. 92.
2   Beevor, p. 105.
3   Howell, p. 14.
4   Woodhouse, p. 13.
5   Long, *Greece, Crete and Syria*, p. 222. Freyberg, 'Report on the Battle for Crete to the New Zealand Minister of Defence', August 1941.
6   *22 Battalion*, p. 65.
7   Ibid., p. 43.
8   Ibid., p. 42.
9   Davin, p. 93; Shores, p. 341.
10   Davin, p. 95.
11   Comeau, p. 89; Shores, p. 342.
12   Shores, p. 342.
13   Davin, p. 95.
14   Clark, p. 55.
15   *22 Battalion*, p. 63.
16   Davin, p. 105, n. 3.
17   Paul Freyberg, p. 297.
18   Shores, p. 338.
19   Author's interview with Anthony Madden, October 2009.
20   Davin, p. 123.
21   *22 Battalion*, p. 37; MacDonald, p. 173.
22   Davin, p. 96.
23   Shores, p. 346.
24   MacDonald, p. 173.
25   Howell, p. 27.
26   *22 Battalion*, p. 66.
27   Comeau, pp. 109–10; MacDonald, p. 175.

28 Shores, p. 341.
29 Stewart, p. 158.
30 MacDonald, p. 178.
31 Ibid., p. 179.

Chapter 18: Hospital Horror

1 *Divisional Cavalry*, pp. 91–2.
2 Kippenberger, p. 52.
3 Captain Karl Neuhoff interview 14 August 1945 by Sergeant H. E. McVeagh, NZ Archives, WA II 1.
4 Hutching, p. 156.
5 *4th & 6th RMT*, p. 82.
6 Ibid.
7 Hutching, p. 156.
8 MacDonald, p. 180.
9 Farran, p. 90.
10 Hutching, p. 157.
11 Kippenberger, p. 54.
12 Captain Karl Neuhoff interview 14 August 1945 by Sergeant H. E. McVeagh, NZ Archives, WA II 1, 447.22/34; Simpson, p. 167; McConnell, p. 75.
13 Taaffe, p. 265.
14 MacDonald, pp. 181, 183.
15 Cox, p. 77.
16 *22 Battalion*, p. 69.
17 Beevor, p. 117.
18 MacDonald, p. 181.
19 Davin, p. 173.
20 MacDonald, pp. 176–7; Beevor, p. 117.
21 Alan Clark, pp. 83–4.
22 Kiriakopoulos, p. 302.
23 Alan Clark, p. 65.
24 Shores, p. 348; Kiriakopoulos, p. 200; MacDonald, p. 188.
25 Buckley, p. 191.
26 Hutching, p. 157.
27 Ibid., p. 192.
28 Farran, pp. 90–1; MacDonald, p. 182; *19 Battalion*, pp. 138–9; Davin, p. 148.
29 Davin, pp. 475–479.
30 Quoted in Barber, p. 60.
31 Kippenberger, p. 113.
32 Cox, p. 78.
33 Ross, p. 68; Cox, p. 78.
34 *22 Battalion*, p. 52.
35 Alan Clark, p. 71.
36 MacDonald, p. 186.

37 Ibid., p. 187.
38 Cox, p. 78.
39 Henderson, *22 Battalion*, p. 71; Alan Clark, p. 72.

Chapter 19: Barbaric Beauty

1   MacDonald, p. 189.
2   Long, *Greece, Crete and Syria*, p. 257.
3   MacDonald, p. 190.
4   *First At War*, 2/1 Bn history, p. 170.
5   Ibid.
6   Lind, p. 20.
7   Beevor, p. 132.
8   Long, *Greece, Crete and Syria*, p. 259.
9   Ibid., p. 260.
10 Beevor, p. 133; Long, *Greece, Crete and Syria*, p. 260.
11 Brune, p. 107.
12 Long, *Greece, Crete and Syria*, p. 160.
13 *White over Green*, 2/4 Bn history, p. 159.
14 Beevor, p. 134; *White over Green*, p. 155.
15 *White over Green*, p. 156.
16 MacDonald, p. 192; Long, *Greece, Crete and Syria*, p. 280.
17 *White over Green*, p. 157.
18 MacDonald, p. 192.
19 Ibid., p. 194.
20 Powell, *The Villa Ariadne*, pp. 111–2. John Pendlebury was wounded in the chest while escaping from Heraklion. On 22 May 1941, German paratroopers propped him against a wall and shot him.
21 Ibid., p. 195.
22 Beevor, p. 117.
23 Davin Papers, quoted in Stewart, p. 175.
24 *22 Battalion*, p. 65.
25 Davin Papers, quoted in Stewart, p. 177.
26 Author's interview with Arthur Midwood, October, 2009.
27 28 (Maori) Battalion, p. 94.
28 Cox, pp. 78–9.
29 *22 Battalion*, p. 54; 28 (Maori) Battalion, p. 94.
30 MacDonald, p. 201.
31 Davin, p. 186; Stewart, p. 178.
32 Long, *Greece, Crete and Syria*, p. 227.
33 Alan Clark, p. 74.
34 Long, *Greece, Crete and Syria*, p. 222.
35 *22 Battalion*, p. 56; Alan Clark, p. 74.

Chapter 20: Losing Maleme

1 Cox, p. 79.
2 Liddell Hart, p. 144.
3 Long, *Greece, Crete and Syria*, p. 231.
4 Ibid.; MacDonald, p. 205.
5 Shores, p. 352.
6 Ibid., p. 353.
7 MacDonald, p. 204.
8 General Freyberg's narratives and papers; Paul Freyberg, p. 304.
9 Paul Freyberg, p. 303.
10 Beevor, p. 156.
11 Comeau, p. 122.
12 MacDonald, p. 207.
13 Freyberg, 'Report on the Battle of Crete to Minister of Defence', August 1941.
14 Winton, p. 200.
15 Beevor, p. 159.
16 Paul Freyberg, p. 303.
17 Long, *Greece, Crete and Syria*, p. 232.
18 Beevor, p. 157.
19 Vasey, Brigadier G. A., '19th Australian Infantry Brigade Account of Operations in Crete 1941', AWM54 535/2/25.
20 Long, *Greece, Crete and Syria*, p. 235.
21 Ibid., p. 235.
22 Green, p. 170; Bragadin, p. 109.
23 Beevor, p. 160, quoting Tom Barratt.
24 Cox, p. 82; Beevor, p. 161.
25 Davin, p. 212; Beevor, p. 163.
26 Davin, p. 216.
27 Long, *Greece, Crete and Syria*, p. 236.
28 Beevor, p. 166.
29 General Freyberg's unpublished narratives and papers, quoted in Paul Freyberg, p. 303.
30 *Purple over Green*, p. 131.
31 Bolger, p. 86; Long, p. 236.

Chapter 21: Holding Retimo

1 Davin, p. 204; *The First at War*, p. 181; Long, *Greece, Crete and Syria*, p. 261.
2 *The First at War*, p. 181; Long, *Greece, Crete and Syria*, p. 243.
3 *The First at War*, p. 182.
4 Long, *Greece, Crete and Syria*, p. 261.
5 Davin, p. 204.
6 Hadjipateras, p. 156.
7 Brune, p. 111.
8 *White over Green*, p. 161.

9   Long, *Greece, Crete and Syria*, p. 284; Davin, p. 205.
10 *White over Green*, p. 162; Long, p. 284.
11 *The First at War*, p. 190.
12 Ibid.; Long, *Greece, Crete and Syria*, p. 263.
13 *The First at War*, p. 191.
14 Ibid., Long, p. 263.
15 *The First at War*, pp. 192–3.
16 Long, *Greece, Crete and Syria*, p. 264.
17 Brune, p. 112.
18 Ibid.; Long, *Greece, Crete and Syria*, p. 264.
19 Ibid., p. 264.
20 Ibid., p. 265.
21 *The First at War*, p. 190.
22 Long, *Greece, Crete and Syria*, p. 266.
23 Brune, p. 115.
24 Long, *Greece, Crete and Syria*, p. 266.
25 Evidence at Student's war crimes trial 1945; Long, p. 233.
26 Long, *Greece, Crete and Syria*, p. 237; Beevor, p. 172.
27 von der Heydte, p. 120; Beevor, pp. 172–3; MacDonald, p. 228.
28 Author's interview with Harry Spencer, October 2009.
29 MacDonald, p. 229.
30 Davin, p. 238, quoting New Zealand Division report.
31 Ibid., p. 239.
32 Davin, p. 239.
33 MacDonald, p. 227; Davin, p. 250.

Chapter 22: Battle of Galatas

1   Davin, p. 158, quoting a letter from Brian Bassett dated 3 June 1941.
2   Michael Forrester interview, Imperial War Museum Sound Archive, 2003.
3   Ibid.
4   Author's interview with Harry Spencer, October 2009; Davin, p. 97.
5   Kippenberger, p. 59.
6   *4th & 6th RMT*, p. 86.
7   Kippenberger, p. 59.
8   Davin, p. 97.
9   Ibid., p. 235.
10 Stewart, p. 336.
11 Alan Clark, p. 136.
12 MacDonald, p. 230.
13 Long, *Greece, Crete and Syria*, p. 238.
14 Davin, p. 251.
15 Long, *Greece, Crete and Syria*, p. 242.
16 Ibid.; Davin, p. 252.
17 Long, *Greece, Crete and Syria*, p. 252.

18 Freyberg, 'Report on the Battle for Crete'; Stewart, p. 359.
19 Long, *Greece, Crete and Syria*, p. 241.
20 Kippenberger, p. 61.
21 Beevor, p. 187.
22 Kippenberger, p. 63.
23 Ibid., p. 64.
24 Thomas, W. B., p. 19.
25 Davin, p. 302.
26 McConnell, p. 135; Kippenberger, p. 65.
27 Beevor, p. 188; Kippenberger, p. 65; Davin, p. 303.
28 Paul Freyberg, p. 307.
29 Davin, p. 309.
30 MacDonald, p. 265.
31 Davin, p. 312.
32 Thomas, W. B., p. 21.
33 Kippenberger, p. 67.
34 Davin, p. 315; Beevor, p. 190.
35 Davin, p. 314.
36 Ibid., p. 315.
37 Ibid., p. 316.

Chapter 23: On 42nd Street

1 Kippenberger, p. 69.
2 Horner, *General Vasey's War*, p. 121.
3 Freyberg, 'Report on the Battle for Crete'.
4 *The Fiery Phoenix*, p. 88.
5 Long, *Greece, Crete and Syria*, p. 247; Bolger, p. 89.
6 Stephanides, p. 62.
7 Long, *Greece, Crete and Syria*, p. 249.
8 Winton, p. 210.
9 Ibid., p. 211.
10 Ibid., p. 211.
11 Long, *Greece, Crete and Syria*, p. 254.
12 Ibid., p. 251.
13 *The Fiery Phoenix*, p. 89.
14 Ibid., p. 90.
15 Ibid., p. 89.
16 Long, *Greece, Crete and Syria*, p. 252.
17 *The Fiery Phoenix*, p. 90; Charlton, p. 176. Reg Saunders later became the first Aboriginal to be commissioned in the Australian Army.
18 *The Fiery Phoenix*, p. 90.
19 Ibid.
20 John Peck interview, Imperial War Museum Sound Archive, 1996.
21 28 Battalion, pp. 119–120.
22 John Peck interview, Imperial War Museum Sound Archive, 1996.

23 Long, *Greece, Crete and Syria*, p. 252.
24 Notes written in 1950 by George Dittmer to General Kippenberger, editor-in-chief of the New Zealand War Histories.
25 Long, *Greece, Crete and Syria*, p. 254.

Chapter 24: Road to Sphakia

1 Author's interview with Arthur Midwood, October 2009.
2 Gill, Volume I, p. 354.
3 Author's interview with Arthur Midwood, October 2009.
4 Freyberg, 'Report on the Battle for Crete to the New Zealand Minister of Defence', August 1941.
5 Davie (ed.), *The Diaries of Evelyn Waugh*, p. 501.
6 Long, *Greece, Crete and Syria*, p. 253.
7 Ibid., p. 296.
8 Stephanides, p. 113.
9 Author's interview with Keith Horton Hooper, April 2009.
10 Author's interview with Arthur Midwood, October 2009.
11 Author's interview with Harry Spencer, October 2009.
12 Davie (ed.), *The Diaries of Evelyn Waugh*, pp. 507–8. Waugh described his experiences on Crete in his 1955 novel *Officers and Gentlemen*, part of his *Sword of Honour* trilogy.
13 Brunskill, unpublished manuscript, IWM.
14 *The Fiery Phoenix*, p. 94.
15 Winton, p. 213.
16 Long, *Greece, Crete and Syria*, p. 304.
17 Author's interview with Arthur Midwood, October 2009.
18 Winton, p. 217.
19 Gill, Volume I, p. 358.
20 Author's interview with Arthur Midwood, October 2009.
21 Stephanides, p. 158.
22 Chania Naval Museum archive, Crete.
23 Gill, p. 359; Stephanides, p. 160; Winton, p. 218.
24 Author's interview with Arthur Midwood, October 2009.

Chapter 25: Deadly Exodus

1 Cunningham, p. 382; Winton, p. 213; Hodgkinson, p. 135.
2 Admiral Desmond McCarthy interview, Imperial War Museum Sound Archive, 1965.
3 Hodgkinson, p. 136.
4 *White over Green*, p. 169.
5 Long, *Greece, Crete and Syria*, p. 291.
6 Ibid., p. 291.
7 Hodgkinson, p. 137.
8 *White over Green*, p. 172.
9 Hodgkinson, p. 138. One account (Beevor, p. 209) claims that a group of

Australians, 'semi-insensible from drink', had to be left below and went down with *Imperial. White over Green*, p. 172.

10 *White over Green*, p. 139.

11 Ibid., p. 142.

12 Long, *Greece, Crete and Syria*, p. 292.

13 *White over Green*, p. 176.

14 Winton, p. 214.

15 *White over Green*, p. 177.

16 Cunningham, p. 384.

17 John Peck's unpublished manuscript, 'Captive in Crete', published with permission of his daughter Barbara Daniels.

18 Paul Freyberg, p. 312.

19 Brunskill, unpublished manuscript, IWM.

20 Clarke, p. 376.

21 *The Second Eighth, 2/8 Bn history*, p. 99.

22 John Peck's unpublished manuscript; Major Henry Marshall, quoted in Long, *Greece, Crete and Syria*, p. 307. The navy called its various evacuation craft 'Skylark' after the pleasure steamers of that name plying England's coasts. The little boats were built at the Skylark Boatyard at Poole, Dorset, and boatmen would shout to holidaymakers, 'Any more for the *Skylark*?'

23 Horner, *General Vasey's War*, p. 131.

Chapter 26: Abandoned

1 John Peck's unpublished manuscript, published with permission of his daughter Barbara Daniels.

2 Le Souef, p. 145.

3 John Peck's unpublished manuscript.

4 Le Souef, p. 147.

5 Lieutenant Roy Macartney, 'An Epic of the Escape from Crete,' Melbourne *Argus*, 9 August 1941.

6 The four men in that boat sailed into Alexandria harbour and their flag is now in the Australian War Memorial. In Melbourne, John Peck's father Harry Peck received a letter from Vera Deakin White, youngest daughter of Prime Minister Alfred Deakin, who was a director of the Red Cross: 'The witness [Jack Thomson] states that on the 1st June, he with two others was on the south coast of Crete when they were joined by a party of four of whom your son was one. Two of the men had a boat which could only hold four and as there were eight in the party by this time, they had to decide who should have the vacant seats. It was decided that a certain sergeant should have one seat and the others drew lots for the last vacant place. The witness was the lucky one and got away to safety.' – Letter from Vera Deakin White, director, Red Cross Bureau for wounded, missing and prisoners of war, to Mr H. F. Peck, 3 November 1941, Peck Papers, AWM.

7 John Peck's unpublished manuscript.

8 Clarke, pp. 379–80.

9   Roy Macartney, 'An Epic of the Escape from Crete', Melbourne *Argus*, 9 August 1941.

10 Letter Roy Macartney to Mrs R. Clarke, 4 July 1941, Clarke archive, Tallarook.

Chapter 27: In Captivity

1   *The First at War*, p. 203; Long, *Greece, Crete and Syria*, p. 272.
2   Long, *Greece, Crete and Syria*, p. 273.
3   Ibid., p. 274.
4   Ibid.
5   *The First at War*, p. 204.
6   Long, *Greece, Crete and Syria*, p. 275.
7   McDonald, *Chester Wilmot Reports*, p. 168.
8   Ibid., pp. 171–4.
9   Ibid., p. 174.
10 Ibid., pp. 175–6.
11 Ibid., p. 177.
12 Churchill, 14 June 1941, PRO PREM 3/109.
13 J. A. B. Crawford, 'Hargest, James 1891–1944', Dictionary of New Zealand Biography, updated 22 June 2007.
14 W. David McIntyre, 'Puttick, Edward 1890–1976', Dictionary of New Zealand Biography, updated 22 June 2007.
15 *The First at War*, pp. 204–5.
16 Ibid., p. 205.
17 Ibid., p, 207.
18 Long, *Greece, Crete and Syria*, p. 310; Damer & Frazer, p. 41.
19 *History of the 2/11 Battalion*, p. 97; Brune, p. 131.
20 Long, *Greece, Crete and Syria*, p. 310; Brune, p. 132.
21 Author's interview with Keith Horton Hooper, April 2009.
22 Le Souef, p. 161.
23 Author's interview with Keith Horton Hooper, April 2009.
24 Ibid.
25 John Peck's unpublished manuscript.

Chapter 28: On the Run

1   Damer & Frazer, pp. 94–5. MI9 was created in 1940 under Norman Crockatt, former head of the London Stock Exchange, and was based in Wilton Park, Buckinghamshire.
2   *History of the 2/11 Battalion*, p. 97; Brune, p. 131.
3   Damer & Frazer, p. 97.
4   Hadjipateras, pp. 292–3.
5   Ibid., p. 99.
6   Brune, p. 133.
7   Brigadier R. L. Sandover, 'Escape from Crete', the 2/11th Battalion Collection, quoted in Brune, p. 134.
8   Ibid., p. 135.

9   John Peck's unpublished manuscript.
10   Letter from John Peck to his stepmother Jean Peck, 12 August 1941, Peck Papers, AWM. Kenneth Huxtable survived the Battle of Crete and was discharged from the army in August 1944.
11   John Peck interview, Imperial War Museum Sound Archive, 1996.
12   Powell, *The Villa Ariadne*, p. 163.
13   Psychoundakis, p. 45. In 1975, the remains of all German soldiers on Crete were moved to a special German cemetery on Hill 107 overlooking Maleme airfield.
14   John Peck's unpublished manuscript, published with permission of his daughter Barbara Daniels.
15   Ibid.; Adrian Gilbert, p. 290; Bunbury, p. 103.
16   John Peck's unpublished manuscript.
17   Bunbury, p. 103.
18   Ibid.
19   John Peck interview, Imperial War Museum Sound Archive, 1996.
20   Duggan, p. 523.
21   Tom Carver, 'Blunder that doomed 50,000 POWs', *Observer*, 1 November 2009.
22   Ibid.
23   Bunbury, p. 127; Adrian Gilbert, pp. 290–1.
24   Tudor, p. 3.
25   Ibid., p. 25.
26   Adrian Gilbert, p. 291.
27   John Peck interview, Imperial War Museum Sound Archive, 1996.
28   Ibid.
29   John Peck's letter to his parents, 27 June 1944. Peck Papers, AWM.

Chapter 29: Belated Justice

1   'Interrogation of General Student', War Office Intelligence Review, November 1945.
2   MacDonald, p. 303.
3   John Peck's citation was published in the *London Gazette* Supp. No. 36961 of 1/3/45. CAG. No. 104 of 24/5/45.
4   Adrian Gilbert, p. 291.
5   'Australian was with partisans', Melbourne *Argus*, 11 April 1945; John D. Peck interview, Imperial War Museum Sound Archive, 1996.
6   Author's interview with Barbara Daniels, September 2009.
7   Duggan, p. 532.
8   Genoud (ed.), *The Testament of Adolf Hitler*, entry 17 March 1945. Author's italics.
9   Author's interview with Keith Horton Hooper, April 2009.
10   Beevor, p. 338.
11   Clarke, p. 507.
12   Author's interview with Louise Morris, April 2009.
13   MacDonald, pp. 304–6.
14   Author's interview with Watty McEwan, December 2009.
15   Davin, p. 523.

BIBLIOGRAPHY

Books

Alanbrooke, Field Marshal Viscount, *War Diaries 1939–1945*, Alex Danchev and Daniel Todman (eds), Weidenfeld & Nicolson, London, 2001

Antill, Peter D., *Crete 1941: Germany's lightning airborne assault*, Osprey, London, 2005

Archer, Laird, *Balkan Journal: An unofficial observer in Greece*, Norton, New York, 1944

Astley, Joan Bright, *The Inner Circle: A View of War at the Top*, Quality Book Club, London, 1971

——*History of the Northumberland Hussars Yeomanry 1924–1949*, Mawson, Swan & Morgan, Newcastle-upon-Tyne, 1949

Australian Dictionary of Biography (ABD), Melbourne University Press, Melbourne, various dates

Avon, The Earl of (Anthony Eden), *The Eden Memoirs: Volume 2 The Reckoning*, Cassell, London, 1964

Baker, Kevin, *Paul Cullen: Citizen and Soldier*, Rosenberg, Sydney, 2005

Barber, Laurie and John Tonkin-Covell, *Freyberg: Churchill's Salamander*, Hutchinson, London, 1990

Barter, Margaret, *Far Above Battle*, Allen & Unwin, Sydney, 1994

Barnett, Correlli, *Engage the Enemy More Closely: The Royal Navy in the Second World War*, W. W. Norton, New York, 1991

——*The Desert Generals*, Castle Books, London, 1999

——(editor) *Hitler's Generals*, Weidenfeld & Nicolson, London, 1990

Bassett, Jan, *Guns and Brooches: Australian Army Nursing from the Boer War to the Gulf War*, Oxford University Press, Melbourne, 1992

Baynes, John, *The Forgotten Victor: General Sir Richard O'Connor*, Brassey's, London, 1989

Bean, Charles, *Official History of Australia in the War of 1914-1918: Volume III – The Australian Imperial Force in France, 1916*, AWM, Canberra, 1941

Beevor, Antony, *Crete: The Battle and the Resistance*, John Murray, London 1991

Bennett, Ralph, *Ultra in the Mediterranean 1941–1945*, Hamish Hamilton, London, 1989

——*Behind the Battle: Intelligence in the war with Germany 1939–45*, Sinclair-Stevenson, London, 1994

Borghese, J. Valerio, *Sea Devils*, Andrew Melrose, London, 1952

Braga, Stuart, *Kokoda Commander: The life of Major-General 'Tubby' Allen*, Oxford University Press, Melbourne, 2004

Bragadin, Commander Marc-Antonio, *The Italian Navy in World War II*, United States Naval Institute, Annapolis, Maryland, 1955

Bramall, Field Marshal Lord (editor-in-chief), *The Desert War 1940-1942*, Sidgwick & Jackson, London, 1995

Brune, Peter, *Ralph Honner: Kokoda Hero*, Allen & Unwin, Sydney, 2007

Buckingham, William F., *Tobruk: The Great Siege 1941–42*, Tempus, Stroud, 2009

Buckley, Christopher, *Greece and Crete 1941*, HMSO, London, 1952

Bunbury, Bill, *Rabbits & Spaghetti: Captives and Comrades 1939–1945*, Fremantle Arts Centre Press, Fremantle, 1995

Calvocoressi, Peter, Guy Wint and John Pritchard, *Total War: The Causes and Courses of the Second World War*, Penguin, London, 1972

Carlyon, Norman D., *I Remember Blamey*, Macmillan, Melbourne, 1980

Chapman, Ivan D., *Iven G. Mackay: Citizen and Soldier*, Melway, Melbourne, 1975

Charlton, Peter, *The Thirty-Niners*, Macmillan, Melbourne, 1981

Churchill, Winston, S., *Their Finest Hour: The Second World War, Volume II*, Cassell, London, 1949

——*The Grand Alliance: The Second World War, Volume III*, Cassell, London, 1950

——*Collected Speeches* (edited by his grandson Winston Churchill), Pimlico Books, London, 2006

Ciano, Count Galeazzo, *Ciano's Diary 1939–1943*, Malcolm Muggeridge (editor), Heinemann, 1947

——*Ciano's Diplomatic Papers*, Odhams Press, London, 1948

Clark, Alan, *The Fall of Crete*, Blond, London, 1962

Clarke, Michael, *My War 1939–1945*, Michael Clarke Press, Melbourne, 1990

Coats, Peter, *Of Generals and Gardens*, Weidenfeld & Nicolson, London, 1976

Collins, Vice-Admiral Sir John, *As Luck Would Have It: The reminiscences of an Australian sailor*, Angus & Robertson, Sydney, 1965

Colville, John, *The Fringes of Power: Downing Street Diaries 1939–1955*, Hodder & Stoughton, London, 1985

Collier, Richard, *1941 Armageddon*, Hamish Hamilton, London, 1981

Connell, John, *Wavell: Scholar and Soldier*, Reprint Society, London, 1964

——*Wavell: Supreme Commander, 1941–43*, Michael Roberts (editor), Collins, London, 1969

Coombes, David, *Morshead: Hero of Tobruk and El Alamein*, Oxford University Press, 2001

Cooper, Artemis, *Cairo in the War 1939–1945*, Hamish Hamilton, London, 1989

Cox, Geoffrey, *A Tale of Two Battles*, William Kimber, London, London, 1987

Cunningham, Admiral Andrew Browne, *A Sailor's Odyssey*, Hutchinson, London, 1951

Damer, Sean and Ian Frazer, *On the Run: Anzac Escape and Evasion in Enemy-occupied Crete*, Penguin, Rosedale NZ, 2006

Davie, Michael (editor), *The Diaries of Evelyn Waugh*, Weidenfeld & Nicolson, London, 1976

Davin, D. M., *Crete: Official History of New Zealand in the Second World War 1939–1945*, War History Branch, Wellington, 1953

Day, David, *The Politics of War*, HarperCollins, Sydney, 2003

Deakin, F. W., *The Brutal Friendship: Mussolini, Hitler and the fall of Italian Fascism*, Weidenfeld & Nicolson, London, 1962

Dean, Peter, *The Making of a General: Lost Years, Forgotten Battles*, University of Sydney, 2007

de Guingand, Major-General Sir Francis, *Operation Victory*, Hodder & Stoughton, London, 1947

——*Generals at War*, Hodder & Stoughton, London, 1964

Department of Veterans' Affairs, *Official Veteran Representatives Biographies*, Canberra, 2001

D'Este, Carlo, *Warlord: A Life of Churchill at War 1874–1945*, Allen Lane, London, 2009

Dictionary of New Zealand Biography (DNZB), Ministry for Culture and Heritage, Wellington, 1998

Dilks, David (editor), *The Diaries of Sir Alexander Cadogan 1938–1945*, Cassell, London, 1971

Eather, Steve, *Desert Sands, Jungle Lands: A biography of Major-General Kenneth Eather*, Allen & Unwin, 2003

Ebury, Sue, *Weary: The Life of Sir Edward Dunlop*, Penguin, Melbourne, 1995

Engel, Major Gerhard, *At the Heart of the Reich: The Secret Diary of Hitler's Army Adjutant*, Greenhill Books, New York, 2006

Evans, Richard J., *The Third Reich at War: How the Nazis led Germany from conquest to disaster*, Penguin, 2008

Evans, Trefor E. (editor), *The Killearn Diaries 1934–1946*, Sidgwick & Jackson, London 1986

Ewer, Peter, *Forgotten Anzacs: The Campaign in Greece 1941*, Scribe, Melbourne, 2008

Farran, Roy, *Winged Dagger: Adventure on Special Service*, Cassell, London, 1948

Farrell, Nicholas, *Mussolini: A New Life*, Weidenfeld & Nicolson, London, 2003

Fenby, Jonathan, *Alliance: The Inside Story of How Roosevelt, Stalin and Churchill Won One War and Began Another*, Simon & Schuster, New York, 2007

Fielding, Xan, *Hide and Seek*, Secker, London, 1954

Foot, David, *Wally Hammond: The Reasons Why*, Robson Books, London, 1996

Foot, M. R. D., *SOE: An outline history of the Special Operations Executive 1940–1946*, Pimlico Books, London, 1999

Fort, Adrian, *Archibald Wavell: The Life and Times of an Imperial Servant*, Jonathan Cape, London, 2009

Forty, George, *The Battle of Crete*, Hersham, London, 2001

Fraser, David, *Knight's Cross: A life of Field Marshal Erwin Rommel*, HarperCollins, London, 1993

Freyberg, Paul, *Bernard Freyberg, VC: Soldier of Two Nations*, Hodder & Stoughton, Auckland, 1991

Fromkin, David, *A Peace to End all Peace*, Henry Holt, New York, 1989

Genisse, Jane Fletcher, *Passionate Nomad: The Life of Freya Stark*, Modern Library, New York, 2001

Genoud, Francois (editor), *The Testament of Adolf Hitler: The Hitler-Bormann documents February–April 1945*, Cassell, London 1959

Gilbert, Adrian, *POW: Allied Prisoners in Europe 1939–1945*, John Murray, London, 2006

Gilbert, Martin, *The Churchill War Papers, Volume III: The Ever-Widening War 1941*, Heinemann, London, 2000

Gill, G. Hermon, *Australia in the War of 1939–1945: Volume I, Royal Australian Navy 1939–1942*, AWM, Canberra, 1957

——*Volume II, Royal Australian Navy 1942–45*, AWM, Canberra, 1968

Gillison, Douglas, *Australia in the War of 1939–1945*, Series 3, *Air*, Volume I, *Royal Australian Air Force 1939–42*, Australian War Memorial, Canberra, 1962

Goebbels, Josef, *The Goebbels Diaries 1939-1941*, Hugh Trevor-Roper (editor), Putnam, New York, 1978

Gooch, John, *Mussolini and His Generals*, Cambridge University Press, New York, 2007

Greene, Jack and Alessandro Massignani, *The Naval War in the Mediterranean 1940–1943*, Chatham, London, 1998

Grey, Jeffrey, *A Military History of Australia*, Cambridge University Press, Melbourne, 1999

——*Australian Brass: The career of Lieutenant-General Sir Horace Robertson*, Cambridge University Press, Melbourne, 1992

Guard, Julie (editor), *Airborne: World War II paratroopers in combat*, Osprey, London, 2007

Gullett, Henry ('Jo'), *Not as a Duty Only: An Infantryman's War*, Melbourne University Press, Melbourne, 1984

——*Good Company: Horseman, soldier, politician*, 1992

Hadjipateras, Costas N. and Maria S. Fafalios, *Crete 1941 Eyewitnessed*, Efseathiadis Group, Greece, 1989

Halder, Franz, chief of the German Army's general staff, *The Halder War Diary, 1939–1942*, Greenhill Books, London, 1988

Harclerode, Peter, *Wings of War: Airborne Warfare 1918–1945*, Weidenfeld & Nicolson, London, 2005

Hazlehurst, Cameron, *Menzies Observed*, Allen & Unwin, Sydney, 1979

Heckstall-Smith, Anthony, and H. T. Baillie-Grohman, *Greek Tragedy*, Anthony Blond, London, 1961

Hehn, Paul N., *A Low Dishonest Decade: The Great Powers, Eastern Europe and the Economic Oringins of World War II*, Continuum, London, 2005

Hetherington, John, *Airborne Invasion*, Allen & Unwin, London, 1944

——*Blamey: The Biography of Field-Marshal Sir Thomas Blamey*, Cheshire, London, 1954

——*Blamey: Controversial Soldier*, AWM and Australian Government Publishing Service, Canberra, 1973

Higham, Robin, *Diary of a Disaster: British Aid to Greece 1940–1941*, University of Kentucky, 1986

Hinsley, F. H., *British Intelligence in the Second World War*, Volume I, HMSO, London, 1979

Hodgkinson, Lieutenant-Commander Hugh, *Before the Tide Turned*, Harrap, London, 1944

Hohne Heinz, *Canaris*, Secker & Warburg, London, 1979

Horner, David, *Blamey: the Commander-in-Chief*, Allen & Unwin, Sydney, 1998

——*Defence Supremo: Sir Frederick Shedden and the Making of Australian Defence Policy*, Allen & Unwin, Sydney, 2000

——*General Vasey's War*, Melbourne University Press, Melbourne, 1992

——*High Command: Australia and Allied Strategy 1939–1945*, Allen & Unwin, Sydney, 1982

——*Inside the War Cabinet: Directing Australia's War Efforts 1939–1945*, Allen & Unwin, Sydney, 1996

——(editor) *The Commanders: Australian military leadership in the twentieth century*, Allen & Unwin, Sydney, 1984

Household, Geoffrey, *Against the Wind*, Michael Joseph, 1958

Hunt, Sir David, *A Don at War*, William Kimber, London, 1966,

Hutching, Megan (editor), *A unique sort of battle: New Zealanders remember Crete*, HarperCollins with the History Group, Ministry for Culture and Heritage, Auckland, 2001

Iatrides, John O. (editor), *Ambassador MacVeagh Reports: Greece 1933–1947*, Princeton University Press, Princeton, 1980

International Military Tribunal, Nuremberg, *The Trail of the Major War Criminals, Volume X*, HMSO, London, 1946–1950

Jackson, W. G. F., *The North African Campaign 1940-1943*, Batsford, London, 1975

Kennedy, Major-General Sir John, *The Business of War*, Hutchinson, London, 1957

Keogh, Colonel E. G., *Middle East 1939–43*, Wilke, Melbourne, 1959

Kershaw, Ian, *Hitler 1936–1945: Nemesis*, Allen Lane, London, 2000

——*Fateful Choices: Ten Decisions that Changed the World 1940–1941*, Penguin, New York, 2007

Kimball, Warren F., *Roosevelt and Churchill: The Complete Correspondence, Volume I, Emerging Alliance*, Princeton University Press, Princeton, 1984

Kippenberger, Major-General Sir Howard, *Infantry Brigadier*, Oxford University Press, Wellington, 1949

Kiriakopoulos, G. C., *Ten Days to Destiny*, Franklin Watts, New York, 1985

Kitromilides, Paschalis M. (editor), *Eleftherios Venizelos: The Trials of Statesmanship*, Edinburgh University Press, Edinburgh, 2006

Knight, Nigel, *Churchill: The Greatest Briton Unmasked*, David & Charles, Cincinnati, 2008

Kuhn, Volkmar, *German Paratroopers in World War II*, Ian Allen, London, 1978

Leigh Fermor, Patrick, *A Time of Gifts*, John Murray, London, 1977

Le Souef, Leslie, *To War Without a Gun*, Artlook, Perth, 1980

Lewin, Ronald, *The Life and Death of the Afrika Korps: A Biography*, B. T. Batsford, London, 1977

——*The Chief: Field Marshal Lord Wavell 1939–1947*, Farrar, Straus & Giroux, New York, 1980

——*Ultra Goes to War*, Hutchinson, 1978

Lind, Lew, *Flowers of Rethymnon: Escape from Crete*, Kangaroo Press, Kenthurst, NSW, 1991

Long, Gavin, *Australia in the War of 1939–1945: To Benghazi*, Australian War Memorial, Canberra, 1952

——*Greece, Crete and Syria*, AWM, Canberra, 1953

——*The Six Years War*, AWM, Canberra, 1973

Longmore, Sir Arthur, *From Sea to Sky 1910–1945*, Geoffrey Bles, London, 1946

McClymont, W. G., *To Greece: The Official History of New Zealand in the Second World War 1939–1945*, Historical Publications Branch, Wellington, 1959

McConnell, Lynn, *Galatas 1941: Courage in Vain*, Reed, Auckland, 2006

MacDonald, Callum, *The Lost Battle: Crete 1941*, Macmillan, London, 1993

McDonald, Neil, *Chester Wilmot Reports*, ABC Books, Sydney, 2006

McGuire, Frances M., *The Royal Australian Navy*, Oxford University Press, Oxford, 1948

McKie, Ronald, *Proud Echo*, Hamilton, London, 1958

Maclean, Fitzroy, *Eastern Approaches*, Reprint Society, London, 1951

Macklin, Robert, *Bravest: How Some of Australia's Greatest Heroes Won their Medals*, Allen & Unwin, Sydney, 2008

Manstein, Field Marshal Erich von, *Lost Victories*, Methuen, London, 1958

Martin, A. W., *Robert Menzies: A Life, Volume I, 1894–1943*, Melbourne University Press, Melbourne, 1993

Martin A. W. and Patsy Hardy (editors), *Dark and Hurrying Days: Menzies' 1941 Diary*, NLA, 1993

Mazower, Mark, *Hitler's Empire: Nazi Rule in Occupied Europe*, Allen Lane, London, 2008

——*Salonica, City of Ghosts: Christians, Muslims and Jews 1430–1950*, HarperCollins, London, 2004

Menzies, Sir Robert, *Afternoon Light*, Cassell, London, 1967

Moorehead, Alan, *The Desert War 1940–1943*, Aurum, London, 2009

Moseley, Ray, *Mussolini's Shadow: The Double Life of Count Galeazzo Ciano*, Yale University Press, New Haven, 1999

Mosley, Leonard, *Gideon Goes to War: The story of Wingate*, Hamilton, London, 1955

Mott-Radclyffe, Charles, *Foreign Body in the Eye: Memoir of the Foreign Service Old and New*, Leo Cooper, London, 1975

Neame, Lieutenant-General Sir Philip, *Playing with Strife: The autobiography of a soldier*, Harrap, London, 1947

Overy, Richard, *Why the Allies Won*, W. W. Norton, New York, 1996

Pack, S. W. C. *The Battle of Matapan*, Pan Books, London, 1961

——*The Battle for Crete*, Ian Allan, London, 1973,

Palazzo, Albert, *Battle of Crete*, Army History Unit, Canberra, 2007

Palmer, Alan W., *The Gardeners of Salonika*, Andre Deutsch, London, 1965

Papagos, General Alexander, *The Battle of Greece 1940–1941*, Alpha Editions, Athens, 1949

Parkinson, Roger, *Blood, Toil, Tears and Sweat*, Hart-Davis MacGibbon, London, 1973

Pettifer, James, *The Greeks: The land and people since the war*, Penguin, London, 1994

Pfennigwerth, Ian, *Australian Cruiser Perth 1939–1942*, Rosenberg, Sydney, 2006

Pitt, Barrie, *The Crucible of War, Volume I*, Macmillan, London, 1986

Playfair, Major-General I. S. O., *The Mediterranean and Middle East, Volume I, The Early Success against Italy*, HMSO, London 1954

Plowright, John, *The Causes, Course and Outcomes of World War Two*, Palgrave Macmillan, New York, 2007

Porch, Douglas, *The Path to Victory: The Mediterranean Theatre in World War II*, Farrar, Straus & Giroux, New York, 2004

Powell, Dilys, *Remember Greece*, Hodder & Stoughton, London, 1941

——*The Villa Ariadne*, Hodder & Stoughton, London, 1973

Pratten, Garth, *Australian Battalion Commanders*, Cambridge University Press, Melbourne, 2009

Psychoudakis, George, *The Cretan Runner: His Story of the German Occupation*, John Murray, London, 1955

Ranfurly, Hermione, *To War With Whitaker: The Wartime Diaries of the Countess of Ranfurly 1939–1945*, Heinemann, London, 1994

Rankin, Nicholas, *Telegram from Guernica*, Faber & Faber, London, 2003

Reid, Miles, *Last on the List*, Leo Cooper, London, 1974

Rhodes James, Robert, *Anthony Eden*, Weidenfeld & Nicolson, London, 1986

——(editor), *Chips: The Diaries of Sir Henry Channon*, Weidenfeld & Nicolson, London, 1967

Roberts, Andrew, *Masters and Commanders*, Allen Lane, London, 2008

Roskill, Captain S. W., *The War at Sea 1939–1945, Volume I*, HMSO, London, 1954

Rowell, S. F., *Full Circle*, Melbourne University Press, Melbourne, 1974

Ruge, Vice-Admiral Friedrich, *Sea Warfare 1939–1945: A German viewpoint*, Cassell, London, 1954

Russell, W. B., *There Goes a Man: The biography of Sir Stanley G. Savige*, Longmans, Sydney, 1959

Schofield, Victoria, *Wavell: Soldier & Statesman*, John Murray, London, 2006

Semmler, Clement (editor), *The War Diaries of Kenneth Slessor*, Queensland University Press, Brisbane, 1985

——*The War Despatches of Kenneth Slessor*, Queensland University Press, Brisbane, 1987

Seth, Ronald, *Two Fleets Surprised: The Story of the Battle of Matapan*, Geoffrey Bles, London, 1960

Shulman, Milton, *Defeat in the West*, Secker & Warburg, London, 1947

Shores, Christopher, and Brian Cull with Nicola Malizia, *Air War: Yugoslavia, Greece and Crete*, Grub Street, London, 1987

Simpson, Tony, *Operation Mercury: The Battle for Crete 1941*, Hodder & Stoughton, London, 1981

Spencer, John Hall, *Battle for Crete*, Heineman, London, 1962

Stephanides, Theodore, *Climax in Crete*, Faber & Faber, London, 1946

Stevens, G. R., *Fourth Indian Division*, McLaren, Toronto, 1948

Stewart, Ian McD., *The Struggle for Crete: 20 May – 1 June 1941*, Oxford University Press, London, 1966

Stoler, Mark A., *Allies in War: Britain and America against the Axis Powers – 1940–1945*, Hodder Arnold, London, 2005

Sulzberger, Cyrus L., *A Long Row of Candles: Memoirs and Diaries 1934–1954*, Macdonald, London, 1969

Sykes, Christopher, *Orde Wingate*, Collins, London, 1959

Taaffe, Brian, *The Gatekeepers of Galatas: The untold story*, Sabicas, Melbourne, 2006

Terraine, John, *The Right of the Line: The Royal Air Force in the European War 1939–1945*, Sceptre, London, 1985

Thomas, David A., *Crete 1941: The Battle at Sea*, Cassell, 1972

Thomas, W. B., *Dare to be Free*, Wingate, London, 1951

Tudor, Malcolm, *Special Force: SOE and the Italian Resistance*, Emilia Publishing, Newtown, Powys, 2004

United States Department of the Army, *The German Campaigns in the Balkan – Spring 1941*, Washington, 1953

von Below, Nicolaus, *At Hitler's Side: The memoirs of Hitler's Luftwaffe adjutant*, Greenhill Books, London, 2001

von der Heydte, Baron, *Daedalus Returned*, Hutchinson, London, 1958

Wason, Elizabeth, *Miracle in Hellas: The Greeks Fight On*, Museum Press, London, 1943

Wavell, Field Marshal Viscount, *Allenby: Soldier and Statesman*, Harrap, London, 1946

——*Speaking Generally: Broadcasts, Orders and Addresses in Time of War (1939–43)*, Macmillan, London, 1946

Willingham, Matthew, *Perilous Commitments: The Battle for Greece and Crete 1940–1941*, Spellmount, Staplehurst, 2005

Wilmot, Chester, *The Struggle for Europe*, Collins, London, 1952

Wilson, Baron (Henry Maitland), *Eight Years Overseas 1939–1947*, Hutchinson, London, 1950

Wingate, John, *Torpedo Strike: With Cunningham in the Mediterranean*, Macdonald, London, 1964

Winton, John, *Cunningham: The greatest admiral since Nelson*, John Murray, London, 1998

Woodhouse, C. M., *Something Ventured*, Granada, London, 1982

Yergin, Daniel, *The Prize: The Epic Quest for Oil, Money and Power*, The Free Press, New York, 1991

Ziegler, Philip, *Diana Cooper*, Hamish Hamilton, London, 1981

Unit histories

6th Division AIF: Johnston, Mark, *The Proud 6th: An illustrated history of the 6th Australian Division 1939–1946*, Cambridge University Press, Melbourne, 2008

2/1: Givney, E. C. (editor), *The First at War: The story of the 2/1st Australian Infantry Battalion 1939–45*, Association of First Infantry Battalions, Sydney, 1987

2/2: Wick, Stan, *Purple over Green: The History of the 2/2 Australian Infantry Battalion 1939–1945*, 1977

2/2: Marshall, Captain Alan John (editor), *'Nulli Secundis' Log*, 2/2nd Australian Infantry Battalion AIF, Sydney, 1946

2/3: Clift, Ken, *War Dance: A story of the 2/3 Australian Infantry Battalion AIF*, P. M. Fowler and 2/3rd Battalion Association, Kingsgrove, NSW, 1980.

2/4: Chrystal, Cecil and Unit History Editorial Committee, *White over Green: The 2/4th Battalion*, Angus & Robertson, Sydney, 1963

2/5: Speed, Brigadier F. W. (editor), *Esprit de Corps: The History of the Victorian Scottish Regiment and the 5th Infantry Battalion*, Allen & Unwin, Sydney, 1988

2/6: Hay, David, *Nothing Over Us: The Story of the 2/6th Australian Infantry Battalion*, Australian War Memorial, Canberra, 1984

2/7: Bolger, W. P. and J. G. Littlewood, *The Fiery Phoenix:The Story of the 2/7 Australian Infantry Battalion 1939–1946*, 2/7 Battalion Association, Parkdale, 1983

2/8: Davis, E. G. (editor), *The Second Eighth: A History of the 2/8th Australian Infantry Battalion*, 2/8th Battalion Association, Melbourne, 1984

2/2 Field Regiment: *Action Front: The History of the 2/2nd Australian Field Regiment AIF*, 2/2nd Field Regiment Association, Melbourne, 1961

2/3 Field Regiment: Bishop, Les, *The Thunder of the Guns: A History of 2/3 Australian Field Regiment*, 2/3 Australian Field Regiment Association, Sydney, 1998

2/11: Johnson, K. T., *The History of the 2/11 (City of Perth) Infantry Battalion, 1939–1946*, Perth, 2000

19 NZ Battalion: Sinclair, D. W., *19 Battalion: The Official History of New Zealand in*

the *Second World War 1938–1945*, War History Branch, Department of Internal Affairs, Wellington, 1954

20 NZ Battalion: Glue, William A., *20 Battalion: The Official History of New Zealand in the Second World War 1938–1945*, War History Branch, Department of Internal Affairs, Wellington, 1957

21 NZ Battalion: Cody, Joseph F., *21 Battalion: The Official History of New Zealand in the Second World War 1938–1945*, War History Branch, Department of Internal Affairs, Wellington, 1953

22 NZ Battalion: Henderson, Jim, *22 Battalion: The Official History of New Zealand in the Second World War 1938–1945*, War History Branch, Department of Internal Affairs, Wellington, 1958

28 (Maori) Battalion: Cody, J. F., *28 (Maori) Battalion: The Official History of New Zealand in the Second World War 1938–1945*, War History Branch, Department of Internal Affairs, Wellington, 1956

NZ Divisional Cavalry: Loughnan, R. J. M. *Divisional Cavalry: The Official History of New Zealand in the Second World War 1938–1945*, War History Branch, Department of Internal Affairs, Wellington, 1963

NZ 4th & 6th RMT: Henderson, Jim, *RMT: Official History of the 4th and 6th Reserve Mechanical Transport Companies, 2NZEF*, Wellington, 1954

Unpublished manuscripts

Brunskill, G. S., 'A Soldier's Yesterdays: The Memoirs of Brigadier G.S. Brunskill', PP/MCR/136, Imperial War Museum

Peck, John D., 'Captive in Crete', Australian War Memorial

Simper, Norm, 'Recollections of a Signalman – 1938–1945', Canberra

Spencer, Harry, 'Lest We Forget', Hastings, New Zealand

Official sources

Australian War Memorial (AWM), Canberra

Department of Veterans Affairs, Canberra

Imperial War Museum (IWM), London

National Archives of Australia (NAA), Melbourne and Canberra

National Archives UK (formerly Public Records Office, PRO), London

National Library of Australia (NLA), Canberra

Official reports

Brunskill, Brigadier G. S., 'The Administrative Aspect of the Campaign in Crete', HMSO, London, 1942

Cunningham, Admiral Sir Andrew B., 'Battle of Matapan', *London Gazette*, 1947

——'Transportation of the Army to Greece and evacuation of the Army from Greece 1941', *London Gazette*, 1948

Freyberg, General Bernard C., 'Report on the Battle for Crete' to the New Zealand Minister of Defence', August 1941

Smith, Major-General A.C., US chief of military history, 'The German Campaigns in the Balkans – Spring 1941', Department of the Army, Washington, 1953

Vasey, Brigadier G. A., '19th Australian Infantry Brigade Account of Operations in Crete 1941', AWM54 535/2/25

Wavell, General Sir Archibald P., 'Operations in the Middle East, 7 February 1941 to 15 July 1941', *London Gazette*, 1946

——'Operations in the Middle East, August 1939 to November 1940', *London Gazette*, 1946

Articles

Roy Macartney, 'An Epic of the Escape from Crete', *The Argus*, 9 August 1941

'Australian was with partisans', *The Argus*, 11 April 1945

Tom Carver, 'Blunder that doomed 50,000 POWs', *Observer*, London, 1 November 2009

'An Empire in Arms', *The Times*, 21 June 1940

'Anzacs Here: Biggest Aid Ever to Britain', *Daily Mirror*, 21 June 1940

John Pudney, 'Empire Warriors Take Luxury Cruise to Battle', *News Chronicle*, 21 June 1940

Rory Carroll, 'Italy's bloody secret', *The Guardian*, 25 June 2001

Field Marshall Earl Wavell, 'The British Expedition to Greece, 1941', Army Quarterly, LIX, January 1950

Other media

Wilmot, Chester, 'The Capture of Bardia', ABC Radio, 14 January 1941

The World at War, Thames Television, 26 episodes, first shown in 1973

INDEX